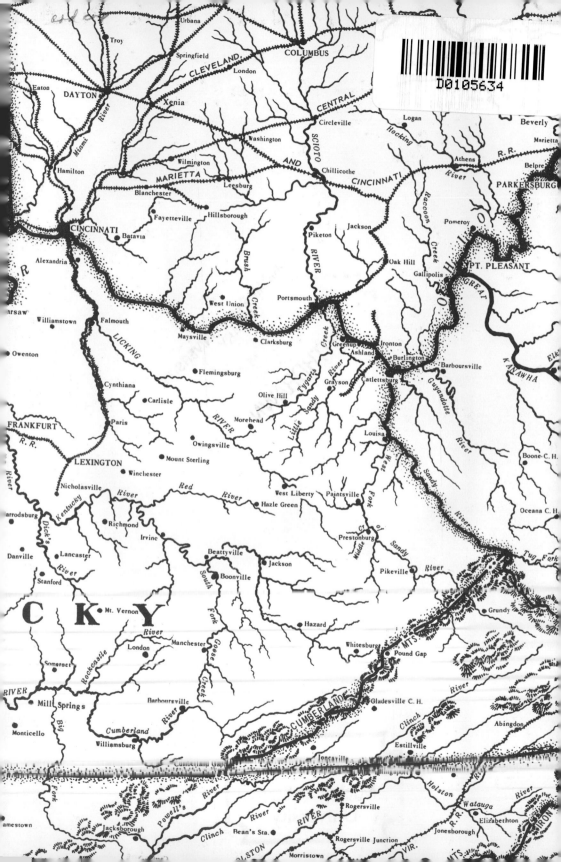

*The Wild Life of the Army:*

# CIVIL WAR LETTERS OF
# JAMES A. GARFIELD

James A. Garfield and his staff in the field, 1862.

*The Wild Life of the Army:*

# CIVIL WAR LETTERS
# OF
# JAMES A. GARFIELD

*Edited with an Introduction by*

**FREDERICK D. WILLIAMS**

MICHIGAN STATE UNIVERSITY PRESS

1964

*For Florence*

Copyright © 1964
Michigan State University Press
Library of Congress Catalog Card Number: 64-20711
Manufactured in the United States of America

# Contents

# Introduction

A week before the Union garrison surrendered Fort Sumter a dashing but distraught young member of the Ohio Senate, gripped by indecision, pondered over the career he should pursue. To his wife he confessed he had never before felt "so sadly, and almost despairingly" over his future.[1] He could not know that a few days later the nation would plunge into a civil war whose driving force would sweep him along and dramatically influence the course of his life. As he envisaged the future there seemed to be three careers for which he was suited—education, law, and politics. Should he settle on one, or, as he sometimes wondered, would a combination of education or law with politics be most rewarding? James A. Garfield had reached one of life's cross-roads, and he knew not where to turn.

Then in his thirtieth year, Garfield could look back on an early life which he viewed in later years with both pride and regret—pride in his conquest of seemingly insurmountable obstacles, regret over having been handicapped from the first by the stultifying impact of want and a crude, uninspiring frontier environment. Born in a log cabin in Orange, just east of Cleveland, he was brought up in poverty. The death of his father in 1833, when James was a toddler, saddled the widowed Eliza Garfield with the responsibility of rearing him and three older children, Mehetabel, Thomas, and Mary. There was always work to be done, either at home or for hire, and like most frontier youngsters James was introduced at an early age to hoeing, haying, cutting brush, chopping wood, and various other jobs, including carpentry. He quickly developed an intense dislike for manual labor and made no pretense about it. His mother remembered him as a rather lazy boy who "did not like to work the best that ever was."[2]

Fortunately for the boy he was blessed with an excellent mind which he determined to train and fill. Until his seventeenth birthday, however, his only formal education came from several years in district schools. Early in 1849, after recovering from an illness contracted during a brief experience at work on a canal boat, he enrolled in Geauga

Seminary, a Free Will Baptist school in nearby Chester, where he studied off and on until October, 1850. From 1851 to 1854 he attended the Western Reserve Eclectic Institute, a school in Hiram, Ohio, founded by local members of the Disciples of Christ. In the summer of 1854 he entered Williams College in Massachusetts, where he graduated in 1856. At all three of these schools he studied hard. To attend the first two he earned money by doing odd jobs and teaching district school. One year during his study at the Eclectic he taught introductory courses in arithmetic, grammar and Greek; and, as soon as he had completed special courses in penmanship and painting, he supplemented his meager income by giving classes in these skills to students. He also began to preach and to conduct Sunday services, activities which he continued as a college student, deriving from them much personal satisfaction, a little extra money, and a number of close friends. After graduating at Williams he returned to Hiram, resumed teaching at the Eclectic and was its Principal from 1858 to 1861. These were busy years. Besides performing his teaching and administrative duties at the Eclectic, he preached quite regularly at Disciple meetings in Hiram and neighboring towns, and in 1860 and 1861 he served as a member of the Ohio Senate.

Physically Garfield was an immensely attractive person. His two hundred pounds were well distributed over a six foot frame. His deep chest, broad shoulders and muscular arms and legs bespoke strength and endurance. His thick neck supported a massive head on which his light brown hair, now thinning, was brushed away from his high forehead. His ruddy, bearded face was round and handsome, with clear blue eyes, a slightly aquiline nose, and a well-shaped mouth planted above a firm chin and a strong jaw.

Naturally curious, well-read, and the owner of a keen, active mind that was more retentive than creative, Garfield was no ordinary man. A gregarious individual, he enjoyed companionship, was a good conversationalist, laughed often and heartily, and frequently displayed his fondness for companions by placing a hand on their shoulders or an arm around their waist. He possessed more than an average allotment of self-confidence and in everything he undertook, whether a game of cards, chess, croquet, or a political or military campaign, he threw himself into the competition with but one thought in mind—victory. Winning was a delightful, elevating experience; defeats were distasteful and hard to take. Towards anyone standing in his way he could be quite ruthless. He was constantly on the watch for opportunities to get ahead. If they failed to appear or were slow in coming, he tended to grow uneasy, and more likely than not he would begin criticizing associates or superiors, not to their faces but in confidential statements to others, including individuals in a position to act on his complaints. While engaged in such undertakings he attempted to minimize risk to himself by couching his criticism in terms which could be explained in the event his efforts misfired. In a sense the work of getting ahead in life was to Garfield a kind of military operation whose objective, success (its essential ingredients were power, fame, and money) was to be achieved by aggressive maneuvers conducted from a position whose flanks and rear were as secure and safe as possible.

As might be expected, during his climb to the top he made enemies, among them erstwhile friends who took exception to what appeared to be studied efforts to twist things and use people to his own advantage. Hattie J. Benedict, the daughter of a Disciple elder, knew Garfield when he was teaching at Hiram, and over the years she seethed with resentment as she watched him hurdle obstacle after obstacle, including the postwar scandals, and go on to greater power and glory in the national government. A Democrat who contributed articles to newspapers, she looked back twenty years in 1877 and wrote a stinging commentary on his hypocritical conduct. She recalled that in 1857 Garfield was "a young man of twenty-six, fresh from college, with boundless energy and ambition large and general, with a charming sociability and freedom of manners which made him appear emphatically a man of the people. His cheerful good-fellowship had nothing in it offensively condescending to the 'great unwashed'—his ready hand was held out for the poorest to shake in those days with delightful democracy—his broad shoulders were thrown back for a full deep-chested laugh with the most obscene joker, who in the future might have a vote to cast for him, as readily as with the most exclusive aristocrat. His [religious] meetings were always well attended and were even more popular with the sinners of the world than with the saints of the church. There was a lack of spirituality about him that grieved the latter, and it was noticeable that revivals never progressed under the spell of his preaching, but the sinners liked to hear his short, sparkling, logical discourses, which did not unpleasantly trouble them with thought of 'righteousness, temperance and judgment to come' and if he did not make converts, he at least made voters." Though the writer conceded Garfield's brilliance, she regarded him as superficial; "he impressed the people strikingly, and few looked deep enough to discover upon how slight a foundation the showy structure of his reputation was built."[3] Despite their obvious bias these observations afford a view of Garfield and his behavior which for various reasons was shared by many.

\* \* \* \*

The 1850's witnessed remarkable changes in many of Garfield's attitudes and activities. At the opening of the decade he was a coarse-mannered, virtually unschooled product of the Ohio frontier, intensely devoted to the teachings of the Disciples of Christ, the church his parents had joined after he was born. The Disciples were followers of Alexander Campbell who separated from the Baptist Church over doctrinal and organizational differences. In particular, the denomina tion stressed adult baptism and strict adherence to the word of God as revealed in the Bible. Garfield's life as a Disciple began in March, 1850, when in accord with a cardinal tenet of the faith he was baptised by immersion.

For several years thereafter his fervent desire to adhere scrupulously to the Disciple creed, which was dedicated to Bible Christianity, induced him to evaluate virtually everything he and others did in terms of Disciple beliefs as he understood them. Sectarianism was an abhorrence, for there was but one fountain of truth—the Scriptures. That a mortal had to interpret them mattered not, so long as he was a Disciple. Such religious devotion naturally colored Garfield's thoughts and behavior, in particular causing him to be prudishly intolerant. Though more than once curiosity took him to services in Presbyterian and Methodist churches, he thought the names were unscriptural and called their places of worship "houses," not churches. At a Methodist "House" he listened one Sunday morning to a *"historical,* rather than a *gospel* sermon,"* and was subjected to more of the same at a Presbyterian "House" in the afternoon. In May, 1850, he attended a service in "the Presbyterian House, listened a few moments and then slept soundly till the exercises were nearly closed. It pains my heart," he complained to his Journal, "to see the ignorance and bigotry that is abroad in the land. I wish that men would let all human traditions alone and take the Bible alone for their guide." At a Catholic service in Muskingum County he was annoyed by the priest, who spoke neither loudly nor distinctly enough to be understood. "He stood with his back to the congregation," Garfield noted with disgust, "and made occasional gyrations and genuflections and changed his garment two or three times. He had two young men to wait upon him and carry his trail (tail). I noticed that the priest (a libel upon the name) seemed the least reverential of all." Garfield worshiped one Sunday in Mayfield and he noted that the town was "a very hard place by reputation and practice." His critical eye focused on other aspects of society—drinking, levity, the bloomer dress, women preachers and agitators for women's rights—and his caustic pen recorded for posterity his opinionated observations.[4]

No less pronounced were his opinions of politics and politicians, which, when considered in the light of his long career as a public servant, are amusingly ironic. As a student at Chester and Hiram Garfield was so absorbed in school and church, and by religious persuasion so unsympathetic toward politics and politicians, that he gave little attention to them. In his Journal he noted without comment the deaths of John C. Calhoun and President Zachary Taylor. For a debate he prepared to argue that "Christians have no right to participate in human governments!" Despite arguments to the contrary, he was inclined to believe it was "like serving two masters to participate in the affairs of a government which is point blank opposed to the Christians (as all *human* ones must necessarily be)." At a Sunday meeting Garfield participated in investigating the subject of voting and its bearing on Christianity. He and the rest of the group concluded that they had "no right to engage in politics." This attitude toward political activity naturally colored his judgments of those involved in it. When in 1851 he visited the Capitol in Columbus, he "was not satisfied with the appearance" of most of the legislators. "Their rubicund, bloated faces spoke plainly of the midnight bowl, and, in my opinion, unfitted them for representing the free people of a great state." A spirited political race left him cold. "Politics," he wrote during the presidential campaign of 1852, "are now raging with great violence. I am profoundly ignorant of its multifarious phases and am not inclined to study it. I am exceedingly disgusted with the wire-pulling of politicians and the total disregard for truth in all their operations. Miserable, low, ungentlemanly trash fills the columns of the political press, unfit for refined feelings, tender consciences, or kind hearts." Election day found him glad he lacked "17 days of being old enough to vote," for he was undecided as to his duty upon the subject. Then he added: "I think, however, I should not have voted had I been 21 years of age." Not until late 1855, when the controversy over slavery began to penetrate his mantle of political disinterest, did Garfield reveal other than almost utter contempt for politics.[5]

As a student he paid little attention to the question of slavery. At Geauga, in 1850, he was induced by a sermon on slavery to read "8 essays on the same subject as connected with Christianity." The writings were, he decided, "conclusive arguments that the *simple relation* of master and slave is not unchristian." The next day he agreed to debate that very proposition. Since only a small minority of the Western Reserve's population remained outside either antislavery or abolitionist camps, Garfield invited harsh criticism by advancing what seemed to his small circle of associates to be pro-slavery arguments. "I love agitation and investigation," he once admitted when his opinions were under fire, "and glory in defending unpopular truth against popular error." Early in October Joshua R. Giddings, the Reserve's fiery abolitionist, spoke in Chester denouncing the recently adopted Fugitive Slave Law. He was, Garfield thought, a "fluent" and "easy" speaker, but "I could not help but consider that the cause for which he was laboring was a carnal one. Not fully settled on that yet." A year later, when Garfield was in his first term at the Eclectic, Professor Jehu Brainard of Cleveland, a reputable geologist, closed a series of lectures with a discourse on the "geological abolition of slavery and an affectionate address upon our duties." Though Garfield was momentarily impressed, throughout his student days at Chester and Hiram he showed little interest in the slavery issue. In the summer of 1852, and again in the spring of 1853, he noted in his Journal that he had begun to read *Uncle Tom's Cabin,* but he made no comment about the book and left no evidence that he ever finished it.[6]

Study, experience, and intellectual maturity gradually and somewhat painfully shook Garfield loose from some of his smugly-held beliefs. "I know not for what reason," he wrote in 1853, "but my mind and peace is [*sic*] continually disturbed by thoughts evil or foolish. They intrude upon my peaceful hours, try to rifle me of holy aspirations and high resolves." Though prayers brought solace and strength, he was conscious of "a spirit of scepticism standing back of my thoughts, and [it] whispers through the courts of reason that all the good results of prayer were the effects of natural causes." Though plagued from time to time by "blighting doubt," his faith remained unshattered. When he left Hiram for Williams College in 1854 he believed firmly that the Gospel made his Disciple brethren "sympathetic and benevolent beyond most others."[7]

Once in college not only did new worlds appear to absorb him in fascinated concentration, but the world in which he lived began to assume substantially greater significance in his thoughts and activities. He became active in extra-curricular affairs on campus; he traveled whenever time and money permitted; and he began to succumb to the lure of the leading political issue of the hour.

In 1855 two abolitionists spoke in Williamstown and impressed Garfield with what was to him an informative and revealing attack on slavery. "I have been instructed tonight on the political condition of our country," he wrote, "and from this time forward I shall hope to know more about its movements and interests." Convinced that a united effort should be made to suppress slavery in every newly acquired territory, he seemed suddenly to be stirred by a crusading zeal. "At such hours as this," he declared, "I feel like throwing the whole current of my life into the work of opposing this giant evil. I don't know but the religion of Christ demands some such action." For all this emotion, Garfield was too intent upon completing his college education to act impulsively. The demands of school and other duties kept him busy and prevented him for the time being both from actively opposing slavery and from entering the political arena. Then too, he still saw real drawbacks in public life, certain aspects of which thoroughly disgusted him. As late as 1857 he wrote disparagingly of politics and the greed, scandal and abuse inevitably associated with it; yet he had become "intensely interested" in the presidential election of 1856, and in the fall of the next year he rejoiced over the Republican victories, hailing them as blows for the cause of liberty. "Slavery," he ventured, "has had its day, or at any rate is fast having it." Thereafter, throughout the late 1850's, there was never any doubt about his hostility to slavery. When in 1857 he confronted a fugitive, an intelligent Negress of twenty-two years, he "could not but feel the enormity of a system which should enslave such as she." Two years later, during the furor over John Brown's raid on Harpers Ferry, Garfield, who never tried to justify the act, felt sympathy for Brown and referred to him on the day of his execution as a brave hero whose "death shall be the dawn of a better day."[8]

When the magnetism of politics finally drew Garfield into active participation the controversy over slavery was a potent facet of its drawing power; but other considerations helped influence him to make the move, not the least of which was awareness that Hiram and the Eclectic, for all their attractions, offered too little in the way of challenge and fulfillment. He had feared as much before returning there from Williams College, and from the moment of his arrival sustained periods of restlessness intruded upon his life with increasing frequency. "In rest," he fretted, "I long for motion. In motion, I pine for rest."[9] To be sure, the want of money and his difficulty in deciding about marriage troubled him immensely, as did various problems at the Eclectic, but what Garfield needed was a change, a change of work, a change of scenery, and a larger, more significant stage on which to act.

Then came an unexpected opportunity. For several years Garfield had been thinking of entering politics, and he had told friends of his interest. Through his teaching and preaching he had become well-known locally, and he had many admirers. More than that, beginning in 1856 he had actually stumped for Republican candidates, and late in 1858 he had impressed hundreds of people who had attended his week-long debate with an atheist on the subject of origin and growth. These activities, especially the debate, had been for Garfield satisfying and inspiring. They had also swelled his following. Thus, in 1859, when the leading candidate for state senator from his district died, friends in Ravenna invited Garfield to stand for the Republican nomination. He discussed the matter with the trustees and teachers of the Eclectic and found it "compatible with my duties [as Principal] to be absent the required time." He accepted the invitation, noting that "if this plan succeeds I shall have gained a step in the direction of my purpose."[10] At the nominating convention Garfield was chosen by acclamation as the candidate to represent Portage and Summit counties.

The Republicans could not have hoped for a more prodigious campaigner. "I delivered," he recalled, "some thirty political speeches averaging about two hours each. The Democrats and a few envious Republicans made me the center of attack and so papers and stumpers were active in secret and open slander and abuse. I returned the fire with interest." In an election which saw Republicans win the governorship and both houses of the legislature, Garfield ran ahead of his party and defeated his Democratic opponent by a vote of 5,176 to 3,746. The step in the direction of his purpose had been successfully executed, and it proved to be a big one.[11]

\* \* \* \*

Although Garfield's work in the Ohio Senate was neither spectacular nor outstanding, it was creditable enough to attract considerable attention and praise, and the experience whetted his appetite for greater political accomplishment. The senatorship gave him the opportunity to display his talents as a clever debater and effective stump speaker. It brought him into close personal association with important and influential figures, including Salmon P. Chase and William A. Dennison who were soon to give active and helpful support in promoting his career; and it gave him a chance to air his views—in floor debates, at political gatherings, and in the Ohio press—to a statewide audience. At first he was cautious and prudent, partly because he lacked experience and wished to avoid mistakes that might prove costly to his future, and partly because he saw no immediate danger to the Union. But by the time the second session convened in January, 1861, he had acquired some seasoning and a good deal of confidence, and secession had convinced him that some measure of violence would be required to save the Union. Resolutely opposed to appeasement and compromise, he identified himself with the extreme antislavery Republicans and urged a firm policy of resistance to Southern disunionists.[12]

As the secession crisis approached climax Garfield was, as already noted, thinking seriously about his future. There was a growing feeling at the Eclectic that he had lost interest in the school, and he realized that others were sharing his assignments in addition to performing their own.[13] Perhaps he should return. For nearly eight years he had been associated with the Eclectic in one capacity or another. In Hiram he had established a reputation as an orator, had begun his career as a preacher, and there and in nearby towns he had conducted services and preached for several years. In Hiram he had fallen in love and married, and there the newlyweds had made their home. In and around Hiram lived many relatives, intimate friends, and worthy associates. The surroundings were familiar, the sentimental attachments powerful, the roots deep. But staying there, Garfield realized, entailed "many unpleasant consequences."[14] Sometimes there was too much intimacy, too much petty jealousy, too much small town gossip. Garfield once urged a friend, whose financial indebtedness to several townsmen was causing tongues to wag, to pay what he owed, adding this quaint reminder: "The financial style of Hiram was always, as you know, based on pennies, and half a dollar is a sufficient sum to sweeten the tea of 40 old women."[15]

More than once Garfield himself had been the target of popular criticism, perhaps the harshest of which came when he was appointed Principal of the Eclectic. His appointment climaxed a protracted and bitter struggle during which his conduct, especially his negotiations with certain members of the board of trustees, became common knowledge. Later, when the trustees fired Norman Dunshee, an able and devoted member of the faculty, and appointed J. H. Rhodes, Garfield's friend and choice for Dunshee's position, school and town buzzed with charges that the new Principal was the prince of politics. Confident in the correctness of their accusations his detractors assailed him re-

lentlessly and subjected his slightest indiscretion to hurtful interpreta-
tion. Their attacks pierced his thin skin and cast him into spells of
anger and depression. Disappointed but not discouraged he set out
to improve the Eclectic's physical appearance and academic program.
So marked was his success that his principalship is referred to as "The
Golden Age" of the Eclectic.[16] "More attention was now given to
education as education," Burke Hinsdale told a Hiram audience in
1900, "and less attention to making preachers." The change occasioned
considerable protest from conservative brethren whose criticisms drew
from Garfield the remark that "the croakers were as thick as the frogs
in Egypt." But young Hiram supported the Principal and by 1861,
under Garfield's leadership, the school was stronger than ever and its
future apparently assured.[17]

Perhaps, Garfield thought, the time had come to break away from
the Eclectic and either turn to law or remain in politics. For some
time he had seriously considered law, but he had strong doubts about
striking out in that direction. Not the lawyers, he wrote in 1859, but
the teachers, preachers, editors and authors were the intellectual
leaders of the day. In the spring of 1861 he all but rejected a career
in law, saying he feared he might soon loath its weary details and
long for a work benefiting others and the "unselfish aims of life." As
for politics, there was much in it that pleased him and much that did
not. He eyed the prospect of running for Congress, fully aware that
public life would leave him longing at times for a quiet secluded
home and select friends. Something distasteful could be found about
each of the careers he was considering. "I can see no one course,"
he wrote on April 7, 1861, "which does not have valid objections
to it, and none which, when taken, will not cause me deep and
poignant regrets." Thus Garfield's dilemma on the eve of the Civil
War.[18]

\* \* \* \*

Once the shooting started Garfield's sense of duty made him impatient to don a uniform; but he wanted a rank commensurate with
his qualifications, which he highly esteemed. At the most he hoped
for a brigadier generalship, and for a time he was unwilling to settle
for less than a colonelcy. The importance of rank was not lost on
Garfield. In a conflict of the magnitude he expected the Civil War
to assume, individuals, except perhaps for a handful, would be ob-
scured by events. Leaders would command attention; successful ones
could expect rewards from a grateful citizenry. To Garfield the relationship between success in the field and political opportunities was
obvious, but friends and associates were nonetheless quick to point it
out. No sooner had the war begun than Governor Dennison, whom
Garfield admired and respected, assured him that successful military
leaders would rule the nation for at least twenty years after the war.[19]
Yet Dennison, cognizant of Garfield's inexperience in military affairs,

hesitated to give him a colonelcy and command of a regiment. Realizing he must have a command in order to lead, Garfield made a prodigious but unsuccessful effort to get a colonelcy. Though his failure jolted him, on the heels of it he declined a lieutenant colonelcy. Then, in August, he accepted an identical appointment in a regiment which existed only on paper. His acceptance, followed by promotion to colonel only weeks later, suggest that Dennison coupled his offer with an assurance of prompt advancement. At any rate, Garfield was given command of the Forty-second Ohio Infantry and ordered to raise the regiment.

As a regimental commander Garfield was in a position to demonstrate from the first those traits of character which qualified him for military leadership. Devotion to the cause, charm, eloquence and persuasiveness as an orator, and a lot of hard work helped him fill the ranks of the Forty-second in about two months of recruiting at a time when volunteers were hard to find. An imaginative and remarkably realistic understanding of the size of the job to be done moved him to study the art of war and to throw himself into the tedious but essential task of training and equipping his men. In camp and field he worked tirelessly, driven, as usual, by his extraordinary ambition. In the absence of mollifying influences such ambition in a military leader can be a prescription to disaster, but in Garfield a sense of justice and concern for the welfare of his men acted as wholesome restraints. He was too decent to impose excessive demands on them or to disregard their welfare. Towards subordinates he tried to be fair; deserving men found him sympathetic and ready to extend himself in providing for their comfort; laggards and recalcitrants found him firm but just in his determination to maintain order and efficiency.

Besides acquiring substantial knowledge of the art of command, he developed a fair understanding of certain principles of war. At a time when the nation's ranking military officers brimmed with maxims expounded in Henri Jomini's *Précis de l'art de la guerre* and placed particular emphasis on the conquest of territory, Garfield insisted that the true objective of an army was the destruction of the enemy's army. To save the Union, he believed it was necessary to subjugate the South—not by taking her cities, girdling her with expeditions, or blockading her ports, but by pulverizing her great armies. To achieve that goal he appreciated the importance of concentrating against the foe, using surprise tactics, and making adequate provision for security; but above all he stressed the efficacy of offensive operations. By word and deed he left little room to doubt his faith in the offensive as the king of the battlefield. In his campaign in Eastern Kentucky his was the aggressor force; in the Shiloh-Corinth campaign, in which he had no independent command, he deplored the snail-paced advance of the Union armies; as Chief of Staff in the Army of the Cumberland he urged his commander to strike, strike, strike; and from the opening gun he insisted that the Union must wage a war of conquest. For an amateur soldier he showed remarkable understanding of the nature of the military challenge the nation faced and of what was needed to meet it.

\*   \*   \*   \*

Most of Garfield's Civil War letters went to Hiram, where his wife Lucretia (Rudolph), whom he called "Crete," and a circle of close friends and relatives lived throughout the war. Lucretia, the daughter of Disciple parents, was an attractive, black-eyed brunette with a keen intellect, firm convictions, an extraordinary amount of good common sense, and a genuinely sympathetic nature. Occasionally she succumbed to self-pity and complaining, but most of the time she showed a pleasant disposition.

She and Garfield had first met as students at Geauga Seminary, but nearly five years slipped by before they became romantically interested in each other. An extremely devout person, Lucretia was quiet, shy, and so inclined to conceal her feelings that Garfield, though confident of her love for him, often feared she lacked the warmth and affection his nature demanded. Their marriage in 1858 ended a long and troubled courtship which survived not only Garfield's romance with another young lady, Rebecca Jane Selleck of Lewisboro, New York, who appears in the letters, but also his deep-seated doubts and fears about matrimony and "its necessitous and hateful finalities."[20] For reasons real and fancied the marriage was severely tested for several years, including those covered by the letters. Happily, Garfield and his wife managed to overcome their difficulties. The arrival of children helped. So did Lucretia's magnificent fortitude and faith when their first child died. Her strength became Garfield's; it assuaged his grief and helped him endure the greatest sorrow he had ever known. Their common loss drew them closer together. In time, with patience, frankness, and understanding, they built a strong and beautiful marriage. Indeed, by late 1863, when Garfield left the army to enter Congress, the marriage had already weathered its most turbulent years.

Garfield addressed some of his best wartime letters to J. Harrison (Harry) Rhodes, a teacher at the Eclectic and its Principal from 1862-1863. Garfield and Rhodes became acquainted when the latter was a student at Hiram. They liked one another from the first and roomed together about two years before Rhodes left to complete his formal education at Williams College. His return to Hiram in 1859 occasioned the controversy, already noted, over the dismissal of Norman Dunshee, whose place on the faculty Rhodes assumed.

Between Rhodes and Garfield there grew an intimate and enduring friendship. To Charles E. Henry, who was close to both men, Garfield's devotion to Rhodes "seemed like the warm love of a big brother for a little sister." The "little sister" was in fact a fascinating personality whose learning, facility with words, subtle humor, friendliness, charm, and ability to unbend without loss of dignity gave rise to more than one prediction that he would achieve considerable success, even greatness. But greatness never came. Rhodes lacked drive; he was, as Henry once observed, "physically indolent." After leaving the Eclectic in 1863, Rhodes entered a law office in Cleveland, where, in consequence of fortunate investments rather than success in law, he was able to enjoy the kind of easy life for which he was temperamentally suited.[21]

At times Rhodes seemed more concerned about Garfield's career than his own. No sooner had Garfield entered the service than Rhodes began sending advice. He begged Garfield not to expose himself needlessly to danger; he stressed the importance of good publicity and asked for help in securing a position on the editorial staff of the Cleveland *Herald*, "for my sake and for your sake." And he admonished Garfield to keep his sword untarnished, for "we are to be ruled by military men for the next twenty years—and perhaps always. . . . The way is before you clearly. The *object* and *aim* of your life is to subordinate all things to political advancement."[22] For news, advice, and active support in promoting his career in politics Garfield leaned heavily on his loyal friend in Hiram.

Garfield's Civil War letters are uniquely significant historical and biographical documents. Although he kept a journal from 1848-1881 which contains a treasure of source material, for one or another reason he sometimes neglected it for weeks and even years on end. Since the greatest gap in that document includes the war years, his wartime letters comprise the most extensive and detailed information he left on this phase of his life. Some of the letters, of course, are disappointingly brief and thin in content; others, including many to his wife and Rhodes, and several to such important people in his life as Harmon Austin, Burke Hinsdale, and Salmon P. Chase, contribute significantly to our understanding of the man and his times.

The letters reproduced below were selected from those written from the outbreak of hostilities to the day he left the Union army, a period of thirty-two months which has been divided into three phases, each of which is presented with introductory remarks and explanatory notes. The letters to Joseph Lay and Corydon Fuller were copied from newspaper clippings (no name or date) in the Garfield Papers. The letter to Wallace Ford (February 14, 1862) is in the Andre DeCoppet Collection at Princeton University. As for the five letters to Salmon P. Chase: April 12, 1863, is in a newspaper clipping (no name or date) in the Garfield Papers; July 27, 1863, is in the New York *Sun*, March 8, 1882; and the other three are in the Chase Papers, Library of Congress. The rest of the letters in this volume are in the Garfield Papers, Library of Congress.

An explanation of editorial policy, adopted in the interests of clarity and readability, is essential. Corrections in spelling were limited to proper nouns, to errors attributable to haste or carelessness, and to words with "ei" or "ie" combinations, such as "receive," which Garfield often misspelled. Ampersands were changed to "and," and dashes, except when properly used, were either omitted or replaced with correct punctuation, as the situation warranted. Garfield often failed to punctuate and was erratic in using commas, capitals, and compounds. Occasionally he underlined words for no apparent reason, repeated words twice in succession, and neglected to underscore such things as titles of books and names of newspapers. In most instances corrections were made. Finally, headings were standardized, paragraphing was supplied, abbreviations were expanded, customary use was made of brackets, and ellipses were inserted to indicate omissions of repetitious or unimportant material. Four dots after Garfield's name at the end of a letter indicate a deleted postscript. The cuts in the body of the text are reproduced from Garfield's original drawings. However, the maps describing the engagement at Middle Creek, Kentucky, and the capture of the reconnaissance force at Thompson's Station, Tennessee, are redrawn from Garfield's sketches which, for technical reasons, could not be reproduced.

The letters range over a variety of subjects, from ordinary remarks about his health and environment to poignant commentary concerning issues, institutions, and individuals. Since Garfield frequently gave rein to his thoughts and feelings, his letters sometimes reveal as much about their author as the men and events he discussed. His morale, subject to sharp and sudden change, was clearly reflected in what he wrote. "Good times," he would say to his Journal when things went well for him as a student at Hiram. There were "good times" in the army, too. When they came, perhaps by way of success against the enemy or a pleasant personal experience, there would be passages glowing with enthusiasm, hope, and humor. But when upset by a Union defeat, the hardships and frustrations of soldiering, poor health, or perhaps worry over family matters, he would fall to complaining, fault-finding, and pessimism. His comments on slavery and emancipation, politics, and military affairs, when compared with those he made in the early 1850's, show a drastic change in his thinking and facilitate understanding of his intellectual development and his growth as a sagacious, shrewd, practical man who aspired, even before entering the Union army, to a seat in the House of Representatives in Washington.

## NOTES

1. Garfield to wife, April 7, 1861. This letter and, unless otherwise indicated, all of Garfield's and his wife's manuscripts, and all Scrapbook material hereinafter cited are in the Garfield Papers, Library of Congress.

2. Quoted in Theodore Clarke Smith, *The Life and Letters of James Abram Garfield*, two volumes (New Haven, 1925), I, 5.

3. Newspaper clipping from the Pittsburg *Daily Post,* October 16, 1880 in Scrapbook (1880).

4. From Garfield's Journal, hereinafter cited as Journal: Methodist and Presbyterian "historical" sermons, October 13, 1850; criticism of Presbyterian sermon and tampering with "human traditions," May 19, 1850; Catholic service in Muskingum County, April 13, 1851; comment about Mayfield, April 21, 1850.

5. From the Journal: Calhoun and Taylor, April 3 and July 10, 1850; Christians in governments, September 5 and 6, 1850; "no right to engage in politics," October 6, 1850; comment on Ohio legislators, February 28, 1851; presidential campaign, August 17, 1852; comment about voting on election day, November 2, 1852.

6. From the Journal: comment on slavery essays, September 29, 1850; "unpopular truth against popular error," September 6, 1850; appraisal of Giddings, October 2, 1850; "geological abolition of slavery," October 3, 1851; reading *Uncle Tom's Cabin,* July 17, 1852 and March 4, 1853.

7. Journal, August 2, 3 and 4, 1853 and June 25, 1854.

8. From the Journal: reaction to abolitionist speeches, November 2, 1855; disparaging remarks about politics, October 8, 1857. Presidential election of 1856, Garfield to Lucretia Rudolph, June 25, 1856. Rejoicing over fall election and comment on slavery's doom, Journal, October 22, 1857. Comment on fugitive slave, Garfield to Lucretia Rudolph, July 4, 1857. Execution of John Brown, Journal, December 2, 1859.

9. Journal, April 14, 1858.

10. Both quotations are from the Journal, August 22, 1859.

11. Garfield to Corydon Fuller, November 9, 1859, quoted in Smith, *Life and Letters,* I, 143.

12. For the major political issues and developments in Ohio during this era, see George H. Porter, *Ohio Politics during the Civil War* (New York, 1911); Eugene H. Roseboom, *The Civil War Era, 1850-1873* (Columbus, 1944); Whitelaw Reid, *Ohio in the War,* two volumes (New York, 1868); William B. Hesseltine, *Lincoln and the War Governors* (New York, 1955); Garfield's senatorship is treated in Smith, *Life and Letters,* I, 140-168.

13. Garfield to wife, March 19 and 24, 1861.

14. Same to same, March 10, 1861.

15. Garfield to J. H. Rhodes, March 26, 1865.

16. See Mary Bosworth Treudley, *Prelude to the Future: The First Hundred Years of Hiram College* (New York, 1950), 79-101.

17. Hinsdale's remarks are in Frederick A. Henry, *Captain Henry of Geauga: A Family Chronicle* (Cleveland, 1942), 598.

18. Garfield to wife, March 10 and April 7, 1861.

19. See Rhodes to Garfield, November 26, 1861, in which Dennison's statement to Garfield is mentioned.

20. Journal, April 14, 1858.

21. For commentary on the Garfield-Rhodes friendship and the latter's indolence, see Henry, *Captain Henry,* 283 and 401.

22. The request for help in getting a position with the *Herald* is in Rhodes to Garfield, November 19, 1861; comment about political advancement, same to same, November 26, 1861. All Rhodes material herein cited is in the Garfield Papers, Library of Congress.

# PART I

## Campaigning in the Army of the Ohio

*In the first phase of Garfield's wartime career, a span of fifteen months in which he served at the front as a brigade leader in the Army of the Ohio, his most important military accomplishment was his successful command of the Sandy Valley campaign in mountainous Eastern Kentucky. There, from December, 1861–March, 1862, he commanded about 3,000 men in the Eighteenth Brigade, which consisted of two Ohio and two Kentucky infantry regiments. Attached to the unit were six companies of Kentucky cavalry and Major William McLaughlin's squadron of Ohio cavalry. The brigade had no artillery.*

*Actually the campaign was a minor one, having little or no bearing on the outcome of the war. It did not, as has been claimed, eliminate a threat to the left flank of Brigadier General George H. Thomas' Union force to the southwest. The Confederate brigade in the Sandy Valley lacked the necessary numerical strength, energetic leadership, supplies, equipment, and transportation facilities to constitute a serious threat to Thomas' left. Indeed, considering the hostility of a large segment of the population, the miserable weather, the wretched condition of the roads, and the ruggedness of the country, almost destitute of provisions, the Confederates might well have been compelled to abandon the Sandy Valley invasion had no Union force been sent to drive them out. But Garfield's command accomplished its mission and gave him a timely victory. After the frustrations of the previous summer and autumn Northern morale needed a boost. Then too, the wish of the Lincoln administration to maintain control of Eastern Kentucky where Unionist sentiment predominated, was, for the moment at least, fulfilled.*

*For Garfield this victory was immensely significant. From General in Chief George B. McClellan and from the commander of the Army of the Ohio, Major General Don Carlos Buell, came words of high praise. Northern papers hailed the campaign as a smashing triumph accomplished under adverse conditions against a numerically superior enemy. Garfield himself contributed to the success story. In Napoleonic*

3

*fashion he issued a proclamation complimenting his officers and men for driving superior enemy numbers from their strongholds and admonishing them to prepare for still greater exertions in the days ahead. To the people of the Sandy Valley he issued another proclamation saying he had come to restore the honor of the Union and to bring back the old banner they all once loved. Both statements were given generous space in the Ohio press. At the same time detailed accounts of his progress against treason found their way into Garfield's letters to his wife and friends and through them, of course, to a larger audience. His promotion to brigadier general, which came in March, also attracted considerable attention. Almost overnight General Garfield became a name familiar to households across the North. For the man who bore that name probably no other event in his life shaped his political future as much as did his success in the Sandy Valley.*

*In April, 1862, Garfield found himself marching towards Pittsburg Landing, Tennessee, at the head of a brigade in the Sixth Division of Buell's army. In that capacity he served for four months, through the Shiloh and Corinth campaigns and the advance eastward across Northern Alabama. In terms of his physical condition and mental attitude this period was the nadir of his service in uniform. Some of the time he suffered terribly with diarrhea and hemorrhoids; he disapproved of Union military leadership in general and West Point leadership in particular; he disliked the way in which Lincoln was prosecuting the war; and all the while he became increasingly fearful that as just another brigade leader in a large army he would drift into obscurity, an alarming thought to one whose interest in running for Congress remained very much alive. Happily for him, late in July he obtained a leave, for reason of poor health, and returned home just before the Republicans of his district convened to nominate a congressional candidate.*

Columbus  
April 13, 1861

*My Dear Harry:*

It is one of those hours of painful weariness, when, between the reaction of a week of intense toil, and the terrible excitement and suspense of the war-news coming direct from the scene of action every few hours, I am completely exhausted. The Senate adjourned today at noon, and the chamber is nearly deserted. It is rainy and dismal outside, and a little group of members is sitting and talking anxiously of the probable fate of the day at Sumter.

An hour ago a telegraphic dispatch announced that the war steamers had crossed the bar, amid a storm of fire from the batteries, and that a flag of distress was hung out from the walls of Sumter, and that the whole interior of the fort was enveloped in dense smoke, indicating that it had taken fire from the red-hot shot from Moultrie. We have just been looking over a large map of the harbor of Charleston and the forts as described by General Carrington,[1] and can almost see the battle. The reflection is so very terrible that Major [Robert] Anderson has been kept there for three months with his hands tied while nineteen tremendous batteries have been erected and brough[t] to bear upon him, and now when they are all ready, he must almost certainly surrender to the traitors or perish.

[April 14]  
Sunday Morning

Cox[2] and I have just returned from the Governor's office to which

[1] Henry Beebee Carrington was Adjutant General of Ohio under Governors Salmon P. Chase and William Dennison.

[2] Jacob Dolson Cox, educator, lawyer, soldier, politician, and author, served in the Ohio Senate, 1860 and 1861, and distinguished himself as a Union general in the Civil War. Among the important offices he held after the war were Governor of Ohio, 1866-1868; Secretary of the Interior, 1869-1870; member of the U.S. House of Representatives, 1877-1879; Dean of the Cincinnati Law School, 1881-1897; and President of the University of Cincinnati, 1885-1889. He also wrote several military histories of the Civil War. Cox and Garfield were close friends and roomed together in Columbus during their service in the Ohio Senate.

5

we were called for consultation.[3] The dispatches show that Anderson has surrendered. The probability is that Ohio will be called upon for men and money, and the Governor has shown us a draft of his message. We meet him again at three p.m. We shall ask for a state loan of half a million, I think. Twenty companies have offered their services as soon as they are wanted. The war has now fully begun.

I am glad we are defeated at Sumter. It will rouse the people. I can see no possible end to the war till the South is subjugated. I hope we will never stop short of complete subjugation. Better lose a million men in battle than allow the government to be overthrown. The war will soon assume the shape of Slavery and Freedom. The world will so understand it, and I believe the final outcome will redound to the good of humanity.

Cox and I have within the last two weeks seriously talked over the prospects of the country and the future of our own lives, and we have resolved that if it be necessary, in order to rouse our people, we will raise companies and go with them into the army. I have no heart to think of anything but the country. If there be any hope in government or the cause of humanity, then justice, religion and patriotism require that our people should stand by the Federal government in every emergency. In a very few days the curtain will be lifted and we shall see whither we are drifting. The military bills which passed the Senate in the early part of the session were lying hopeless on the table of the House till Friday, when the attack on Sumter swept them through. They will be of great service in a crisis.

We have agreed to adjourn on the 23rd, but I fear we shall not be able to do so. I am distressed at being kept away from Hiram so long. I want you to let the school know how greatly I desire to be with them, and that I shall be there as soon as possible. At this crisis of affairs it would be unwise to adjourn, but I think we shall surely be through as soon as the 20th, if not the 23rd, which last I still hope for. Let me hear from you fully in regard to your own feelings on the school, war and your thoughts generally.

Do our Mecca prospects look any better?[4] With kindest love I am as ever your brother,

James

[3] William Dennison, a native Ohioan, graduated at Miami University in 1835, studied law, and was admitted to the bar in 1840. He practiced in Columbus until 1848, when he was elected as a Whig to the Ohio Senate. In the 1850's he engaged in banking and railroad enterprises. He turned Republican in his politics and served as Governor of Ohio, 1860-1862, and as Postmaster General of the U.S., 1864-1866. In his message to the Legislature, Dennison recommended an appropriation of not less than $450,000 to be used for organizing, arming and equipping the military forces of the state.

[4] From 1859-1861 a wave of speculation in oil swept the township of Mecca, Ohio. On November 9, 1860, Garfield himself invested some money. Huge sums were spent to sink hundreds of wells; land prices skyrocketed and the boom town of Dixie sprang up. But by early 1861 the bubble had burst and Dixie, later known as Oil Diggings, became a ghost town.

Columbus
April 14, 1861

*My Dear Crete:*

After a long delay I received yours of the 11th. Indeed, Crete, I have not omitted writing to you for a week and a half at any time since I came here. My trip with Corydon[5] did however break into my custom to some extent. But surely you were joking on the first page of your letter. My memory is quite excellent. I remember that I haven't heard from you for nearly two weeks till last night. Ain't we even now? My whole effort to get a place for Corydon has proved a failure. We found numerous obstacles in the way when we reached McArthur [Ohio] and he remained several days after I returned, but accomplished nothing. He went from here to Mishawaka, Indiana, hoping to get a place in an office there. Put down as a memorandum $35.00 which I lent him.

I have been quite well for the last week, but the work and exciting news have made me exceedingly tired today. I can see nothing now before us but a long and sanguinary war. The wanton attack on Sumter and the surrender of Major Anderson can result in nothing else than general war. When I see the outrageous meanness of the Democracy, and the timed and cowardly course of many of the Republicans, it makes me long to be in the strife and help fight it out. It seems to me, that even in the revolution there was no greater need of men to stand by the country and sustain its authority. A resolution has been adopted by both branches of the Legislature to adjourn on the 23rd. I very much desire to get away by that time, but I fear we shall not. The war news is causing great excitement and I presume we shall be kept a week longer.

Then the little dear Trot[6] is creeping about the floor! Is it a new trick? You have said nothing about it before. I will get her a willow cart when I come home. Does she attempt to talk any yet? It will seem so very strange to hear her. Do you think she will remember me when she sees me? I guess not. I had a letter from your father a few days ago in regard to the theological department and my staying another year. I have answered the letter. Who is moving in reference to the theological department?[7]

I wish we were so situated here that you could come down and stay

[5] Corydon E. Fuller, Garfield's friend and classmate at the Eclectic; author of *Reminiscences of James A. Garfield* (1887).

[6] The nickname of Garfield's first child, Eliza, born on July 3, 1860. Sometimes Garfield referred to her as Mrs. Polk, the little grump, and the little cogger.

[7] Because of dissatisfaction with the quality of sermons delivered by their preachers, a number of congregations of the Disciples of Christ in and around Hiram petitioned the trustees of the Eclectic to expand the program of study for young men planning to enter the ministry. The trustees, one of whom was Garfield's father-in-law, explained that when the school's debts were paid they hoped to establish a theological department. The matter was given considerable attention in 1861 and for a few years thereafter, but the school never organized a theological department.

the rest of the term. It would be a great pleasure to me. I have felt so all winter but I knew that with Trot it could not well be done. If I should go to Congress we would move there for the winter. (Isn't this a fine specimen of unhatched chicken?) Cox and I are spending all our leisure time in reading military science and the campaigns of Napoleon and Wellington. I will try to write a letter to Trot as soon as I can. The little *grump*. She don't care anything about me. Kiss her though and write in her journal for me. Please don't *fail* to write to

*Your* James

Columbus
April 17, 1861
10 o'clock p.m.

*My Dear Harry:*

I [see] that [the course of events] I foreshadowed in my letter of Sunday is hastening to take the form of reality. The all absorbing and intense excitement which fill this city and state and whole nation has no parallel in our history. It has swept everything before it. The million war bill[8] I sent you had but one dissenting vote in the Senate, though Judge Key[9] and I had a debate on it which inspired me more than I have been before moved. Today my treason bill,[10] which has received the jeers of Democrats and their journals, passed the Senate with but eight dissenting votes. Yesterday, a dispatch from Washington requested two regiments (780 men each) to be at Washington this week. Before night they were promised to be here in 24 hours. They will reach the city in an hour from now and tomorrow start for Washington.[11] Hundreds have volunteered in the city within two days. I

[8] The bill passed by the Senate on April 17 provided for a state loan of a million dollars for raising and equipping the Ohio militia. William Newman of Portsmouth, who represented the Seventh District (Adams, Pike, Scioto, and Jackson counties) raised the lone dissenting voice. The next day, however, he requested and received permission to change his vote, which he did. The Cincinnati *Gazette* (April 18, 1861) attributed Newman's switch to popular outcry against him, especially in his own district.

[9] Judge Thomas M. Key, a Cincinnati Democrat who became a colonel and judge advocate on McClellan's staff, actually supported the bill, though he regarded it as "an unwarranted declaration of war" against the seceded states. Key denounced Lincoln's policy toward the South, accused the President of usurping power and of moving in the direction of a military despotism; yet he opposed secession and supported the Union.

[10] The treason bill, reported by Garfield on April 15 and passed by the Senate two days later, provided a penalty of life imprisonment at hard labor for any Ohio resident found guilty of giving aid and comfort to the enemies of the U.S.

[11] Troops began to arrive in Columbus on April 17, and on the following day two regiments (three months) were organized from twenty militia companies then in the capital. Early in the morning of April 19, without waiting for arms, uniforms, or equipment, the regiments entrained for Washington only to encounter an exasperating delay en route.

was just sent for to address a tremendous mass meeting at the Armory Hall. They were calling for me, and I went over and spoke to them a short time. Not ten minutes have passed since morning without some dispatch which adds new fire to the excitement.

There can be no doubt that we are now entering upon a terrible and bloody war. We have fought the battle of argument and have conquered. The American people have learned to bear talk of any kind and all kinds, but an act has meaning to them.

There is nothing now left but war and I do not hesitate to say that our duty to God and the country requires us to accept the issue. In this war, triflers and loafers will not meet the emergency. True, strong men, who comprehend the issue and are willing [to] meet it, are needed. I have offered the Governor my services in any capacity he may see fit to appoint me. He may not require me to enter the army now, he may not at all. It is thought by some that a brigadier generalship will be assigned to me, but this is not probable. I have thought it my duty to tell you these things in confidence, to be shown only to Crete and Almeda,[12] and such others as you may think it entirely prudent to. I have no doubt I shall go home next week and take my place in the school till the end of the term; still, this may not be so. It will be important to keep the school quiet and as free from the general excitement as possible. I want to hear from you all immediately and fully in the whole premises.

I would do nothing wrong or rash, but there is something due to the state from the position I hold.

Your good letter was received and read with pleasure. I am very glad to hear the school is doing so well. Tell Burke[13] I will try to answer his letter soon. My dear Harry, my heart answers fully to all your expressions of love.

With love to all our dear circle, and hoping to see you soon, I am

*as ever your brother,*

James

[12] Almeda Ann Booth, intimate friend and colleague of Garfield, taught at the Eclectic from 1851-1866, save for one year during which she studied at Oberlin. At Hiram this learned young lady exerted a strong influence in shaping Garfield's character and career. Unfortunately, only a few of Garfield's letters to her are extant.

[13] Burke Aaron Hinsdale, educator, preacher, editor, and author, was a close friend and correspondent of Garfield for many years. At the Eclectic (renamed Hiram College in 1867) Hinsdale was a part-time student, 1853-1860, and a teacher, 1860-1864 and 1869-1883. He was President of Hiram College, 1870-1883. In 1883, after serving four years as superintendent of schools in Cleveland, he became a professor in the University of Michigan. He wrote books on religion, education, history, and government, and edited a memorial volume, *President Garfield and Education* (1881), and *The Works of James A. Garfield,* two volumes (1882-1883). In May, 1862, Hinsdale married Mary E. Turner, who is mentioned in later letters.

Columbus
April 28, 1861

*My Dear Crete:*

I have been too busy during the whole of the past week and even now, though it is Sunday evening, I have but a short time which I can snatch away from work. I left Ravenna on the evening train Tuesday and finding I could not make the connection at Cleveland, I stopped off at Newburgh. Saw mother for an hour, made a speech in the village to a large audience, and staid over night at John Clapp's.[14] I reached here Tuesday forenoon and on Thursday went to Cleveland to help organize two regiments.[15] Returned Saturday morning. Cox has been appointed one of the brigadier generals and leaves tomorrow morning at five o'clock to organize a camp at Loveland. He takes about 1,200 men with him.

It now appears probable that I shall be elected Colonel of the 7th Regiment now at Cleveland. If so I shall probably be ordered into camp before the week is ended. If not, my military history will not begin just [yet]. The more I reflect on the whole subject, the more I feel that I cannot stand aloof from this conflict. My heart and hope for the country are in it and I could do no justice to the every day duties of life. I found in the camp a[t] Cleveland a company of Oberlin boys. More than half of them were students. Charley Bowler and W. D. Ringland were among them.[16] Their Captain was a theological student.[17]

I am every day impressed with the character of the men who are going into this war. A few days ago there came a company from Ironton on the Ohio River. They were mostly members of a Methodist Church in that place. When they reached here there were no quarters for them in the camp and the Senate, House, and Supreme Court room were already full. They were obliged to sleep on the marble floor of the rotunda. Before lying down for the night they gathered into a corner

[14] John H. Clapp was the husband of Garfield's cousin, Phebe Boynton. Clapp, who entered the military service as a captain in the Second Ohio Cavalry Regiment, died on October 5, 1861, from injuries received when thrown from and trampled by his horse. See Garfield's letter to Phebe, October 8, 1861.

[15] Garfield went to Cleveland to help organize the Seventh and Eighth Ohio Infantry (three months) regiments. Hereinafter infantry units alone are not identified as to branch of service.

[16] Bowler and Ringland, formerly students at the Eclectic, joined the Seventh Ohio. Bowler, a sergeant, was killed at Cedar Mountain in August, 1862.

[17] Giles W. Shurtleff had been a member of the Oberlin Theological School and a tutor in Latin. His contingent left Oberlin for Cleveland on April 25, 1861, and became Company C of the Seventh Ohio. The company took the name of Monroe Rifles in honor of Oberlin's politician professor, James Monroe. These soldiers received their first training in field service at Camp Dennison, near Cincinnati, where they became known as the praying company. Shurtleff was taken prisoner in the engagement at Cross-Lanes, Virginia, August 26, 1861, and was exchanged and returned to his regiment in October, 1862. He subsequently became Colonel of the 5th U.S. Colored Troops and was breveted a brigadier general in March, 1865.

and held a prayer meeting. Their officers led in prayer and they sang finely. One song was "I'm glad I'm in this Army." Ungodly men who looked on were moved to tears, and one old fellow said to another who made some s[l]ighting remark, I'll whip the first *damned* man that makes sport of them. Such men will fight.

I shall know in a few days my own course. . . .

Kiss Trot, dear soul, and receive my love.

*Your* James

Governor's Office
Springfield, Illinois
April 30, 1861

*My Dear Harry:*

While Governor Yates[18] is preparing some papers, I take the time to write a few words. I left Columbus yesterday morning at 3½ o'clock and arrived here via Crestline, Ft. Wayne and Chicago at 6 o'clock this morning, having ridden nearly 600 miles. I find the whole West, so far as I can see in Indiana and Illinois, stirred to its depths on the subject of the war.

Besides taking home with me 5,000 stands of arms, I am to open negotiations with the governors of Illinois and Indiana with the design of obtaining permission of the General government to divide the forces of the Union into two grand armies, all east of the mountains to be called the army of the East and to take charge of Washington and the sea coast, and another to be called the army of the valley, who shall take the whole line of coast from Pittsburgh to Cairo, and shall open a way down the Mississippi River. As there is but one major general west of the mountains called for in the requisition, and he is from Ohio (General G[eorge] B. McClellan)[19] it will be a work of some difficulty to get all the states of the valley to submit to the leadership of Ohio. I am to try my power of diplomacy to effect this purpose.

The members of the Illinois Legislature are a strong, muscular, rough looking set, but I like the bearing of the Governor.

I must wait here till I can get the guns shipped and then go with them. We dare not trust them alone, lest some scamp should get them away. I hope to be in Columbus again by Thursday. Let me hear from you soon.

[18] Richard Yates, Governor of Illinois, 1861-1865; U.S. Senator, 1865-1871.

[19] On April 23, Governor Dennison appointed George B. McClellan a major general of Ohio Volunteers with command of all Ohio forces. McClellan accepted the commission and took office that day. On May 13, however, he received a commission (dated May 3) as major general in the Regular army with command of the Department of the Ohio, which then included the states of Ohio, Indiana, and Illinois.

The colonelcy will probably be decided before I return. I fear my absence will affect it unfavorably.

*Truly your brother,*
James

Columbus
May 3, 1861

*His Excellency, Governor Dennison,*
*Dear Sir:*

In conformity with your instructions of the 29th *ult.,* I visited Springfield, Illinois, and obtained from the Quartermaster General, by order of the Governor of Illinois, five thousand muskets and accouterments and shipped them via Lafayette and Indianapolis to Columbus for (55) fifty-five cents per hundred weight. The invoice and shipping bill are herewith submitted. I also communicated to Governor Yates your views concerning the consolidation of the army of the Mississippi Valley, and am glad to report that they met with his hearty concurrence. I desire to acknowledge my obligations to Governor Yates and Quartermaster General [John] Wood for the prompt aid they rendered me in the accomplishment of my mission.

*Very respectfully,*
J. A. Garfield

Columbus
May 5, 1861

*My Dear Crete:*

Last evening I received your good letter, the first word I have heard from home since I left there two weeks ago. The rapid succession of events has made this past fortnight seem more than a month long. I am exceedingly gratified and my mind much relieved to hear that the school is swinging back again into its usual orbit. I have been fearful that it might break under the strong outside pressure. Patience is now among the prime virtues and the whole country should learn to practice it. I returned from Springfield on Wednesday evening, having undressed myself only twice during a whole week.

But before I detail any of my doings, I will vindicate myself from the mysterious suspicions which are giving my dear friends anxiety about me. I don't remember what I said in my letter that should give you an idea that I was using any means not quite honorable to secure a good post in the army. If I used any expressions which indicated any such thing they were unfortunate and did me injustice. In the first place I do not feel about this matter as I do about ordinary offices.

To seek a place of usefulness in the army seems to me rather meritorious than otherwise. When I hear that Ben Wade,[20] John Sherman,[21] A. G. Riddle[22] and other men of that character have enlisted in the ranks, I say it is done for buncombe and is an unmanly piece of demagogism.[23] I should even regard it so in myself. I know the time may come when it might be the duty of all men of every class to go into the ranks or to take any other position where they can aid the country, but that time has not yet come. I looked the field over, and thought if I went into the army I ought to have at least as high a position as a staff officer. My friends thought so likewise, and generously offered to aid me in obtaining such a position. The Governor would have given me one still higher if he had had one in his gift.

I went to Cleveland for two purposes. One, to see that the Reserve was fairly represented in the regiments to be formed. The Governor sent me for that. The other was to see whether I could honorably obtain the colonelcy. I accomplished the first, and for the second, I met with favor from all the companies I saw. I should have been elected before now but for my absence to Illinois. The Governor of his own accord delayed giving the order for the election till my return. While I was gone, Tyler[24] of Ravenna, whom I had aided in various ways and who

[20] Benjamin F. Wade of Ohio, U.S. Senator, 1851-1869.

[21] John Sherman of Ohio; member of the U.S. House of Representatives, 1855-1861; U.S. Senator, 1861-1877, 1881-1897; Secretary of the Treasury, 1877-1881; Secretary of State, 1897-1898; defeated for nomination as Republican presidential candidate in 1880 by Garfield, who had placed his name before the convention.

[22] Albert Gallatin Riddle of Ohio; lawyer, congressman, and author; member of the U.S. House of Representatives, 1861-1863; author of several books including *The Life, Character, and Public Services of J. A. Garfield* (1880).

[23] The rumor that Wade, Sherman, and Riddle had enlisted in the ranks was unfounded.

[24] Erastus B. Tyler, a businessman and soldier, was a brigadier general in the Ohio militia when the Civil War began. On May 7, 1861, the officers and men of the Seventh Ohio, impressed with Tyler's military background, elected him Colonel of the regiment, a position Garfield coveted. In the two weeks prior to the election, when Tyler emerged as a formidable candidate, Garfield redoubled his bid for the colonelcy and the contest assumed political overtones. A number of men worked hard for the Hiram candidate. John H. Clapp, William Bowler, and others circulated among the officers and men at the Seventh's encampment in Cleveland. In Columbus, Governor Dennison's private secretary, William T. Bascom, did what he could to help. Just before the election, when Garfield appeared to be in difficulty, Bascom wired Clapp that it was important to have Garfield elected and that all his friends must "rally at once." In Ravenna, Halsey Hall's *Portage Democrat,* a Republican paper, sided with Garfield. After the election, the paper leaped to Garfield's defense against charges of seeking the colonelcy; but all the while Hall was complaining to his Hiram friend about the tactics being used to defeat Tyler. After the latter's victory, Ravenna's *Weekly Portage Sentinel,* a Democratic paper, ran an editorial (May 29, 1861) entitled "The Colonelcy of the Seventh Regiment." Garfield, said the *Sentinel,* is "without military education, experience, or training," refuses to join the ranks, and attempts "to leap from the walks of a private citizen to the position of a military chieftain." He is interested in *"self"* not country, said the paper. The *Sentinel* denied the contention of the *Portage Democrat* that Gar-

had told me he would aid me in the election, turned in and offered himself as a candidate and by bargains and brandy got an informal ballott by which he was elected.

But the regular election has not yet been held. I do not know how it will turn. I may not be elected but I shall do all I can justly to secure his defeat, for he has acted treacherously. Several Cleveland men have been doing what they could for me. John Clapp is now here and the 7th Regiment will be here this afternoon. I shall, if for no other reason than to defeat Tyler, go before them as a candidate. My trip to Illinois was wholly on the Governor's war business, and was not only no part of my own interest, but if I fail, that trip will be the whole cause of it. For it gave Tyler a chance to say what he pleased and he was very unscrupulous. I am not conscious of any act in the whole matter which I would not willingly have known. I will not spend any time with this now. But I am glad you spoke of it, and I want you to tell me fully of any reports or rumors which throw a suspicion upon my course. I know and appreciate the spirit in which you wrote about it and I thank you for it. I should know soon the outcome of the whole matter. Give my love to all and kiss Trot a hundred times for me.

*Ever your* James

[P.S.]
Tell Burke I will secure those military books for him as soon as I can. The market has been emptied and they have been waiting for supplies.

Hiram
June 4, 1861

*Captain Hard,*[25]
*Dear Sir:*

In an editorial of the *Portage* [County] *Sentinel* of May 29th I notice that you are referred to as authority to prove that I was instrumental in getting your company ruled out of a regiment because they would not support me for the colonelcy. I saw in an article in the *Summit County Beacon* over your signature a complaint that your company was not received into the 19th Regiment and some "civilian" was charged with being concerned in keeping you out. I did not know to

---

field never sought the colonelcy, charging that there was "scarcely an officer in the Seventh Regiment whom he did not importune personally or besiege through his friends." In an earlier post-election issue (May 15, 1861) the *Sentinel* gloated over the defeat of the "Hon. Rev. J. A. Garfield, Esq., A.M." After accusing him of "overweening ambition," the paper said: "As Mr. Garfield assured our volunteers four weeks ago that he would be with them on the tented field in a short time, we presume he will soon enlist as a private!"

[25] Pulaski C. Hard became a captain in the Twenty-ninth Ohio in September, 1861, and resigned in March, 1862.

whom you referred, but the appearance of your name in the *Sentinel* in the article referred to, leads me to conclude that your statement in the *Beacon* has reference to me. I presume you have no desire or intention of doing me any wrong, but I was exceedingly surprised when I read the statement in the *Sentinel*.

The first knowledge I ever had of you or your company was when I heard that an Akron company had been disbanded, and shortly after saw your card in the *Beacon*. I had no knowledge whatever of the formation of the 19th Regiment and did not know what companies were rejected from it or what ones were received into it till several days after its formation when its list of companies was published. I was sent to Cleveland near the close of April to aid in the formation of the 7th and 8th regiments, but at that time no Summit county company had been accepted by the Department at Columbus. I cannot conceive how I have been represented as in any way concerned with your company or with the 19th Regiment. I write this in justice both to you and to myself. I am not personally acquainted with you but I am unwilling that any man should be led to misunderstand me in such a way. If there be any thing in this matter which requires explanation I shall be glad to know it. I will esteem it a favor to hear from you.

Hoping that there may be no misunderstanding or injustice between us, I am,

*Truly yours,*
J. A. Garfield

Hiram
June 8, 1861

*J. H. Clapp, Esq.,*
*Dear Sir:*

Yours was received last evening. I can hardly understand why there is so much delay in mustering in the new regiments. I will have some letters sent to the Governor if it can be done without exciting suspicion of plotting. There seems to be in the community a perfect crazy determination to make it out that I [am] making great exertions to secure a place. So strong is that feeling that I think it will be unwise for me to do anything to increase this feeling. I don't know but some handle will be made of your being at Columbus, if it is generally known. I hope you will take extra pains to keep down suspicion and remark. A few judicious friends will accomplish as much good, and less harm can result than if there were a great number. I don't want to pay too much attention to rumor, but I really feel that my reputation in two or three counties is in danger, and [that] a lot of un scrupulous men who want me out of the way are pushing the matter with all the strength they can command.

If I can get the appointment without making a great effort, I believe that I might redeem myself from the obloquy they have attempted to heap upon me. But I would rather not succeed in it at all than to give much opportunity for slander. I shall trust the whole matter to your judgment and prudence, and shall hope to hear the result soon.

Our Commencement closed finely. All well.

*Yours truly,*
J. A. Garfield

Cleveland
June 14, 1861

*Dear Crete:*

I returned from Columbus last evening. Harry and I go to Bedford this afternoon. I go to Wheeling tomorrow. Shall be early next [week?] at home. Army question will be decided by that time.

Have only time for a word for the Mahoning train is just off.

Joe[26] is well.

*Truly your*
James

Hiram
June 18, 1861

*Governor Dennison,*
*Dear Sir:*

I have waited until the limit is reached, at which I was to communicate with you in regard to my appointment as Lieutenant Colonel of the 24th Regiment.[27] I very much desired to go into the army, and felt that I could not remain away from the conflict. But such is the condition of my personal affairs, and my relations to those with whom

---

[26] Joseph, Lucretia's brother, was mustered into the Twenty-third Ohio as a private in June, 1861. He was transferred to the Forty-second Ohio in March, 1862, and served as a sergeant until July, 1864, when he was mustered out. All the members of the Rudolph family appear in later letters. Lucretia's father, Zebulon, married Arabella Mason. Zeb, as he was called, was a carpenter, a member of the Disciples, and a founder and trustee of the Eclectic. The children not yet introduced were Ellen, usually called Nell or Nellie, and John. The latter died in Lexington, Kentucky, in 1862, leaving his wife, then twenty-four years of age, and four children.

[27] On June 22, 1861, Samuel A. Gilbert was appointed to the position declined by Garfield, and the Twenty-fourth Ohio, whose first commander was Jacob Ammen, did most of its campaigning in the western theater.

I am in business connection, that I feel compelled to decline the place. This I do with great regret, but with the hope and belief that a few months may find me at liberty to follow the promptings of my heart and take any post to which the country may see fit to call me.

Should Congress make an additional levy of troops, I shall still hope to be ready for any work at which I may be needed. With many thanks for your kindness and confidence,

*I am,*
*Truly yours,*
J. A. Garfield

Hiram
June 28, 1861

*Dear Brother Austin:*[28]

I have intended for several days to write to you, but I have felt that the deep grief which has fallen upon you and your family was too sacred to be broken in upon by subjects so foreign from it. I know I cannot enter into your feelings, nor can any one but yourself, but you know that you have all my sympathy and affection in your deep bereavement.

I have finally decided, as you have doubtless heard, to decline the appointment tendered me by the Governor. I confess to you that it was more of a struggle than I have passed through for years. I found that my heart was pretty thoroughly set on going into the army and I had also much pride to struggle with in the matter. But I made this compromise with myself: "There are plenty to take that place now. But if there shall hereafter be more levies, and greater necessities, I can go then with the full approval of my own judgment and that of my friends." I went to Columbus and had a long and full visit with the Governor on the subject and agreed to let him know my decision by the 19th of June. When that date arrived I wrote him my decision.

Brother Robison[29] and I have visited Wheeling and Bethany. We

[28] Harmon Austin was a prominent member of the Disciples of Christ in Ohio. A successful businessman in Warren, he was well known locally as a host to public figures. He was also Garfield's close friend and for about two decades his political lieutenant in Trumbull County. Austin's wife, Minerva, his daughter, Nellie, and Minerva's sister, Lottie, appear later. Two weeks before Garfield wrote this letter, Austin's eldest child had died at the age of twelve.

[29] John P. Robison founded and for many years led the Disciples of Christ congregation in Bedford, Ohio. He also travelled with Alexander Campbell through the state preaching at Disciple meetings, and he was a trustee of both the Eclectic and Bethany College. Although he graduated at the Vermont Medical College (1832) he abandoned medicine for business. As a member of the Ohio Senate, he played a conspicuous role in getting Garfield promoted to brigadier general. Loud, aggressive, self-confident, and crude, Robison was to many people an unattractive personality. For a number of years Garfield's wife disliked him; but she had a

had a very pleasant time. The college classes were disbanded nearly two months ago. It is a deserted looking place, I assure you. That splendid structure standing unfinished and abandoned. There is too much invested there to be lost. It must and will someday be redeemed, I am sure.[30]

Professor Pickett[31] was a rabid secessionist and had gone home to Kentucky. Professor Pendleton[32] has had a severe trial. His friends and family are in the heart of old Virginia and are strong secessionists. He voted for secession, but I believe his heart is inclined to be right. We had a long conversation which I believe will result in good. I love him very much. Brother Campbell[33] is for the Union, but his son, wife, and daughter sympathize with the South. It is sad to see a family so divided. . . .

Brother Campbell is getting very much broken. He cannot last long, I fear. He frequently says in a very mournful way, "I shall never see peace in this country again." . . .

You see in the papers what the convention has done. It is a great and hopeful move, and the principle involved in it seems to me the straightest road out of our present difficulties.

Brother Robison has written to Brother Errett[34] (I suppose you have also) and as soon as we know at what time he will be at home, he wants you and me to go with him to see Isaac and talk the proposed plan all over. I hope to hear from you soon and know what you are thinking on the whole subject.

I dread to go into the school for some reason this coming year. It must be small and the pay will be hardly sufficient to keep me and my family. Pecuniarily considered, it is a ruinous course for me to take. I am anxious to know what is to be the result of the theological effort. . . .

---

change of heart and grew fond of him. Robison remained close to the Garfields and was their next-door neighbor during the years they lived at Lawnfield in Mentor.

[30] During the academic year 1860-1861 the enrollment of Bethany College was one hundred and five. When Garfield made his visit, there were rumors that the school was closing. In July, however, the board of trustees announced that they had no thought of suspending Bethany's program. The college remained open, but, of course, the enrollment declined during the war years. "That splendid structure" referred to by Garfield stood where the Main Building now stands. Late in 1857 a fire destroyed it, but rebuilding began promptly and continued until July, 1862, when lack of funds brought operations to a halt with much work still to be done inside. The building was not completed until 1870.

[31] Professor J. D. Pickett taught Spanish and English literature in Bethany College from 1858-1861.

[32] William Kimbrough Pendleton, Vice-President of Bethany College, 1845-1866; President, 1866-1886.

[33] Alexander Campbell was the founder of the Disciples of Christ. In 1840 he established Bethany College in Western Virginia and was its President from then until his death in 1866.

[34] Isaac Errett, author, educator, and Disciple preacher, was being consulted about establishing a theological department at Hiram.

I am busy preparing some public addresses I have to deliver by and by.

With much love, I am

*Truly yours,*
J. A. Garfield

Hiram
July 8, 1861

*My Dear Smith:* 35

I remember that you were so kind as to intimate to me before we left Columbus that a correspondence between us would be pleasing to you. There was a pleasant and hearty frankness in our intercourse which always made me feel so much at home with you that I must protest against silence and non-intercourse. Since I left you I have found no one with whom to splinter a lance on banks and bullion, or *communism* in general as you are pleased to style the majority of corporations.

You know I was looking toward the army when I last saw you. I received a regimental appointment but after mature deliberation and not a little struggle with the blandishments of Bloody Mars, I resolved to decline and follow a little longer the inglorious path of an innoxious [innocuous] civilian and a retired (used up) politician.

I have, since I left Columbus, been plunging again into the closing work of our academic year, and since the term closed have been running about some and trying to do some political and miscellaneous reading. Another 4th of July oration lead me to read over again the history of the Constitution and confirmed [me] in my love for [Alexander] Hamilton and weakened my regard for [Thomas] Jefferson. I believe the next half century will see the fame of those two men change places in the popular estimation.

I was greatly pained and disgusted at the result of your congressional district's election. Wasn't there some intrigue in that matter? It is outrageous in a time when men of decisive opinions are needed to have such a man as the Honorable R. A. H.36 in Congress. Tell me how it occurred. I had hoped to see you there now. I suppose the Union cry did it.

I want to give you my views on the Union movement for our state

35 John Quincy Smith, member of the Ohio Senate, 1860 and 1861, and of the Ohio House of Representatives, 1862, 1863, 1872, 1873; member of the U.S. House of Representatives, 1873-1875; U.S. Commissioner of Indian Affairs, 1875-1877; U.S. Consul General to Montreal, 1878-1882.

36 Richard A. Harrison of London, Ohio, was elected as a Union Democrat to the U.S. House of Representatives to fill the vacancy created by the resignation of Thomas Corwin and served from July 4, 1861 to March 4, 1863.

and legislative tickets this fall. The feeling in that direction is so strong and widely diffused that I think it will be quite likely to control the nominations, but I see only disaster in it. I observe that in most places the movement means to put a Democrat at the head of the state ticket for governor. I would like to know by what rules of equity that party makes such a claim. In all strong Democratic counties they are putting up their own regular tickets. Here on the Reserve where they have no strength they are all patriotic for the Union and a Union ticket. Indeed they are among our loudest and busiest Union men. The result will be that Democratic counties will have Democratic members in the legislature, and strongly Republican counties will have Union Democrats, and the general assembly will be Democratic. Pugh[37] will be senator and the congressional districts will be put in a horrid shape. I fear this result cannot be averted. Our men are taking the bait and will be caught unless some strong measures can be taken to avert the calamity. The Democratic leaders here are aided by a bevy of fossil Republicans who hope to ride into power on the wave of the war. Give me your thoughts on this subject. I hope your section has learned from its Harrison experience not to get bitten so again.

Shall you be in the [Ohio] Senate again next winter? I hope you will. Or have you thought still more of the lieutenant governorship? I would rather see you a senator but will be glad to aid you whenever and where ever I can. Let me hear from you. Present my regards to your good wife, and believe me,

*Ever and truly,*
J. A. Garfield

Hiram
July 12, 1861

*My Dear Burke:*

Shortly after my last letter to you was written, I received yours. I delayed writing, hoping that I might be able to say that we would, several of us, visit you before this, but so many things have intervened that I find we cannot yet set a time, if indeed we can come at all this vacation. Harry will, however, be there before he returns. He goes home to Massillon next Monday. I start for Michigan with Brother[s] Robison and Austin on Monday. Crete goes to Princeton, Illinois to visit her brother John and I go round there to come home with her. We shall probably be gone about two weeks.

I spent nearly two weeks before the 4th in constitutional readings.

[37] George Ellis Pugh was a member of the Ohio House of Representatives, 1848-1850, and of the U.S. Senate, 1855-1861.

I read Curtis,[38] *The Federalist*,[39] and parts of Hildreth[40] and Bancroft,[41] and a few chapters again in de Tocqueville.[42] The chief point I made in the speech at Burton was that Jeffersonianism was now fully tested and had proved a failure. The Kentucky and Virginia Resolutions contained the germ of nullification and secession, and we are today reaping the fruits. Hamilton was right in his main propositions. Hereafter he and Jefferson will change places in the popular estimation, at least in the estimation of statesmen and thinkers. All my readings confirm this. Have you ever observed how severe Hildreth is on Jefferson? He hardly allows that there was any patriotism or manliness in him. He makes him out a mean-spirited intriguer. By the way, I think we ought to have Hamilton's *Works*[43] in the Library.

Since the 4th we have had some company, some business, some play and some reading. We should have visited you during that time but the negotiation was going on about the trip to Michigan and I could not tell when we should go.

I hardly knew myself till the trial came how much of a struggle it would cost me to give up going into the army. I found I had so full[y] interested myself in the war that I hardly felt it possible for me not to be a part of the movement. But the consideration that there were so many who could fill the office tendered to me, and would covet the place, more than could do my work here perhaps, that I could not but feel it would be to some extent a reckless disregard of the good of others to accept. If there had been a scarcity of volunteers I should have accepted. The time may yet come when I shall feel it right and necessary to go, but I thought on the whole that time had not yet come.

I was very glad to read your reflections on the subject. I felt them very fully. Indeed, I look forward to a separation from Hiram as an event filled with much that is sad and trying. I believe a man can never leave any place where he [has] done earnest work that gave him thought and anxiety for any great length of time without such feeling. The first school house in which we taught is always a more marked object with us than any other one.

I am perplexed for a subject for my address at Oberlin. I wish you would suggest some themes which you think would be appropriate.

---

[38] George Ticknor Curtis, *History of the Origin, Formation, and Adoption of the Constitution of the United States,* two volumes (1854-1858).

[39] The eighty-five articles written in defense of the Constitution by Alexander Hamilton, John Jay, and James Madison appeared in book form in the spring of 1788 under the title *The Federalist*.

[40] Richard Hildreth, *History of the United States,* six volumes (1840-1852). A strong Federalist bias is evident in the early volumes.

[41] George Bancroft, *History of the United States,* ten volumes (1834-1874). The first eight volumes appeared before the Civil War. Volume VIII treated the years 1774-1776.

[42] Alexis de Tocqueville, *Democracy in America,* two volumes (1835, 1840).

[43] John Church Hamilton, editor, *The Works of Alexander Hamilton,* seven volumes (1850-1851)

Write me at Princeton, Illinois. I shall be there in ten days from this time.

We are having a very pleasant, quiet time here—Harry, Almeda, Crete and I. Harvey[44] is coming back in the fall. I expect a small school.

I am anxious to know the result of our negotiations with Errett.

Give my love to your folks. Crete and Almeda join me.

Hoping to hear from you, I am as ever,

*Truly yours,*
J. A. Garfield

Detroit
July 30, 1861

*My Dear Crete:*
I have been quite well with the exception of my arm. I have not been able to write scarcely at all, and each motion of my pen now gives me acute pain. But still it is much better than when I left you. I found, by John, that a letter had come from the Doctor and was sent to Monmouth on Monday but the surliness of the Post Master kept me from receiving it. I reached Chicago in the evening and the next morning left on the propeller for Milwaukee, where I arrived at noon. At 4 P.M. I took the boat for Grand Haven, which I reached at 10½ P.M. It was somewhat rough and for once I was sick and vomitted. It was hard to be sick alone but I was sick but a short time. I went on to Grand Rapids and next morning went to visit my uncles.[45] I had a good visit and at two o'clock Sunday morning I reached Muir and found Doctor [Robison], [and] Brothers Jones[46] and Austin. After a brief visit we came on to this place.

I very much wish you were here now. I should be greatly inclined to go right on home but still I hardly feel as though I ought to go by and not see the Port Austin friends. A boat goes out tonight and I go on it. I cannot get back till the next boat returns. It arrives at Port Austin on Wednesday evening or Thursday morning and leaves on Sunday. That will bring me here on Monday. If you could be here on Monday evening we could go to Cleveland on the evening boat but I think you cannot do that without leaving on Saturday.

[44] Harvey W. Everest was a student with Garfield at Geauga Seminary and at the Eclectic. He taught for several years at the Eclectic and was its Principal, 1861-1862, 1863-1864. Later he was President of Eureka College in Illinois and of Butler University in Indiana, and he made an unsuccessful attempt to establish Garfield University in Wichita, Kansas. At his death in 1900 he was Dean of the College of the Bible, Drake University, Iowa.

[45] Jerry and William were the sons of Aseneth and Caleb Boynton. Aseneth was the widow of Thomas Garfield and grandmother of James A. In 1835 Jerry and William moved to Byron Township, Michigan, where each purchased land, farmed, married and raised families.

[46] Jefferson Harrison Jones, a Disciple preacher who became Chaplain of the Forty-second Ohio, was one of Garfield's most intimate friends.

I think, therefore, this is the best plan. You leave there on the midnight train, Monday night, or I believe it is at 2 o'clock Tuesday morning, and come directly through. It will give you a stop of an hour in Chicago and bring you here at 6 o'clock P.M. when we will take the evening boat. This will cause me to wait a day and night at Detroit, but I will accept the invitation of Brother Hawley[47] who lives on Woodward Avenue and who wants us both to stop and visit him. Now let me be definite. What I have written on this page is written with the belief that there is not [a] 2 o'clock train Monday morning from Princeton. If however there is, I want you to take it, and it will get you here in time for the Monday evening boat. Have John find how this is. If you can start then you may reach here an hour before I do and in that case, I have agreed that you will call at Brother Hawley's. I enclose a card of direction and you can order the omnibus to take you there. Now if this last plan can be adopted, I want it done. If not I will await you for Tuesday evening.

My wrist and you are both tired with these details.

Give my love to Johnny and Mattie. Doctor [Robison] and the whole company here send love. I have been very lonesome without you and our precious little Trot. Kiss her for me a great many times and kiss yourself for me in the glass.

> *With much love I am*
> *ever your*
> James

Hiram
August 7, 1861

*Governor Dennison,*
*Dear Sir:*

I have just returned from a trip of two weeks to the west and found your favor of the 28th *ult.* asking me to accept a lieutenant colonelcy awaiting me. I regret that I was not here at the time.

I now write to inquire if the lieutenant colonelcies are all disposed of, and, if not, to inquire at what time I should be needed to go into camp. If I should not be needed under two or three weeks I hope I could accept the appointment. Will you also mention whether the colonels are to be West Point men?

I shall be pleased to receive an early answer. With many thanks for your kind remembrance of me,

> *I am,*
> *Very respectfully,*
> J. A. Garfield

[47] Richard Hawley, a Detroit businessman and sometime city official, was the proprietor of Richard Hawley & Son, Maltsters. He was elected to the Michigan legislature in 1864 and again in 1877.

Cleveland
August 14, 1861

*My Dear Crete:*

I have concluded to go. Shortly after I arrived, I went to the telegraph office and sent a dispatch to the Governor saying I was ready to go, and asked him if I should leave on the next train. It is now past eleven and I have not heard from him. Probably from the lateness of the hour he failed to get my dispatch. The reason for my asking him the question was that from the tardiness of my response he may have concluded I was not going and have filled the place. If I get an answer tonight I shall know certainly all about it. If not, I shall go to Columbus in the morning and stay if I am still wanted. I presume there is but little doubt but that I shall stay. So far as I am concerned, it is settled.

But I have arranged to send you a dispatch from Columbus, which is to be sent out in the bundle of papers on tomorrow evening's train. See that the boy gets it. In that I will let you know the final result. Until that time I want my absence kept entirely within the circle of yourself and the teachers. Let there be no hint of its purpose.

Concerning my decision, you know how much of a question was before me. The only new view since I left home was the bad news from Missouri[48] and the slowness with which recruits come in. In case I am not needed I shall come back on the first train and be home Friday morning. In any other case you will soon hear from me. With kisses for yourself and Trot for more than a day, I am,

*ever yours,*
James. . . .

Cleveland
August 15, 1861

*Dear Mother:*

I expected to see you before now but have not been able to do so. I was gone to the west over three weeks—and visited Uncle[s] Jerry and William and the rest of our folks in Michigan. They were all well. When I came back I found the Governor still wanted me to take a place in one of the new regiments and after thinking it over fully I have concluded I ought to go. I hope you will agree with me and will feel that it is all right. I shall go to Columbus today, and shall be there several weeks. I shall come home in the course of a few weeks and spend some time before I go into service, and I will surely save time for a good visit with you. Now I hope you will not feel in any

[48] Federal troops were defeated in the Battle of Wilson's Creek, Missouri, August 10, 1861.

way uneasy about me. You will certainly have no reason to for a long time yet.

I want you to write to me soon. Direct to Columbus. Care W. T. Bascom.[49] I will write you oftener than I have heretofore. Give my love to the girls and all our folks and let me hear from them all.

*Ever your affectionate,*
James

Cleveland
August 15, 1861

*My Dear Crete:*

I have spent the morning in writing letters and have not much time left. I have written a short letter to mother, and I want you to write her again soon.

I hope you will see that your father and mother do not think that I went away recklessly and without reason. I intended to see them before I left but was so hurried that I could not.

I should have left you some money if I had thought of it when I left, but Harry owes me some and you can get it of him till I see you again. I want you to have the piano taken special care of, for I fear it will get injured in that room. You had probably better make no change in regard to our rooms and board till I come home. Please see that my books do not get scattered and lost. Send word to Mr. Beardsley of Freedom, by his boy [Byron P.] who is in school, that I may not be able to meet the appointment to speak at his place and he had better not depend upon me. I don't know what my regiment is yet, nor whether it is yet formed, or where it is to go. I shall write to you soon after I arrive and learn something. You must write me often. I shall want to know all that transpires. . . .

Love for Trot and you as ever,

James

Camp Chase[50]
August 19, 1861

*Dear Friends at Home:*[51]

I cannot have any privacy or solitude for the next 24 hours and so

---

[49] William T. Bascom, journalist and politician; clerk of the Ohio Senate, 1856-1050; private secretary to Governor Dennison; editor of the Mount Vernon *Republican,* 1865-1867; and Secretary of the Republican State Central Committee for several years. During their senatorships Garfield and J. D. Cox roomed together in Bascom's home. Bascom did considerable work to get a satisfactory military appointment for Garfield.

[50] At Camp Chase, near Columbus, recruits were organized, trained, supplied, and mustered into the Union army.

[51] The letter was addressed to Rhodes.

will not try to write personal letters but will give you all such general items concerning my doings as can be written between spells. I arrived in Columbus Thursday evening, and on Friday morning was ordered to Camp Chase by the Adjutant General for general duty until my regiment is organized, which may not be for several weeks.

I reported at camp and was placed on General Hill's[52] staff for the present and was appointed Officer of the Day for today. Having no quarters yet assigned me, I slept that night on a pile of straw, and the next morning went into Columbus to make some purchases. I engaged my uniform but it will not be done for a week. Meantime I bought a suit of cheap blue blouse and a regulation cap, for I am required to be in full uniform when acting as Officer of the Day. I staid Saturday night at Mr. Bascom's and received letters from two of you, which I will answer more particularly as soon as I get time.

I intended to write on Sunday, but I went to visit the Governor, and he needed my assistance nearly all day, and at 6 P.M. I was obliged to return to camp; and not yet having any blankets, I accepted the invitation of a major, former stage actor in New York and Cincinnati, to share his blanket with him. This morning at eight o'clock I took command of the brigade and police guard of 200 men, and am to sit up on duty till 8 tomorrow morning. I have been exceedingly busy, having taken all the spare time I have had from 8 A.M. till now (4½ P.M.) to write so much of this letter. To give you an idea of the nature of my work, I send you a sketch of the camp, containing 160 acres.

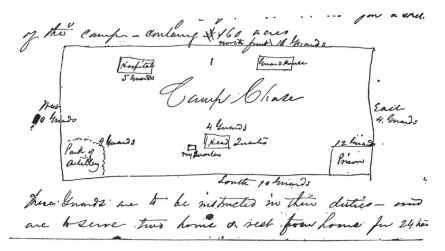

---

[52] Brigadier General Charles W. Hill commanded Camp Chase for a few months in 1861. He was Adjutant General of Ohio, 1862-1864, and commander of the 128th Ohio, 1864-1865.

These guards are to be instructed in their duties, and are to serve two hours and rest four hours for 24 hours.

As Field Officer of the Day, I issue passes to and from the camp, and arrest or reprimand any one for disorderly conduct. Six secession prisoners came in about noon, whom I had to take in charge and give a receipt for. One was a hard old hunter, a leather stocking kind of man, who had killed several Federal pickets in western Virginia. All the letters that the 40 prisoners write or receive have to be read by the Field Officer of the Day. I have just had the pleasure of reading some eight or ten. The Governor intimated that I might be sent to Old Point Comfort with a company of prisoners in a few days, but this is not at all certain.

Last night a splendid mounted battery of 6 rifled cannon fully mounted and equipped left here for St. Louis. A regiment of infantry goes tomorrow morning.

We shall soon organize a school of instruction for officers and men and go into it with all our might. I am glad that some weeks are to elapse before we shall take the field, for I want all I can gleen from direct study and practice. I think I know how great a practical problem it is to make men learn to lose their individuality and merge it in the mass, consent to be parts of a machine to be controlled by [us ?].

I have the greatest anxiety for the school and for you all. It seems to me, I think more about it than I should were I there with you. I hope you will think it no form of complaint when I urge you to write to me as often and as lengthily as your work will allow you to. I have gone into this as no ornamental work or holiday sport, and I feel deeply the need of all the strength of that conversing with you to keep me feeling that support and hopefulness of heart which I desire to cherish. I shall try to [write] some of you very often, and however long or short my career may be, I will let you know fully what it is.

From present appearances it is probable that all the Ohio troops in the next several months will be sent to the valley with Frémont.[53]

I am obliged to add that the purchases I have been compelled to make have completely exhausted my present exchequer, and I shall have to ask some of you to send me $25.00 by next mail if you can do it without distressing yourselves. I will send you back a due bill. I must ride round the camp and prepare for the night watch as it is 5¼ o'clock. To our three or four,

*Always yours,*
James

---

[53] Major General John C. Frémont commanded the Department of the West with headquarters in St. Louis, July–November, 1861.

Camp Chase
August 22, 1861

*My Dear Crete:*

Your good letter was received Saturday night and the trunk came at the same time. I am not very well, being still hard pressed with my usual malady [diarrhea]. But I have commenced to take medicine, and I think it will relieve me soon.

Before I write further I wish to apologize for the looks of this letter. I was suddenly called on to act again as Officer of the Day for today and came away here leaving my pen at my quarters, and so must write, if I get in time for the mail, on foolscap and with this old steel pen.

I was very thankful for the many little comforts you had enclosed in the trunk. I find them all coming in play. I will not say much more about my feelings in leaving you and all the dear associations at Hiram, not the least among which is our darling little Trot; but I will say that while I shall at all hazards keep up my heart and work with my might in the duty before me, I shall nevertheless feel very greatly the need of such full and frequent letters from you all as shall make me constantly feel the full knowledge and sympathy of you all.

And our darling! tell me all about her, her changes, developements, and try not to let her memory of "papa, papa" fade away. Have her say it, so that when I come she may know to call me. I think I have no unmanly feelings in regard to the future and my own share in it, but I have more sadness at the thought that should anything befall me she would not remember me. I know how a child feels under such circumstances, and that by experience. Please copy these last few sentences in her journal. And now with these lugubrious thoughts we will dismiss all that style of talk and look at the bright side which is always the right side.

I am entering on the work of the camp with success and shall hope to be able before I leave to be intelligent and efficient. It is a little odd for me to become a pupil again, but I come into it easily and have no fear of very disastr[o]us failure in learning duty. I think I must have a lot of flannel shirts, but you may wait until I learn more about what style will be needed. I want you to have the piano seen to, and as good care taken of it as possible. I must receive at least $15 per term for the use of it, over and above the expense of tuning. I cannot now tell how soon I will be at home, but probably in two or three weeks.

Perhaps Wall[54] had better see if Mr. James will not pay the note

---

[54] Wallace John Ford, friend and correspondent of Garfield for many years; attended the Eclectic and became a trustee of and fund-raiser for the school; secretary to Garfield during part of his first term in Congress; businessman in Pennsylvania and later editor of the *Geauga Leader* (Burton, Ohio); late in life moved to California where he died and is buried.

of $50. I want to let the larger amounts lie at interest as long as I can.

Since I began this letter I have probably given a hundred orders. Among other things held a trial and sentenced a sentinel to 3 days imprisonment on bread and water for sleeping on his post.

Kiss Trot for me and get her fingermarks on your letter in some way if you can. Ever yours and hers.

James

Columbus<br>August 25, 1861

*J. H. Clapp, Esquire,*
*Dear Sir:*

I received your letter enclosing $5 for which accept my thanks, as I was nearly strapped. I immediately forwarded letters of recommendation to the Governor and wrote one to him myself. Last night I came here from camp to see him personally but found he had gone to Delaware, not to return until Monday.

From what I learn from the books of the Adjutant General, I think that most if not all the majors are appointed for the regiments now forming, but I have no doubt you can succeed soon, if not now. I will press it.

Ford has bought a horse for me, but I don't know but I shall need another. What kind of a horse [is the] $100 gelding you spoke of? How much time could you give me on him? Please answer soon.

*Yours truly,*<br>J. A. Garfield

P. S.
I shall be home in the course of two weeks, I presume.

J. A. G.

Camp Chase<br>August 28, 1861

*My Dear Governor:*

I have a friend, Mr. W. H. Clapp[55] of Hiram, for whom I wish to solicit the appointment of Regimental Adjutant. He was formerly a pupil of mine, afterward for three years a merchant, and when the war broke out joined the New York 71st Regiment, one of the most

---

[55] On September 20, 1861, William H. Clapp was appointed a second lieutenant, Company A, Forty-second Ohio. The company consisted mostly of students and graduates of the Eclectic. In 1862 Clapp was promoted to first lieutenant and in the following year to captain and adjutant of the regiment.

efficient in the service. He entered it as a private, but was promoted to the command of leading sergeant in his company and acquitted himself with great bravery in the battle at Manassas. His regiment was in the severest of the battle, and he received commendatory letters from his company and regimental officers, which I can procure for you, if you desire it. I should feel great confidence in entrusting the Adjutancy of the 42nd in his hands, and from my intimate personal acquaintance with him, I know of no one I should prefer for that post.

*Very respectfully,*
J. A. Garfield

Camp Chase
August 30, 1861

*My Dear Friend:* [56]

I was very desirous of seeing you before I left home, but the pressure of the time forbade it. It was not without rigorous self-examination and, I may add, a struggle of no ordinary character within myself that I entered upon this field of duty. But now that I have flung myself and all my plans of activity into the scale of war, the struggle and questionings are all over, and I am busy and cheerful in the work of tearing down the old fabric of my proposed life, and removing its rubbish for the erection of a new structure. As a mental phenomenon, the work is a curious one. I find so many lines of connection with the world I deem to have left that I cannot altogether and at once sever myself from it. There is one matter of public concern on which I wish to confer with you before I take full leave of political life for the present.

I see many of our journals in a considerable spirit of generosity expressing themselves in favor of a Democrat for Governor, most of them having David Tod[57] as the man. Aside from the fact that

[56] Luther Day of Ravenna; lawyer and judge; member of the Ohio Senate, 1864; Judge of the Ohio Supreme Court, 1865-1875; father of William R. Day, an Associate Justice of the U.S. Supreme Court, 1903-1922.

[57] In 1861 the Union party—a new war party consisting of Republicans, Democrats favoring vigorous prosecution of the war, former Whigs and supporters of the American party—nominated David Tod, a lawyer, businessman, and Douglas Democrat as its candidate for governor. Like Garfield, a number of Ohio's leading Republicans, wishing to endorse the national administration by sending a Republican to Columbus, opposed Tod's nomination. In the election Tod scored an impressive victory and served one term, 1862-1864, being defeated in 1863 for the nomination as candidate of the Union party. For all of Garfield's misgivings, Tod ardently supported the national administration. Lincoln admired and respected the Governor and in 1864 invited him to become Secretary of Treasury. According to one account Lincoln once said, "Governor Tod of Ohio aids me more and troubles me less than any other governor."

I do not regard Mr. Tod as the man for the place, I wish to say that I do not think it a wise policy to select any Democrat for the Governorship. I trust you will understand that I do not say this from any partisan feeling. I want to see a full representation of Democrats on the ticket. It would be a fatal mistake and a great wrong not to have it so. But in my judgment, if we want to give an earnest and patriotic support to the Federal administration in its war measures, we can best do it by electing a governor who stands out as an acknowledged friend of the administration. Were I a Democrat, I think I should insist that no one of my party should take that place. I hold to this, not because the Republican party has the greater numerical strength in the state, nor because of my sight of them, but because it would be an implied censure of your president and mine to elect a man to be his intimate and confidential co-worker, who could not in conscience be his political friend.

This difficulty would not rest against any other member of the state government. I have no pet choice for the governorship. I desire to see a man of conservative views, of thorough business ability and round about common sense made Governor, but it seems to me to elect a Democrat at this crisis would be unwise, to elect Mr. Tod would be a fatal blunder. I am anxious to hear from you and know your views on this question. I feel that very much depends upon the 5th of September Convention.

I have seen with peculiar pleasure your name mentioned, and always with approval, for the Supreme Judgeship. It may be the strength of personal preference that influences me, but, be it what it may, I rejoice that the time has come when I can hope to welcome your name on the ticket of my choice. If there is any way in which I can serve you in this matter it will give me great pleasure to do so. I have conversed with several gentlemen of prominence in Columbus, and the proposition has met with very general favor.

I shall hope to see you here on the 5th *prox.*, and I shall be very glad to hear from you before that time.

Do you think there could be a company of infantry raised in Portage [County]? I very much desire to have at least one company of our boys in my regiment. Will you present my kind regards to Messrs. Hall[58] and Taylor,[59] and believe me

*Very truly yours,*
J. A. Garfield

[58] Lyman W. Hall and his son Halsey were the proprietors and publishers of the *Portage County Democrat* (Ravenna). This paper, whose name was changed in 1875 to the *Portage County Republican-Democrat* and in 1877 to the *Republican-Democrat,* gave Garfield helpful support during his political career.

[59] Ezra Booth Taylor, lawyer in Ravenna to 1861 and thereafter in Warren, Ohio; Judge of the Court of Common Pleas of the Ninth Judicial District of Ohio, 1877-1000, succeeded Garfield in the U.S. House of Representatives, 1880-1893

Camp Chase
August 30, 1861

*Dear Mother:*

Your kind letter was received and read with great pleasure. I am very well, though I had a diarrhoea for several days after I came here; yet I am all right again. I hope you will not allow yourself to feel troubled about me in the least, certainly not for a long time yet. My own regiment is [not] yet commenced, and will not be for two weeks. It will probably be five or six weeks before I shall actually go to the seat of war. I am very busy now in camp studying and doing a great variety of camp duties. I live in a board shanty, whitewashed outside and in. It is about 20 by 15, and is divided into two rooms. Outwardly it appears thus:

In the front room are two windows one on each side. In one corner is a table, at which I am now writing. In the other is a cot bedstead with one quilt and one blanket to go over me, and a thick comforter under me. Pants and coat make a pillow. A little piece of board with three shingle nails in it makes my candlestick. In the back room I have a little shelf with a tin pail and cup on it and a wash dish. Three chairs complete the outfit. So you see I am very comfortable.

I board with General Hill and so have not had the experience of regular soldier fare in regard to living. I have got on a flannel shirt for the first time, and it does all the scratching I need. I shall now want to use the woollen socks which you have been so kind as to knit for me. When I go home I shall get them. I can't tell the precise time when I shall visit you, but it will be in the course of two or three weeks, perhaps sooner.

My reason[s] for going into the army are many, but chiefly because the men of military experience were most all now in the service, and still more were needed for the new regiments. The Governor wrote to me again and I felt it would not be manly or honorable for me to stay away from the contest longer. I am sure, when you think it all over, and think how great and good a cause we have to fight for, you will not regret that you have furnished one son for it. I know you think better of me now for having gone. I assure you, I did not go from any mere desire to be in battle and gain a name. I went in with a full understanding of the perils and sufferings incident to war. I hope you will not have cause to be ashamed of me, whether I come out of it or not.

And now keep up good courage. Tell Mary[60] I am thankful that she wrote to me, and ask Hitty[61] if she won't, just for me, write me a letter too. She has never written me a word. All the rest of our family have. I want to hear from Thomas.[62] I will write to him. In order to insure my letters to reach me you must direct [to] J. A. Garfield, Lieutenant Colonel, 42nd Regiment, Camp Chase (near Columbus).

> *Ever your own,*
> James

Camp Chase
August 31, 1861

*My Dear Crete:*

Your last was received in good time, but it would seem that you did not receive mine till several days after it was sent. You had better direct to Camp Chase, and they will come here without delay. I am much better than I was when I last wrote. Indeed I am now almost entirely well. The water here is chalybeate, or strongly tinctured with some other mineral and is almost as laxative as hygiene pills, so I drink as little of it as possible and use cold coffee instead.

I am having my first experience in a woollen, and it is the first time I could ever truthfully cry "enough" on the subject of scratching. I think, however, I shall get used to it before long. I wish you would overhaul my woollen socks, for I shall take them with me. I also shall need a pair of sleeping shirts, made large around the neck and considerably longer than those I now have. . . . I wish you would enquire

[60] Mary, Garfield's sister, married Marenus Larabee, a farmer, and lived in Solon, Ohio.

[61] Mehetabel or Mehitabel, Garfield's sister, married Stephen Trowbridge, a farmer, and lived in Solon.

[62] Thomas, Garfield's brother, married, raised a family, and now lived in Solon. In 1867 he settled on a farm in Jamestown, Michigan.

the price of soft flannel and estimate what shirts and drawers will cost so that I can see how much will be saved by having them made at home. I think it will be well to have mother come out to Hiram to help you make them up if we conclude to have them made at home.

Then the Honorable O. P.[63] would not sign the petition. Well I am very glad that I did not want him to sign it. Indeed I did not know that *such* a move was on foot. Don't think the petition has been received at Columbus but may be it has. I am now broken into the work so that I get along very finely, only I ought to have my regiment here and under drill. Have you seen the horse yet that Ford has bought? I am fearful it is putting a good deal of money into a target. Still I want a good horse. I am practicing a good deal in riding and am getting some skill.

Does Trot walk yet? I want to see her move about by the time I come home. Bless her little soul, how I want to see her. Tell Nellie to write me. If I knew where Joe is I would write to him, but I do not. The news of the defeat of the 7th casts a gloom over every body. Tyler is greatly blamed for being taken by surprise.[64] Perhaps however he was not in fault.

With love to yourself and Trot, I am

> *Ever and ever your*
> James

Camp Chase
August 31, 1861

GENERAL LETTER No. 2

*My Dear Friends:*

I have thought that it might be pleasant to you and to me to gather up occasionally into a general letter the miscellaneous events and reflections incident to my life in camp, and so I will take a few moments of this fine morning for that purpose.

One of my chief afflictions here is the presence of myriads of flies and after ten days of the most perplexing torture, especially when trying to sleep in the forenoon after 24 hours watch. A few

---

[63] A few days earlier Garfield's wife had written that Oliver P. Brown of Ravenna had refused to sign a petition urging the Governor to promote Garfield to colonel. In 1862, Brown was an unsuccessful opponent of Garfield for the Republican nomination as congressional candidate.

[64] On August 26 at Cross-Lanes in Western Virginia, Confederate troops surprised and routed Tyler's Seventh Ohio, which lost two killed, twenty-nine wounded, and 110 captured. No formal charge of negligence was ever made against Tyler, who was promoted to brigadier general in 1862 and breveted a major general in 1865.

days since I went into the city and bought a few yards of pink musquito cloth, and so I am sitting at my table with this cloth over the paper and inkstand and me, while legions of flies are on the outside, and, like Virgil's winds, *"fremunt circumclaustra."*[65]

The enclosed scrap of dirty paper shows you our regular programme of daily duties, so that if one is inclined to work there is plenty to do. The duty of instructing the guard in their duties as day and night sentinels has been committed to me and so every morning at eight I am obliged to make the same speech over again, which seems very much like the explanations which we make at the beginning of a term, when we assign rooms and [deliver ?] "Rules and Regulations."

It is very unfortunate for the service that regiments should be hurried into the field with so little preparation. Immediately after the death of General Lyon,[66] the 27th Regiment was hurried off to Missouri before half of its companies had had two days' drill.[67] When the news of Colonel Tyler's defeat reached us, the 27th under Colonel Ewing[68] (son of Thomas Ewing, with whom I have formed a very pleasant acquaintance) was filled up from other half-formed regiments and last evening left for the valley of the Kanawha. I should dread the responsibility of taking such a regiment into the field. They went out of camp at dusk last evening with arms and three days' cooked rations, thoughtless and jubilant. As the cloud of their own dust shut them in, I came back sadly to my hut, repeating Byron's splendid stanza of "the unreturning brave."[69]

## My New German Friend, Lewis Kempner

A few days since, while on drill, instructing the guard, I saw a sprightly German in the uniform of a United States regular, who seemed to take peculiar interest in all the movements of the manual. When the drill was over I spoke to him in German and found him

[65] See the *Aeneid,* I: 56.

[66] Nathaniel Lyon, 1818-1861, was killed in the Battle of Wilson's Creek on August 10

[67] The Twenty-seventh Ohio, commanded by Colonel John W. Fuller, left Camp Chase for St. Louis, Missouri, on August 20.

[68] Hugh Ewing commanded the Thirtieth Ohio, which left Camp Chase for Western Virginia on August 30.

[69] In describing soldiers going into the Battle of Waterloo, Lord Byron wrote (*Childe Harold's Pilgrimage,* Canto III, Stanza 27):

> And Ardennes waves about them her green leaves,
> Dewey with Nature's tear-drops as they pass,
> Grieving, if aught inanimate e'er grieves,
> Over the unreturning brave,—alas!
> Ere evening to be trodden like the grass
> Which now beneath them, but *above* shall grow
> In its next verdure, when this fiery mass
> Of living Valor, rolling on the foe
> And burning with high Hope shall moldor cold and low.

very intelligent. I finally invited him to my hut and the result is a very peculiar and intimate acquaintance and friendship. He staid with me one night till nearly midnight. I will give you his story.

He is of wealthy Silesian family and his mother is a widow, not of the wealthiest, but perhaps the middle class. He was confidential clerk to a Herr Leipziger of Breslau, the head of one of the richest wine firms in the world. The firm has branch houses in Russia, Holland, Italy, France, England and New York, and Lewis has frequently visited all the European branches of the establishment on its business.

Herr Leipziger has an only child Jenny, a blond, yellow-haired, blue-eyed girl of 17 with whom Lewis had associated almost as a brother for the last three years, the old Leipziger never dreaming that there could be any danger of love between the clerk and his daughter. Some miles out of the city the old Herr owned a fine farm and summer residence at which Jenny spent much of her time. The head farmer turned out to be a defaulter and Lewis was sent out there to overhaul the books and discover the extent of the robbery. He was there three weeks and during that time his love for Jenny culminated to the height of rapture. When he speaks of that visit his German enthusiasm knows no bounds.

On his return to Breslau he obtained an interview with Mein Herr and asked [for] the hand of Jenny. The old man was thunder-struck. He had intended Jenny for a very rich old bachelor of 40 and told Lewis so, whereat the young lover went into transports of rage and grief. [He] declared that if that was the decision he would leave his employment and quit Europe immediately. [The] old man expostulated, told him to remain, would be glad to keep him and treat him as a son but not as Jenny's husband. Lewis told him he could not stay on the continent where Jenny was and not know that she was his, demanded to see her; a fifteen minute interview was granted, Lewis's mother being present. Jenny vowed never to marry another and to marry him when he reached legal age (24).

In three days he was on board a Hamburgh steamer bound to New York. This was last December. He came to Cincinnati, had money enough but was very unhappy. In a few weeks the war broke out. He had read American history in Germany. I have seen but few young men of his age (21) so intelligent on American history as he. His whole nature is fired up with the love of our Institutes and our Freedom. He knows many of Körner's, Schiller's and Goethe's songs for *Freiheit* by heart. He comprehends the issue with great clearness. At the first call he joined the regular army for five years. He said he could not live without Jenny and he was glad of a chance to bury his suffering in the activities of war. He is a splendid scribe and the Colonel of his regiment at Newport Barracks offered to obtain for him a clerkship at

Washington but he would not take it. Night before last he came and read me an eight-page letter to Jenny. It was written with great power and when he went away he said I must not talk so much of Breslau. I can sleep none tonight. Near midnight I passed him through the lines to his hotel where he has been sent to enlist recruits for the regular army.

I have twice been out with the officers to practice at target shooting with the revolver and have thus far come off best shot thanks to my little rifle [*sic*] and a steady nerve. Inclosed please find an Irish bull which pleased me very much.

Sixteen more prisoners of war were brought into camp yesterday. They are a hard looking set of the species of the "great unwashed." Cincinnati is having another periodical scare. She has now asked the Governor to draft 50,000 men for her protection. I hope the 42nd will not be sent to guard slaughtering and pork packing establishments.

Now I am quite in doubt whether a letter of this kind is worth my time to write it or yours to read it. I should like to know. But whatever the letter may be, I am ever your

James

Columbus<br>September 28, [1861]<br>4 o'clock A.M.

*My Dear Crete:*

I hope I shall not again be obliged to delay writing to you so long as I have done this time, but I know you will not blame me when you know what I have had on [my] hands. This is the third night that I have passed in succession without regular sleep. When I reached Columbus I worked incessantly for two days and most of the nights to get my regimental quarters in condition, and to get blankets and other comforts for the boys. Before this was accomplished other companies began to turn in. We now have five companies in the regiment, and it has been the hardest work of my life to secure the necessaries for their comfort.

I have dragooned and chased down nearly every state officer, and at last started on Thursday evening (not having gone to bed at all the night before) for Cincinnati, where we had made requisition for all our stores. The articles were not in the warehouse of the Quartermaster, and so I went to the contractors one by one and appealed to them, and at 10½ o'clock last night (having ridden to Cincinnati the night before) I took the train and am here waiting for the carriage to take me to camp. I think I am right in saying I never was so tired in my life. I never tried to write before when my hand trembled as it does now from sheer exhaustion. But the unprecedented rapidity with which my regiment has been filling up has given me much harder work than I shall have by and by.

So please don't be troubled about my health which [is] excellent, except the occasional pressure of the old trouble. Dr. Wilcox[70] did not send me the medicine. I don't know why. But I will try to get some soon. My surgeon will be here Monday, and then I promise you I will try to attend to myself.

I was greatly disappointed at not seeing you in Ravenna, but then as you said it was such a crowded day that we should not have had much quiet for visiting. I hope when I get into camp I shall find a letter from you. Indeed you must not fail to write if I do. I assure you my heart is with you all the moments I have any leisure to think.

The boys are all well except Charley Raymond who has been quite sick, chiefly because he was terribly homesick. He has not been sworn in yet, and I have concluded to send him home as soon as he is able to go.

I think I shall get arrangements soon to have you come into camp and stay a week or two. Probably Lieutenant Clapp will bring his wife also. I will let you know when the teacher and friends of Company A had better come down. We have established our regimental mess, and were I not too weary I would describe our cook and meals, but for now I must stop. Give my love to all our friends. Kiss Mrs. Polk for me.

*Ever your*
James


Camp Chase
October 2, 1861

*My Dear Harry:*

The drums have just beaten the signal called "Taps" which means for soldiers to put out the lights in all their quarters and retire. This gives me a moment of solitude and my time for study on the lesson for tomorrow. But I take a few moments from it to say that the time of our departure draws near, and I do not believe we shall be here more than two weeks longer, if so long. Now I must take no denial but that you shall all according to agreement come down here and spend a Saturday and Sunday with me in camp. I think one week from next Saturday is the time, and you had better start on the Friday evening train from Hiram, leave Cleveland on the 5 o'clock train Saturday morning, reach Columbus at 11, and be in camp in time to take dinner with us. Write immediately and tell me how many of you we can rely on, and we

[70] Sylvester K. Wilcox, a local physician and surgeon, practiced in Mantua and Hiram townships.

will have arrangements to meet you at the depot in Columbus. I am sure we will have a fine time.

I have six companies already, and two more expected tomorrow. I have a fine brass band and a good field band. We will give you a taste of camp fare and camp life. I have never been more than two-thirds as busy as I am here and with the usual abdominal exception am thoroughly well. If the friends that come will bring a box of something for the table it will brighten up the countenance of our darkey cook, the Professor, as well as your friends.

With much love to all,

*I am ever yours,*
J. A. Garfield

Camp Chase
October 8, 1861

*My Dear Crete:*

I took the medicine last night, which Dr. Wilcox sent me, and am quite sick this morning. But after a little vomiting and purging I think I shall soon be better. I hope a course of medicine will set me right. I have not been very unwell since I wrote you last, but just enough to keep my system in a constant state of irritation and depletion. I will make a vigorous push to get into proper shape. The work is yet very pressing but I am getting the regiment in such shape that it will by and by be easier to manage it.

I have written three or four letters home to different ones and though more than a week has passed since I first set the time I have not heard a word from any one of them whether you are coming or not. I expect you and hope that you will not disappoint me. I have written to Harmon Austin and wife and Lottie according to your suggestion to come down with you. I have also written to Harrison Jones to come and preach on Sunday. I want to know as soon as possible about the number that will come. We will arrange it so that you can all have a touch of camp life. I hope the friends will bring some eatables, and we will try to have a good time. I think you had better bring Trot if you can do so without too much trouble. Still you must do as you think best in the matter. I don't know how long we shall be allowed to remain here in camp, but I think you had better come prepared so that if it seems best, you can stay a week or so. I can't yet tell whether it would be best or not and indeed, I don't know as it will [be] best to bring Trot at all. Do as you think best.

Bring Joe's watch, and I will let you take mine. Bring a couple pairs of sheets to use while you stay. Do let me hear soon.

*Ever your*
James

Camp Chase
October 8, 1861

*My Dear Harry:*

I have just received your letter. I supposed there would be a large number of persons who would come down to see us with you all next Saturday. Of course I should love to have you come with the rest but I would love still more to have you come when we are in the field.

I wish you could be with me but there is no post open in the regiment which [is] good enough for you. If you really wish to go into the service I think some appointment can be obtained for you.

In regard to regimental colors, I am glad to hear of the movement which is begun in Hiram. Nothing adds so much enthusiasm to a regiment as that which adds to the equipage and pride of its appearance. In a banner is symbolized an army's honor in its country's glory, and if the affection of friends at home can also be expressed in it, it will add wonderfully to the éclat and spirit of the regiment. The stand of colors presented to was magnificent [*sic*], costing $150, and was considered very cheap at that. It don't become me to make suggestions, but I know of nothing that could do more for the 42nd than to receive such a stand from their friends at home.

The Government has not yet furnished a single banner for the army in this war. It is indeed the duty of the War Department to do so, but the requisition I made on the Department a few days since was returned with the answer that there were none. I am lotting largely on the visit.

I have not received a letter from Almeda since I left home. Is she sick? Hoping to see you soon and to hear from you often.

*I am, dear Harry,*
*Truly yours,*
J. A. Garfield

Camp Chase
October 8, 1861

*My Dear Cousin [Phebe M. Clapp]:*[71]

I have not till this moment heard of the terrible blow which has fallen upon you. Had I heard in time I should have gone to you at once.

I know there are no words which can be spoken by any human being which can bring consolation to your heart or in any way help to rebuild the shattered fabric of your household love. Few women have

[71] Phebe, a daughter of Amos and Alpha Boynton, was Garfield's favorite cousin. She attended the Eclectic and later became a member of its faculty. In 1857 she married John H. Clapp whose violent death, already noted, was the occasion of Garfield's letter.

been called to mourn so noble a husband. I have loved and admired him and for a long time we have intimately counselled together. I too, feel the loss, oh how deeply for myself and for you. If I live through the war I hope I may in some manner be able to serve you.

With all the love of a cousin and brother, I am

*In grief, yours,*
J. A. Garfield

Camp Chase
October 26, 1861

*My Dear Harry:*

This has been a peculiarly beautiful autumn day, and for the first time for a good many weeks I have enjoyed the subdued splendor, the wonderfully mild beauty of the Indian summer afternoon. Your good letter was received very opportunely. I read it this morning, just before we assembled for preaching on the green turf of the parade ground. You have written me many good letters, but none that has come home to my heart so sweetly sad, and yet so tenderly welcome as this. The very contrast of your quiet with my unrest makes you long for activity and me for rest.

Your reference to the closing days of the full term made my heart swell till I could not breathe quietly. I have always felt at those closing hours of terms that teachers and students came all "with naked hearts together," and measured the strength of each other's influence and the power of their mutual love. Those were always very sacred moments to me. I remember the first full term which closed on me in Hiram and I delivered a valedictory. I remember another which brought tears to Burke's eyes as he was leaving school, forever as he then feared. The reflection that all these are past forever with me brings a stifling sense of bereavement which I never have felt on such a subject before.

I have always hitherto in all my absences referred my life and its activities to our little circle of friends as the base of operations and estimated every event according as it stood related to that basis. But now there is no basis. We can draw no diagrams on the sea. Much less can we centralize a life which is launc[h]ed out on the uncertain currents of war.

You could not have named a book which I more desire to read than Hodson's.[72] I have heard of it and shall buy it the first opportunity. I long for some one like Tom Brown[73] to lead me in the war. I feel

---

[72] William Stephen Raikes Hodson, *Twelve Years of a Soldier's Life in India: . . . ,* edited by George Hewett Hodson (1860).

[73] Hero of *Tom Brown's School Days* (1857) and *Tom Brown at Oxford* (1861), by Thomas Hughes. Although many readers insisted that these volumes were autobiographical, Hughes maintained that Tom Brown was a fictional character.

my sympathies every day cling more to the Tom Brown style of men. I believe they are the true men of this new time.

My nature is perversely peculiar. It seems that just now, when I need to be hard and almost unfeeling, my sympathies are weaker than ever. I never felt so much need of love and tenderness. I am lavishing my caresses on my horses. They have both been hugged and patted a score of times this past week, and several times at midnight, and I am fancying that there is a sort of secret understanding between them and me, a mute sympathy, when they lay their velvety noses against my cheek and pretend to bite my beard. I remember it when they are galloping with me on parade and wonder if they do too. I don't know but other men have similar experiences. I noticed the Major the other day looking at his horse who (horses do not belong [in] the grammatical category of thing[s] and brutes) was threatened with the lung fever, and he said, "I had rather have the lung fever myself than to have him have it."

A late occurrence has put a wider gulf between me and the men. I was so proud of them that I was willing to warrant that they were not engaged in any irregularities like breaking guard, *etc.* But lately I found a few had been engaged in it, and last night I spent nearly all night in scouting. This morning found five of my men in the guard house. It has touched my pride [and] roused all my determination, till I now feel that I must be the scourge of many rather than the cooperant friend and leader. I feel, therefore, much more isolated tonight than I have ever done [been] in camp before.

I hope you will come and see me again. I dare not go out into the depth of my desire to be in our dear little circles at Hiram tonight. I feel it much more than I would like to have any one here know. When I think that only a few hours' travel would bring me to you all, I ask myself whether I can plunge away where distance as well as duty will separate us still more inexorably.

I am getting on very well. The regiment is taking shape under my hand, and I feel by degrees a growth in the organic life of it which makes me hope for its ultimate success. My own health is very good. I was at Cincinnati a day and a half during the convention of the American Missionary Society. I made a little speech there under peculiar circumstances which created as much sensation as anything I ever did. Brother Jones or Robison can tell you about it if you happen to see them. I have not the time to tell the details of the affair.

I don't know what to say in regard to your next winter. The correspondent matter would depend a good deal upon what kind of an arrangement you could make with the *Herald.* I very much wish you could raise fifty or eighty recruits for the 42nd. The minimum would have been reached long ago, but for the failure of the new system [of] recruiting by second lieutenants.

Write me again soon. Tell Burke to write and believe me never more than now,

> *Your own brother,*
> James

Camp Chase
October 27, 1861
Sunday night

*My Dear Crete:*

I intended to have written before this but I had to go to Cincinnati and it crowded my work. I received your good letter, and it together with the whole visit makes and leaves an impression on my mind and heart which will give me hope and joy in a great many dark hours. I am very glad indeed that you came down and staid with [me]. I shall feel much happier in going out into the field than I should if you had not come. I cannot but feel a strong regret that I could not have seen our precious little Trot. Could she have been here at that last sacred and solemn night when we kneeled together almost here where I am now sitting, it would add a great comfort to my remembrance of the dear week in camp.

I am now quite well and am in hopes that I shall acquire a hardy and more constant health than I have hitherto had. I am drilling the regiment every day with a more severe discipline than ever, and I think I can see their growth marked and increasing. The ranks however are filling up slowly. We have now 755 on our rolls. We are constantly harassed by rumors that we are to leave immediately, but none of them are at all reliable.

Monday morning

At this point I was interrupted by calls on business and had to try several cases of misdemeanors and early this (Monday) morning I was ordered to report as Officer of the Day. So here I am in for it. You remember something of what the duties are. I am beginning to tire of the monotonous routine of camp duties. I hope we may soon be sent away to active service. The thought of remaining during the winter would be unendurable. Still I have not much fear of being kept here.

I saw Major Casement[74] of the 7th when I was in Cincinnati, and in a private conversation he surprised me very much by saying in the most positive and vigorous terms that Colonel Tyler was a coward and one of the meanest and most unmanly men he ever knew. He then went on to say that the feeling was becoming quite universal among the officers, and that they were now becoming aware of Tyler's per-

---

[74] John S. Casement, major in the Seventh Ohio until May, 1862; Colonel of the 103rd Ohio, 1862-1865; breveted a brigadier general in 1865.

sistent attempts to injure Cox and build himself up at his expense. I of course said nothing which could be made use of and I hope I was not deficient and regret that any one in the public service at a time like this should prove himself unfit for the post; but I am obliged to confess that I felt that if any one was to be found unworthy it should be one whom I had so much reason to believe was unfit for command. How much was said because *I* was the auditor, I could not tell; but I think he represented the case fairly. I am sure that Cox's fame will shine brighter hereafter and I believe Tyler has been the chief of his detractors.

Fifty-nine more prisoners came in yesterday. We have now nearly 300 in prison. I wish I had time to tell you about my trip to Cincinnati but I have not.

Love and kisses to our dear little Trot and to yourself.

*Ever your* James. . . .

Ashland
October 30, 1861

*Dear Mother:*

I left camp last evening to raise the tenth company for my regiment. I came to this place and made a speech last evening. I shall probably stay here nearly a week. I did think of going home to see if I could not raise a company or part of a company there, but I think shall not do so. I really do not want to go home again and say the goodbyes over again. I have enjoyed excellent health most of the time since I have been in camp. I am working very hard and my men are learning the drill very rapidly. I know of no regiment which has done better in the same length of time, and I hope to make it a regiment that will do good service for the country and make a mark for itself.

We had a fine visit from the Hiram folks a few weeks ago. Crete and Almeda staid a week in camp. I think they enjoyed themselves very well. I have now in camp 760 men and more coming in every day. I have two horses, and very good ones too. I did not get the old stallion you were so much opposed to, but I have younger horses. I have two servants (colored gentlemen); one cooks for me, and we call him "Professor." The other takes care of the horses. . . .

If I knew how long we should stay in camp I should insist on your coming down to see me. But we may be sent off any day. I want you to write to me often and I will try to keep you advised of all our movements. Give my love to Thomas and the girls, and a large and strong share to yourself. I am still, as ever,

*Your son,*
James

Ashland
November 4, 1861

*My Dear Crete:*

I did not expect to be out making speeches again but here I am at it at the rate of two or three a day. I found if the regiment was ever to be filled up, we must do it ourselves. We selected Ashland County because it had not sent its full quota to the army. I should have gone home, but I really felt that I could not go through the ordeal of separation again.

This is a hard place to work in but we have got the ice fully broken. There is here a set of men who have not given up their partisan prejudices and are still more than half in sympathy with the South. Added to that there is a style of over-pious men and churches here, who are too godly to be humane. Commencing Wednesday evening I have made eight speeches and have raised 36 volunteers. They all refused me their churches for last evening except the heretic J. N. Carman, who has been ostracized by the Disciples of this place. He went on to the platform of the Town Hall with me and I address[ed] a very crowded house. I felt particularly free, and I believe I never succeeded better for an hour than I did in characterizing the Christianity of Ashland and all people who were afraid to "do good on the Sabbath Day." I then called for volunteers and six of the best young men in town and the teacher of the Union Schools and a Methodist preacher came forward. So I think we shall succeed. Indeed I told the Adjutant General that I should never return to the regiment till I brought a company.

I have not heard a word from Augustus[75] and I am very anxious to do so. Show this to Harry. I have received his letter and am in hopes to hear that he has done something in the school. I should have been glad if Harry had concluded to go as captain of a company.

Give my love to all our folks and write me at this place. I shall not leave before next Friday. Tell Almeda and Harry to write. Love to Trot and yourself.

*Ever your*
James

Medina
November 17, 1861

*My Dear Crete:*

I expected to have been in Camp Chase within a few hours after

[75] Frederick Augustus Williams entered the Forty-second Ohio as a captain. He distinguished himself in the Sandy Valley campaign and was promoted to major in March, 1862. That same month he contracted typhoid fever. He returned to his home in Ravenna and died there on July 25, 1862. His sisters, Mary and Sophia, are mentioned in a later letter.

I left you on Tuesday morning, but about fifteen minutes before I left for the train I received a letter from Major Pardee[76] urging me to come to Medina and help raise a company. I stopped off at Grafton and rode 30 miles to Lodi and made a speech that evening, and up to this time I have been going just as I did in Ashland. I am to ride 30 miles today and speak twice and tomorrow morning [before] I leave for Camp. I think now there is nothing that can turn me aside from seeing the regiment. I am told they went down to Columbus in full force to see me when I was to have arrived last Tuesday. I am very weary of speaking I assure you and yet I believe I did as well in the Court House here yesterday as I have often done. I staid over night with Burke once since I came here, and saw Eleanor and Frank Stiles. We have up to this time obtained 63 names in this county and I think we can get a full company. If we do I shall take two of our fragmentary companies and put them into one, and thus we shall be nearly full to the maximum.

I have become exceedingly anxious for the condition and welfare of the regiment. It is now nearly three weeks since I saw them and I very much fear they will begin to feel that I am neglecting them.

I am very glad I went home and saw you again. I think we shall both have more cheerful recollections of our parting than we did before. We had a very fine visit taking it all in all. When you find some one of the boys who are coming down to camp I wish you would send my rifle and bullet moulds if you can, send also the globe sight that goes with the rifle. I think I can get some comfort out of "my pretty gun."

With love to all, especially to Trot and yourself, I am

*Ever your*
James

Camp Chase
November 23, 1861

*My Dear Crete:*

I have only time for a word. I want you to go to my papers and find a few copies of my Senate Report on Treason and send four or five copies to N. H. Swayne,[77] Esquire, Columbus.

We have 917 men on our rolls and the Major is coming in today with about 70 more. No news about time of leaving camp. I have learned the pleasing intelligence that I can draw no pay for any time

[76] Don Albert Pardee, soldier, lawyer, and jurist; a major and member of Garfield's staff, September, 1861-March, 1862; promoted to lieutenant colonel in March, 1862, and served until October, 1864, when he was mustered out; Judge of the Second District of Louisiana, 1868-1880; appointed by Garfield as Judge, U.S. Circuit Court, Fifth District, and served, 1881-1919.

[77] Noah Hayes Swayne of Ohio; lawyer and jurist; Associate Justice of the U.S. Supreme Court, 1862-1881.

I have spent before my regiment was full. My colonelcy and pay begin from this time.[78]

The work of getting ready for marching is immense. I am glad you agreed to let me write you only a line once in a while. . . .

Love to all,

> *Ever yours,*
> James

> Sunday evening
> December 1, 1861

*My Dear Crete:*

After a long struggle and a good deal of difficulty I have arranged and harmonized the new recruits from Ashland and Medina. We now have 1,009 men and officers and have changed in some instances the letter of our companies. In order that you may know the companies should they be referred in the papers, I will give you a list of them:[79]

| [Company] | [Commander] | [Commander's Home Town or County] |
|---|---|---|
| A. | Capt. F. A. Williams | Portage |
| B. | " W. H. Williams | Medina |
| C. | " T. C. Bushnell | Ashland |
| D. | " J. H. Riggs | Noble |
| E. | " C. H. Howe | Lorain |
| F. | " H. H. Willard | Portage |
| G. | " C. P. Jewett | Cuyahoga |
| H. | " S. M. Barber | Ashland |
| I. | " R. B. Lynch | Logan |
| K. | " A. Gardner | Bellefontaine |

In line of battle they stand in this order

> Three contiguous counties—170 Medina men
> scattered through
> these three

| *Portage* | | | | *Ashland* | | *Lorain* | | | |
|---|---|---|---|---|---|---|---|---|---|
| A | F | D | I | C | H | E | K | G | B |
| \| | \| | \| | \| | \| | \| | \| | \| | \| | \| |

↓ Front

We have lately got our arms, a fine French rifle, and the boys are well pleased with it.[80] We know nothing of our future, but we are still living

[78] The organization of the Forty-second regiment was officially completed on November 26. The date of Garfield's rank was August 14, but his commission was not issued until December 14, when his regiment was ordered to the field.

[79] Garfield's list of company commanders has been standardized.

[80] According to the historian of the Forty-second, the men were issued the ponderous Belgian rifle with ordinary lance bayonet and were on the whole disappointed with it.

on the hope that we shall be ordered to move southward very soon. I shall not be surprised if we receive marching orders tomorrow, but shall not be surprised if we do not receive them for a fortnight. I have given up thinking about [leaving]. Meantime I wait and work. . . .

My pretty gun came down in good condition. I have sent it to Columbus to have it repaired more thoroughly.

Tell me how you are getting along. I hope you are practicing a good deal on the piano. I am exceedingly anxious that both you and Trot should be good players. How is the blessed little darling? Kiss her for me. Does she do any new things? Tell me about them.

I send you a warrant from Crittenden warranting my watch to run one year. If it should stop, send it to him and send word about the warrant. Do you hear from Joe? It is now time they were joining us if they are going to be transferred. Jones has been appointed Chaplain and has accepted.

*Ever your own,*
James

Columbus
December 9, 1861

*My Dear Crete:*

It will be a month tomorrow since I left home, and yet I have received but two letters from you and none from Almeda. Your last letter was received more than three weeks ago. I do not find fault for your letters may have miscarried, but I am exceedingly troubled in not having heard from you.

The immense work of organizing a thousand men, getting them properly officered, armed, and equipped, and making out sixty full company rolls, together with the usual routine duties of drill and discipline, have filled the past month full to overflowing. We are now seeing our way clear to get off into the field after so many long delays. Nothing now but the hopes of getting our pay will detain us here till the end of the week. But if by waiting a week long[er] our men can be paid, we will wait. I am very well satisfied with the condition of the regiment, and every day feel more confidence in it and trust in the success of its performances, if I and other officers do our full measure of duty.

I am in the city this morning on business and take a moment to drop this line to you. I would, were it possible, run up and see you once more before I leave, but indeed I hardly feel as though I can leave without seeing you all again. But I know this cannot be and so I must be content. Do let me hear from you. Direct as usual, I think it will reach me before I leave. If not it will be forwarded. Kiss our darling and believe me now as ever,

*Your own,*
James

Headquarters, Department of the Ohio
Louisville, Kentucky
December 17, 1861

*My Dear Harry:*

I arrived here 3 P.M. of yesterday and after a bath reported myself at headquarters, found the General out, but his Adjutant General made an appointment for me to meet him (General Buell)[81] at his hotel at 9 P.M. I did so and had an interview of three quarters of an hour. He is a direct, martial-spirited man and has an air of decision and business which I like. He told me at once that he knew of me and that knowledge had led him to put me in command of the expedition to drive back the rebels from Eastern Kentucky.

You remember that Williams was driven back from Piketon.[82] He and Humphrey Marshall[83] have returned with an increased force variously estimated at from 2,000 to 6,000 men including cavalry and artillery. The General says the information is so vague and his own knowledge of the country in that section is so limited that he must entrust the management of the expedition to my discretion.

In order that you may understand the scope and purpose of the movement, consult the map in connection with the following statements: The 40th Ohio Regiment goes today to Paris; the 16th Ohio to Lexington. They, in conjunction with several fragmentary regiments, are to move eastward and oppose the progress of the rebel force whose vanguard is now supposed to be as far west as West Liberty. Meantime the 42nd is to form a junction with a Kentucky regiment now at Louisa, and as soon as the rebel colum[n] has passed, fall upon their rear and cut off their retreat. This is the general plan, but all the details of it are committed to me.

The work will be positively enormous, for a large share of the Kentucky forces are as yet unarmed and undisciplined. It is a horrible country, fully as rough as Western Virginia and the General intimates that I cannot leave there before spring. He said (and I fully agree with

[81] Don Carlos Buell, brigadier general and from March 21, 1862, major general, commanded the Department of the Ohio which now included Eastern Kentucky.

[82] At Piketon on November 8-9, 1861, a Union brigade commanded by Brigadier General William Nelson engaged a Confederate force of about regimental strength under Colonel John S. Williams. Williams, who was retreating southward from Prestonburg, was defeated and forced to withdraw to a position near Pound Gap on the Kentucky-Virginia border. He was soon joined by the regiments of Brigadier General Humphrey Marshall's brigade, and the entire force crossed into Eastern Kentucky and headed north. Since Nelson's brigade had been withdrawn for duty elsewhere, a call went out to Garfield to lead an expedition against Marshall.

[83] Humphrey Marshall of Kentucky graduated from West Point in 1832 and led a Kentucky cavalry regiment in the Mexican War; member of the U.S. House of Representatives, 1849-1852, 1855-1859; minister to China, 1852-1854; became a brigadier general in the Confederate army in 1861. In the first winter of the war Marshall led a brigade into Eastern Kentucky on an unsuccessful campaign, the turning point of which was his clash with Garfield at Middle Creek. Marshall became a member of the Second Confederate Congress and after the war returned to Louisville, where he practiced law until his death in 1872.

him) that he would much have preferred to have me with him in the grand column, but yet he said I would have a much greater chance for distinction. The territory I am to command covers more than 6,000 square miles. I must go to studying geography. The General told me to make memoranda of such a plan and such questions as I might think important, and call on him this morning. I made out the following:

### I. Queries

1. Extent of my authority in reference to
   (a) Command, Discipline, Court Martial, etc.
   (b) Contracts, Purchases, Transportation, and Passes.
   (c) Local Troops and Extent of Territory.
2. Statement of the number, character and condition of forces to be placed under my command.
3. Suggest modes of communication between the parts of my force, and my mode of obtaining information of strength and plans of rebels.
4. Some idea of [what] the expenses per 1,000 men should be in the conduct of the expedition.
5. What policy shall I pursue toward local rebels in reference to their persons, slaves, and other property?
6. Shall I establish more than one depot of stores and if but one, where?
7. Shall commandants of regiments under my command report to these headquarters directly or through me?

### II. Wants

1. More Tents; 2. Dress Coats; 3. A Bakery; 4. Blank[et]s; 5. Mechanics; 6. Muleteers; 7. Money; 8. A Battery of Artillery.

Armed with these queries and wants I came to the General's headquarters and at the door ment [met] one of his aids, who to my great surprise and pleasure was a college class mate of mine, A. F. Rockwell.[84] I am writing this in Rockwell's office, waiting until the General is ready to see me. Whether I shall [be] equal to the occasion may rationally admit of doubt. But we shall see and I shall try. A part of the work, that of getting information, is quite like the work of Hodson and his guides.

Of course all that I wrote you in regard to my interview with the General and the plan must only be shown to our circle at Hiram.

---

[84] Almon F. Rockwell of New York, a classmate of Garfield at Williams College, was an aide-de-camp to Buell. He became an intimate friend of Garfield. After the war they were neighbors in Washington and they and their families were together frequently. In 1880 Rockwell helped manage Garfield's presidential campaign and in the following year Garfield appointed him overseer of Federal buildings and grounds in Washington.

The General has sent for me and I must close. God bless you all. Read this to Crete and Almeda. I will write to Almeda next and give an account of my interview with the General.

*Ever yours,*
James

Steamer *Bay City*
Off Maysville, Kentucky
December 20, 1861

*My Dear Crete:*

I will continue my journal from the point I left off in my letter to Almeda from Louisville. I spent Tuesday and most of the night in making arrangements with the heads of the various departments for stores and full outfit for the brigade. In the evening General Buell sent a request for me to go and see him, which I did and spent an hour more with him. At 6 o'clock Wednesday morning I left, according to instructions, for Lexington and Paris. At the former place I found Jacob Heaton[85] and the 16th Ohio Regiment. After two hours' delay I went on to Paris [and] made arrangements for quartering the 40th Ohio, which arrived 9 P.M. that night.

In the morning I started the 40th on the march eastward and gave them orders, a copy of which I will enclose you if I can get a chance to send this letter off on the Ohio side. Otherwise I will not send it. I also left orders for Colonel Wolford[86] to send 4 companies of his cavalry along with the 40th and the remaining two companies to hasten across the country to Catlettsburg to join me there. I then left for Cincinnati, where I met Wallace and Harry and in about an hour was on board the steamer bound up the river. Wallace is aboard going up to Pittsburg. Charley Hoadley is clerk of the boat.

It is rumored that the rebels are coming down in force to attack Catlettsburg and that the people are very much alarmed. I believe I told you that Colonel Moore[87] of the 14th Kentucky had retreated from Louisa to Catlettsburg in consequence of the superior numbers of the enemy. I intended to stay in Cincinnati to transact some important business, but hearing of the troubles I concluded to hurry up at once. I intend to move the whole force up the valley as soon as possible.

I am now feeling badly in reference to this brigade matter, for fear

[85] Captain Jacob Heaton was a commissary officer who later served on Garfield's staff in the Twentieth Brigade, Army of the Ohio.

[86] Colonel Frank Wolford commanded the First Kentucky Cavalry Regiment.

[87] Laban T. Moore of Kentucky, lawyer, congressman, and soldier; member of the U.S. House of Representatives, 1859-1861; Colonel of the Fourteenth Kentucky, 1861-1862.

it will separate me from the 42nd. I would rather stay with them all the while than to command a brigade a few months and then go back to them and find them changed in their habits and affections. I have found that the cavalry sent me from Ohio are not armed with carbines for which I am exceedingly sorry. I shall endeavor to see that they are supplied as soon as possible. Such has been the rapidity with which events have occurred to me, and such unexpected ones, that I hardly know how I shall like the change, though I think I shall like the additional inspiration of increased work.

One column (the 40th) passes through Mt. Sterling where Brother Munnell[88] lives. I saw several prominent Disciples at Paris and received valuable assistance from them.

I am exceeding[ly] anxious to receive frequent and full letters from you and I want you to send me any papers that make criticisms on my course. Kiss Trot for me and give my love to all our friends.

Ever your
James. . . .

Headquarters, 18th Brigade
George's Creek
December 25, 1861

*My Dear Crete:*

An express rider is just about to leave for the mouth of the river. I have been writing dispatches for the last two hours. We are now within 18 miles of 2,500 rebels who have four guns. Our scouts have been very near the enemy's pickets. We are waiting for our Kentucky regiments to come up and have General Buell to send us artillery. As soon as these arrive we shall attack the rebels at Paintsville who are now fortifying the place. We may be attacked where we are but I do not expect it.

Conceive of my great hurry and pardon this brief note. God grant you may now be enjoying a merry Christmas. I am exceedingly anxious to hear from you. I have had no word, letter or paper since I left Camp Chase.

Love to all.

Ever and forever,
Your James

[88] Thomas Munnell, a graduate of Bethany College, taught history, languages, and literature at the Eclectic, 1850-1852, 1853-1855.

Headquarters, 18th Brigade
Camp Moore
January 1, 1862

*My Dear Crete:*

Just as I had given up that my scout, who was sent to Colonel Cranor[89] with the message to move on to Prestonburg, had been captured, I am [able] to rejoice, more than [over] any news I ever received in my life, by the arrival of the faithful "Kit Carson"[90] fifteen minutes ago. He has been shot at, twice surrounded by enemies, once escaped by strategem, and once, when aid[ed] by a party of Union men, fought and captured several prisoners.

Colonel Cranor left McCormick's Gap yesterday morning and is now moving via Hazle Green toward Prestonburg.

I have organized a system of spies and scouts which is giving me full and satisfactory information of the doings of the enemy. He is now entrenched on a hill three miles back of Paintsville on the Prestonburg road and is fortifying still more.

I dare hardly hope that I shall capture a whole army, and I always feel very reluctant to say I think I shall do a thing when I may fail of succe[e]ding. But I do think I am getting into a position from which I have good ground to hope that I shall capture him. I cannot tell you how deeply alive to the scheme in hand are all the impulses and energies of my nature. I begin to see the obstacles melt away before me and the old feeling of succe[e]ding in what I undertake gradually taking quiet possession of me.

In all this, don't think I am so absorbed that I do not often have sweet thoughts of home and all that I love. In the lulls of work there comes to my heart fairer visions of all these than ever greeted me before. Your very dear letter, one from Almeda and one from Burke were received day before yesterday and were thrice welcome I assure you. It was the first word I had had from home.

We have effected an arrangement by which our letters will be brought to us twice a week from Ashland, a place near Catlettsburg. Tell all our friends to direct to Ashland, Boyd County, Kentucky.

Jacob Heaton is just going down the river and will take this hasty note. I write on a board and [am] sitting on a box with a dozen officers talking around me.

Harry Jones wrote you for me, a few days ago, and wouldn't let me see it.

I send you the lock you asked for. Love to all. Now and ever,

*Yours and Trot's,*
James

[89] Colonel Jonathan Cranor commanded the Fortieth Ohio.
[90] Not to be confused with the famous Christopher (Kit) Carson.

Paintsville
January 13, 1862

*My Dear Crete:*

You have doubtless heard before this that we have had a battle with the enemy. I have just returned from Prestonburg and now find my first breathing space since we left this place. I will endeavor to give you a history of the whole affair. I hardly know where my last letter left us, but I believe it was at Camp Pardee, on the head of Tom's Creek. At that place I held a council of war as to our future movements, or rather the time when we should make the advance. The council was composed of field officers, plus Harry Jones who is a privileged character in all our deliberations. I sent off another messenger to Colonel Cranor telling him I would attack the enemy's cavalry at the mouth of Jenny's Creek, and the question before the council was what day shall we make the attack. I have always believed in the success of vigorous and well directed audacity, and I wanted to move the next day (Saturday). There was but one man who agreed with me and that one was Major Pardee. The rest all agreed on Monday. During Saturday and Sunday I planned and conducted a series of little maneuvers intended to mislead the enemy in regard to my own intentions. I believe I was entirely successful. Some day I hope to tell all of you about them in detail.

On Monday morning I moved down to the mouth of Muddy Branch with the infantry, for the sake of getting at the river where I could get our stores up by boat, and could also attack Paintsville should the enemy be there. I left the cavalry back at the forks of Tom's Creek, with orders to attack the rebel cavalry while we attacked his infantry. During the night in our camp in the woods (which we called Camp Jones), I planned a night expedition of two companies under Captain F. A. Williams to go and occupy Paintsville and learn whether the enemy were making any demonstrations upon us. This he did very successfully and returned to me before morning.

Early the next day (Tuesday), I moved on with the whole force and occupied this place. It was rumored that the enemy had learned of my plan to surround him and cut off his supplies and was retreating from his entrenched camp. I built a temporary bridge across Paint Creek, which was then very high, and started two expeditions to start from here at the same time. The cavalry under Colonel Bolles[91] of Virginia (whom General Cox had sent to me) were to ford the creek two miles above here, at the mouth of Jenny's Creek, and drive the enemy up that stream. I led eight companies of the 42nd and two of the 14th Kentucky across the pontoon bridge and formed them at the mouth of a deep ravine just as dusk came on. The rebel scouts had

[91] Colonel William M. Bolles and three hundred troopers of the Second Virginia Cavalry had arrived on January 6, having been sent by Cox, commander of the Kanawha District in Western Virginia.

been seen to retire for the wooded cliffs on the further shore of the creek as we were completing the bridge. I had full reason to suppose they were in the hills.

We moved up the dark gorge with caution, throwing forward pickets and scouts, and at eight o'clock entered the deserted fortifications of the rebels where their camp fires were still smoldering, and the scattered remnant of their stores lay in sad confusion. The frozen tracks of thousands of feet were plain under the light of the new moon.

While sitting in the deserted house which had been General Marshall's headquarters, I received a dispatch from a messenger saying that the enemy's cavalry were in full at the mouth of Jenny's Creek, that our cavalry had skirmished with them, and they had concealed themselves in ambush. The messenger was sent to know whether they (our men) should make the attack in the night or wait till morning. I sent back an order for them to get as near to the ambush as possible without making the attack, and I would march across the hills and attack the rebels in the rear. I then moved forward. By some failure of the message the Virginia cavalry made the attack before I came to the road on which the enemy were, and chased them five miles, kill[ing] six, wounding several and losing two killed and one wounded.

I marched on and built two bridges that night and reached Paintsville just as the sun was rising. It was the hardest march I ever made. But it had a fine influence on the regiment. It schooled them to danger, for there was not a half hour of that gloomy night in which we did not have reasonable apprehensions of an attack. Then too for the first time the regiment was under fire, for two companies of the 14th Kentucky which I had ordered to be posted as pickets had got off into an out-of-the-way hill which we passed on our return. They mistook us for an enemy and fired on us.

The next day was spent in scouting to learn the route the enemy had taken. I found the river was up so that he could not cross to take the road to Piketon, but he had turned southwestward and was retreating up a branch of Jenny's Creek. Such was the terrible state of the roads and the exceeding depth of the mud, that our supplies had come up very slowly, and I could not for several days get provisions enough to warrant a pursuit with my whole force.

I felt as though we had (as General Marshall has since said) outgeneralled the enemy, but I was unwilling he should get away without a trial of our strength. Our forces were very much exhausted and our sick list large. I found we had about enough hard bread for 500 men [for] three days. So I organized an expedition to consist of two movements. One of 500 cavalry to pursue the enemy [and] harrass him in the rear, while the infantry should take a circuitous route and if possible flank him. (The 40th Ohio, fearing that the retreating enemy might cut them off if they went according to orders to Prestonburg, had turned aside and joined me here on Wednesday.) I took 300 picked men from the 40th [and] 42nd Ohio, and 14th Kentucky respectively, and 200 from the 22nd Kentucky, and with three days' rations of cra[c]kers in their haversacks I started on Thursday noon along the river bank toward Prestonburg. The cavalry went up the Jenny's Creek route. You will understand the routes from the enclosed map.

When we had marched ten miles and it was fully dark, as we were ascending a deep gorge, we came to a place almost at the crest of the hill where trees had been felled across the road to prevent our passage. [Sergeant] Jasper Ross with a small body of sco[u]ts was in advance and a few cavalrymen with him when from behind the fallen trees a volley of a dozen muskets was fired upon them, but the balls went whizzing above our heads. Company A was immediately sent out as skirmishers to clear the coast and we felt our way inch by inch till we reached the mouth of Abbott's Creek, where 200 of the rebel cavalry had been two hours before.

I there learned that the whole body of the rebels was encamped three miles above on Abbott's Creek. I took my men up a very high hill and on its top, without fire[s] (for I wanted to keep the enemy ignorant of our position) the boys bivouac[k]ed on their arms. I went to a house and made inquiries of the people about the enemy and wrote an order and sent it by a courier to Colonel Sheldon[92] to follow me with all haste with every man that was able to march, for I then knew that we were within striking distance of the enemy. Before I had finished my dispatch a messenger reached me from the cavalry column saying they had approached near to the rebels who had planted their cannon so as to rake the road in rear of them, and he requested a reinforcement. He had sent the request to Colonel Sheldon and to me also. At half past twelve o'clock I climbed the hill and rolled myself up in the blanket, while the cold drizzling rain poured down upon us during the whole night.

At three in the morning I turned out and called up the boys to take their crackers and prepare for the march. I assure you it was a very dreary prospect. The deepest, worst mud I ever saw was under foot, and a dense cold fog hung around us as the boys filed slowly down the hill side. We went one mile up Abbott's Creek, built a bridge and crossed over one mile more to the mouth of Middle Creek. On the passage over the ridge, our scouts began to meet theirs and skirmish with them.

We moved slowly up Middle Creek, feeling our way by sending scouts on the hills on each side [of] the creek. On the way up we took one prisoner and two horses. As we passed around a point of hill where a plain stretched away before us, two or three hundred

---

[92] Lionel Allen Sheldon entered the Civil War as a lieutenant colonel in Garfield's regiment. He later became its colonel. After the war he was a member of the U.S. House of Representatives from Louisiana, 1869-1875, and Governor of the Territory of New Mexico, 1881-1885.

of their cavalry dashed out toward us but soon fell back behind a ridge which ran near half way across the valley. They seemed to be posted behind the ridge in force and their officers rode up on its point and looked at us through their glasses. I ordered two companies to pass up to a crest that commanded the ridge, and come down and take it if they could; if not, call for more help. The main body had to wait in the plain.

Meantime, for the sake of brass [?] and audacity, I ordered a battalion drill, and we formed squares and wheeled from column into line, while the long line of our rear was trailing round the hill into the plain. I was willing the rebel officers should see the drill and should see the troops file on, but I did not want them to look till the whole line was in sight. I wanted them to leave off looking when they might have a vague impression of numbers and hosts, yet unseen, coming on. So I stationed a sharp shooter to fire at them just before the rear of our column hove in sight. This drove them back. After a few shots from our scouts we advanced and occupied the ridge, whose termination is called Graveyard Point. As we passed around this point the enemy's cavalry were seen in the plain. Our scouts crept along its skirts near the foot of the ridge (bbb—see splendid drawing [on page 58]).

From the enemy's motions I was satisfied we were near his main body and I did not want to wait for a long reconnoissance, so I took my cavalry escort of ten, added a few mounted citizens who were armed and were following with us, and ordered them to charge across the plain so as to draw the enemy's fire and thus induce him to reveal his position. They made a very gallant charge along the road half way across the plain, when the whole Virginia regiment stationed behind the ridge at G fired on them, but strangely enough without effect.

I immediately ran up Graveyard Point to the rock (A), an isolated crag which gave me a splendid prospect of the plain and all the hills. I sent two Kentucky companies along the ridge—bbb—and two companies under [the] command of Captain F. A. Williams to [who] forded the creek, which was nearly waist deep, and passed up the ridge as indicated on the drawing. I gave this command almost the moment after the rebels fired on the cavalry. Hardly a minute more had elapsed when boom went a cannon, followed by another throwing a 12 pound shell which struck at H, within two feet of Adjutant Olds,[93] who was leading on a company of scouts. The shell tore up the earth in the midst of the company, but did not explode. Had it done so, it would almost have annihilated the company.[94] The Adjutant

[93] Captain William W. Olds, Company A, Forty-second Ohio, campaigned with the regiment down to May 1, 1863, when he was killed in action at Thompson's Hill, Mississippi.

[94] Nearly all of Marshall's shells were duds. The historian of the Forty-second Ohio said that the enemy guns momentarily checked Garfield's skirmish line, but when fired against the main force "were badly trained and the shells buried them-

Explanation

- - - Road
/////// Rebel Regt
# # Rebel Cannon
T T T T T T Rebel Cavalry

a. my position during battle on
   a high rock.
:·:·:·:·: My reserve —
b b b b b — rocky ridge, high.
c c c c c rocky ridge
d. d. d. " " " terminating in
D. a high rocky point
E. a very high point — rocky
F Rocky Point not so high as D & E
+ + + + + Capt Williams route
mmmmm Maj Pardee's "
eeeeee Col Monroe's "

remained till he reconnoitered the position and saw the rebel cannon, their cavalry at I, and their infantry at KKK. He then returned to Graveyard Point. This was about half past twelve.

There was then a lull till Captain Williams reached to within thirty rods of F, when a terrible fire opened upon him from the enemy who had concealed themselves behind the ridge and rocks. The Captain rallied Company A around him a[nd] commenced one of the most terrific fights which has been recorded in this war. The enemy came charging down upon him from F, shouting like demons. They however made this mistake. The ridge was so narrow that not more than two or three companies could fight on it to advantage. Captain Williams' men could nearly all get hidden behind trees, while the rebels came down in such masses as to make a splendid mark for our Hiram boys. After a scattering fire on the ridge bbb, the Rebel regiment at G was withdrawn and sent up the hill on the other side of the creek.

I then ordered Major Pardee with 90 men to cross and support Captain Williams. He went up along the track (∿∿∿∿∿) as indicated in the drawing, but had hardly reached M before a fire was opened upon him all along the ridge LDE. The whole ridge swarmed with rebels. Our little force was the focal point on which concentrated the fire from the whole semicircle of hills. The Major pushed on, fighting his way till he joined Captain Williams and both charged forward on the enemy, who were now so near that the combatants shouted and talked to each other while they fought.

When they came so close that the rebels at L and D could not tell whether they were firing on friends or foes, they turned their whole fire upon me and the reserve around me. I have no doubt but that a thousand rifle balls came within a foot of me. They cut the twigs, splintered the rock, and cut a canteen which hung beside me. I directed the reserves, consisting of 300 men, to fire upon D and L. Such terrific volleys I had never seen. The hill trembled under the recoil. The enemy fell back over the ridge but the sharp shooters hidden behind rocks kept up a random firing especially at me and Harry Jones, who stood beside me on the rock and acted as my aide-de-camp during the battle. He is brave as a lion.

I then sent Colonel Monroe[95] of the 22nd Kentucky to cross the creek at the foot of Graveyard Point, and charge up the point cccc to L and D. There the enemy, holding the two points named and the ridge ddd, met the Colonel and another fierce conflict followed. After one

---

selves harmlessly in the mud." In his official report Garfield said: "During the fight he [the enemy] had fired 30 rounds from his guns, but they were badly served, as only one of his shells exploded and none of his shot, not even his canister, took effect."

[95] Lieutenant Colonel George W. Monroe, second in command of the Twenty-second Kentucky.

hour's constant firing, the enemy was driven from those three points to the high rock, E. Before this I had sent Colonel Cranor, 40th Ohio, to reinforce Captain Williams and Major Pardee, and these, fighting most fiercely, drove the enemy inch by inch back to E, which towered above all our boys.

My reserve was now reduced to a mere handful, and the agony of the moment was terrible; the whole hill was enshrouded in such a volume of smoke as rolls from the mouth of a volcanoe, thousands of gun flashes leaped like lightning from the cloud. Every minute the fight grew hotter. In my agony of anxiety I prayed to God for the reinforcement to appear. I had sent back word to Colonel Sheldon to display the banner as his column came in sight. I was just ordering my whole reserve into line and was going to lead them up the hill myself, when I looked behind us and saw the Hiram banner sweep round the hill. I shouted to our boys to look. They saw, and such a shout of joy never greeted my ears. The reinforcement on double quick returned the wild shout and the fighters on the hills heard, saw and returned an answering shout.

The enemies saw and heard likewise; a rebel colonel mounted the hill on horseback and shouted three times to his men to retreat. Seven Ohio boys leveled their rifles at him and fired. Horse and rider tumbled back over the hill.[96] They were driven in dire confusion. Night closed in upon us. I did not dare to pursue in the night, lest we should fire upon each other. We brought off our dead and wounded, built our camp fires, and lay down on the field, while the rain and the darkness covered us. Scarcely had the last gun been fired when a glare of fire lighted up the hill where the enemy's camp had been. He was burning his baggage and fleeing. He left 85 of his dead on the field. His wounded cannot be less than 150. He has acknowledged 100.[97] In the morning my cavalry came up. They had lagged ingloriously behind. I ordered them to pursue. They followed six miles and brought back some prisoners and trophies. I moved the column back and occupied Prestonburg, taking a considerable quantity of stores.

But the men were weary almost unto death, and I came back yesterday to this place to recover the strength of my brave boys. That we lost so few is hardly less than a miracle. One only was killed on the field, two have since died of their wounds, not more than twenty were wounded. Men who have been in other battles say they never saw such fierce and terrible fighting. I can never tell you how full of love

[96] In his official report of the engagement Garfield claimed that an enemy field officer was found among the dead. Marshall's official report contains no reference to the name or rank of any of his casualties.

[97] In his official report Marshall said that he had 1,500 men in action, lost eleven killed and fourteen wounded, and claimed that after the fight the enemy "withdrew from the field, leaving me just where I was in the morning." Garfield reported losses of three dead and eighteen wounded in a victory which ended with the enemy "burning his stores and fleeing in great disorder."

and pride my heart is toward our Hiram boys. Men of other regiments and other states do not hesitate to say they were bravest among the brave. Many of them shot even when they were faint from the loss of blood.

General Marshall sent a letter a few days ago to his wife in which he stated his force in full. He acknowledged having over 4,000 men and a chief of engineers who was a graduate of West Point.

I would dearly love to go home and see you. But the men and officers all want to go. I know it will not do for me to leave and I must make up my mind to stay till the war is over.

I have written this to be read to all our friends by whom you think it will be well to be seen. I have had but two letters from you. Do let me hear from you all.

*Ever truly your*
James

Headquarters, 18th Brigade
Paintsville, Kentucky
January 26, 1862

*Dear Mother:*

It has been a long time since I have heard from you or from Thomas and the girls. I very much want you all to write to me even though I do not write to you as often as I would like to. You can hardly conceive the amount of work I have had on hand since I came into this valley. I hope you have some map large enough to show you the location of this Sandy Valley, which lies along the boundary of Virginia and Kentucky. Catlettsburg is the village at the mouth of the river where we landed about the 19th of December. The Union troops which had been located at *Louisa,* a town 28 miles from Catlettsburg, had fled in great fear from the rebel army which was pushing its way down the valley. Humphrey Marshall, a very prominent man and a general in the rebel army, was in command of an army of 5,000 men and was raising recruits as fast as he could. I sent a part of the brigade under my command to go from Paris eastward toward Prestonburg, intending to cut off the enemy's retreat while I should come up the valley and drive him back. It is the worst country to get around in I ever saw. There is not room enough to form a regiment in line for want of level ground. The roads are very bad, indeed almost impassable, and we were obliged to make them all over before we could get along with our teams. The 42nd regiment had 150 wild mules which had never been broken, and we were obliged to work a long time to get them so that they could haul our wagons. In three weeks, however, from the time I landed in Catlettsburg, I had marched with my division over 75 miles, and had driven General Marshall from his fortifications and followed him fifteen miles, fought him five hours, and scattered his army. His whole army has now gone away, part of it to Virginia and the rest close to the Virginia line at Whitesburg.

So you see I have been in a battle and have not been killed nor wounded. Brother Jones was by my side through the whole fight and acted as aid-de-camp. Hundreds of bullets came very near us, cut the twigs above us and the rock on which we stood. Our boys acted very bravely. We had only one man killed and 20 wounded. Two of the wounded have since died. You have seen the accounts in the papers I presume. It was a terrible sight next morning to walk over the battle field and see the horrible faces of the dead rebels stretched on the hill in all shapes and positions.

They ran in the night, leaving most of their dead unburied.

We are now resting and doing nothing but send[ing] out small scouting parties to drive away or capture little bands of rebels secreted in different localities. I have two such expedition[s] now out, and have a good deal of business on hand in the way of holding trials of rebel prisoners, giving passes, getting our provisions up the rivers, and all the other thousand things that belong to the management of our army.

My health is very good, though I have been considerably troubled with diarrhoea. I am better now. I have slept out on the ground in the rain a number of nights since we came but it has not hurt me at all as I can see. I don't know how long we are to stay here, but I am inclined to think we shall not leave before spring.

I want you to write me a long letter, and I want you to tell me all the news of the neighborhood. I don't get the Cleveland papers till they are two weeks old. It takes letters a long time to get here. In order to insure them to reach me you must direct them to Catlettsburg, Boyd County, Kentucky, and they will be sent on to me.

Where is Thomas? I want him to write to me, and Mary also. Give my love to Mary and Hitty and to all the children. Tell them I have got a secession flag which was taken on the battle field. I hope to bring it home some time.

With much love, I am now as ever,

*Affectionately your son,*
James


Headquarters, 18th Brigade
Camp Buell, Paintsville, Kentucky
January 26, 1862

*My Dear Crete:*

Your good letter accompanied by the elegant little gift for my wrists was duly received. I cannot tell you how much pleasure it gives me to catch now and then a glimpse of home through the medium of your letters. I do hope you will make them more frequent, even though mine are not as thickly sown through the months as we would both desire. Think of it! I have received but three letters from you since I left Camp Chase. I have never been so shut out from the world before, and you can hardly understand it when I tell you that it is quite a relief for me to get hold of a paper two weeks old. This country is terribly broken up in its social and commercial relations. There has not been a regular mail to this place since the first of last September. The only way we get our mail is by having a messenger to make a trip of 60 miles after it.

For several days after the battle I was quite sick but I am much better now, indeed, nearly well. I have now fixed my headquarters with a wealthy farmer, and have a fine room and am getting along nicely. General Marshall's brigade seems to be dissolved. He retreated eight miles the evening that the battle closed and hurried on twelve miles more the next day. There he halted a few days. I was preparing my stores and getting ready to follow him when his two Virginia regiments left and went to Virginia, and the remainder of his force retreated to Whitesburg near the Sounding Gap.[98] I have sent out two small expeditions to cut off some small bands of rebels in the neighborhood of Grayson on the Little Sandy, and Piketon on the Big Sandy. This done, and I cannot see much else for us to do here unless Marshall should get reinforced and return, which I don't believe he dare try again.

I believe I have never made a more favorable impression of myself than I have upon the Kentucky regiments under my command and upon the citizens of this [valley]. They have the most extravagant notions of my doings here and hereafter. Marshall, I find, had a wonderful reputation and was accounted one of the bravest men in the South. He is a graduate of West Point, was a colonel in the Mexican War, won great honors at the Battle of Buena Vista, was a long time in Congress, was minister to Russia, *etc., etc.* I should suppose he would feel exceedingly mortified at the result of his campaign in Kentucky. General Buell sent me an intercepted letter from Marshall to his wife in which he stated his force to be 5,000 and rapidly increasing. He had an engineer (a West Pointer) who laid out his fortifications for him. I hope some day we will go up this valley together and visit all these places. I can never tell you about them so that you can appreciate them as you can to see them.[99]

It may be that we shall stay here in winter quarters, though I have not yet received orders from General Buell.

I have had a new adventure lately. There were some four days and

[98] The original name of Pound Gap, a mountain pass on the Kentucky-Virginia border which connects the Big Sandy Valley with the South.

[99] In September, 1871, Garfield made a trip to the Big Sandy Valley but his wife did not accompany him.

nights of most violent rains and the river was so swollen that steam-boats dare not come up. Indeed, it was a fearful sight. The river raised nearly 50 feet. We were getting short of provisions. I went down to Catlettsburg last Sunday and ordered our boats to go up at once. The captains of boats said it was impossible to go up and the attempt would be dangerous in the extreme. They utterly refused to try. I took command of a little steam boat, and on Monday, 3 o'clock P.M., started against the warning of all the boatmen. I found that my old canal experience was then very valuable to me. I took the helm and stood at it night and day, with the exception of about six hours, till Wednesday near noon, when we reached this place with a load of provisions just as the last was being eaten. There were a few times in the night, in the midst of the fearful current and the drift of fallen trees sweeping down, when we came very near sinking. Once the current wheeled us entirely around and drove us forty rods down stream before we could stop. The men on board implored me to stop, but I thought that our boys might be starving and I had some pride to do what I had undertaken, and I pushed on. So you see I have turned sailor at last.

I have today written a long letter to mother. I hope she is not feeling uneasy about me for I think we shall have but little more fighting for some time. I want you to tell me all about our precious little Trot. Give my love to Father and Mother and Nell. I want to hear from them all. I ask what I believe I never did before, the news of the neighborhood. Send me copies of the Portage *Democrat*. I don't see it.

*Ever and forever your*
James

Headquarters, 18th Brigade
Camp Buell
February 12, 1862

*My Dear Harry:*

I have been flat on my back for six days and though I have dictated a good many business and official letters and managed the brigade from the bed, still I have not been able to wield the pen till today. Even now I dare not venture out of doors. I have lost nearly 20 pounds of flesh by the vaccination, cold and fever. But it happened just in a time when I had got matters in such a shape as to be quite manageable. I have moved two regiments and a few companies besides on to Piketon, and as soon as I am able shall go up with the 42nd and the 16th Kentucky, which has lately been added to the command. Instructions from General Buell allow me [to] drive all rebels from the soil of Eastern Kentucky. So you see I have some work again.

Your last good letter of the 6th contains more good muscular statesmanship in it than anything you have written. I tell you I admire it very much, and I am very glad of this opportunity to speak a few words on the general bearings of the war. It is true, I have not had much conversation nor time for a great deal of reflection on the great governmental revolution now going on, but yet, I have a few well defined conclusions which are being forced upon me as the war advances. That this war will result fatally to slavery I have no doubt. This assurance is to me one of the brightest promises of the future. But I am equally clear that a declaration of emancipation by the administration would be a most fatal mistake. The logic of argument wielded with the varied power of all the minds that have labored on this theme has not brought the people of the North even, up to the necessity. Nothing but the terrible logic of events will do it. That logic is at work and will surely do its work, but not yet. General McClellan is weakly and wickedly conservative on this point and the President nearly as bad. But out of the very weakness and timidity of our leaders I draw the hope that thus God has willed it, that He is the commander-in-chief of our armies, and there is no central iron will making ends for the war and effectually thwarting the Divine purpose. If McClellan will discipline and mobilize our people into armies, and let them meet the enemy, God will take care of the grand consequences.

I believe in Beecher's Thanksgiving Sermon.[100] It is the best political philosophy Beecher ever wrote. I suppose you have read it. If not I beg you do so at once.

My address to the people of this valley, which the papers have been pleased to call a proclamation,[101] is designed to effect one purpose— to weed out from the war here the infernal devil that has made this valley a home of fiends, and converted this war into a black hole in which to murder any man that any soldier from envy, lust or revenge, hated. I have a soldier now under arrest, and whom I expect to sentence to death in a few days for shooting a prisoner (a neighbor of

[100] On November 26, 1861, Henry Ward Beecher, famous Congregationalist minister, delivered in his Plymouth Church a sermon entitled "Modes and Duties of Emancipation." In it he declared that in the Civil War, God and Liberty were fighting slavery and the devil; that the war would destroy the doctrine of state sovereignty and win freedom for all men everywhere; that emancipation, already begun, should be consummated by constitutional processes; and that programs must be developed to prepare the Negro for citizenship.

[101] In Paintsville, on January 16, 1862, Garfield issued to the citizens of the Sandy Valley a formal statement setting forth the objectives of his campaign. He had come, he said, "to restore the honor of the Union," to offer its enemies "the alternative of battle or unconditional surrender," to protect loyal citizens and their property, to give like protection to those in rebellion who laid down their arms and supported the Federal government, to restore peace, to redress wrongs done by the enemies of the Union to loyal citizens, and to urge all Unionists to abandon their private feuds and "let a liberal-minded love of country direct their conduct towards . . . [their enemies]."

his) in cold blood. If these people are ever to live together again in peace, I think the reconciliations ought to be begun while the army is here. I know there is not the vindictiveness which suits these blood-thirsty Kentuckians in that proclamation, but I know this, it has brought me more than 70 deserters from Marshall's camp since the battle, men of no brains who had been scared into the rebel army and whose lives are not worth to the country what the bullet would cost to kill them. Yet their desertion has aided to disorganize his army, and these poor fellows will slink off home glad to escape the sufferings of an inglorious campaign.

Let the war be conducted *for the Union* till the whole nation shall be enthused, inspired, transfigured with the glory of that high purpose. Let all the deeds of valor add their glory to that purpose, all the blood of noble men that die in the fight hallow it, all the love [of] the people for the fallen ones sanctify and exalt it, till the integrity, indivisibility, and glory of that Union shall gather round itself all the hero-worship, pride and power of the nation, and then, perhaps not till then, they will love the Union more than slavery and slay the python because it[s] slimy folds roll toward the cradle of our infant Hercules (for the Union spirit is yet an infant compared with what it is to be). Again I say read Beecher if you have not.

Harry, come and see us during the vacation. I think you had better. Perhaps you will conclude to stay. I will see that the expense is some-what mitigated. *I want you to come very much indeed.* I am glad to hear you say that Almeda is happy. God bless her. You are very good to her I hope and believe. You and I have never yet summed up the magnitude of our debt to her. Give her my love. I, too, hope to make a part of that dear circle once more, and that hope is stronger than it was the day I left you. Write me often. You must mirror the spirit of the time for me, for I am shut out from the great world of doctrines and philosophy.

> *Ever and forever,*
> Your James

Headquarters, 18th Brigade
Camp Buell
February 14, 1862

*My Dear Wall:*

I have been confined to my room for the last six days but I have dictated business letters and managed the brigade nevertheless. Your kind letter of the 5th was received a day or two since but this is the first day I have been able to sit up and write. I received one letter from you some weeks ago, but I was then so overwhelmed with busi-ness that I could not answer it. I am glad to hear from you and I want you to write me often, even if I don't have the time to answer. You can hardly conceive the amount of work I have on hand, and as usual I have to see to everything in order to be sure it is all going on right.

I am moving the whole brigade on up to Piketon as fast as I can, and shall go on myself as soon as I am able to ride. I hope to strike a blow through the gates of the Cumberland Mountains soon. We have a great deal of sickness but not so much as they have down the Great Valley. It really seems as though the rebellion is beginning to feel the blows of the Federal government now.

I am glad you are in the Senate as reporter of the *Herald*. I sometimes think I should like to be in my old seat again, but if I were I suppose I should pine for the activity of the field.

In reference to my promotion,[102] of which you speak so kindly, I have never said a word in reference to it in way of expressing a desire for it. If any such thing comes up I want it to be because the great cause of the Union will be advanced by [it]. It don't become me to say how that is. At any rate I am glad that my friends are pleased with my management of the Eastern Kentucky campaign. I have never told the difficulties and drawbacks which I met at every step up this valley; not the least was the constant, timid croaking of a lot of officers who were not willing to risk anything for the sake of success.

I hope some day to see you and all my friends in Ohio, but I have no prospect of doing so till the war is over. I appreciate and fully reciprocate your kindness to me. Don't feel any more as you wish[?].

Let me hear from you. My hand is not yet steady, as you see.

*Ever yours,*
J. A. Garfield

Headquarters, 18th Brigade
Camp Buell
February 15, 1862

*My Dear Crete:*

I will begin this letter with a chapter of ailments. With the exception of a few days just after the battle I have been very well indeed, until about twelve days ago when I began to feel the effects of vaccination. I had been exposed to the small pox and was vaccinated immediately after. I had been very much worn down by working several nights in getting our boats loaded and had taken a severe cold. I had the most excruciating pain in my head and back and indeed through

---

[102] Soon after Garfield's victory in Eastern Kentucky a campaign was launched to get him a brigadier generalship. Led by Dr. John P. Robison and William T. Bascom in Columbus, and Salmon P. Chase in Washington, the effort succeeded. About March 19, Garfield received official notice of his promotion, which was dated January 10, the date of the engagement at Middle Creek.

all my bones. Then the camp fever set in and dried up the pustule before it had matured. I have only been able to sit up till three or four days ago. I am now quite weak and find I have lost much flesh. With the exception of pains in my bones, which appear to be rheumatic, I am now quite recovered. During much of that time, I kept up my business by dictating letters and giving orders, but till three days ago I was not able to carry a pen with steadiness. There! I hope not [to] use up another page in telling my sorrows.

I am moving the brigade on to Piketon, and as soon as I can get ready shall move on to the Pound Gap where there is said to be a force of the rebels holding that pass through the Cumberland Mountains.

A late letter from General Buell intimates that as soon as the soil of Eastern Kentucky is entirely cleared of rebels, I with a part of the brigade would be called to another field. I hope this may be so. I will not trouble you with a history of the peculiar difficulties which surround me in this valley. Just now for instance the water in the river is so low that boats cannot go up. There is now a considerable snow on the ground and it is quite cold. If the river should freeze up it would be a terrible thing for us. We are quite at the mercy of this river, and we have had the most favorable winter for good water that has been known in this valley for many years.

Unconsciously to myself I have scribbled away still on things gloomy and distressful. The fact is I have for a few days been feeling more depressed than at any time since I entered the service. For many reasons, personal to myself, I have been feeling that I would be glad to be out of the perplexities of war and enter again the pursuits of peace, but I am perfectly aware that a few weeks of quiet would make me desirous of being in the strife again. Still I have no expectation of abandoning the fight until it [is over] or I am done. There are many indications now which seem to me to show that the rebellion is soon to be crushed. Many think the war will be over by June. I, of course, am not so sanguine as to hope that, but think [it] will be shorter than I had supposed.

Your two good letters of January 25th and February 3rd came by the same mail and were received about five days ago while I was sick. I think our mails are now more sure, and we shall receive letters more certainly than hitherto. You had better direct to Catlettsburg for our communications are now more direct with that place than any other. Or perhaps you had better direct to Piketon, via Catlettsburg.

I was very much struck by your remark concerning my canal experience. It does indeed seem to be a strange part of my history and did not seem to subserve any purpose in the general plan, but if I had not understood the management of a boat, and that too in a degree better than most boatmen, no amount of will power on my part could have got that load of provision up to the boys and they must have suffered. There have been a great many instances in this campaign which are either special providences or very wonderful coincidences. I am inclined to believe the former.

I am growing deeply anxious to know how our darling little Trot is developing. I can't tell you how much I desire to see you both. Have you established such a relation between yourself and her as will lay the basis of both strong control and equally strong affection? I beg of you to guard your heart and not let her get so long an arm of the lever as to develope her power to the prejudice of discipline and control. I dare not hope that many children will come up with as much will and as little restraint as I did, without being ruined. You say she shows a great power of will. I am glad of it. It is very necessary to give point and force to her character. But what was an aid to a thunderbolt of boy like me would make her unlovely. Tell all about the terms of your acquaintance with her. Is she being petted a good deal by others? That way lies great danger. Your task with her is harder than mine with the brigade.

In regard to the loan to John, you may do as you please. Take a note with your father as joint signer and it will all be right. I fear my Mecca matters will sweep off what little we have. I shall no doubt come out of the war not more than even with the world. That gives me a great deal of anxiety. I cannot endure the thought of not having a fund in store for Trot's education. Should anything befal[l] me, I leave it as the concentrated sum of my most earnest wishes that she be provided with means for education of the most liberal kind. I have no fears but that it will be done in some way, but I feel so great an anxiety to have part in it, to leave some of my own hand and heart prints in her nature and education.

What do you think are the prospects of the Eclectic? It would be a great grief to me to have that school dwindle away. Write me fully about it, and give me a look from the inner temple. I tell you, Crete, there is infinitely more satisfaction in feeling that we are embalmed in the hearts of those we have benefitted and blessed than to be in the blaze of a sort of fame which has only the blare of trumpets and the breath of words. But here I am again letting the dusk run down through my fingers. I may as well confess that this enervated feeling of bodily weakness has left me in the valley. I will be on the hill tops again soon.

It is not now in my power to do anything for John but it may be by and by. If so, I shall be most happy to do so. Give my love to him and Mat and all the rest. Ask Harry if he don't think we can make some terms of settlement with Cowdrey and those others in Mecca whom we owe.

*Ever and forever, your*
James

Headquarters, 18th Brigade
Camp Buell
February 15, 1862

*My Dear Smith:*

Your very kind and welcome letter was duly received and I assure you, my dear friend, I am grateful to you for it. My recollections of our friendship are of the most pleasing character. It was one of the few thoroughly intimate confidential friendships I formed during our senatorial term, and I rejoice to bear away with me one such bright remembrance from all the trash and selfishness of political life. I think of you very often in these stirring times and I see your name now and then in the stray papers which occasionally find their way into this God-forsaken valley.

For your earnest words of cheer and congratulation and your manly feeling of fellowship with me I am very grateful. My work in this valley has been full [of] anything but promise, and it has been only by vigorous audacity that I have been able to succeed. But I do believe the work I was sent to do has been pretty thoroughly accomplished. I am beginning to feel encouraged in regard to the war. I believe Ed Stanton[103] is taking hold of matters with more muscle than has been used since the contest began. Oh, if the powers will only push on the work and follow up the late advantages at Somerset [Kentucky] and Fort Henry! Let the great Tennessee & Virginia Railroad be taken and the grand lever on which the rebellion hangs will be broken. I am hoping we shall be allowed to pass through the gates of the Cumberland and strike a blow near the fulcrum at Abingdon [Virginia] or Knoxville. I am now moving the brigade forward to Piketon and if Sir Humphrey stands fire I shall try to have another interview. But his brigade seems to be dissolved. His Virginia regiments have gone, and I issued a notice to the inhabitants of the Sandy Valley which has induced several hundred of his Kentucky troops to desert him since the battle.

I would be very glad to sit down with you and talk over this wonderful chapter of American history and political philosophy—the rebellion and the war! Some day I hope we may. I am sorry you were not made Speaker, and sometimes I long to be back again among the quiet scense [scenes] of peace and in the work of civil life.

Do write to me again. Tell me the news and your views of the outside and inside movements. You can hardly conceive how completely we are shut out from the world. Oh the blight that slavery and ignorance have left on this land! Surely this country is not worth fighting for, it must be a war of principle.

[103] Edwin McMasters Stanton succeeded Simon Cameron as Secretary of War in January, 1862.

Let me hear from you, I say again. Remember me to your good wife, and remember that I am

> *Ever and forever,*
> *Your friend,*
> J. A. Garfield

Headquarters, 18th Brigade
Piketon
February 23, 1862

*My Dear Crete:*

It seems to be my fortune to have a constant round of strange adventures. While I was sick I kept moving the brigade, company by company, forward to this place and when four days ago I got well enough to make it prudent for me to leave, I had the 22nd Kentucky, the 40th Ohio, one company of cavalry, and six companies of the 42nd already up here. The river had been greatly swollen by rains and a large steamer came up easily over the shallowest places. Still the river was falling. We were detained by breaks in the machinery so that we did not get here until yesterday at 10 o'clock A.M. It had commenced to rain at 4 o'clock in the morning and continued to rain in fearful torrents till near midnight last night. I have never seen the fearfulness of water before. I detailed 200 men to take our stores further up the bank and save them. We commenced early in the evening and worked till after midnight. I was conquered for the first time. In one hour the water rose twelve feet. It surrounded the camp of the 40th and they barely had time to get away their guns and ammunition and save themselves.

This morning discloses a fearful scene. The house where I am staying, which is sixty feet above the usual level of the river, is now surrounded. A wild river roars around it on all sides. It is forty rods to the shore. Two large steamboats are up in the principal street of the village. House[s], stacks of wheat and hay, gigantic trees, saw-logs, fences, and all things that float are careening by with fearful velocity. The terrified people of the village have fled to the hills when they could, or have carried their goods to the upper rooms of their dwellings and are waiting, terror-stricken, [at] the mercy of the flood.

At day break I got a horse and rode through a current, which came very near sweeping me away, to look after the safety of my dear 42nd. I found them safe but Captain Williams' tent was out of sight under water. The noble fellows had given up most of their tents, which were on tolerably high ground, to the women and children who had fled from their houses. Company A and two others of the 42nd are surrounded on an island adjoining the one on which I am. Most of the tents of the 40th are gone. All are under water. Many horses are drowned. I hope no men are lost. I presume $50,000 will not near repair our loss. It is a strange place to be in, where one is utterly powerless to do anything. I hope the flood has reached its height. Three inches more and it will swash through the room where I am sitting. I tremble for the sickness and suffering which must follow. Four battles would not be so disastrous to us. I am very much worn down, but my anxiety for the boys and the immense amount of work to be done in consequence of the flood will, I think, keep me from being sick. I have sent for the steamer's yawls to get up a line of communication with the different parts of the brigade. They will be at the door soon.

I am stopping with [a] Disciple family, the finest in the place; but they are all secessionists. It is one of the painful facts of the rebellion that nearly all the most cultivated and enlightened people in this country, at least, are on the side of the rebellion. This probably grows out of the fact that the leaders of the rebellion were the aristocrats of the South, and they have led off that element with them. The men are as well as could be expected in such a country.

Poor Baldwin Bently[104] is gone. He was a noble, brave boy. I cannot tell you how that regiment grows into my affections. Every hardship they suffer makes them dearer to me. The latest news we have gives me hope that the end of the war is not far off. It would be so great a good if the grand army of the valley could take Nashville and sweep up the great rebel road, let us join it at Abingdon and make an attack from the rear on Richmond and the Potomac. But let us have patience. I expect never to see you till the war closes, so let us hope that the blood that must be shed may flow fast and finish this terrible work. But I would rather it should flow for seven years in reddening torrents, than that the great national question should not be gloriously, fully and finally settled.

The water has begun to fall. The sun is breaking out and is gilding the devastation. I must take the yawl which is now coming and gather up the fragment which the anger of the river-god has left us.

Try to tell Trot how much I love her and how I long to take her in my arms again. I have not heard from you in a long time. The communication will be very slow now [as] it is 100 miles in a direct line to the Ohio, 140 by river. Do write me often. You have no idea how much I long for letters. Give my love to all our family and friends, and remember now as ever your affectionate and flooded

James

[104] Baldwin Bently of Mantua, a private in Company A, died of disease on February 10.

Piketon, Kentucky
March 3, 1862

*My Dear Harry:*

I have been for three hours continually writing and dictating orders and dispatches to send down by the boat, and now as the crowd of men are going on board and the little steamer is coaling, I will scratch a few words to you in answer to your very good letter of the 21st. Be assured, my dear brother, that I am deeply grateful for all your kind words and many assurances of that affection which [is] all the dearer to me because it was formed in those quiet days when we talked with naked hearts together with all [the] unselfishness of honest love. You are wrong to intimate that our spieres [spheres] can ever be so different, or any gulf so widen between the currents of our lives as to make you any less dear to me, or your thoughts and experiences any the less valuable and interesting. If each does his duty, wherever his lot may fall, God will bless us both and make the life of each valuable to the other.

For the past ten days I have battled with a foe more formidable than the legions of Marshall. The waters have played frightful havoc with our campaign. It was truly appalling, but I am struggling to conquer our losses and shall succeed. It will delay the forward movement, which was almost ready, for at least half a month; but I have come to requite such interferences as a part of God's plan in the management of my life and my work. So I am very cheerful and happy in the wreck which the flood has made.

I thank you for your congratulations in regard to the promotion, though I do not yet know whether it has been made or not. I have had no official notification of the fact. I hardly know whether to be more pleased than saddened by it. It makes me very sad to think of being separated from the 42nd. I cannot tell you how strangely and powerfully my whole being has been drawn out in love for that body of men. The very sound of the word Forty-second has a strange charm [in] it. It seems to me that I could never love any other like it. But I am reassured by this thought, that I have never by word or written sentence made any approach to forwarding the movement or inviting it. Had I done so I should feel I was moving the plans of God, and should not succeed.

I have not yet heard from Almeda, and it has now been almost a month since I have had a line from her. I hope she will be happy and will write to me *ex pleno animo* [from the whole heart].

Harry, the chances of this war in reference to my own life make me anxious, for the sake of Crete and Trot, that my Mecca obligations should be cancelled, and I released from any claims in the case. I wish you would go or send some one and find out [on] what terms [I] can be fully released from the whole matter. I don't want it to hang up an incubus upon what little means I might leave in case of my death. If you will do this at once and write me the best terms you can get, I will try to raise the money and cancel the obligation. Now I hold you to your promise to write me soon and often. I know this is not a worthy return for your noble letter, but it is the best I can do *cum calamo currente* [with hurrying pen]. Give my love to Harvey and tell him I shall be very glad to hear from him.

The news from along the lines is full of hope. It may be that the green leaves will see us home. God grant it. I am not quite well again. I regret you did not conclude to come to us in vacation.

*Ever and forever yours,*
James

Headquarters, 18th Brigade
Piketon, Kentucky
March 10, 1862

*My Dear Crete:*
Yours of February 24th is just received. There has been no mail, except a few stray letters for nearly three weeks. The terrible state of the river and the weather have made it nearly impossible for me to get or send news. Till yesterday our latest papers were February 25th. I cannot comprehend why you had not received my letter. There has been no gap between them as long as the time you stated, though there was a space of nearly two weeks in which we got no regular mail sent to the Ohio.

So far as our stores are concerned, we are rapidly recovering from the effects of the flood, but we are suffering terribly in health in consequence of the exposure incident to the high waters. There has never been so fearful a condition as our sick list now exhibits. It is really alarming. There are over 400 sick in the hospital at Ashland, and I am this morning sending nearly sixty more. I hope you will not mention this outside the family. I am doing everything in my power to aid those who are sick, and to prevent the well from falling sick. But this country is stripped of every comfort. We need relishes, like pickles, sour-kraut and other antiscorbutics, but not a thing of the kind can be got here. Fifty have died within the last four weeks. Twenty-two of them from the 42nd Regiment.

I declare to you there are fathers and mothers in Ohio that I hardly know how I can ever endure to meet. A noble young man from Medina County died a few days ago. I enlisted him, but not till I had spent two hours in answering the objection of his father, who urged that he was too young to stand the exposure. He was the only child. I cannot feel myself to blame in the matter, but I assure you I would rather fight a battle than to meet his father.

Two Hiram boys came to me last night in tears and besought me to send them home. They said they had been taking the doctor's medicine for several days and were getting no better. They all have a terrible dread of the hospital. Captain Williams came with them. He broke down and cried too. I told the boys I had been wrestling with sickness myself as with a giant enemy and they must do the same. I talked to them till they felt brave, and then sent them to Captain Williams' tent to have him bathe them, soak their feet, and give the Hygiene pills.

I am glad to say they are better this morning. They are Cyrus Mead and Chapman.[105] A large number of officers are sick. I dare not tell you how small a number of that noble regiment can be mustered for duty. This fighting with disease is infinitely more horrible than battle. We have had but little snow till since March came in. For two weeks we have had mingled snow and rain, and horrible mud. I am alarmed but not discouraged. I dare not be that. I hope, and with grounds for it, that April, at least, will bring us settled weather and restored health. I suppose we are not worse off, perhaps not so bad as those in the Great Valley. This is the great price of saving the Union. My God, what a costly sacrifice!

When I read how considerately and with what distinguished attention the Government is treating the rebel officers who are now prisoners of war, I am fired with the deepest indignation. The 1,200 nabob officers who were allowed to wear their side arms and be attended into Camp Chase by their slaves,[106] and then find fault that "Gentlemen were put into such a muddy and uncomfortable camp," and when I remember that that camp was good enough for me and my noble boys to drill in for three months and nobody complained that we were ill used. If the severest veng[e]ance of outraged and insulted law is not visited upon those cursed villains who have instigated and led this rebellion it will be the most wicked crime that can be committed. The blood of hundreds of the 18th Brigade will before summer be crying from the ground to God for veng[e]ance.

I don't want you to feel alarmed to the extent that our present condition would indicate, for I have great faith in the power of will to resist disease. Particularly I desire that you shall not feel alarmed for me. The efforts I am making and must make to strengthen others will, I believe, keep me well.

I have now accomplished all in this valley I was ordered to. I have written to General Buell for further instructions. On my approach to

[105] Cyrus A. Mead of Freedom, formerly a student at the Eclectic, was a private in Company A. He died of disease on March 27, and Elam H. Chapman, also a private in the same company, died the following day.

[106] In March, 1862, complaints from outraged citizens led to an investigation by the Ohio Senate of conditions in Camp Chase, then a Union prison. The investigators revealed that about fifty slaves and more than twenty Free Negroes were servants to captive Confederate officers. This shocking revelation, together with other disclosures of lax discipline and extensive privileges to inmates resulted in the speedy adoption of corrective measures.

this place, the remnant of Marshall's force fled through the Pound Gap and is now scattered all the way from Gladesville to Abingdon. I have not yet received official notification of my promotion, but presume the accounts of the matter are correct. I am very sad at the thought of being more widely separated from the 42nd. Indeed it has been a serious question with me whether I would accept or not, though I presume I shall. I have been doing the duties of the position ever since I came here.

I enclose a note to Joe. I shall have his name added to the rolls. Tell him to buy [bring] a large supply of Hygiene pills with him. Also tell him to buy DeHart's work on court martials for me.[107] I hope you and Trot are well. How are [you] treating her health? There is much danger of being over cautious of her. The half-naked, half-starved children of this valley are rarely sick. Don't make her a house plant. Tell me all about it. Give my love to the family and all who inquire. Ever and forever,

*Your* James

Steamboat *Piketon*
Big Sandy River
March 19, 1862

*My Dear Crete:*
I will try to scratch you a few words as well as the jiggling of this little boat will let me. On Monday evening I returned from the expedition to the Pound Gap. It was one of the dreariest roads, and the most dreadful state of weather we have had yet. I took 600 infantry and one hundred cavalry. Started on the 14th, went 15 miles the first day, and 21 the second. It rained and snowed nearly all the time. I enclose you a map of the route.

On Sunday morning the 16th I started with the column of infantry to climb the mountain, where no one supposed we could ascend; the cavalry was sent around to attack the enemy (500 strong) in front and draw off his attention. It took us two hours to climb the mountain for it was nearly a mile and a half from foot to summit. We then crept silently along the ridge and came within 200 rods of them before they saw us. They immediately formed in line of battle, but we had no sooner formed and fired a few vollies among them than they fled ingloriously. I fired one shot among them and the boys say I felled one, but I think and hope not.

We then took possession of their camp, where they had left everything but themselves and what guns they had in their hands. The roads being so bad, and having no means of transportation, I set on

[107] William Chetwood DeHart, *Observations on Military Law, . . . and Practice of Courts Martial, . . .* (1846) .

fire and destroyed a larg[e] amount of stores and all their huts to the number of sixty. There were many curious trophies saved by the boys. I have all their official documents, among them several letters written by General Marshall. In most respects it is the completest thing we have accomplished but it lacks blood to give it much place among the movements of the time. There were seven of the enemy's [soldiers] killed and wounded. None of our boys were hurt. Better to gain a bloodless victory. I was in my saddle and travelling on foot 18 hours of one of the days.

I have received the brigadier's commission of which so much has been said. It bears date of January 10th, the day of the battle.

I am glad to inform you that one hour ago I received orders to move my brigade to Bardstown, Kentucky. So we shall go down the river soon. Direct my next letter to Bardstown, Kentucky. I enclose you some trinkets. Tell Joe to meet us at Cincinnati, March 25th. I was delighted with your good letters. Bless the little darling that is getting so smart and good. Ever your and hers.

> *Love to all,*
> James

Burnet House, Cincinnati
March 30, 1862

*My Dear Crete:*

I arrived here today and have stopped off to do some business and go down in the next boat which will be here in the morning with the remainder of our men. I have received your letter by the hand of Rogers. I should be exceedingly glad to go home and see you, but I know it is of no use to speak of it.

The sickness is still fearful in the brigade, and when a man gets sick there seems to come over him a conviction that he is going to die, and that hastens his death. [Cyrus] Mead died last night while I was in Ashland. [Elam H.] Chapman and [Frank B.] Cowles of Company A have also died within the last 48 hours. Captain F. A. Williams is very sick with the Typhoid Fever. I have brought him here and got a good private house for him. I shall telegraph for Sophia or Mary to come down and stay with him. I don't know [that] I could endure his loss, should he die. He is one of my very best officers. I am in an agony of anxiety about him. Still he is not past strong hope of recovery.

The boxes of goods you sent are here but they have not yet been opened. I know nothing as yet of our future destination. I presume, however, it will be with the grand army. I hope I shall have a few weeks to recruit my men and drill them in brigade movements before we get into column again. It is due to the me[n]. I cannot tell you how I dread the approach of the hot season away in the South for my men. My anxiety in their respects makes me very unhappy. I will hold out no expectation about getting home. It may be possible that I can get away for a few days from Bardstown, but I hardly expect it. If I can get a chance at a bank before I leave in the morning, I will send you some money.

I am trying to see if I can do anything for John. It would give me great pleasure if I could. Joe arrived safely and looks better than I ever saw him.

I enclose you a picture of Governor Dennison which I received today from Mrs. Dennison. Also a letter from her. Governor Dennison's history will yet be vindicated. I have all along said as I now say that he was one of the wisets [wisest], most honest, capable and faithful governors Ohio ever had.[108]

Have I ever told you about my contraband Jim?[109] If not I will do so in my next. Tell me.

An[d] now to Trot and yourself I give again, and from the soil of home, as ever my love,

James

I thank father for his letter. I will try to get time to answer it before long.

Cincinnati
March 31, 1862

*My Dear Harry:*
Your letter I have just found here. DuBois'[110] references are excellent, but it surprises me that he has not had some place before now if he is really all his vouchers say of him. I am greatly troubled in regard to my staff. I don't know what my rights are, fully. I shall call on General Buell and discuss the whole matter. I am greatly disappointed in not seeing you here on my arrival. I stopped off yesterday noon and shall go down on the steamer that brings the last detachment of the 42nd. I am expecting the boat every minute. I should have been very glad had [I been] able to come up home and see you all before going away south, but it is impossible.

I send you two holly trees which grew near the battle field. I want

---

[108] Dennison remains to this day a controversial figure. Historians disagree sharply in appraising his wartime leadership. For a balanced and sympathetic treatment of his governorship, see Eugene H. Roseboom, *The Civil War Era*, 380 ff. But William B. Hesseltine, *Lincoln and the War Governors*, 153 ff., condemns Dennison as an inefficient and incompetent executive.

[109] See Garfield's letter to his wife, May 27, 1862.

[110] Cornelius J. DuBois of New Haven, Connecticut, served about two years (1861-1863) as a private in the Seventh New York and nearly three months in 1864 as adjutant of the Twentieth Connecticut.

them planted in the Seminary yard for me. They are the old English Holly of poetry. There are but few places in America where they grow wild.

In a few days I will be able to send you some money if you still find it necessary. I hope we may successfully draw on our debtors and thus settle the matter.

Captain Williams is very sick. I think he is a little better this morning. Write me often. My address will be Bardstown, Kentucky.

> *Ever yours,*
> James

Louisville, Kentucky
April 2, 1862

*My Dear Crete:*

I have never so fully realized the fickleness of fortune, and the chances and changes of war as this morning. I arrived here in the night, last night, with three regiments, all promising ourselves great pleasure in a new and broader field of operation. Ten minutes after my arrival dispatches were placed in my hand ordering my regiments turned over to the command of General Morgan,[111] and myself to report to General Buell at Nashville or where-ever he may be in the field. No hint is given of my destination, but it is supposed I am to be assigned a command in the forces that are now gathering to attack Corinth. No matter, in fifteen minutes I leave. I have wakened Colonel Sheldon and Major Pardee to bid them good-by. I dare not let the 42nd Regiment know I am going. It might make a scene. I know it would nearly break me down. Whether I shall ever see them again in the war I cannot tell. One thing is sure: I am their General no longer.

The omnibus is at the door. Farewell, you shall hear from me soon. As ever yours and Trot's,

> J. A. Garfield

Headquarters, 20th Brigade
In camp 48 miles south of
Columbia, Tennessee
April 4, (8P M ) 1862

*My Dear Crete:*

If my life were not so much like a series of strange and odd dreams, I should be inclined to think I had been dreaming during the last few

[111] George Washington Morgan, soldier, lawyer, and congressman, was appointed brigadier general of volunteers in November, 1861. He succeeded Garfield in Eastern Kentucky in March, 1862, when he was appointed commander of the Seventh Division, Army of the Ohio.

days. When I wrote to Harry from Columbia, I was about ready to leave that place at sunset of Thursday. General Negley[112] gave me an escort consisting of one sergeant and eight cavalrymen, and furnished me a trooper's horse. The beast would not gallop, but was a very fast and hard trotter. Till dark we passed through one of the most delightful tracts of country I have ever seen.

The residences of General [Gideon J.] Pillow and Right Reverend Major General [Leonidas] Polk are very magnificent. The ditch-digging General is worth two millions of dollars.

Making our way past camps and transportation wagons almost innumerable, we reached the headquarters of General Thomas[113] at ten o'clock where I obtained a new escort, but kept the hard trotter and in an hour was in the saddle. General Buell was moving on to the front of the Grand army as rapidly as he could and I knew my only way to catch him was to go in the night. At 3½ o'clock in the morning I reached General Buell's tent 3[3] miles south of Columbia. In half an hour the General was up and after taking breakfast with him he assigned me to the 20th Brigade in the 6th Division.[114] The men were already under arms and were to march at 6 o'clock.

You can imagine how well prepared I was in regard to general outfit. Horse, servant, books, sword, pistols, blankets and mess chest were in Louisville and my trunk had been committed to the uncertain chances of a quartermaster's wagon at Columbia. I had no baggage but my overcoat, and that was needed for the rain began to fall in torrents by six. The General ordered a trooper to dismount and give me his horse, which trotted, only not so hard as my equine companion of the night before.

Thus mounted I assume command of the 20th Brigade, consisting of

[112] Brigadier General James S. Negley commanded the Seventh Independent Brigade, Army of the Ohio. Later he led a division in the Army of the Cumberland, distinguished himself at Stones River, and was promoted to major general. After rendering able service in the Tullahoma campaign, he was driven from the field at Chickamauga and relieved of his command. A court of inquiry, requested by him, cleared him of charges of cowardice and desertion but he was never reassigned a command.

[113] Brigadier General (three weeks later he was promoted to major general) George H. Thomas commanded the First Division, Army of the Ohio. Later, in the Tullahoma and Chickamauga campaigns, he led the XIV Corps, Army of the Cumberland. His heroic stand at Chickamauga (Garfield was by his side during most of it) won him the sobriquet, Rock of Chickamauga. He succeeded Rosecrans as commander of the army and won additional laurels at Missionary Ridge and Nashville.

[114] Garfield succeeded James W. Forsyth, an Ohioan, as commander of the Twentieth Brigade in Brigadier General Thomas J. Wood's Sixth Division. Wood, of whom Garfield became severely critical in private correspondence, later headed a division in the Army of the Cumberland. At Chickamauga he acted on a faultily-worded order from Rosecrans, withdrew his division from the line of battle, and created a gap through which Confederates poured to rout the Union right and center.

the 64th and 65th Ohio, and the 13th Michigan and 51st Indiana regiments. The Colonel who had been in command (a West Pointer) delivered the brigade to me and away we went with a train of 85 wagons drawn [by] 510 mules. After a march of 15 miles I have encamped in a large field in the regular order of encampment, and, having got supper with one of the colonels, I have borrowed a blanket and am now ready and willing to lie down and rest, only I thought I would write a word to you before I slept.

The two Ohio bands have just been before my tent serenading me. I hardly know for what, only they seem to have heard of me and appear glad that I am here. But no matter what other regiments may be to me, I mourn like a bereaved lover for my dear old 42nd. If possible I shall get it with me, but I fear not before the great battle comes off. . . .

Having slept but one night in the last three, I must try [to] sleep a little. In the midst of this great army I am alone. The tent is very large and is more than 600 miles from you and Trot, whose I am with a love which reaches out through the night and the distance and asks God's blessings upon you.

*Ever your* James

Battlefield, 12 miles from
Corinth, Mississippi
April 9, 1862

*My Dear Crete:*

I sent a letter to you from Savannah, just [as] I was embarking my brigade to go to the battle. We landed from the steamers at a place called Pittsburg, nine miles above Savannah about half past one o'clock. The battle had been raging since early dawn, and the enemy were just beginning to fall back slowly. General Wood met [sent?] orders for us to proceed to the front with all possible dispatch. I hurried my brigade on and reached the front before three o'clock. I was there halted to await further orders; for an hour we stood amid the roar of the battle, the shells bursting around us occasionally and the grape shot falling on all sides of me and my staff. We had ridden forward to watch the indications and await orders, but the tide [of] battle swept on and as the sun went down our division was ordered to the extreme front where we bivouac[k]ed during the worst night of mud and rain I ever saw.

Yesterday morning we pursued the enemy in an armed reconnois-[s]ance between three and four miles, when we were attacked by 800 Texan Rangers and as many more Alabama cavalry. The[y] made a most de[s]perate attack, driving back our advance (a regiment of cavalry and one of infantry), killing 19 and wounding 40 with nearly an equal loss on their side. They were, however, soon driven back and their camp destroyed. On the whole this is no doubt the bloodiest battle ever fought on this continent, in which has been mingled on our side both the worst and the best of generalship, the most noble bravery and the most contemptible cowardice.

General [Ulysses S.] Grant was encamped on the west side of the river with a very large army, and on Sunday morning, very early, he seems to have been surprised by an overwhelming force of the enemy who came down with a front line of battle three miles in length and a long column supporting it in the center. General [Albert Sidney] Johnston was in supreme command, [P. G. T.] Beauregard in the center, [Braxton] Bragg and [William] Hardee on the wings. By some criminal neglect, not yet explained, their approach was not discovered till fifteen minutes before the attack.[115] This vast column moved on sweeping Grant's advanced brigades before it like leaves before a whirlwind, here and there; some brave officer formed his line and withstood the shock till the long line of dead and wounded was greater than the living. In this way the enemy drove on for four miles, till our force was driven to the steamboat landing, where it must have been annihilated or captured but for the two gunboats which sent shells with terrible effect into the columns of the enemy, and forced him back from the river. Thus night closed in over a most disastrous day for our arms and our honor.

It was the enemy's evident intention to cut off Grant before General Buell should arrive via Nashville and Columbia. In the night, however, our column reached the river and began to cross.[116] Early next morning the battle was resumed, both parties having been strongly reinforced.[117] Inch by inch the enemy were driven back over the ground they had captured, and as night closed in, our line of battle, five miles

[115] At dawn of April 6, the first day of Shiloh, a small Federal reconnaissance force engaged advancing enemy pickets nearly two hours before the main body of Confederates struck Major General Ulysses S. Grant's army. Yet most Union officers were not expecting a general attack until minutes before it came. Thus surprise was an important factor in Confederate successes of that day. Garfield's charge of criminal neglect is unfounded. Also, not until the night after the first day of fighting did the Confederates form a line with corps side by side. The reorganized line, from left to right, was commanded by Hardee, John C. Breckinridge, Polk and Bragg. P. G. T. Beauregard was second in command when the battle began. He succeeded General Albert Sidney Johnston, the commander, who was killed on the first day. It is of interest that years later, when Garfield went to New Orleans concerning the disputed presidential election of 1876, he sailed down the Mississippi River on a steamer with Beauregard, who related the history of Shiloh. "It was curious to hear the story of the battle by the rebel commander," Garfield wrote his wife on November 21, 1876.

[116] The first of Buell's troops at Pittsburg Landing were in Brigadier General William Nelson's Fourth Division. They arrived late in the afternoon (about 5:00 p.m.) and formed on the Union left, next to the Tennessee River, where the Confederates had been stopped not only by the gunboats *Tyler* and *Lexington*, but also by Colonel Joseph D. Webster's well-placed, fifty-gun battery and its supporting infantry.

[117] The Confederate army received no re-enforcements at Shiloh.

in length, had swept the enemy back over a space of six miles. Such a scene as this 30 square miles presents beggars all attempt at description. If I live to meet you again, I will attempt to tell something of its horrors. God has been good to me and I am yet spared. After returning from our reconnois[s]ance last evening, we slept again on the ground without blankets. It rained heavily for three hours the latter part of the night. Today we are beginning to bury the dead. I presume we shall soon move on Corinth.

My health has never been better, though I am entirely without camp equipage. My horses and servants, trunk, mess-chest, are all back. Indeed I have nothing of my own, save the clothes on my back. When they will be here I do not know. I shall telegraph for them today.

I have almost been glad that my dear 42nd is not with me, there has been such terrible exposure of the soldiers here. But oh, how I grieve at our separation!

Kiss our precious little Trot for me a hundred times. God bless you and her with the richest of his infinite love. Remember me to father and mother and all the family. Tell Harry and Almeda I wrote to them a short time before I reached Savannah.

My letters must be address[ed] to me, Commanding 20th Brigade, 6th Division, Army of the Ohio, via Nashville, *to follow the Brigade.* This voluminous direction will cause letters to reach me, and I hope a great number will come.

> *Ever and forever your*
> James

> Headquarters, 20th Brigade
> Field of Shiloh
> April 21, 1862

*My Dear Crete:*

After the lon[g]est space that ever intervened between your letters to me when away, yours of the 5th *inst.* was received. But it was on the way during the confusion and almost entire suspension of the carrying trade consequent upon the great battle, and so only reached me a few days ago. It is the only word from northern Ohio I have had since I left the Big Sandy. I assure you, my dear Crete, I have never been in so much need of letters from home as since my arrival here. Still, I am getting along as well [as] it [is] possible for me to, without the 42nd.

I am by slow degrees recovering from a violent attack of bloody dysentery which was accompanied by an incipient attack of piles. I never suffered such acute and crushing pain in my life as I did for 40 hours during that attack. I should probably be entirely well but for the severe and continued rains. There has not been four hours' cessation of heavy cold rain for the last three days and nights. From Saturday morning to

Sunday evening I was on outpost duty with my whole brigade, and it rained continually. I was wet through and through and the effect has been rather bad on my malady, but I am so much better today that I believe I have seen the end of this attack.

My pickets and videttes were so far out that they could occasionally see the pickets of the enemy. I found a group of twelve tents in the woods beyond our pickets, where there were 30 wounded rebels attended by a surgeon and a few soldiers. We sent them food and what comforts we could, but dead men were lying in among the living, and sight and smell were terrible. We buried the dead, and were in hearing of the commands of the officers of the rebel outposts. The horrible sights I have witnessed on this field I can never describe. No blaze of glory that flashes around the magnificent triumphs of war can ever atone for the unwritten and unutterable horrors of the scene of carnage. I hope you will find a sketch of the battle of Sunday and Monday, written by "Agate" of the Cincinnati *Gazette*.[118] It is, in the main, very correct and is one of the best battle sketches I have seen.

I am still in a rather unpleasant condition in regard to my personal arrangements. I left Louisville with nothing by [but] my trunk, overcoat and a belt pistol. The trunk I was obliged to leave at Columbia to be brought forward on a government wagon, but I have heard nothing of it since and fear I never shall. It contained all my clothing, letters, commissions, *etc.*, so that I have not even a change. When the Aid Society[119] was down with a steamer for the wounded, come down from Cincinnati, I found Dr. Beckwith, and a Mrs. Noble of Cleveland, and also Mrs. Wilcox of Painesville who came as representatives of the Aid Society, and they gave me a pair of drawers and undershirt. But for that I should have been wearing the same underclothes more than three weeks.

---

[118] Agate was Whitelaw Reid who, soon after Sumter fell, became a war correspondent for the *Gazette*. His story of Shiloh appeared on April 14, 1862. Accompanied by an excellent map showing principal roads and water courses, and the disposition of Union troops, the thirteen-column article, though erroneous in spots, is a classic of the battlefield reporting of the Civil War.

[119] To aid the fighting men and needy families of soldiers, Cleveland residents founded on April 20, 1861, the Soldier's Aid Society. Later in the year it became a branch of the U.S. Sanitary Commission. Like its sister organizations, the Cleveland society sponsored numerous activities, including concerts, balls, lectures, plays, and fairs, the proceeds of which enabled it to disburse food, clothing, bedding, medical supplies and hospital furniture valued at nearly a million dollars. After the Battle of Shiloh the Cleveland society used boats chartered by the Sanitary Commission to carry supplies from Cincinnati to Pittsburg Landing, and to return with sick and wounded destined for hospitals or home. Dr. John Strong Newberry, noted physician, geologist, and secretary of the Western Division of the U.S. Sanitary Commission, accompanied the first post-Shiloh cargo sent by the Cleveland society. So did Mrs. B. O. Wilcox and Mrs. Stanley Noble of the Painesville branch, who represented the society. The Dr. Beckwith mentioned by Garfield may have been either S. R. or David H., who were Cleveland surgeons.

I do not hear from my horse or from Green.[120] I hear incidentally that my boy Jim, who came over to me at the Battle of Middle Creek, was kidnapped at Louisville, but was rescued by a writ of habeas corpus. This circumstance caused a panic among the Colored men connected with the 42nd and Professor went home, partly because he was sick. The Major wrote me he believed it was because I was gone. At last accounts Green was feeling blue about coming down here, and I am inclined to think he thought prudence the better part of valor and has gone home. Still I hope to see him and my horse Bill. I have telegraphed to Captain Plumb[121] and Heaton, now in Cincinnati, to send for my horse Harry, now in Elyria where I sent him when I found what a country we had to operate in, in the Sandy Valley.

I have chosen Ben[jamin B.] Lake (lieutenant in a cavalry company in Piketon) as one of my aids. He will be here in a week or two. You remember him when he was a student in Hiram. A few days since I met his father (Brother Constant Lake of Wooster) here in search for his son Joseph. He was nearly distracted. His son belonged to an artillery company, and was very sick with the typhoid fever. When the battle was raging, and while his companions were gone for a [team ?] to take him out of danger, he arose from his bed and in his wild fever delirium ran down to the landing. He was seen on the shore amid the hurrying crowds, and that is the last trace we can discover. His father has searched for days and has now gone down the river to search the hospitals through to see if he may not in his wildness have got on a boat among the wounded and been taken below. Faint hope! but it is a father's.[122]

Dear little Trot! How is she tonight? Did you know that I am farther away from you now than ever before? There are a thousand miles between us tonight. I need not tell you how great a joy it would be to me could that space drop out and bring me to you. Do write me long and frequent letters. Tell me what you hear about the 42nd as well as the friends at home. I met George Garfield[123] a few days ago. He is in a cavalry company here.

[120] A Cleveland Negro who was for a time Garfield's hostler.

[121] Captain Ralph Plumb was assistant quartermaster on Garfield's staff.

[122] Benjamin B. Lake, one of Garfield's classmates at the Eclectic, served in the Sandy Valley campaign as a lieutenant in Major William McLaughlin's First Squadron of Ohio Cavalry. Lake was reassigned in April, 1862, as Garfield's aide-de-camp. Constant Lake, father of Benjamin and Joseph, was a hardware merchant in Wooster. Joseph, a corpulent young man, enlisted in Captain Andrew Hickenlooper's Fifth Ohio Battery which fought at the Hornets Nest in the Battle of Shiloh. Though hospitalized for three days prior to the battle, Joseph took his position by his gun and remained until he collapsed and was carried to the rear. He wandered to the Tennessee River, somehow got aboard a boat and was carried to St. Louis where he died in a hospital.

[123] Garfield's cousin George was the son of Thomas Garfield, the younger brother of Garfield's father. Uncle Thomas, who is mentioned later, was a farmer in Newburg, Ohio.

I send you in this $50.00, a $30 treasury note, and two ten dollar bills. I should have sent you some before, but I could not get the proper exchange. I have sent some money to Dr. Robison to invest for me. Tell me when you want money and how much. Give my kind regards to all the family and friends.

*Ever thine and Trot's,*
James

[P.S.] Did I tell you how to direct? I believe I did, but here it is again. 20th Brigade, 6th Division, Army of the Ohio, up Tennessee River.

Lick Creek, Tennessee
12 miles from Corinth, Mississippi
May 1, 1862

*My Dear Crete:*

I have been busy settling up my army accounts connected with the Sandy Valley since noon of today; and now at midnight, when the rest have gone to their tents, I will sit and write once more to you. Do you know that I have not heard from you since the 6th of April, the date of your last letter. I have just concluded to send Captain Ralph Plumb (of Oberlin) back to Cincinnati to close up some of our Sandy Valley accounts, and being so near I have directed him to go to Hiram and see you. From all I can learn I have reason to believe that my letters have not reached you. I have written you not less than five since I left Cincinnati. It is said that they are retained till they are three weeks old so that the contents of the mails shall communicate no intelligence which might injure the cause of the Union army. I regard it an absurd and foolish policy and a very wicked course to pursue toward the friends of the army who may be in such great anxiety to know the fate [of] their soldier friends in the battle. Be that as it may, I have now the satisfaction of feeling sure that what I write will reach you. There is no trouble in the mails coming this way, or at least others get letters though I do not average three per week from the whole world.

I have been very unwell during the last ten days. When the bloody dysentery left me, the piles set in, an[d] I suffered more in 48 hours about one week ago than I ever did in the same length of time in my life. I have been quite bad with them ever since and am so yet, though I believe I am still improving. It has been very hard for me to ride on horseback.

We have had a succession of heavy rains, the severest I have ever seen, and it has made camp life in these woods very uncomfortable. But I believe the rainy season is now nearly over, and we shall continue the advance movements which we began two days ago. The whole of this great army will move forward, as we now think, to fight another great battle. I do not see how a fight can be avoided except by the flight of the rebels, which we have no right to expect.

I have tonight drawn my pay for the last four months, amounting to a little more than $1,300. I owed some of this, which I have paid, and have sent $1,000 to Dr. Robison and asked him to deposit it in the Bank or some other equally safe place for me. In order that you may fully understand the state of my affairs, I will say that I have saved all I could out of my salary, and, besides what I have sent you, I have deposited $2,000 with Dr. Robison since I came to Kentucky. Colonel Sheldon had $600 belonging to me, which he sent to Dr. Robison about the time I left Louisville to come here. A few days after I came here, I sent the Doctor a check on New York of $400, and now I send him $1,000 making in all $2,000. About one week ago I sent you $50 in a letter which I hoped would do till I could hear from you, and I will then send you whatever amount you need. Please tell me how much you need. I desire as a matter of policy to draw in the small amounts that have been owing me for a long time, and get what we have concentrated into so small a compass that it may be got at when needed. I have put enough in the hands of Dr. Robison to aid Trot considerably by the time she would be able to need it, and I want an eye kept constantly to her future, even if our own is not secure. You do not know how frequently I think of her and of the difficult task she would have to carve out an education of her own. Bless her dear little soul. I still hope we may live to see her the pride and joy of both our hearts in the sweet days of peace.

I have just today got my trunk, and so far[e]well to the flannel shirt that I have worn just 30 days. I am delighted to see the old trunk, soiled and bruised as it is. I have had a long talk with Captain Plumb who can tell you every thing about me here that I could not write in a long time. He will bring my Harry horse down with him, and anything you may send. I want you to send me your picture and Trot's together. Now don't fail to do so. Get one taken while Captain Plumb is there. He was with me in the Sandy Valley and will be with me here. He is a noble man and a good officer. I cannot but believe you have written to me, and that the letters are detained. I was never so anxious to hear from you as now. Give my love to the family all. Kiss the dear little one and remember and love me ever as your own, James.

Headquarters, 20th Brigade
In the field 9 miles from
Pittsburg, Tennessee
May 1, 1862

*My Dear Harry:*

You can't imagine how glad I was to receive last night your letter of April 20th. It was the first word I had heard from you since I left

Cincinnati one month ago. For the last months I have gone on writing to you all with the utmost confidence that you were receiving my letters. Being so entirely alone here, I felt more than usually anxious to hear from you all, and was unusually punctual in writing. I have, since I left Cincinnati, written to Almeda oftener than once a week and have sent several long letters to you. In one or two instances I sent a letter by some person who was going to Ohio, but in all others I committed them to the mail.

Judge then of the mortification and indignation I felt when I learned a few days since that the war authorities here had detained all mails going out from this camp since the battle. There are said to be cords of letters still held at Savannah with the absurd notion that they are thus keeping back any information of the army's strength which might prove injurious. Every scribbler for a newspaper can send by private hand or carry his letters, while letters from soldiers to friends who are agonizing to know of their welfare [are] committed in confidence to the public carriers of the government. As near as I can learn there has been no letter received here in answer to any letters sent by mail from the battlefield. One of my letters to Crete was sent by a private hand, and I only know from your letter that she probably received it. My last letter from her bears date of April 6th. Not long ago I sent her a letter enclosing $50, and of course I am in doubt whether she will receive it.

Now to give you assurance of my faithfulness and constant remembrance of you all, I will say that I have written more than fifty pages of this kind of paper to you and Almeda within the last four weeks and a half. While sitting on my horse at Savannah and seeing my brigade march on board the steamers which were to take us to the battlefield, I wrote a pencilled letter to Almeda, and just as I was going on board I found H. W. Johnson, to whom I gave the letter with a request that he would mail it at once. I have in these letters written fully my impressions about the war and its management, slavery and its relation to the army, *etc., etc.* I have had but one letter from Almeda, and that bore [the] date of April 13th which I immediately answered. Now I want you all to understand that there is no embargo upon mails coming to us. Indeed they come with great regularity and certainty, and you may feel sure that all you write will reach me. This is Virgil's Hades, of which you know he says *"Facilis decensus Averni. Sed rediie gradum,"* etc.[124]

We have lately advanced five miles and are now within cannon shot of the Mississippi and Alabama line. Yesterday I rode "down to Alabam," but still didn't get "out of the wilderness." The old Hyrcanian Forest is not more dense and mysterious than this. Right in the midst of these clustered trees we frequently come upon a deserted cotton-field with its dead stalks and ruins of an old house and its surrounding Negro

[124] See the *Aeneid*, VI: 126-129.

huts. We started for a continuous advance but when we reached the bank of Lick Creek, we found that the enemy had obstructed our advance by felling an immense number of trees, and we are now at work with thousands of men to remove these incumbrances and to build corderoy roads over the swamps. It will be some days before we can move on. The enemy seems to be retiring, but whether he intends to give up the Mississippi River without a fight is not known. Still I believe the decisive battle is yet to be fought, or rather I begin to believe it must be a series of battles rather than any one battle. There is still an immense stretch of country between here and the Gulf which it will take a long time to occupy.

In one thing I fear we have been mistaken. We have believed in a suppressed Union sentiment in the South. It is my opinion, formed against my will, that there is not enough Union (unconditional) feeling south of Kentucky to plant the seeds of public faith in. The fact can no longer be denied that the white slave interest is inveterately hostile to the Union, and I am most thoroughly persuaded that the Union can never live in these states, except upon the "broken body and shed blood" of slavery. My heart and hope have been down into the depths since I came here. I find an attempt so persistent and almost universal that I have come to believe there is something amounting almost to a conspiracy among leading officers, especially those of the regular army, to taboo the whole question of anti-slavery and throw as much discredit on it as upon treason. This purpose is seen clearly both in their words and acts. I have been made deeply indignant at many things which I hope some day to tell you. So far from these things influencing me, I find myself coming nearer and nearer to downright abolitionism. But here I have found consolation and hope. I find the rank and file of the army steadily and surely becoming imbued with sympathy for slaves and hatred for slavery.

A command in the army is a sort of tyranny and in a narrow and ignoble mind engenders a despotic spirit, which makes him [the commander] sympathize with slavery and slaveholders. There is at the same time in the position of a soldier in the ranks that which makes him feel the abridgement of liberty and the power of tyranny. I find my reasoning on this subject vindicated by the fact that there is a growing hatred of slavery among the rank and file of the army. It is an observable fact that soldiers generally hate their enemies much more thoroughly than officers do. It is particularly so in this war, and I observe that they are in their reflections linking slavery and the rebellion together in an indissoluble bond. When as at Nashville our soldiers were obliged to stand ground at the gates of wealthy rebel nabobs and be insulted and abused by the very men and women whose persons and homes they were protecting, they cannot but be taught the lesson that slavery and its military hate the man who walks in any humble path of duty.

Before God I here second my conviction that the spirit of slavery is the soul of this rebellion, and the incarnate devil which must be cast out before we can trust in any peace as lasting and secure. It may be a part of God's plan to lengthen out this war till our whole army has been sufficiently outraged by the haughty tyranny of proslavery officers and the spirit of slavery and slaveholders with whom they came in contact, that they can bring back into civil life a healthy and vigorous sentiment that shall make itself felt at the ballot-box and in social life for the glory of humanity and the honor of the country.

This is then my hope, that when we shall return to civil life—alas, how few—when the temporary distinctions between officers and men are broken down, when generals and privates stand on the grand and beautiful equality of American citizens, there shall go up a voice of power and might that shall [be] resistless for freedom. I live in that hope, and if this shall ever be realized, the thousands who have fallen on the bloody field, or gone down to the silence of death in the terrible fever wards of the hospitals, will not have died in vain. I may not review this subject again soon, for the time is full [of] duty and stir[r]ing events. But I have taken the time to say this much now, as I have an opportunity of sending this letter to you by a private hand which will not be held back by the military embargo on the mails.

Ten minutes ago my trunk arrived, but in consequence of this same embargo on the mails I have not heard from my horse, servant and baggage at Louisville. I welcome the arrival of clean shirts, for the woolen one which now graces my form has been there just 30 days.

In reference to the matter of using my name on the Eclectic Catalogue, I have no objection as relates to myself; still, I should want to know that it would be entirely agreeable to all concerned. You know I would love to have my name still associated with you, where it has so happily and pleasantly been so long. I have been thinking I would try to write something for the students on that occasion, but I presume I can't. I hope you will try to come here, on to me, in vacation. I will secure a pass for you and, so far as I can, a fare ticket.

My position here is in some respects very unpleasant, though General Buell designed to compliment me by calling me here. I am unfortunately under the immediate command of General Wood, a very narrow, impetuous, proslavery man in whose prudence and patriotism and brains I have but very little confidence, and a shamefully rough, blasphemous man, quite destitute of fine or manly feelings. It is rumored that I am to be placed in command of a division, though from the peculiar condition of things here at this time I don't think it can be done at present. There is so much red tape here, every thing going through so many hands, I don't feel as though I can personally accomplish much where I am, but yet I will try.

Since I began this letter we have had orders to prepare for a rapid march. I must get ready. I presume you will get my letters by and by all in a pile. But now I beg of you not to stop writing to me, even if I am not able to get my letters sent through to you. . . . I am nearly well, but have been greatly afflicted with the piles. Love to all.

*Ever yours,*
James

Headquarters, 20th Brigade
In Camp, 9 miles from Corinth
May 4, 1862

*My Dear Crete:*

Immediately after leaving Captain Plumb on the boat at Pittsburgh Landing, I returned to camp and at 5 o'clock yesterday morning we broke up our encampment and moved forward to this place, or rather this deserted field. I pitched my tent in a little sassafras grove, and here we received orders to prepare for battle early next day (that is today). About 4½ o'clock in the afternoon a fierce cannonading [commenced] a few miles to the left. We turned out and stood under arms, but in about an hour the cannonading ceased. We passed the night very pleasantly, drank sassafras tea for breakfast, and are now waiting orders to move forward. The fight last evening may have changed the aspect of affairs to such an extent that we may not move forward today. I hope not, for there is a sentiment, wide spread in the army, even among those who are hard men and blasfemers, that battles begun of the Lord's Day are not a blessing to the attacking party. I presume, however, there will not be more than a reconnois[s]ance and mutual maneuvering to feel of the enemy and learn where he is located. In this calm Sunday morning of anxious waiting I sit by the rough desk in my tent to write again in the hope that this will reach you before May is gone.

The past night and the morning thus far have been strangely quiet for the camp of a great army. There is the peculiar quiet and subdued manner which characterizes men who are on the eve of great events in which their own lives are at stake. I rode along in the woods this morning and saw little groups here and there seated on the leaves in low, earnest conversation, sometimes a little group with a Bible in their midst, sometimes a man by himself reading a pocket-worn letter. Men who are usually rough, address each other with more than usual gentleness of manner. All this tells me that these men will fight with great desperation.

It is understood that General Mitchel[125] is moving up to form a

[125] Brigadier General Ormsby M. Mitchel, commander of the Third Division, Army of the Ohio, did not participate in the Corinth campaign. In April he left Murfreesboro, Tennessee, descended upon Northern Alabama, and secured control of about one hundred miles of the Memphis & Charleston Railroad, along which Buell's army was to advance toward Chattanooga after the fall of Corinth.

junction with us and every thing indicates a very great battle. There has been no battle where the preparations were on so gigantic a scale as this. Since the battle of Shiloh we have been reinforced by Pope's Command, 20,000 strong,[126] and the remaining brigades of Grant and Buell, and all our arrangements of forage and provisions betoken vast operations.[127] God grant that this may be the last great bloody sacrifice of the war in the Mississippi Valley. I would not write you on the eve of battle if my letter would reach you before you could hear from me in any other way, for I would not give you the anxiety consequent upon such a letter. But I know that long before this letter reaches you, you will have heard the results of matters here. I have written you so frequently and so fully of late that you will have a full knowledge of all my doings hitherto.

I am still in great anxiety to hear from you, not having had a word since April 6th. Yesterday I received a letter from Dr. Robison, dated April 23rd, so you see there is no obstacle in the way of letters reaching me. I trust you will not fail to write to me very frequently, so that letters may keep reaching [me] by and by, even though they should be of old dates when they come. I am very glad to know that Captain Plumb will visit you soon and carry the hand grasp I gave him directly to you. You will not forget, I hope, to send me your picture and Trot's. Is she growing in size and beauty? Does she learn to talk rapidly? Tell me about her.

Harry wrote to me asking me to allow my name to go down on the catalogue as President of the Eclectic. Do you know anything about it, why he wants it? Tell me about it. Why don't Nellie write to me? I wrote last. I think I have answered father's letter, though I may be mistaken. I know I intended to do so. My trunk has come, but not Green nor my horse. I am riding a little yellow Texan horse which we captured from the Texan Rangers in our reconnois[s]ance the day after the Battle of Shiloh.

Give my love to all our dear friends and brethren. I hope you and they are enjoying a sweet and peaceful Lord's day in the church. I have never longed so much as now for a quiet day in church and a good religious sermon from some good man.

Ever and forever I am yours and Trot's,

James

[126] On April 21, Major General John Pope, fresh from successes at New Madrid and Island No. 10, joined Halleck and commanded the left wing in the Corinth campaign. In June, Pope was called east and given command of the Army of Virginia. After his defeat in the Second Battle of Bull Run he was relieved of his command and sent to the Department of the Northwest to handle Indian problems.

[127] Major General Henry W. Halleck, commander of Federal forces in the West, took personal charge of the Corinth campaign and on April 30, he reorganized his command into three wings: the right under Thomas, the center under Buell, and the left under Pope. The reserve was placed under Major General John A. McClernand. Halleck's command now included new brigades, as well as old ones, which arrived after Shiloh. In July, 1862, Halleck was called to Washington as military advisor to Lincoln and given the title General in Chief of the Union Armies.

Headquarters, 20th Brigade
In the field 6 miles from
Corinth, Mississippi
May 8, 1862

*My Dear Mother:*

Your welcome letter of April 25th was received half an hour ago. I can assure you I was very glad to hear from you and our folks in Solon and Orange. It has been a very long time since I have heard from home. If you have had reason to complain of my not writing to you, you may know how I feel to pass more than two months without hearing from any of you either by letter or paper. I very seldom get any paper from home, and the last letter I got from Crete was dated the 6th of April. I don't understand how it is possible for her letters to be delayed so long if she has written at all. Since I wrote you last I have been quite sick with bloody dysentery and piles, but I am now quite well.

The great army here has been slowly advancing toward Corinth; but the weather has been so very bad, such a great amount of rain, that our advance has necessarily been slow. Our advance guard is across the Mississippi line. The lines of the enemy have gradually fallen back as we approached. We have been expecting a battle every day for a long time, but it may be a week or ten days yet before we meet the rebels in full force. I was out with my brigade a few days ago beyond the Mississippi line and met a considerable force of the rebels. They fired three cannon shot (shell) at us but didn't do any harm. I captured two of them and drove the rest back. One rebel fired at me when I was not more than 20 rods from him, but he did not take good aim and so I am still spared to try them again.

I don't want you to feel uneasy about me. You want me to do my duty as much as I want to do it, and if I do it well and come through safe we will all be glad. If I should not be permitted to survive the war, you will, I hope, still have the satisfaction of knowing that I did not flinch in the hour of danger. Ellis[128] is in my brigade and is well. George Garfield is in the same division, and I see him almost every day. He is a good soldier, is a sergeant, and is well liked by his officers.

A few days after the great battle I met Marcus and William Morton. They and Noah are all in the 25th Missouri Regiment and were in the fight.[129] I hadn't met Marcus before since the time when I made him a cap of Burdock burrs. His voice is as grim and heavy as it used to be.

The weather is now warm and pleasant and the Southern summer will soon be here in all its glory. I have become so accustomed to living

---

[128] Garfield's cousin Ellis Ballou, of Muskingum County, was a sergeant in the Sixty-fifth Ohio.

[129] Marcus enlisted at Gallatin, Missouri and served from 1861-1864, and William A enlisted at Cameron and served from 1861-1865. Both were lieutenants in the Twenty-fifth Missouri. Noah Rhodes, who enlisted at Flora, Illinois in 1861, was a private in that regiment.

in a tent that I would hardly know how to get along in a fine house. You would be amused to see my furniture. My bed consists of crotches driven down into the ground, and small poles laid across. A few leaves spread over them, and one blanket under and another over me make me very comfortable. Our food is substantial if not luxurious, though I will not deny that I should be exceedingly glad to sit down to one of Mary's good dinners. You know, I think that you and she can get up about the best dishes to suit my taste.

By the way, why don't she write to me? I wrote to her a long time ago, but have not heard. You have no idea how much I love to receive letters away here out of the world.

Do you know I am further away from you than I ever was before? I am nearly 1,200 miles from you. By looking on the map you will see that Corinth is just across the Mississippi line.

I wrote a long letter to Thomas just before I left the Sandy Valley. Did he get it? I want him to write to me. You will, I hope, write to me again as soon as you receive this. I am glad to hear from Uncle Amos' folks.[130] I think of them very often. Give them my love.

I am sorry to hear that you have been unwell. You must not worry about the war or me. I hope we shall both come out all right. I know the war will. Give my love to Thomas, Marenus and the girls and all the family.

*Ever and always your affectionate son,*
James

Headquarters, 20th Brigade
In the field 6 miles from Corinth
May 9, 1862

*My Dear Crete:*

I have written you so frequently and sent in so many different ways that I cannot doubt that you have received some of them at least. Why

---

[130] Amos Boynton of Orange, a half brother of Garfield's father, married Alpha Ballou, a sister of Garfield's mother. He raised his family on the farm next to Garfield's birthplace. A stern, hard-working farmer, Boynton was known by neighbors as a kind, considerate man with remarkable common sense and impeccable integrity. By stepping into the void created by the death of Garfield's father, Uncle Amos exerted a strong paternal influence over the fatherless boy. Boynton was the father of seven children: William A., Henry B., Harriet A., Phebe M., Silas A., Mary C., and Bentley who died in infancy. William, who was about three years older than Garfield, died at the age of twenty-nine; Henry, a year younger than William, attended the Eclectic and returned to farming the family homestead in Orange; Silas became a prominent physician and in 1881 attended Garfield after he was shot; Harriet married Daniel Clark and made her home in Bedford; Phebe, as already noted, married John Clapp and lived for many years in Hiram; and Mary, who went by her middle name, Cordelia, married Alonzo Arnold and became a resident of Grand Rapids, Michigan.

I have not had anything from you since the 6th *ult.* I am wholly unable to understand. I have just received a letter from mother dated April 25th, also one from Circleville, Ohio, date[d] April 30th. I really have no heart to write any more and get no acknowledgement of their receipt. I write this to say that our expected attack has been delayed, and though we may move further any day, I don't think a general attack will be made under a week or ten days. I made a reconnois[s]ance a few days ago across the Mississippi line to within 4½ miles of Corinth and took two prisoners. The enemy fired three shells at us, and one rebel fired at me from a house 100 yards ahead but missed his aim. I am now quite well.

Anxious to know if you are still alive, I am as ever,

James

Headquarters, 20th Brigade
2 miles from Farmington
6 from Corinth
May 12, 1862

*My Dear Crete:*

The dead silence is at last broken. Last evening's mail brought me letters, one from you dated April 26th (postmarked 30th), and one from Harry, dated March 31st, remailed from Bardstown; none from Almeda. In my last (a short, short note) to you May 9th, I felt as though I could not write again until I heard whether my letters were received or not.

Since then we have moved from the Hamburg and Corinth road around to the Hamburg and Farmington road. We are now three miles farther to the left wing of the army and about the same distance from Corinth. The enemy made a fierce attack on General Pope near here last Friday,[131] and we were sent here for the double purpose of supporting him and to extend the left of our army around so as to possess the Florence [&] Memphis Railroad and put ourselves between General Mitchel and the enemy, so that he can come up as a reserve if necessary.

There has been but little fighting for the last two days. General Curtis[132] came in last night with the advance of his army to reinforce

[131] Pope had advanced to a point about a mile and a half from Farmington, Mississippi, where his right flank was exposed because of Buell's failure to keep up. On May 9 the Confederates drove in Pope's pickets and attacked his main line. It held, but the Federal loss was nearly 180 killed, wounded, or missing.

[132] Major General Samuel R. Curtis commanded the Union Army of Southwest Missouri which had won a significant victory two months earlier at Pea Ridge, Arkansas. Curtis did not join Halleck, as Garfield reported; he remained in the trans-Mississippi West and in September became commander of the Department of the Missouri with headquarters in St. Louis. He did, however, send infantry reinforcements to Halleck.

us, and though the enemy still greatly outnumbers us, we have confidence in our superior discipline. I think it is the policy to cut off the enemy's retreat by river and rail, and force him to a general battle or a surrender. His river egress is nearly shut up and all his railroad avenues of retreat, except the direct southern one, are in our grasp. It would be wiser for us to consume a month in hemming him in than it would be to dash upon him and beat him in battle, only to allow him to slip out at the back door and make another stand farther back. His army cannot number less than 150,000 men,[133] but a large part of that force is made up [of] conscripts who neither serve willingly nor intelligently. It is rumored but not confirmed that General Sigel[134] has arrived with General Curtis. I hope this is so. I have great faith in that General and his fighting.

My health is now quite restored. You would hardly know my sunburnt face which is fast acquiring a saleable color. Before this I presume Captain Plumb has seen you, and I hope he will soon return with messages from you. It will be a great joy to see one who has lately seen you. I saw Wall[ace] Ford a few days ago. He will be in Hiram soon. I should have [been], how glad, to have been with you at Newton Falls.

Your reflection in reference to the effects of the war upon my tastes and feeling coincide precisely with my own.[135] But I have not much fear that this wild life will unfit me for the joys of peace which I so much long for. I greatly desire to see the end of it and lay aside the terrible work. Still it would be just like my perverse nature, if I should ever see quiet life again, to be restless and long for turbulence. There will probably be turbulence enough to satisfy the most storm-loving disposition for [the] next few years.

I am still grieved at not hearing from the 42nd. When you write, tell me what you hear from them. My last intelligence bore [the] date April 12th. They were then just leaving Louisville. I have heard from Major Williams a little later than your letter and he was then better. I have suffered greatly in reference to him. I know of no man in the army whose death would crush me so terribly as his. He is a true man and one of my dearest friends.

I hope you will receive sometime the volume of letters I have written

---

[133] The Confederate army had about 75,000 men; the Union about 100,000.

[134] Franz Sigel fought with Curtis at Pea Ridge and had just been promoted to the rank of major general for distinguishing himself in that battle. Sigel remained with Curtis until later in the month, when he was called East. In June he was assigned to Pope's Army of Virginia, in which he led a corps in the Second Battle of Bull Run. Shortly thereafter Garfield met Sigel and continued to admire him. But in October, 1862, his faith in the German officer was shaken considerably by Major General Irvin McDowell, who disliked Sigel as much as Sigel disliked him.

[135] "I hope," Garfield's wife had written on April 26, "the honors you may win . . . [in the field] may not unfit you for a return to a life of peace and quiet, and a love for all those pursuits which have been so much your delight."

you within the last six weeks. I will try to get time to write to Dr. Briscoe if possible.

I cannot finish this page now, for I must go out on duty for a few hours. Kiss the little one and tell her if you can that I love her, and you.

Love to the family.

*Ever your*
James

Headquarters, 20th Brigade
In the field 3 miles from Corinth
May 19, 1862

*My Dear Harry:*

Your very welcome letter of the 9th was received last evening, which made me very happy. Your expressions of confidence and affection make me feel the joy and pride of a lover. I assure you everything you say to me is most fully appreciated and reciprocated.

Since I wrote to Almeda two days ago we have advanced about three miles. We have been constantly skirmishing with the enemy's outposts for three days, forcing him gradually back toward his entrenchments. We are now locating our permanent camp and erecting defensive works from which we shall go out light-armed and without baggage. We are now in plain hearing of the cars at Corinth. Hitherto, the whistle of the locomotive has been to me a symbol of peace and enterprise, and now when we have been so long in the wilderness the sound of the whistle, which should welcome us to civilization, is the harbinger of most terrible barbarism and strife.

It is wonderful with what a spirit our soldiers carry on this war of outposts. For two days the pickets of the two armies have been watching each other across large wheat fields and sharpshooters on both sides have been hunting each other with the eagerness and nonchalance that we would hunt squirrels. They creep out behind stumps and trees and fire away at each other, laughing as merrily as though it were a holiday sport. One of my men was very severely wounded yesterday. There were nearly a dozen in all killed and wounded, and yet the boys kep[t] on as if nothing had occurred or could occur that was in the l[e]ast unpleasant. Now, while I write, there is a constant cracking of Springfield rifles out on the picket lines, a little more than half a mile distant.

Our operations are assuming the character of a regular siege. The exciting nature of our work keeps almost every one from reflection on the terrible phases of our work. I cannot help feeling a strange fascination fro[m] witnessing the operations of our pickets. I was out nearly all day yesterday watching the effects of our shots and watching the operations of the enemy through my field glass. While watching them, they brought up a field howitzer within ¾ mile and fired a dozen shells at our boys, who kept firing away at long range. The distant puff of smoke, the report of the howitzer, followed by the smoke of the bursting shell and the dull *thud* of its explosion, concluding with the cloud of dust rising from the field where it struck, formed a series of exciting and even fascinating phenomena. I suppose I have heard 200 rifle shots since I began this letter. The left wing of our army (Pope's) now lies east of Corinth and faces toward the west. Buell's army occupies the angle between the east and north lines.

I am growing exceedingly anxious to see the end of this war. I begin to feel that I am losing great opp[ort]unities for growth. When I do get time for thought, I find myself looking back to what I have acquired as food for reflection rather than looking around me at what I am now grasping. This, I believe, is the truest indication that growth has measurably stopped. The old man looks back upon his past for comfort because his present growth is insufficient to afford him any food. It is somewhat so with me in matters of purely intellectual growth. Still, if I live through this war, it will have been of very great service to my mind to have been plunged into the midst of this peculiar kind of activity, and I shall return to intellectual life with much greater zest.

If the battle comes off soon, I hope you will visit me. Come to Pittsburg Landing and if you have any difficulty in reaching me, write from there and you will soon hear from [me]. I will be able to make it very pleasant for you. Don't fail to come. You can find a boat at Cincinnati directly for this place.

I dare not think of Congress now, though I should be pleased to take part in the legislation of the next few years.[136] If the people should of their own motion see fit to call me to that place, of course I should be greatly pleased; but it seems to me now it would be almost a mockery for me to lay any plans for a life over which I have so little control, and on the continuance of which I have no pledges.

Why don't Almeda write to me? April 12th was her last. I have

[136] On May 9 Rhodes had written Garfield that if he would agree to run, the Republicans of the Nineteenth Congressional District (newly created and made up of Ashtabula, Geauga, Mahoning, Portage, and Trumbull counties) would nominate him as candidate for the U.S. House of Representatives. A little later Garfield received more letters from friends who were actively supporting his candidacy. In his replies, Garfield tried not to appear as a man seeking office. He indicated he would submit to the will of the people, and left the impression that he had not expected to be a candidate. In fact, however, he and his wife had discussed the subject over a year earlier and he had agreed, if elected, to take her with him to Washington. Nor were his ambitions a household secret. They were long known to O.P. Brown, who became one of Garfield's rivals for the nomination. On April 17, 1861, Garfield learned from his wife that "O.P. says that you will be a terribly defeated man if you attempt to oppose him! ! He bestows upon you the following encomium: 'Garfield has an interest everywhere . . . but in the Kingdom of Heaven.' You may go to Washington though, notwithstanding his opinion. . . ."

written you both several times since Plumb left. He has not yet arrived.

My horse "Billy" is sick at Louisville.

Give my love to all our circle, to Burke when you write. I hope he will finish his course after he is married.

*Ever and forever yours,*
James

Headquarters, 20th Brigade
3 miles from Corinth
May 20, 1862

*My Dear Almeda:*

Our life here is so active and eventful of late that I must write a few words frequently. I wrote Harry yesterday morning, and just as I was closing up that letter, an order came from General Halleck for us to entrench our position. I threw 3½ regiments forward, ran a line of half a mile through a point of woods and along a crest in a field, and before sunset we had completed the rifle trench, which, in connection with the work of other divisions, makes a line of four or five miles. My advanced regiment was thrown forward a quarter of a mile beyond our work and a constant skirmishing was kept up, which toward evening grew quite warm. A part of my line was at one time driven back but was immediately reinforced. There is a house in an open field six or seven hundred yards beyond our lines, which the rebels filled with sharp-shooters, and from which they kept up a constant fire. One of my men was killed and three wounded. Toward sunset the enemy open on us with shells. Major [Seymour] Race (of the Cleveland *Herald*), in command of our division batteries, replied grandly with fourteen shells which burst far back in the enemy's lines. We trained a battery on the house and threw a few shells into it which despersed the rebels very soon.

The night was comparatively quiet, but I was awakened by the sound of distant cannon and rode out three miles along the lines. I could plainly hear the drums of the enemy. Three deserters came in to me last night while I was out with the advance. They were all Northerns and were greatly rejoiced to get away. One was an Ohio boy from San dusky who had been forced into the rebel service at New Orleans. He found a brother in the 3rd Ohio Cavalry here whom he had not met for nine years. The other two were Germans, noble fellows, one from St. Louis and one from Detroit. I love the Germans more and more every month. The[y] report the rebe[l]s on short rations, and say we shall be attacked by them soon.

I cannot describe to you the constant occur[r]ence of events which would be of the most exciting character. I have heard a number of cannon and hundred[s] of small arms since I began this letter. It is really wonderful how men can become accustomed to danger and alarm. I have just ordered a regiment forward to the trenches, and shall go out myself in a few minutes.

I will leave this sheet unfinished, and add more this afternoon. It is now 8 o'clock A.M. It has been very hot weather for ten days. Last night we had a glorious shower. No letter from you since April 12th, Almeda dearest, why is this? I have had two from Crete, one from Harry, and several from central and southern Ohio. Why not from you? Do write to me. Did you know how greatly I desire to hear from you, I am sure you would write. Your letters will be quite sure to reach me. The last from Harry came through in eight days. Good bye till evening.

9 o'clock P.M.

Another busy day. We have finished the intrenchments, cut away the underbrush and made roads leading from our camps to the trenches. It rained last night and gave us water. We are very thankful for the muddy gift. It made our coffee look as though there was milk in it. Brisk firing has been kept up nearly all day between the pickets. My men took the log house and burned it. One of our men was wounded, but my 64th boys placed four rebels hors du combat. It is still raining and my poor 64th are away in the storm. Now and then a gun booms through the darkness. We stand under arms from 4 o'clock in the morning till broad daylight. This we have done for nearly a month. I am very tired tonight but otherwise I am quite well. This afternoon I saw a paper of the 16th *inst.*

I am rejoiced to see an increasing number of signs of national awakening on the subject of emancipation. There are a few quiet indexes of healthy growth which I have noticed with surprise. The most remarkable is that the American Tract Society[137] is talking a little about the sin of slavery. Edward Everett[138] in an oration at Chicago incidentally gives the history of British emancipation (see also

---

[137] The American Tract Society was organized in New York City in 1825. Its purpose was "to diffuse a knowledge of our Lord Jesus Christ as the Redeemer of sinners, and to promote the interests of vital godliness and sound morality, by the circulation of Religious Tracts, calculated to receive the approbation of all Evangelical Christians." By mid-century the society had issued hundreds of books and leaflets and was a powerful voice speaking out against such things as lying, profane swearing, drinking, levity, novel reading, breaking the Sabbath, and sleeping in church. But in the 1850's it came under sharp attack for failing to take a stand against slavery. In fact, its policy was to publish proslavery but not antislavery literature. Relentless opposition from Northern abolitionists and antislavery people brought results. By 1860 the society was issuing some antislavery literature. The increased hostility to slavery generated by the Civil War was responsible for the more pronounced change of policy of which Garfield spoke.

[138] The famous Massachusetts clergyman, educator, orator, and statesman. An eloquent speaker and tireless champion of the Union cause, Everett lectured

"Clotilde and the Contraband" in *Harper's Monthly* for May).[139] The old pro-slavery Democratic party is trying to rise from the dead to keep down the tendencies toward growth. I hope we may "hasten slowly" but surely in the right direction.

It were useless to wish what wants so fill my hungry heart tonight, the sight of you all once again and now. Events are every hour thickening here, and the great contest must be come [coming] very soon, if it comes at all. I believe the enemy will fight, and with great fierceness. We expect a mail tomorrow and I hope it will bring me a letter from you. You are "the half of my surviving soul," and this great silence grieves me more than I can tell you.

*Ever and forever your own,*
James

In Camp near Corinth
May 27, 1862

*My Dear Crete:*

I have just learned that Colonel Hazen[140] is to leave for home today noon, and I will take a moment to write a word by him before he goes. I have been greatly rejoice[d] by the late gifts of the mail which has now become quite regular. I have received four letters from you since May 9th, besides one by the hand of Captain Plumb. Your last of May 18th, post marked the 20th, reached me yesterday evening. It was a joy I assure you to converse with one who had seen you all, and it was a peculiar delight to see the semblance of your face and Trot's. They are very good pictures. Trot is growing finely I am sure.

---

throughout the war to large audiences in towns and cities across the North. One of his noblest efforts was his excellent address delivered just before Lincoln's immortal one at Gettysburg.

[139] A short story about Clotilde, a twenty-year old French orphan whose father had exiled himself for freedom by leaving France for America. Although she lived in the South, Clotilde refused to hide her Union sympathies during the Civil War. More than that, she helped a slave escape! Discovered and threatened with imprisonment, Clotilde was rescued by wealthy Archibald Ralston, a handsome young Southerner of similar sympathy. They fell in love, married, and fled the South, becoming exiles for freedom.

[140] Colonel William B. Hazen, a graduate of West Point, entered the war as commander of the Forty-first Ohio. At Shiloh he led the 19th Brigade in Nelson's Fourth Division, Army of the Ohio. Hazen, whose behavior at Shiloh Garfield casts under a cloud of suspicion in his next letter, was not among the dozen officers singled out by Buell for special commendation. But Buell reported that others who had won honorable distinction had been commended in the reports of his subordinate commanders. Buell endorsed those commendations, among which was Nelson's tribute to Hazen for carrying his brigade into action and maintaining it there most gallantly; and for capturing "the battery which so distressed us," before being forced to fall back on his reserves. Nelson's division of 4,500 men suffered 710 casualties, 400 of them in Hazen's brigade. Hazen was promoted to brigadier general in November, 1862.

For three days picket firing has nearly ceased by common consent. Indeed the pickets are becoming so friendly that they frequently go out into an open field in fron[t] and sit down and chat together between the lines.

We have been building heavy intrenchments, and it looks now as though we were to make the regular approaches of a siege. It seems to me to be of the last importance that Memphis and Mobile should be taken. If that be done, we cut off the rebels' supplies and compel them to come out and fight us on our own ground or to surrender where they are. I would be very glad if this cup might be permitted to pass, and we not drink it. But all speculations as [to] the time, place, mode and result of so great a battle are vain.

My health is now exceedingly good. Captain Plumb brought Green and my two horse[s], and also a good cook. For the first time since I left Camp Chase I am living well in the eating line. We have a French cook who gets up soups, *etc.*, and you know, when I have good soup, my wants are nearly all supplied. I was delighted to see my horses again and I really fancied they knew me and I am sure they will soon, for they each get hugged a half dozen times a day. Green is a good servant and knows more about horses than any one else I am acquainted with.

I promised to tell you about my Jim. Just as the last guns were being fired at Middle Creek, a Negro, fully armed and equipped and dressed in rebel uniform, braving the fire of both parties, clim[b]ed down the hill side and came to our men and said he wanted to see the commander. The boys brought him to me and he gave himself up, saying [that] he was the servant of Colonel [Robert C.] Trigg of the 54th Virginia, [that] he was in the battle of Bull Run and tried to get away there, but could not, and that on the opportunity being offered he came away. I kept him in camp a few weeks and found him to be very intelligent and thoroughly honest and faithful. I took him with me and told him he should go with me to Ohio when the war is over. He is greatly attached to me and I believe he would die for me cheerfully if it were necessary. The unsettled state of the country made me hesitate to bring him so far away as this from a free state, and so I let him go with the 42nd to serve Brother Jones and William Clapp. I have lately written to him that he must remember my promise to stand by him, and [that] if anything should happen to me, he is to make his way to Ohio and find you, and that you will see that he has a home. I intend to keep him with us if I return. He is learning to read and has much more than ordinary Negro talent.

I must close. Love to all, especially Trot and yourself.

*Ever your*
James

P.S. I would send money by Colonel Hazen but I haven't it to spare.

J.

Headquarters, 20th Brigade
2½ miles from Corinth
May 28, 1862

*My Dear Harry:*

Yours by the hand of Captain Plumb was received on the 24th. I had received one by mail a short time before. I am glad that the mails are becoming somewhat regular again. I should have written you yesterday by Colonel Hazen but we were ordered to the front to support Mc-Cook's division,[141] which went out on a reconnois[s]ance to discover the position of the enemy and take possesssion of a high ridge.

I am exceedingly mortified that Hazen should go home now. I am sorry to tell you that he has fallen in the estimation of many of his best friends here. (Of course, what I now write will never be mentioned outside of our circle.) When I reached Pittsburg Landing it was one o'clock P.M. of Monday. The battle was at it[s] height of fury and the heaviest firing was five miles away from the Landing. As I passed up the bank at the head of my brigade, I met Hazen coming down to the river! ! ! I shook his hand and asked him how the battle was going. He replied, "It is a terrible fight, and the issue is still doubtful. My brigade is terribly cut up." I hurried on, thinking no more about it, presuming that his command had been relieved by fresh arrivals. He afterward told me that in the fight he got separated from his brigade and could not find them for some time and in his search came out at the Landing where he met me. Very soon I began to hear talk among the officers of Nelson's division reflecting on his conduct and saying that he left his brigade fighting and went to the Landing and got dinner on board a steamboat. One of his own regiment (a field officer) told me he did not see Hazen after 10 o'clock A.M. It has become a general impression that his conduct in that matter cannot be explained consistently with the highest sense of duty and honor. Nelson has his pets, and he mentions Hazen favorably in his official report, but you will observe that General Buell omits his name in the list of specially approved officers.

But what pains me chiefly is this, that I know by Hazen's own remark to me that he goes home for the purpose of going or sending to Washington to secure his confirmation as brigadier, and that too under the plea of sickness. There is hardly a more perfect picture of health in the army than he was yesterday when he started. He left at three o'clock when his own brigade had been ordered to the front and when the roar of cannon and musketry for more than a mile along the line were in his ears. I have been and still am a friend of his and would have made al-

[141] Brigadier General Alexander McDowell McCook of Ohio commanded the Second Division, Army of the Ohio, in the Corinth campaign. Later, as a major general, he commanded the XX Corps, Army of the Cumberland, in the Tullahoma and Chickamauga campaigns. He was blamed for the Union defeat at Chickamauga and relieved of his command, but a court of inquiry cleared him of responsibility. McCook, a graduate of West Point, remained in active service until 1895. He died in 1903.

most any sacrifice to have prevented his taking so suicidal a step. He may come back with stars on his shoulders, but I fear that many will have fallen from his reputation. Let it be remembered that he went on *sick leave*. For myself, I would much rather die here away from all my friends than to go home on the eve of a battle.

Hazen's leave expires in 20 days. Now I think you had better come with him if he returns by the way of Hiram. I send you a pass, and in order to make it sure to be respected, I call you a member of my staff, which will be literally true if you will consent to be a volunteer aid-de-camp while you are here. You must not fail to come. I see no hope of my going home till the war closes, though I may apply for a furlough after the battle. I could get one, I presume, but I shall leave no room for indinnations [indignations].

My relations are more pleasant than heretofore. General Buell frequently calls on me for special service, and General Wood seems to feel as though he needed my aid in managing the division. He has always treated me with respect. He is only a tyrant where he dares to be. He could not live and treat me as he has treated some officers.

I cannot but feel an interest in what you say in reference to Congress, and I am free to confess that I would like to be a member of the next one. Please write to me more about it. If the people of the district should see fit to elect me of their own choice, I shall be gratified. I remember to have promised Almeda not to use the military as a stepping stone to political preferment, and I shall make no effort. But if the people want me, they can say so even if I should not be out of the army till December.

Write me fully about Commencement. I have not seen a *Portage Democrat* for more than a month. Tell Almeda I thank her for the seven commercial note pages she has written me since the 20th of March.

My love to Burke when you write him.

*Ever yours,*
James


Near Corinth, Mississippi
May 28, 1862

*My Dear Brother Austin:*

A fight has been raging all day along a front of more than five miles. It has been mainly skirmishing and artillery work, and I have held my brigade in the trenches as a part of the reserve. The fight closed with the going down of the sun; nearly a hundred wounded were brought in, and some prisoners, and I have returned to camp to rest my men and be ready to go out with them tomorrow to the front. I have set down in my tent weary and in the hushed stillness of the camp. I have a little space for memory and reflection.

Of the places in Ohio where my mind rests with most pleasure, your own home is next after Hiram, and I will not tie up my tent for the night till I have written a word to you and yours. I have not heard from you for a long time, only as I read an occasional line in Brother Rhodes, boasting of his pleasant visits at your home, which always makes me wish the thousand miles of space were dropped out between us and I could be seated by your grate enjoying your society and the family's, and at the same time paying my respects to the Sunday evening bowl of bread and milk. I assure you, the blessings of peace, home, friends, Christianity and Christian worship never seemed so dear and inestimable to me as they do now in the moments of calm between the events of this terrible war.

Of course, my heart is fixed upon prosecuting the work to its bloody end, and I am hopeful and cheerful in the performance of the duties which fall to my lot; yet I feel more keenly than ever before the worth of a calm civil and peaceful life. Indeed, it is the glory of the volunteer service as compared with the regular that the volunteer turns aside from his plans of life to perform a terrible and disagreeable duty, hoping to live through it and return as soon as possible to his old life. An officer in the regular army adopts war as a profession and makes fighting his trade. War is his harvest, peace is his famine.

The fate of Corinth must soon be decided. If the enemy still determines to maintain himself at Corinth, there must be one of the bloodiest battles of the war. If he retreats, his forces will be greatly disheartened and demoralized and our army will feel chagrined at losing the game we have been trying to bag for more than 50 days since the Battle of Shiloh.

My health is very good though I have been quite sick several times since I have been in the service. I want to hear from you to know how the movements of the day seem to you. I have been so long accustomed to compare views with you that I need to hear your thoughts again. . . .

But I must close. It is our hour to go to the picket front.

Give my love to all your dear family. Won't Minerva and Lottie write to me? With much love, I am as ever,

*Your brother,*
J. A. Garfield


Headquarters, 20th Brigade
Iuka, Mississippi
June 7, 1862

*My Dear Crete:*

About the time of the fall of Corinth, after an uninterrupted month of good health, I was revisited by my old complaint which I should have been able to check in a few days had we not been ordered away on a heavy march in the extremely hot weather. Three days' hard marching aggravated my disease and gave me something of a fever. I have not been out of my camp now for six days and most of the time have been confined to my bed. I weigh lighter than I have before for twelve years. But I presume it will be better for me not to be so fleshy. I am much better now, and though weak, have regained my appetite and shall soon be well. We are now in a high healthy region where for the first time since we reached the Tennessee we have found good water.

Do not feel alarmed for my health; we have more to hope for when I am getting better than when I am entirely untouched by disease. This attack has cleansed my system of its bile and has done me good.

One of my staff officers, Captain Farrar,[142] is going home to Ohio and will take this letter along, where he can change the money I shall give him into a draft or check, and so it will be save [safe]. I enclose you fifty dollars.

It will be six weeks to my next payday, when I can send you more. We are repairing railroad and thus establishing a new base of military operations.

Yours of the 26th was received last night. Give my love to Burke and Mary. I hope you will pardon this brief note. I will write you again when I have more strength and less dizziness of head.

Love to Trot and all,

*Ever yours,*
J. A. Garfield

To Mrs. J. A. Garfield
  Hiram, Portage County,
  Enclosed $50.00
P.S. Pardon this signature and address, written to forefend the loss of the enclosure by mail.

*Your* James

Headquarters, 20th Brigade
Iuka, Mississippi
June 7, 1862

*My Dear Mary:*

For the last five days I have been quite sick, and while we have not been marching I have kept [to] my tent. I had a severe attack of the diarrhoea and a slight attack of fever. During that time I have not attempted to write or do any work which was not indispensably necessary. This morning I am feeling better but am quite weak. I have not weighed so little for ten years. But it is better for me not to be fleshy in this hot climate. You can hardly conceive how different everything looks here from what it does in Ohio. The people have finished harvesting their wheat more than a week ago. It is almost time for new potatoes and other garden sauce that we don't see in Ohio till late in July.

---

[142] Captain William M. Farrar of the Sixty-fifth Ohio, brigaded under Garfield.

Well, after nearly two months of expectation and preparation and a good deal of skirmishing, the rebel army ran off from Corinth without risking a general battle. I had been in a number of picket fights and had been several times shot at, and expected there would be another great battle; but they left and the next day we occupied the town. You can form no idea of the desolation which great armies leave in passing through a country, and particularly where they encamp for a considerable time. It will take a great many years for this part of the country to regain its prosperity and happiness. Shortly after Corinth was evacuated we were sent to this place about 30 miles east of Corinth to repair some railroad bridges that were burned.

We have encamped in a woods of mingled pine and oak and where for the first time in two months we find good water. . . . And my staff officers have clubbed together and hired a Frenchman from Cincinnati to cook for us and we have good fare now, good I mean for camp life. I have not seen a cup of milk for nearly three months and it is a long time since we have had any good butter. One gets accustomed to getting along with but very little. My tent is just 8 feet by 10, in outward form something like this:

The front curtains tucked up for summer and daytime. The room inside is furnished with a cot, desk and trunk, and from the side hang my sword and pistols. As the tent is now pitched it faces the East and is arranged thus:

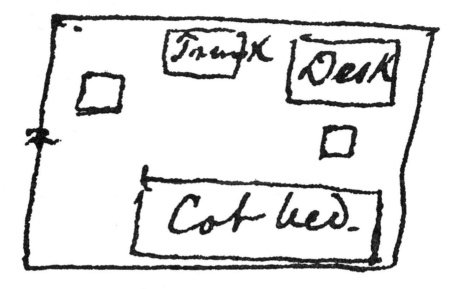

The two small squares in the figure are camp stools. Ten yards from the tent my horses are hitched and every morning since I have been sick, Green brings them up to the tent door to see me. They put their noses down in a very affectionate way and I fancy they know I am not quite well. They are noble horses and I am greatly attached to them. The[y] have never injured me, although "Aunt Eliza" thought I would have to be tied on. One of them (Billy) was with me in the Battle of Middle Creek. The other one (Harry), a stallion, was never in battle but is a brave noble fellow. They both get hugged every night before I sleep, when I am well.

I see George Garfield frequently. He was not in the Battle of Shiloh but he is a brave man and a good soldier. He has been in several skirmishes.

Ben Fisher's oldest boy is in the army here and I saw him a few days ago. I am well acquainted with General Rousseau[143] and as soon as I get a chance I will go and find George Larabee.[144]

[143] Brigadier General Lovell H. Rousseau commanded a brigade in McCook's division and later, as a major general, he led a division in the Tullahoma and Chickamauga campaigns. After serving through the war and one term in Congress, he re-entered the army. He died in 1869.

[144] A brother of Marenus, the husband of Garfield's sister Mary.

I am cheerful and happy as any one can be in such fierce business as killing men; but I hope the war will be over soon, and I very much desire to see you all again. I think we shall refit the Memphis & Charleston Railroad and go over and liberate East Tennessee. That is now our intention.

Give my love to Mother, Hitty, Thomas, Marenus and all our folks in Solon and Orange. I wonder why Henry Boynton don't write to me? I wish he would, and all the rest of our folks. Hoping to hear from you again and also from Mother and Thomas. I am now as ever and forever,

*Your affectionate brother,*
James


Headquarters, 20th Brigade
Army of the Ohio
In the field near Corinth, Mississippi
June 9, 1862

*President [Mark] Hopkins, D.D.*[145]
*Williams College, Massachusetts*
Dear Sir:

Please find enclosed a draft on New York for sixty dollars ($60) payable to your order. You will remember that you loaned me forty dollars ($40) in the last year of my college course (1856) from a fund which Christian benevolence had placed at your disposal. The enclosed amount will probably cover the interest, and enable you to aid some student hereafter whose necessity may be as great as mine was then. It was a great favor to me at that time, but it was only one of the many and greater favors for which I have to thank you.

I had hoped to visit the college at its next Commencement, but the escape of the rebels from Corinth leads me to doubt it. I try to see God's hand through this darkness and believe that the issue will redound to His glory. With many kind remembrances of the college and much gratitude to yourself, I am

*Very truly yours,*
J. A. Garfield

[145] Mark Hopkins, educator and theologian, went to Williams College in 1830 as Professor of Moral Philosophy and Rhetoric. He became President of Williams in 1836 and served to 1872. His inspiring performances in the classroom and pulpit, and his logic and high thinking left a lasting impression on Garfield. It has been said that Garfield once expressed his concept of an ideal college as consisting of a log in a woods with Mark Hopkins on one end and a student on the other. Whether he said that or not, it comported with his conviction that superb teaching was the most important factor in education—a conviction which grew out of his refreshing experience with Mark Hopkins as a mentor.

June 10, 1862

*My Dear Crete:*

By some oversight Captain Farrar went away without the letter and it lies here yet. I have now received yours of June 2nd. It is a great comfort to me to hear from you regularly and to know that you and the dear little one are well. Of course everything in her growth and happiness are full of interest to me. I am, however, made anxious by the confession made in your last letter where you say: "she is such a little mischief that she nearly gets the upper hands of me some times." Her young intellect knows almost instinctively where the vulnerable point in parental authority is, and just when is the opportune moment to storm it. When you ask her what you shall do for such mischief and she recommends "pak" as a remedy, I fear it indicates that your authority has followed the track of your medical faith and become homeopathic to some degree. Of course I am at so safe a distance from her witcheries that I can give advice of so staid and proper a kind as this without committing myself for inconsistencies. I will say concerning your passage about spanking as another has said of smoking: "It does not make me love you less, but it makes me sad that you should not show more strength in resisting the temptation to such weakness." Seriously, is there no danger that you are letting her will ~~get~~ remain too undisciplined? You see, I changed the word from "get" to "remain," for the will of a child is in the beginning wholly untamed and undisciplined. I have no doubt that gentleness of spirit is to a great extent an acquired possession, and that only by control. Please write me a letter about it.

I am taking some purgative medicines and so am not so well today though my general health is improving. . . . Since I have been sick here, I have been indulging in novels. I have read Bulwer's *Strange Story* and Dickens' *Great Expectations*.[146] Almeda sent me a book just before I left the Sandy Valley which was locked up unread in my desk and is now in Cincinnati. Tell her about [it]. I have never acknowledged the receipt of it, though I have intended to, but forgot it when I have been writing to her. I hope to read it some time. With much love to you and Trot and all, I am

*Ever your*
James

[146] Edward George Bulwer-Lytton, *A Strange Story* (1862), and Charles Dickens, *Great Expectations* (1861).

Headquarters, 20th Brigade
Iuka, Mississippi
June 10, 1862

*My Dear Harry:*

Yours of the 27th *ult.* is at hand. I have been flat on my back since we left Corinth, or rather since we reached this place. Three hot days' marching when diarrhoea was doing its best for me, brought on a slight attack of camp fever, and between the two I have been kept in the ambulance or on my bed ever since. I have grown quite thin. I was weighed this morning and could only pull down 170 pounds. I am giving myself to a thorough course of medicine and have some ground for believing that I shall be permanently better when I get the bile once out of my system. It may be better for me in this hot climate to be thinner. I have fancied that the two weeks [of] breathing the breath that came from the great rebel camp with all its sickness and offal, has half poisoned my system.

We are now 30 miles east of Corinth, repairing the Memphis and Charleston Railroad. It is a higher region, and here for the first time since we reached the Tennessee we find good air and water. We are reopening the railroad to form a junction with General Mitchel, and I suspect we will then move on to the liberation of East Tennessee. Strangely enough we do not yet know where the rebel army have gone.[147] This of itself fixes disgrace upon our generalship.

It makes me indignant to see the attempts made by General Halleck to show that "the enemy were furiously cannonaded and forced to make a hurried and disastrous retreat."[148] There could be no greater falsehood. Our cannonading was wholly a work of outposts. We threw shells into the bushes with light artillery but not one shot was fired from any of the hundred heavy siege guns that for ten days could have filled Corinth with shells. In any one of those ten days in which our splendid army lay chafing with impatience and asking to be lead to battle, a column of 25,000 men could have made a reconnois[s]ance which would have compelled a full knowledge of the enemy's works, strength and operations, but no such reconnois[s]ance was permitted and no officer or soldier of our army saw even the enemy's outer earth work till the whole camp was deserted.

The matter treated of in your last letter is indeed of grave importance as it stands related to my own future, and I am very glad you have introduced it. I will give you the impressions that the first views of the matter makes upon my mind, and I start out with the

[147] After evacuating Corinth the Confederates retreated southward about fifty miles to Tupelo, Mississippi.

[148] Garfield was probably referring to Halleck's three reports of May 30. In different words than Garfield used, Halleck spoke of Union artillery bombardments, of Corinth in flames, and of vast quantities of arms and accoutrements discarded by the "flying troops."

confession that I do not feel comfortable in present surroundings. You have divined the situation quite perfectly. While a battle was imminent, I felt my duty to meet the issue was paramount to every other consideration. If now the war in the west is substantially ended, and its future operations are to consist of holding positions[?] here and there, and keeping down guerrillas, then I shall feel that I can much better serve the country in some other capacity. Let the war be what it may, if I am to serve under such a weak and narrow man as I now obey, I shall feel that I am doing the country but little good and myself but little credit. I confess freely [that] as a matter of choice I would greatly prefer a seat in Congress to my place in the army, or indeed to any place which West Point management will be likely to assign me. So much for my *preferences*.

I believe I entered the service with patriotic motives and in good faith, and with no small struggle made in offering of myself. I cannot for a moment think of taking any course which may even by inference throw a shadow of suspicion upon those motives as being for political and demagogical purposes. And should I resign, go home and seek the nomination to Congress, it seems to me that the whole year's work would be misconstrued. I would rather be reduced to a residuum of 100 pounds than have such a shadow fall upon a year's work, which I hope may be a pleasant one for me to reflect on hereafter. I greatly desire to visit home and if the war continues may do so, but I have felt I can hardly do even that without having it misconstrued. No, I have concluded that I will take no steps whatever in the matter and will only think of the thing in the very improbable event of its being spontaneously tendered to me in my absence. I shall be very glad to hear from you farther on the subject and to know whether there is any serious talk in the premises.

I believe your Commencement exercises are to be held day after tomorrow. I need not tell you how much I would love to be there. . . .

I have all along cherished the hope that I might be through in time to attend the Commencement at Williams this year, *sed aliter Deo videtur* [but God's thought is otherwise].

My surgeon recommends me to go home 30 days to recruit my health, but I think I will be able to get along without it. I shall expect you here in vacation. I think I can make it pleasant for you and not very expensive travelling. Do come. Love to all.

*Ever your*
James

Headquarters, 20th Brigade
Near Iuka, Mississippi
June 12, 1862

*My Dear Mother:*

Your good letter of May 27th is received. I had written to Mary a few days before it came. I have been very bad with the diarrhea, but am getting better now. If I have much more trouble with it, I shall get a leave of absence and go home 20 or 30 days for my health. We march today eastward toward Decatur and Chattanooga for the purpose of liberating the oppressed Union men of East Tennessee. I think it is a healthier country with better air and water there than here.

I see Ellis every day as he is brigade postmaster and attends to all our mail matters. William Perdew is in my brigade. You probably remember that he went to school to me there at Blue Rock and that I whipped him once.[149]

Today is Commencement Day and I suppose you are at Hiram. It is the first time I have been absent since 1856. I had hoped the war would be ended by this time and that I might have been there too today.

It is ten months today since I joined the army, and if our generals don't manage better than they did here at Corinth it will be ten months more before the war is ended. I believe, however, the heaviest of the fighting is over, that is if McClellan succeeds in beating the rebels at Richmond.[150] If we get around to East Tennessee I shall possibly have an opportunity of seeing my 42nd Regiment again. I assure you it would give me great joy to do so. You must write me all about Hiram, the Commencement, and how Trot and Crete are getting along. Why don't Thomas write to me? I wrote him a long letter just as I was leaving the Sandy Valley, but have never had an answer.

You must not worry about me for if I get very sick I shall go home. I hope you are taking good care of your health. Go and stay with Crete just as often and long as you want to. She loves to have you with her and so does Trot, I am sure. She is nearly two years old and I have not been with her more than six months. Isn't it too bad. I expect the little thing won't know me when I get home. Give my love to all our folks and let me hear from you again soon.

*Ever your son,*
James

[149] In the spring of 1851 Garfield taught in a log schoolhouse in Blue Rock, Ohio. His students ranged from "little scholars" to "large" ones, two of whom eloped. He found the boys in the class generally disobedient and defiant, and the parents uncooperative and critical. All in all it was an unpleasant experience which he abandoned after fifty troublesome days. On at least two occasions he thrashed disorderly boys, one of them being William T. Perdew. In June of 1862 Perdew was a private in the sixty fifth Ohio in Garfield's brigade.

[150] McClellan, now in the critical phase of his Peninsula campaign, had just fought the Battle of Fair Oaks (May 31 and June 1) and was preparing for his assault on Richmond, which was destined for failure.

Headquarters, 20th Brigade
Tuscumbia, Alabama
June 14, 1862

*My Dear Crete:*

We reached this place early this morning, having marched since daylight. We spend the day here taking in a supply of forage and provisions. We shall move on tomorrow morning. Our immediate destination is Decatur. It is very severe on our poor boys to march in such hot weather in this sultry climate. For two days we have passed through a splendid country. Great plantations with magnificent residences fill this rich valley of Tuscumbia.

No one who sees the splendor and luxury of these wealthy planters' homes can fail to see that the "Peculiar Institution" has great charms for the rich, and yet no one can fail to see that it is the poor man's bone. We pass these fine plantations and see the slaves toiling for masters and masters' sons who are in the rebel army fighting us, and we let them stay at their toil. A regiment preceeded us a few days ago, and as it passed a cotton-field the whole drove of slaves came to the road and shouted for joy saying, "now we are free!!" One who acted as a for[e]man for the rest said, "take us with you, we will work, we will do anything for you." The Union colonel answered with terrible blasphemy which I will not repeat: "Go back to your plough you black villain or I will put a bullet through you." The poor slaves went back to suffer not only their terrible bitter disappointment but all that is in store for them in consequence of this expression of their wishes. I could chill your blood with the recital of horrors that have resulted to slaves from their expectation of deliverance and their being abandoned to death at the hands of their overseers. But I have not time nor heart to write these things.

The first day's march nearly exhausted me. Yesterday I stood it better and today I am quite strong. I shall be busy drawing my supplies and preparing for the march.

Direct your letters as before and they will follow me. I presume the address will be changed when we reach Decatur, but I don't know what it will be.

Love to Trot and all.

*Ever your*
James

Headquarters, 20th Brigade
Tuscumbia, Alabama
June 23, 1862

*My Dear Crete:*

On the 19th *inst.* I had just received yours of the 19th of April, written just two calendar months before. Where it could have been all that time is quite a mystery. I[t] bore no indications of having been missent, and came with no other postmark than Hiram. Notwithstanding its age I was glad to receive it. It alarms me to think we are getting so old. You wrote on your 30th birth-day and [I am] now but four months behind my 31st. *"Sic anni fugaces labuntur* [So the fleeting years slip by]" and away we go with them. We are thirty. Do you remember what the philosopher poet says of us?

"At thirty man suspects himself a fool," and then he gives us such a glorious prospective future in the next line: "Knows it at forty," *etc.,* and then after leading us through the decades dismisses us with the cheerful hope of his last four words, "then dies the same."[151]

In the letter before me you refer to the matter of Joe's pay. It was the business of Captain McIlrath[152] to make out a full final statement of his pay and clothing account in duplicate, accompanied by a regular discharge. Nobody can do that but the captain of his old company who has the company books and all the company accounts. If Joe has not got that, he must write to Captain McIlrath and get it. Tell him so in a letter. Why don't the boy write to me?

This is the eighth day I have presided seven or eight hours per day over the deliberations of a General Court Martial,[153] and still the work piles up. I have been slowly recovering from my sickness, till day before yesterday I had a backset, and a return of my besetting trouble. I begin to fear that I shall be perpetually subject to this kind of attack while I stay in this climate. I am anxious to get on into the uplands and mountains of East Tennessee, both for the sake of active work and better air and water. I have no doubt it will be much healthier there than here, and then I hope to meet again my old friends of the Sandy Valley region.

Just now I was surprised by a burst of music about ten feet to the rear of my tent. It is a little band of slave minstrels who have come up from the village to visit our colored people and to serenade me. The rude music is really charming. I wish you could hear it, only you would be displeased at the "Julinth" portion of the entertainment. Do you remember that feature of Negro performances which you and I heard somewhere? Poor fellows! How can they sing songs? They told Green if the army would only protect them they would follow us to the

[151] Edward Young, *Night Thoughts,* Night I, Line 417:
"At thirty, man suspects himself a fool;
Knows it at forty, and reforms his plan;
At fifty chides his infamous delay,
Pushes his prudent purpose to resolve;
In all the magnanimity of thought
Resolves, and re-resolves; then dies the same."

[152] James P. McIlrath entered the Twenty-third Ohio in June, 1861, as a captain and was promoted to major the following month. The difficulty over Joe Rudolph's pay was occasioned by his transfer to the Forty-second Ohio.

[153] The accused was a lieutenant in the Fifty-eighth Indiana.

end of the world. But they get no [illegible word] from an American army. We seem to be as much their enemies as [are] their masters.

I am so unwell, you will excuse me for not writing more. I have a sort of dizzy feeling in the head and a sickness at the stomach super-added. I hope you have written me fully about the Commencement and have sent me a programme and catalogue. Love to all and especially to Trot.

*Ever your*
James

The poem you sent me, "In State,"[154] is exceedingly fine. It is greatly admired by all to whom I have shown it.

Headquarters, 20th Brigade
Tuscumbia, Alabama
June 25, 1862

*Dear Brother Austin:*

Your very welcome letter of the 16th *inst.* reached me today. I assure you I was very glad to hear from you and yours again, and I trust there will not be so long a silence between us again.

After the evacuation of Corinth (an event which I am compelled to regard as disgraceful to our generalship) the Army of the Ohio immediately began to repair the Memphis and Charleston Railroad and since that time my brigade has been hard at work marching and building up bridges where one army or the other had burned them. I have for the last ten days been serving as the President of a General Court Martial and several of my regiments have gone on to repair the road eastward. I start to join them tomorrow morning at 3 o'clock and so I take a few moments of the evening before to write to you. In about three days I hope [to reach] Decatur, Alabama and I presume we shall go thence to Eastern Tennessee to liberate the Union men there from the terrible bondage which they have suffered.

Since I last wrote you I have had a severe attack of dysentery and camp fever combined, which confined me to my tent or to the ambulance for two weeks. In that time I lost nearly 30 pounds of my weight. I am better now, though I fear the low country and bad water will not allow me to recover so fully as I could wish. I expect better things of the region to which we are going, and there I hope to meet again my dear old 42nd.

My heart sinks down very low when I see the mode in which the war is conducted. Until the rebels are made to feel that rebellion is a crime which the Government will punish, there is no hope of destroy-

---

[154] Forceythe Willson's poem depicting the terrible fighting and suffering in the Civil War, which ends with the Union victorious.

ing it. I declare it as my deliberate conviction that it [is] better in this country, occupied by our troops, for a citizen to be a rebel than to be a Union man. Everything they have is protected with the most scrupulous care, especially their property in human flesh. Besides the General Order of General Halleck to prevent contrabands from coming inside our lines,[155] every means is taken to show the people that the Union army is just as ready as possible to keep "the institution" secure.

Not long ago my commanding general sent me an order to have my camp searched for a fugitive slave. I sent back word that if generals wished to disobey an express law of Congress, which is also an order from the War Department, they must do it themselves for no soldier or officer under my command should take part in such disobedience. We have marched scores of miles past splendid plantations waving with corn which the planters boast openly is intended to feed the Southern army. While masters and masters' sons are away in the rebel army, the slaves under the whip of their drivers toil on in the fields we are passing and dare hardly look up at us.

A few days since, as an advance brigade passed by a field with 40 of these human cattle at work, the whole gang came to the road, threw up their hats and shouted, "Now we are free. We will go with you anywhere; we will work for you, fight for you, do anything for you, only let us go with you." The colonel in command of the regiment thus addressed drew his pistol and with terrible oaths said to the leading slave who spoke for the rest, "Go back to your work or I will put a bullet through your blue heart." This performance has been praised as a "very proper course to be taken under such circumstances." We do not even inquire whether a black man is a rebel in arms or not; if he is black, be he friend or foe, he is to be kept at a distance. It seems to me hardly possible that God will let us succeed while such enormities are practiced.

Our weak and timid management at Corinth in letting the enemy escape will greatly protract the war. I agree with you that it is not to be as short as we had supposed. I had hoped that we might all go home before the autumn was passed by [but] my hopes of that are becoming very weak.

My personal affairs at home need my attention for a few weeks, but I have acted on the resolution to see the end of the war first. If it is so very long, I may yet go for a short time.

I am greatly obliged for your kind expressions of confidence and approval of my efforts hitherto. Concerning my future, of which you have spoken, I am always glad to hear your views and to consult your judgment. As you have requested it I will speak without reserve. I am

[155] After receiving reports that fugitive slaves were feeding information to the enemy, Halleck, on November 20, 1861, issued orders directing their exclusion from within Union lines. From across the North a storm of criticism descended on the General, who defended his orders as military, not political.

serving in my present capacity cheerfully and, I hope, acceptably to the country, and I am willing still to do so. I entered the service in good faith, at some considerable sacrifice of my own plans and purposes, and I am wholly unwilling to do anything which will throw a doubt upon the motives which have governed me and make me appear to have done this only to serve myself to something else. I would far rather die here without ever seeing my friends again than to have the shadows fall upon that year of my life, whose motives my own heart so fully approves. I would not therefore abandon my work here to seek another field, even if it were tenfold more honorable, if by so doing I should seem to shrink from any duty.

But on the other hand I will say that while the war promises to be a long one it still appears to me that the great battles of the war have been fought or will have been all fought as soon as the Richmond question is settled. To remain in the army and follow the military as a profession was never any part of my plan. I have always intended and still intend to resign my commission as soon as the active work of the war is done. It seems to me that the successful ending of the war is the smaller of the two tasks imposed upon the government. There must be a readjustment of our public policy and management. There will spring up out of this war a score of new questions and new dangers. The settlement of these will be of even more vital importance than the ending of the war.

I do not hesitate to tell *you* that I believe I could do some service in Congress in that work, and I should prefer that to continuing in the army. I have not expected a nomination. I have said nothing about it except in answer to a letter from Professor Rhodes. I do not, of course, know what is the feeling in the new district, but it does not seem to me probable, when there are several prominent men in the field who will press their own claims, that the people will of their own accord choose one who is away from them and whose future depends upon the uncertain chances of war. I cannot say what is best under the circumstances so well as you can. Should the people of their own motion, without any suggestions from me, choose to nominate me for Congress, I should esteem it a mark of high favor. But I should be unwilling that my name should go before a convention and be rejected. I must therefore commit the decision of this matter wholly to my friends and I particularly desire you to help me in determining whether I shall allow my name to be presented or not. I have received several letters on the subject which I have not answered as yet. From what is written in these, I should think it quite probable that were I there, the success would not be very uncertain.

I hope you will not think that I feel any impatient anxiety on the subject. I do not. Indeed, I have more than once shrunk from the thought of the dangers which will beset the course of any man who shall buffet the next stormy four years of public life that lies before the nation. I hope to hear from you very soon and very fully on this whole subject.

Give my love to your wife [and] to Lottie and Nellie. I would be exceedingly glad to hear from Lottie. Tell her I solicit a letter from her and then I will make it necessary for her to write another in answer to mine.

Direct your next to Decatur, Alabama. To follow the brigade.

*Very truly your brother,*
J. A. Garfield

Headquarters, 20th Brigade
In Camp Near Decatur, Alabama
July 5, 1862

*My Dear Crete:*

By some unaccountable delay your letter of June 9th did not reach me till last night, though I had ten days ago received one from Harry mailed at Solon, June 16th. One also came last night from Harry mailed at Newton Falls, June 28th. There would seem to be some fault at the Hiram office. Till last night I have had no mail since we left Tuscumbia ten days ago, but we are now in railroad communication with the North and I hope our mails will be more regular and rapid.

I am sorry to have to tell you that my health is not only not improving, but getting worse. I have kept hoping that each attack of my besetting disease would be the last, but it has lately returned with a vigor and stubbornness which I am quite unable to control. I had begun to regain strength and weight, was weighing 177 pounds, but the last week has run me down to 168, and I am suffering a good deal of pain as well as weakness. If I do not get better soon I shall get a sick leave to go as far as Cincinnati if not all the way home. Still I am hoping to be able to work on till I can set myself right, though I have not been so much discouraged about my health since I came into the army. We have rebuilt over a hundred miles of railroad and are now lying still with no apparent aim or future purposes. It has been supposed we were going into East Tennessee, at [and] it may still be our destination; but there seems to be no vigorous symptoms of any movement. General Mitchel has accomplished a good deal, but his men have committed the most shameful outrages in the country here that the history of this war has shown. He (General Mitchel) is reported to have resigned. At any rate he has gone to Washington to see about his future in some way.[156]

---

[156] The most serious acts of pillage and plunder were committed by Colonel John B. Turchin's 8th Brigade. Turchin, together with other officers, was court-martialled (see the next four letters) and dismissed from the service. The verdict was never

A number of people have written me about running for Congress this fall. I have not determined what to say about it, until I can learn more of the state of feeling throughout the district. I would, of course, rather be in Congress than in the army if there is to be no more active service, for I have no taste for the dull monotony of camp life, and then I believe I can dispose of my life to more advantage than to confine it to the inglorious quiet of a brigade camp. Still, I am very unwilling to do anything that would look like a desire to leave my place in the army, nor will I as long as my health will hold out. It is that which made me say I might go as far as Cincinnati, if I did not go clear through home, should I continue unwell very much longer. To go home just now would, I fear, be misconstrued into a purpose to make political capital for myself. I have been [so] thoroughly dead *militarily* since I came to the Tennessee that I hardly see how I can be sufficiently remembered to make my return a matter of much comment; still it might be, and I don't [know] why it is, but I have a more than usual horror at being hauled over the coals of political persecution again. What do you hear said about the congressional matter?

I wish you would send me a catalogue of the Eclectic and also tell me about the Commencement. Have you received a letter fr[om] me enclosing $50? I sent it about the 12th of June.

I thought of our little darling a thousand times on the 3rd and wondered how many of her birth-days I should be permitted to enjoy with her. Dear little creature, I cannot tell you how anxious I am for her growth in beauty, health and intelligence.

Yesterday we had a celebration of the 4th. I was hardly able to sit up but the officers of the division insisted that I should speak and I went out and spoke about 20 or 30 minutes. I did not know but I had lost the trick of speech, but I found the old feeling coming back to me with all its memories of other days. We had a very pleasant time though a strange one.

Several Disciples of the vicinity have been here to visit me. There is a church in the village of Mooresville near by and they have sent up wanting me to speak to them on Sunday next. If I am not too unwell I have a notion to speak to them.

I hope to hear from you again in regard to what you think about the matters referred to above. Love to all.

*Ever your*
James

---

executed, Turchin having been commissioned a brigadier general of volunteers before it was announced. Mitchel, then feuding with Buell and upset by the outrages he had tried to prevent, submitted his resignation. It was refused. He was then called to Washington. In September he was transferred to Hilton Head, South Carolina, to command the Department of the South and the X Army Corps. There, on October 30, he died of yellow fever.

Athens, Alabama
July 9, 1862

*My Dear Harry:*

I am again President of a Court Martial now sitting in this place for the trial of Colonel Turchin, one of the brigade commanders under General Mitchel. I cannot sufficiently give utterance to my horror of the ravages and outrages which have been committed by General Mitchel's army. There has not been found in American history so black a page as that which will bear the record of General Mitchel's campaign in Northern Alabama. He has fought no battle worthy the name and yet his overweening self-conceit has filled the columns of the press with his praises and procured him another star. I fear his reputation will not be enhanced by the incidental revelations of this trial. This town, which contains some of the finest village residences I have ever seen, was, by Colonel Turchin, given up to pillage and in the presence of the Russian (Colonel Turchin) was sacked according to the Muscovite custom.

The grand army of the West is now spread out over a front of 300 miles from Memphis to Stevenson, and should the rebel army who occupies some point or points in the south of us choose to strike a blow upon any part of our line, I do not see what is to hinder his breaking through our thin line before we could mass our forces and effectually resist him. There is positively no accounting for the wonders of scientific strategy!!![157]

I have just seen Colonel Hazen and from my conversation with him I have almost given up the hope of your coming to me this vacation. I have delayed answering your last two letters in hope of seeing you. I greatly wish you were here to spend a few weeks with me. I am sorry to tell you that my health is very bad. I am well in every respect, except that the diarrhea has hardly let go of me since the evacuation of Corinth. If I don't mend soon I shall be compelled to quit the field for a time at least. I am anxious to hear what turn the congressional matter will take. I can not get away from the court-martial while I am able to sit up, for it is the most important one that has yet been called in the West. But if the court closes up its work in a reasonable time, I shall try to get home a little while, always provided there should be no battle imminent.

July 10, Evening

I have come away to my room after a weary day of presiding over a court composed of myself and six colonels, and with a captain of the regular army as Judge Advocate. There are a good many intricate questions of law constantly coming up which I must decide and which gives me now and then a little intellectual exercise.

[157] Seven weeks after these lines were written Bragg began his invasion of Kentucky.

I am stopping with a wealthy planter [Dr. Benjamin W. Maclin] who has the finest house in town. I do not wonder that the slave aristocracy is so fascinating to a man of wealth. When once a man is rich, wealth flows into his coffers easily and bountifully. Their homes are luxurious with magnificence and wealth. Herein lies the great vicious self-deception of their social system. They pursue such a course with their slaves and [as] to render it manifestly true that the mass of their blacks are wholly incompetent to direct the business of their own lives. Then they point us to their slaves and say with an air of triumph, "These people are infinitely better off here than in freedom. We are religiously bound to take care of them."

The effect of the war on slavery depends almost wholly upon the length of the struggle. President Hopkins in [a] letter to me received today says: "It is for the Southern people themselves to say whether the abolition of slavery shall be the result. Their present course indicates that it must be."

I have lately had a letter from Senator Smith who was on a visit to Washington when he saw several leading senators who said I must be put in command of a division. I have no notion in reference to the matter whether such will be the result or not. I cannot accomplish much for the country or myself as I am now situated. General Wood grows smaller and smaller in proportion as emergencies loom up.

Can't you send me some paper containing the account of the Commencement? Send a catalogue also.

I hear you think of marrying soon. Is it so? Tell me about it and your plans for the future. I have wanted to know more about yourself for a long time. You haven't said anything on the subject of your plans, whether you have chosen law or the ministry.

Give my love to Libbie and write again soon. I think you had better direct to me at this place, though a letter will reach me if only the Army of the Ohio is added to my name.

*Ever your*
J. A. Garfield


Athens, Alabama
July 17, 1862

*My Dear Crete:*

Your two favors, one of June 27 by the hand of Colonel Hazen and the other by post, dated July 6th, were received within a few days of each other and since I have been in this place. This is the 13th day of the court-martial and we have only just closed the evidence for the prosecution. The case is a very important one, but exceedingly tedious in the almost endless extent of its details. The horrible character of the outrages which have been committed here are in striking contrast with the character of the officer (Colonel Turchin) who is charged with the responsibility of allowing their perpetration.

From the accounts we had heard of him and his doings we had expected to meet as fierce and brutal a Muscovite as the dominions of the Czar could produce. But though he is a Russian by birth and education, yet when he came into court we met a fine manly figure with broad expansive forehead, mild blue eye[s] with an unusual depth of piercing intelligence which at once won respect. Though he was suffering from the effects of fever, which gave him a most severe headache, he was not excused by the court and for ten days he has sat patiently while citizen after citizen (rebels all) have rehearsed and we have recorded the outrages of the men under his command. Though by a fiction of military law, the prosecution has been striving to fix upon him the responsibility for robbery of citizens and rapes of female slaves, yet during all that time he has borne himself so much like a noble-souled man that he has quite won my heart.

In conversation with me [him] today I gathered his history as follows. He was educated in the artillery school at St. Petersburg and after serving some time in the army entered the Imperial Military Academy and there graduated, winning a place on the Imperial Staff. During the Crimean War he was Colonel on the Czar's staff and had the control of 30,000 men. There are few places in the American army that afford more honor or emoluments than that, but said he to me: The dream of freedom was before my eye and in my heart and I could not rest. I abandoned my post in the army, gave up my serfs (for I owned a number) and came to America. I had studied engineering in my native land, and having settled in Chicago, I became an engineer on the Illinois Central Railroad. When the war broke out I was called to command a regiment and have lately been nominated by the President as brigadier-general but I do not want a military position. I left the art of war in the old world to reap the peac[e]able fruits of freedom in the new, but since I have been in this army I have tried to act for the best interests of this noble country. I have tried to teach rebels that treachery to the Union was a terrible crime. My superior officers do not agree with my plans. They want the rebellion treated tenderly and gently. They may cashier me, but I shall appeal to the American people and implore them to wage this war in such a manner as will make humanity better for it. I have tried to give you the substance of the thoughts of a man who will probably be dishonorably dismissed from the army in a few days, but who nevertheless has won my heart and whom I will always be glad to call a friend.

My duties are exceedingly unpleasant. Colonel Stanley, a brother senator in 1860-1, and Captain (Professor) Edgarton of Cleveland are both to be tried before us.[158] I am glad to tell you that I am consider-

[158] Timothy R. Stanley commanded the Eighteenth Ohio in Turchin's brigade. The charges against Stanley were dropped on the ground that he had acted under

ably better; indeed, I have got almost entirely well since my last letter. I am stopping a[t] Dr. Maclin's, a wealthy planter, where I have a fine room and the best of accommodations. I take a shower bath every morning. Doesn't that astonish you! Tomorrow, during a recess of the court, I go out with him nine miles [to] visit his plantation and 95 slaves.

As I have long expected, the enemy has run through our extended lines and cut off several important lines of communication. We have been cut off from Nashville several days and our whole army is on half rations.[159]

Again I repeat the sad truth that we have no generals. In this respect the South has far outstripped us.

How long I shall be on this court I cannot tell—I fear a long time. Write me at this place and it will reach me whether [I am] here or not. Give my love to all the folks, especially to Matt and her numerous family. Kiss our dear Trot for me. I thought of her on her birth-day but was too ill to write.

> *Ever yours,*
> James

Huntsville, Alabama
July 24, 1862

*My Dear Harry:*

Your live letter of the 10th so full of healthy gossip and good sense reached me on Sunday the 20th. Situated as you are you can have no idea of the pleasure which such a letter brings to me. You know the human mind perversely longs for all that it has not, especially what it has small hope of attaining. You may be sure I followed you spiritually through all your excursions in Warren on the 4th. . . .

Soon after [reading your letter] I was doomed to the tedious and inglorious work of this most tiresome court-martial. I began to get better in physical condition till at last I had been lead to believe I was permanently recovered. On Sunday last the venue of the court was changed to this place. I had come down here on Saturday evening to see my brigade which had been ordered forward to Stevenson. It had got through this place and I remained here. I returned Sunday night in excellent health and spirits, but awoke next morning with headache, fever and diarrhea accompanied with severe fits of vomiting. I was very sick during the day, sent for a surgeon, took a powerful

---

Turchin's orders. For the same reason Warren P. Edgarton, commander of Battery E, First Ohio Light Artillery Regiment, was acquitted.

[159] The destruction of Union communications was being accomplished by Confederate cavalry under Generals Nathan Bedford Forrest and John Morgan. On July 13 Forrest's troopers descended upon Murfreesboro and captured the town and its Federal garrison of about 1,400 officers and men.

emetic, and spouted forth floods of "irrepressible bile" not of the Horatian but of the Esculapian kind. I tell you, Harry, it is far from pleasant to toss on a bed of pain alone in a hot sweltering room hundreds of miles away from those who care especially for your life and comfort. But I am better now, though very weak. With the exception of part [of] one day I have since continued to preside over the deliberations of the court, though I have been allowed a cot to lie on and have thus been enabled to work and be sick at the same time. Just now I am threatened with returning health but am so weak as to be quite spiritless.

I am almost inclined to be delighted at the raids behind us, the cutting up of our railroad and telegraphs behind us. It will do us good to have a few score towns in Kentucky, Indiana and Ohio plundered. It is particularly pertinent that these things should happen, especially such brilliant exploits as the giving up of Murfreesboro, while General Mitchel is being persecuted and Colonel Turchin is in his third week of trial for not dealing quietly enough with rebels and their property. It may bring our people ultimately to understand the beauty of West Point and the terribleness of a broken and ruined government. The regular army is as rotten as corruption can make it. You can hardly imagine how my lofty views of West Point have been lopped off one by one. There are but few sprigs left on which I can hang fair confidence, much less admiration. Look at the shameful distribution of Halleck's army. I have written it in a dozen letters that our lines would be broken up and the rebels be behind us any day they choose to be. If we are not gobbled up in detail it will only be *per gratiam hostium* [through the grace of the enemy].

I have lately received a letter from P. R. Spencer, Sr.,[160] forwarded to me by Crete. Did you see it? In it he proposes that Portage County should move in the congressional nomination. I wrote him in answer as I have written before that I must leave the matter wholly to my friends. You tell me you think my name may be committed to the tender mercies of a convention. I wish you would give me the ground of your confidence. There are some few points of the matter as it appears to me which looks a little singular. I have not heard a word from L. W. Hall or Halsey for several months, nor has anyone told me how they stand on the congressional question. But I am inclined to the belief, strange as it may appear, that they are for O. P. Brown. My supposition arises first from their silence both in not writing to me nor sending the *Democrat* for a long time, and second in the fact, which I accidentally discovered in the advertising columns of a late number of the *Democrat,* that young H. P. Hall is in partnership with Brown as an attorney. Am I right in my hypothesis? These sentences of course must not go outside our circle. If the *Democrat* is for Brown it will

---

[160] Platt Rogers Spencer of Ashtabula County, Ohio, was a noted penman. Garfield became acquainted with him at the Eclectic in Hiram, where Spencer conducted one of his writing schools.

be a strange exhibition of human nature after all the past. Be assured I am not anxious in the matter and shall lose no sleep nor have one diarrhea less or more if O. P. Brown or any other man is chosen. I will not, however, promise that I should keep perfectly free from nausea should *Bombastes Furioso*[161] be reared and raised and born into congressional life for the next quadrennium.

In regard to the new levy of troops and your own course, I am hardly clear in my own mind except in this; I think the time has now come when you ought to go into the service. I hate to say this, Harry, for I had all along thought our little Hiram circle had sacrificed enough and it was a matter of great comfort to me to know that you were still there and the circle not dissolved. But now the great death struggle of the nation approaches and a terrible exertion of our people may bring us through the darkness. But I do not want you to go unless you can have a position worthy both [of] yourself and the country. Now what shall that position be? First of all, I would have you with me if it were possible. I am taking the matter into earnest consideration and if I can make an opening I shall be most glad to do so. There is a matter now pending in my brigade which may result favorably soon. Second, if the first is not successful, I want you to have a field office in one of the new regiments now raising in Ohio. As the regiments will be sent into the field without much time for preparation, I would rather you should be lieutenant colonel or major under some good colonel. I am trying to get Lieutenant Colonel Pardee of the 42 made colonel of a new regiment and I should be glad to see you with him if you cannot be with me. Write me again before you decide the matter and I may know more. I received Burke's *Prospectus* last evening. Almeda says he writes her that "He is trying to realize that he is a married man." *Verb. sap.* [*Verbum sat sapienti:* A word to the wise is sufficient].

Wearily, wearily stretches the work of the court-martial. I think I would decline the honor of being Lord Chief Justice of the King's Bench. Do write to me.

*Ever your*
J. A. Garfield


Cleveland
August 2, 1862

*By Telegraph from Louisville, Kentucky*
*To Mrs. Garfield:*

I am sick. Shall reach Cleveland Monday. Meet me. Bring Harry and Almeda.

J. A. Garfield

---

[161] William Barnes Rhodes, *Bombastes Furioso*, Act 1, Scene 4:
"Who dares this pair of boots displace,
Must meet Bombastes face to face."

August 5, 1862

*By Telegraph from Cleveland*
*To Mrs. Garfield:*
I am here unwell. Will wait at Weddell.[162] Answer.

J. A. Garfield
Brigadier General

Howland, Trumbull County, Ohio
August 27, 1862

*Dear Sir [General Buell]:*
Your note of the 13th *inst.* asking an explanation of an enclosed paragraph from the Louisville *Journal* of August 6th in relation to the trial of Colonel J. B. Turchin was forwarded to me from Stevenson and is just received.[163] I am greatly surprised at the paragraph. While I was in Louisville I neither saw the editor of the *Journal* nor did I divulge to any one the sentence of the court-martial. The only circumstance I remember from which the paragraph could have originated was the following. I was too ill to leave my hotel, and while waiting for the Cincinnati boat, several acquaintances, residents of Louisville, visited my room. During the conversation one of them remarked that he had just heard that Colonel Turchin had been dismissed from the service and asked me if it were so. I answered: "It may be so, the sentence was not published when I left, though it may be by this time." My remark may have been taken as a confirmation of the rumor, and by some means found its way into the *Journal.*

I had not seen the paragraph till now. It does me great injustice and annoys me exceedingly. I will be particularly obliged if you will allow this letter to be shown to Colonel Turchin and to the members of the court.

*Very truly, your obedient servant*
J. A. Garfield
Brigadier General, Volunteers
U. S. A.

[162] The Weddell House, a four-story hotel on the northwest corner of Superior and Bank streets, opened its doors in June, 1847. Its luxurious accommodations and outstanding meals attracted numerous distinguished guests.

[163] The *Journal,* citing as its authority a member of the court, reported with approval that Turchin had been cashiered from the service. Since the court's decision had not yet been announced, Turchin called Buell's attention to the article.

# PART II

*Sojourn in Washington*

Garfield remained in Ohio until after the Republican nominating convention. Though weakened by illness, he kept a watchful eye on political developments. All the while a group of reliable supporters labored sedulously for his nomination as Republican congressional candidate from the Nineteenth District. Garfield himself studiously avoided doing or saying anything that might be interpreted as office-seeking. When asked whether or not he was a candidate, he replied that he would accept the nomination if it represented the spontaneous wish of the people. Just before the convention he and his wife retired to Howland Springs, where he was resting when the delegates gathered in Garrettsville.

Although the other candidates were on the scene, Garfield's absence probably mattered little. He was in capable hands, was well known as an educator, preacher, and state senator, and was still receiving popular acclaim as a successful military leader. Furthermore, his opposition to slavery appealed to voters imbued with the abolitionism of Joshua Giddings, who had been ousted from Congress a few years back by John Hutchins, the incumbent and Garfield's chief rival for the nomination. Still, the contest was close. Not until the eighth ballot was Garfield nominated, defeating Hutchins by the narrow margin of 78 to 71.

The successful candidate, his health nearly restored, now had to face the fact that he still wore the Union blue and had a star on each shoulder. But he had no desire to return to Buell's army at the head of a brigade, and he probably heaved a sigh of relief when Secretary of War Edwin M. Stanton called him to Washington for an assignment to duty.

Quite unexpectedly his stay in the national capital stretched into four months. An eventful period it was, for the country and for Garfield. On the national scene there was the Battle of Antietam, fought while Garfield was en route to Washington; there was the dismissal of McClellan, followed by the Union defeat at Fredericksburg; there was the Confederate invasion of Kentucky, an aftermath of which was

131

*the dismissal of Buell and the appointment of Major General William S. Rosecrans as commander of the Army of the Cumberland, an event pregnant with meaning for Garfield; there were the fall elections and the proclamations of emancipation; and, along with all, there was a swelling tide of anti-Lincoln acrimony.*

*For Garfield, whose letters disclose his deep concern about all of those developments, his sojourn in Washington offered unusual opportunities to circulate among the nation's mighty. Shortly after his arrival in the city he became the house guest of the powerful, prestigious Secretary of Treasury Salmon P. Chase and his vivacious daughter Kate, the belle of Washington society. Almost daily he brushed elbows with leading political, business, and military figures. Accordingly, the Washington that emerges from his letters is not a city of streets crowded with uniformed men, office-seekers, and run-of-the-mill people; rather, it is the seat of power whose only apparent seamy side is the wily intrigue of inordinately ambitious and hypercritical men, scheming and plotting for personal gain and glory.*

*Although Garfield relished associating with Washington officialdom, his pleasure was dampened by anxiety over his next duty and its delay in coming. As the letters show, the War Department seriously considered him for three different assignments, but for one or another reason each fell through. In the midst of annoying uncertainty came an important, though temporary appointment—that of serving on the court which tried and convicted Major General Fitz John Porter. The trial dragged on about five weeks, with the verdict against Porter coming late in January, 1863. Before then, however, Garfield had left Washington on orders assigning him to duty in the Army of the Cumberland.*

Howland
September 2, 1862

*Dear Mother:*

I had hoped to visit you long before this and to have been back in the army by now. But I have improved very slowly and though I hope I am steadily and surely recovering, yet I am still too weak to go back and the doctor thinks I had better stay here a few days longer, perhaps ten days longer before I try to go around much. It was impossible for me to have any quiet or rest at Hiram or indeed any place where I was well acquainted. This has been a very pleasant quiet place though for a while the people from Warren came out here in such numbers that we were obliged to ask to be left more alone. The yellow has pretty nearly disappeared from my skin and I am feeling quite restored except in my strength, and in that I am gaining.

Crete and Trot are well. Crete will write in this letter. We wrote to you when we first came here but have not heard from you. Why don't you write to us? I had hoped to be able to attend the Bedford meeting but I fear I shall not.

They are holding the congressional convention for this district today at Garrettsville. I may be nominated, but I don't know how it will turn out. I have done nothing about it and I really don't care much about it. If I am nominated I shall still go back to the army till the new Congress meets, which will probably be a year from now; it may be more. I presume I am the only candidate that will not be at the convention. If the people of the district want me, I take it that it is their business to tell me so and not mine to coax them to have me.

Be sure and write to us right off. Direct to Warren and we shall get it sooner than to direct here. Love to Mary and Hitty and all our folks. I shall hope to visit you all as soon as I am able to do so.

Your affectionate son,
James

133

Hiram, Ohio
September 12, 1862

*My Dear Burke:*

Yours of the 4th was forwarded to Warren, thence reforwarded to Hiram and reached me last evening. A few days after you left here, I went with Crete and Trot to Howland Springs in Trumbull County, about four miles east of Warren. It was a quiet, farmer's home, shut up in the woods on a hill and was just what I needed in the way of quiet and rest. We staid there three weeks and got back here on the 9th. I have been slowly, very slowly, but steadily improving in health and strength. I was never a fat man and hence my 43 pound loss was a loss of muscle, which comes back very slowly. I have gained 9 pounds, however, since I came home and I believe I have now got freed from active cause of disease. But I am still so weak as to feel quite unequal to the duties of the field.

I have lately received a telegram from the Secretary of War ordering me to report to him in person at Washington for orders as soon as I am able. I think I shall be able to go to Washington by the middle of next week, and by the time the new command is assigned me, and my staff and equippage can be extricated from the maze of Kentucky and Tennessee strategical complications, I shall hope to be able to take the field for active service. I have no idea what post is to be assigned me, but Governor Dennison thinks I am destined for a division on the Potomac. If under McClellan, may the gods deliver me. If under Sigel, I rejoice.

The war is now strangely mixed, and the days are sufficiently dark; but if we have any generalship (which we may reasonably doubt) we will take advantage of the nearness of the enemy to our border and strike them a worse blow than we could have done so far in on their own soil. When we push the war pendulum back southward again, it ought to swing further in consequence of the great northward sweep it has just now taken. The most deplorable feature of the present situation is that our generals seem to have no confidence in each other, nor the people in them. Governor Dennison writes me that the army at Washington is in a most fearful state of discouragement and demoralization. What has become of McClellan's boasted power of organization and disciplining of armies? General Cox's Kanawha brigade is said to be the finest corps in the whole Capitoline army, a fine comment of West Pointers and Civilians!!

I believe our greatest danger just now is that [Jefferson] Davis will take the wind out of Lincoln's sails and declare universal emancipation as the condition of foreign acknowledgement. If he does this the day is lost to us forever. If Lincoln anticipates him we are safe.

I think your theory of the difference between European and American warfare is correct. We can never hope for peace till we crush up or disperse their heavy armies and remove the active cause of the sectional feud. It may be a philosophical question whether 11,000,000 of people *can be subdued,* for we need no longer disguise the fact that this is the thing to be done before there can be union and peace.

In regard to the congressional nomination I hardly know whether to be sad or gratified. I am certainly gratified at the fact that I took no part in steering the nomination and did not even attend the convention, though all the other candidates were there; but I feel in some degree sad at the prospect of being for a series of years brought out into public life, when I would perhaps get more growth in the quiet of private study. Still I don't know but I grow faster in storm than calm. I suspect I do. The next four years in Congress will probably be as fatal to political longevity as the war is to personal life and health. The people will not attribute the burdens and serious troubles of the next few years so much to the philosophical causes as to their legislators, and so I suspect Congress will be the scapegoat for the press and people—especially for demagogues. I would not, however, wish to be cowardly and shirk the responsibility of thinking and acting because the times are dangerous. So I shall try the rough sea, if the bulletts will let me.

I was very glad to hear from you and particularly glad to know you were doing so well in your school and in speaking. Your incident with the bigot at York was interesting. The world decidedly moves in liberality.

Remember me affectionately to Mary. Crete sends love. The school is doing well, 180 students. Let me hear from you as soon as you know where I am to be.

*Ever yours,*
J. A. Garfield


Cleveland, Ohio
September 16, 1862

*Mason Raymond*
*Dear Sir:*
I intended when I was in Hiram to see you and find out what disposition you intended to make of the note I hold against you. But I was too unwell to do much business and hence failed to see you. I have requested Professor Rhodes to see you for me. If you want to keep the money another year, I am willing you should do so either by paying the interest that has already accrued or by giving a new note covering interest and principal. If you desire to make this arrangement, Mr. Rhodes will attend to it, or in case you wish to pay it you can pay it to him.

*Very truly yours,*
J. A. Garfield

Monongahela House, Pittsburgh
Wednesday Evening
September 17, 1862

*My Dear Good Crete:*

You did not expect a letter so soon. The fact that my trunk was left led me to think it most safe for me to wait here for its arrival, as it might be lost if I should go on without it. Then I found myself somewhat sleepy and tired and I took the leaving of the trunk as one of the "providential interferences" to give me some more rest. I am sorry that Green did not go with me, and yet my future is so indefinite that I can't tell what is best. It may be just right that he didn't come. He forgot to bring my revolver along. I hope it will come with the trunk for I shall need it. The trunk will be along at 3 o'clock tomorrow morning, at which time I take the train for Harrisburg. I shall go to bed in a few minutes and try to rest before starting.

When I got here I was quite weary, but I took a good bath and have just taken a frugal supper. I caught myself eating warm bread and, remembering your wishes, it was a great pleasure to lay the tempting "hot roll" away, while I thought of you and wished you were with me. I cannot tell how glad my heart is at the remembrances of my visit with you. It has been so much more than I have dared to hope for the last two years and more that my soul is full of thanksgiving. If this still, lone room could now be filled with your dear presence I would not even be tired or sick. I do not me[an] to say *I am sick,* for I think I am coming right up out of the valley; but it would make my heart so light and happy if you could be with me now and shed around me the brightness of the new light, that I might breathe the fragrance of the "alabaster box," which, so long sealed, has been broken at last.

Everything conspired to make the visit dear to me, and its close was worthy of its whole course and character. Our little darling never put her arms around my neck and hugged and kissed me so lovingly as in the farewell embrace. You walked and talked with me till the train whistled, and you tossed a sweet kiss after the flying train. It was all as my fondest wishes could ask and it all augurs good for the future. I shall hope soon after my arrival to receive a dear letter with a heart full of love from you.

I send you a slip from the *Portage Democrat* which I found as I came along the road. Mother may be pleased to read it.

The news today looks still more encouraging. God grant we may soon see the end of the war, though I dare not hope that the end is very nigh. As I draw nearer Washington my own future looks more and more uncertain. It seems as though the individual would be lost in the magnitude of the whole great movement.

I must close and rest. I will read a chapter in the little Testament for you and me, and ask God to be with you before I sleep. And now, my precious darling, with my heart very warm and full of love to you, and with my best "God bless you" and warm kisses for you and Trot, I give you good night. Ever and forever

*Your own,*
James

Willard's Hotel
Washington, D. C.
September 20, 1862

*My Precious Crete:*

I reached here yesterday morning at 9½ having spent the previous night at Baltimore. I was quite tired but am now feeling very well. My ankle is still sore and a little lame. I have been pretty busy since I came, doing some little errands from [for] friends and for myself. I took dinner at 4½ last evening with Secretary Chase at his house. His daughter Kate is quite a belle here from what I learn. They have a fine residence and live in splendid style. Mr. Chase seems to be the only member of the Cabinet who stands firmly up with Stanton (or more properly Stanton stands up by him) for the vigorous prosecution of the war for freedom's and the Union's sake. Chase is, I believe, by far the strongest man in the administration, and he seems to be thoroughly imbued with a moral and religious sense of the duties of the government in relation to the war. My interview with him and Stanton yesterday was satisfactory so far as they are concerned. They would give me any place in their power, but Stanton said it would be difficult to give me any place which would save me from West Point. . . .

I wrote you from Pittsburgh and have been anxiously watching the Ebbitt House Post Office to find your letter, but it has not yet come. I shall hope to get it today. I found that House not a pleasant one and so came here. The board is heavy both in quality and cost ($17½ per week) but it is central and I hope not to be here long. I have not yet come to any conclusion about where I would like to go. Of course I would like to go to Cumberland Gap and Stanton wants me there but says he cannot do it now without wronging General Morgan.

I did think about going to Port Royal, but General Hunter thinks the Government is bound to neglect that or any other place where Negroes are to be treated as men.[1] I may go across the river and visit General Sigel this afternoon.

I have drawn my pay for July and August, amounting in all to $632.48, and I enclose you draft on New York for $500. Remember

[1] Earlier in the year Major General David Hunter, then commander of the Department of the South, issued an order freeing the slaves in South Carolina, Georgia, and Florida. Hunter was overruled by Lincoln, who insisted that military emancipation was his responsibility.

that is even better than currency, so do not allow any discount on it. I have also sent to Uncle Thomas the $50 I borrowed of him. I want you to pay Dr. Robison the $50 I borrowed of him and make just as large a payment on the notes I gave Harry as you can consistently with your first chores and your own wants. I set no limit but your own judgment in regard to the extent of your purchases for housekeeping.

Make a special effort with Wall[ace] Ford and Esquire Udall to get the amount they owe me for soliciting, and use it to take up the Harry note. Write me fully about your management of this matter.

I have felt very lonely without you since the Wednesday morning when I was so sad to leave you and so glad to love you. I am still both, and your letters will be read and kissed in lieu of your dear self. Bless and kiss the little darling for me. God bless you and her, prays ever your own

James. . . .

Willard's Hotel, Washington<br>Monday, September 22, 1862

*My Dear Harry:*

I think I have reached as peculiar a phase of my life as any I have yet met. I have come here in obedience to an order from the Secretary of War. He tells me to take a few days to reflect and as soon as I determine where I want to go, let him know and he will send me as soon as wherever I wish if it is in his power. At the same time says he doubts if he shall be able to get me any where, where West Point will not get its hands on me and do with me as it pleases.

Since my visit with him I have been looking around as much as my weak health and a sprained ankle would let me. And I am as far from seeing a satisfactory way forward, and even farther than in the beginning. I find that General Sigel is under a quasi ban of West Point, and a place among his Dutchmen would neither be personally desirable nor would it promise very much for the future.

I went this morning to see General Banks,[2] whom I consider one of our first generals. He was very kind and wanted me with him, but is now in a tempor[ar]y command and does not know what his own future is to be. In short, it is quite impossible to see any way to usefulness or distinction that does not go down before West Point first. I feel more gloomy at the prospects of the way viewed from here than from any other stand-point.

Judicial blindness seems to have seized the President and most of his cabinet. He is almost a child in the hand[s] of his generals. Indeed he recently told a delegation from Chicago that he could not grant a cer-

[2] Major General Nathaniel P. Banks was then in charge of the defenses of Washington.

tain request of theirs, which [he] regarded perfectly proper to be granted, unless General Halleck concurred. But he would give them a letter to the General introducing them and their business. What shameful humiliation when the President becomes a petitioner before one of his subordinates.

My regret at losing the command of the Cumberland Gap forces in consequence of my sickness is very poignant indeed. The more I look the whole matter in the face the more I am inclined to believe that it will be my fate to be put again under some West Pointer and command only a brigade. It will not be so if Stanton can help it, but I doubt if he can prevail against the odds of the close corporation. I would take my leisure hours in going about the public buildings and seeing the sights, but I am quite disinclined to go and alone. I want to enjoy these things with some friend. I wish you were here with me. Indeed I am quite foolishly and childishly lonesome, and this feeling is not a little enhanced by my being unwell. I am more disgusted at McClellan's late operation of lying still a day and two nights after the great battle, and letting the rebels cross the river and get safely away before he began the pursuit or renewed the attack. It confirms my opinion of his utter want of audacity and vigor. There is great bitterness here in regard to him. If this nation dies, it will die in consequence of the timidity of its rulers.

I had a long interview with John Hutchins[3] in which he endeavored to convince me; 1st, that my election to Congress would be void if I held my commission at the time of the election; 2nd, even if the election should be valid I would forfeit my right to the seat if I did not resign by the fourth of March. I am looking into the matter and am sure his first position is incorrect, and I think the second is. At any rate there is a large number of officers in the same boat and we will try to see that no harm befalls the whole crew.

Do write to me. Direct here. I think I shall go to see Sigel and Cox before I choose a field.

*Ever yours,*
James

Willard's Hotel, Washington
September 25, 1862

*Dear Brother Austin:*

. . . . I reached here last Friday without being much exhausted. I soon saw the Secretary of War and the President. They told me to rest a few days and meantime if there were any field that I would prefer, they would give it to me if they could. I have been pretty quiet and

---

[3] Member of the U.S. House of Representatives whom Garfield had just defeated for the Republican nomination as congressman from Ohio's Nineteenth District.

have been steadily improving. I am now nearly well again, and by the time a place is ready for me, I shall be ready for it.

They are now talking of putting me in command of Florida. I shall know in a few days. If I go to Florida it will be to open the way for taking 20,000 northern men there to settle upon the confiscated lands of the rebels. In this way the Government proposes to make the seceded states loyal by giving them a loyal population.

I am rejoiced at the President's proclamation. It give[s] us light in the midst of the darkness and shows us the beginning of the end. The people will hail it with great joy.

My visit home was an exceedingly pleasant one and I hope it was so to my friends. I look back with peculiar pleasure to my stay in Howland for a large share of the pleasures. I am indebted to you and Minerva and Lottie. I hope it was as pleasant to her (Lottie) as it was to Mrs. Garfield and myself. If I return I shall surely visit there again.

I had a visit with John Hutchins here a few days ago. He was very friendly and we had a very comfortable time. He thought there was some doubt about my election being valid if I s[t]ill held my commission at the time of the election. I differed with him and we looked into the law. He finally gave up that point but thought I would have to resign on the 4th of March. I have looked into the matter further and talked with Governor Chase and General Banks. They agree with me that I will not need to resign till the Congress meets. I want you to tell me if there is any agitation of the question in the district. Don't forget to send me any accounts there may be against me.

Love to Minerva and Lottie. Would they write too? Direct as per heading of this letter.

*Very truly your brother,*
J. A. Garfield

Washington
September 26, 1862

*My Dear Harry:*

Your kind letter of the 24th is received this evening. I have not had a word from home till tonight, and now I have two letters from Crete and this from you. In my last to Almeda I spoke of the Florida expedition. It is still on the tapis, and I have been busy for two days in studying the geography of the State and planning a campaign and making estimates of what will be necessary for making it a military and political success. There are many features of the project that please me, though on the who[le] I believe I would rather command a division in the Grand Army if McClellan were not at its head.

I am very glad to read your letter. There is such a strong cheerful healthy tone in all you write. I am alone, slightly homesick, not feeling as if I amount to much, and I will gossip a little to you and then go to bed. I have been so much busied with my own destiny in a military way that I have not done a great deal of visiting. Professor [Jehu] Brainard is here and I have visited with him a good deal. We went through the Patent Office several times and also visited the Smithsonian. I had a long visit with General McDowell who regards himself a victim of McClellan's jealousy.[4] He is a very frank honest man I think. Cassius Clay[5] is here and is jubilant over the proclamation. Indeed all the men who are worth talking to are in favor of it now that it has been promulgated. Mr. Lincoln did it himself and when he called the cabinet together to read it told them he did not ask their opinion about publishing it, only he would be glad of any suggestions in reference to its language and special points. Only two members (Chase and Stanton) were really in favor of it.[6] Chase sent for me yesterday to ride out with him to see General Hooker, who is considered one of our best generals.[7] You know he was wounded in the foot on the 17th *inst.* He says McClellan never can be a soldier, has no

[4] Accused of blame for the Union defeat in the Second Battle of Bull Run, Major General Irvin McDowell asked to be and was relieved of his command. When he met Garfield he was in Washington awaiting action on his request for a court of inquiry. Bad feeling between him and McClellan dated back to the spring of 1862. McDowell then commanded a corps in McClellan's Army of the Potomac. When McClellan began moving the army by water to the Peninsula for an attack on Richmond, he intended to take McDowell's corps with him. This was all changed when Lincoln, fearing that Washington was being left without adequate protection, sent McDowell southward by land with orders to provide at all times for the safety of the Capital. McClellan, angered by having to give up over 30,000 men, blamed McDowell for disrupting his plans. McDowell advanced to Fredericksburg and was given command of the newly created Department of the Rappahannock. As McClellan went up the Peninsula and closed on Richmond, calling along the way for more and more men, Lincoln decided to send McDowell to him. On the eve of the latter's departure, however, news of Major General Thomas J. (Stonewall) Jackson's victory at Front Royal in the Shenandoah Valley reached the White House. Lincoln, believing Jackson could be isolated and destroyed, ordered McDowell into the Valley to help do the job. This, of course, infuriated McClellan. Again he blamed McDowell, whom he believed to be pulling strings to retain a separate command for himself. McDowell failed to trap Jackson in the Valley and likewise failed to help McClellan in front of Richmond. He was then assigned to Pope's Army of Virginia and commanded a corps in the Second Battle of Bull Run. McDowell was convinced that the hostile criticism of his conduct in that battle came largely from McClellan and his friends, and that McClellan was jealous of him.

[5] Kentucky abolitionist who had recently returned from Russia, where he had served as the U.S. minister. Soon after his return he was appointed a major general, but he refused to fight until the abolition of slavery became a war aim.

[6] When on July 22 Lincoln informed his Cabinet of his intention to issue an emancipation proclamation, Stanton and Attorney General Edward Bates were the only members to give the President enthusiastic support. Chase soon joined them, preferring Lincoln's program to no program.

[7] Major General Joseph Hooker was wounded while leading a corps at Antietam. In January, 1863, he was given command of the Army of the Potomac, but he was relieved late in June after his defeat at Chancellorsville and his failure to stop General Robert E. Lee's second invasion of the North. Though a failure as an army leader, Hooker performed ably and rendered valuable service as a division and corps commander.

dash, no boldness in him, and is the curse of our army. It is a disgraceful thing that an administration whose every member (Halleck too) has no confidence in a general and [can] yet have not enough spunk to turn him out.

Chase said to me: "If I had been the President I would have arrested McClellan for his failure to support Pope and ordered him tried, and if he had been convicted of what I believe him to be guilty of, I would have had him shot!" Among his other very sensible sayings was the following, which you will recognize as full of wisdom!!! He said to me, "Garfield, I would rather have you for Secretary of War than any other man I know." He then proceeded to give me an analysis of the War Department. Spreading out his fore and middle finger so as to form a letter "V", he said, "There (end of forefinger) is Stanton, full of propulsive energy, strong and sincere, but impatient of delay and restraint, and feeling at times completely disheartened by the perplexities of his position; hence fitful and lacks balanced steadiness. There (end of middle finger) is Halleck, with immense brain, clear, powerful intellect, full knowledge of his work but as cold as a stone, cares not one penny for the work only as a professional performance, has no more heart about it than the shoemaker who pegs away at a boot. Here (junction of knuckles of fore and middle fingers) is the President, with a great noble heart, most anxious to do his duty, but don't know how and has not the power and independence to shake of[f] the shackles of West Point. If Lincoln's heart, Halleck's head and Stanton's executive energy could be united, it would make a magnificent Secretary of War or President"—alias me!!!

Chatted half an hour today with Secretary [of Navy Gideon] Welles who looks very venerable and seems as imperturbable as a sleeping Rip Van Winkle. Took tea this evening with Eli Thayer[8] and Governor Stanly of North Carolina.[9] The latter is a nice *little* man, would make a good, discreet, careful clerk *"et ne plus ultra* [and nothing more]." The Governor came in from Altoona today. I can see no other reason for their meeting than to cut a flam. Tod is here today with Hoffman[10] hung to his tail, or rather it is *Asinus cum cauda* [An ass with its tail]. Hoffman's wife has a much more sensible taste, if the Warren people have truly informed me. Old General Wadsworth[11] is here (lately

---

[8] Massachusetts educator and congressman who advocated military colonization of Florida. The proposed expedition was never undertaken.

[9] Edward Stanly, lawyer and congressman, had been appointed Military Governor of North Carolina in May, 1862. It was hoped that he could recapture the loyalty of the state's population, but his mission was a failure from the beginning and ended with his resignation in January, 1863.

[10] Benjamin F. Hoffman, Governor Tod's private secretary. For many years before the war these two men had been partners in a law firm in Warren, Ohio.

[11] Brigadier General James Samuel Wadsworth, then in his fifty-fifth year, was unsuccessful as the Republican candidate for Governor of New York in 1862. After

nominated Governor of New York). He is a noble looking old fellow. I like Hooker to[o]. He has got a fighting blue eye. I have seen also Schurz,[12] Banks, Cadwalader,[13] Casey,[14] [and] White,[15] who with Tom Ford[16] and Trimble[17] of Ohio are under arrest for the Harpers Ferry infamy, *etc., etc.* I have met [Henry] Root, a college class mate who is a surgeon in the army, and I am told Harry Hopkins is Chaplain in the hospital.[18]

If I go to Florida and you don't have a school, you had better go along and make a tropical tour during the winter. I would be very glad to have you do so. Your views of my reputation are right and I don't expect much from the war, not more than what a Minie ball may give me. I hope Almeda will write to me. I have written her twice. I suppose I should if she never answered. Love to her and to all.

*Ever thine,*
James

Washington
September 27, 1862

*My Precious Crete:*

Your two dear letters of the 19th and 21st were received last evening. I had inquired every day at the Post Office but by some means

---

his political defeat he fought at Fredericksburg and Gettysburg, and was mortally wounded in the Battle of the Wilderness.

[12] Brigadier General Carl Schurz then commanded the Third Division, XI Corps, Army of the Potomac.

[13] Major General George Cadwalader, a member of the board to revise U.S. military laws and regulations, served on the military commission that investigated the surrender of Harpers Ferry to the Confederates on September 15, 1862.

[14] Major General Silas Casey had distinguished himself when his division received the initial Confederate attack in the Battle of Fair Oaks. From August, 1862, until the end of the war he commanded a division defending Washington, and he was a member of the Porter court-martial.

[15] Brigadier General Julius White had commanded a brigade in the force at Harpers Ferry which Colonel Dixon S. Miles had surrendered to Stonewall Jackson. The military commission appointed to investigate the affair praised White for able and courageous action.

[16] Colonel Thomas H. Ford of the Thirty-second Ohio had commanded the defense of Maryland Heights, a key position which he had abandoned to the enemy. The commission found Ford incompetent, censured him for surrendering his position without sufficient cause, and recommended his dismissal from the service. On November 8 he was cashiered.

[17] Colonel William H. Trimble of the Sixtieth Ohio had commanded a brigade at Harpers Ferry. The commission found nothing censurable about his conduct.

[18] Henry Hopkins, oldest son of Mark, was called Harry by family and friends. He graduated at Williams College in 1858 and was ordained a minister in the Congregational church in 1861. After serving for the duration of the war as a chaplain in the Union army, he held pastorates in Westfield, Massachusetts and in Kansas City, Missouri. He was President of Williams College, 1902-1908.

they had either been delayed on the way or covered up in the mass of matter, not having been directed to my hotel here. I had become very lonely without a letter from you, but do not, my darling, think for one moment that I doubted you or supposed you had not written. I have no words to tell you how precious these two letters are to me. It is indeed a "baptism into a new life" which our souls have received and which, after so many years of hoping and despairing, has at last appeared in the fulness of its glory. I bless our Good All Father who has brought us through it all and I trust our love will be all the more perfect, being made so through suffering.

You write as you never wrote to me before, and my pen is in the hand of my heart as it has not been for years. It is a joy to me to sit down and let my heart write itself out to you, and yet I tremble in the very fulness of my joy. It is not, I trust, the trembling of doubt or fear but of joy, the trembling that one feels when the danger is past and the light of hope, peace and safety beams gladly in upon him. Bless your dear true heart for the sweet words you have written to me.

My heart followed you back to Uncle's and shared the loneliness with you. But you, my dear, have our blessed little one to be with you, and I have only the great world. You can fondle and kiss your companion and be kissed in return. Mine is a great unlovely, unloving, unkissing comrade to be frowned and whipped into respect even.

For the last three days I have been busy in the study of Florida, its geography and topography, and in planning a campaign there. It is still unsettled where I am to go. I think [it] will be Florida or South Carolina. If they determine to retake Charleston I shall choose the latter. If not, the former. I somewhat dislike to be under General Mitchel, but I am resolved not to be faultfinding. The President and War Department has trouble enough without my adding to it, and they are kind to me. I should have written to you oftener, but I have been hoping every day to hear from you and waiting so as to have the pleasure of acknowledging your letter. I sent you $500 on the 20th which I hope has been received before now.

I see by the papers that Spalding[19] is nominated. I am sorry, though I suppose he is a good man.

Give my love to all our folks. I am getting better and stronger every day. I have scarcely had a symptom of diarrhea since I left home. I am sorry I did not bring the diarrhea medicine. Kiss Trot a score of times and receive my love. Ever, anew and forever, your own James.

[19] Rufus P. Spalding, a Cleveland lawyer and congressman; member of the Ohio House of Representatives, 1839-1852; Associate Justice of the Ohio Supreme Court, 1849-1852; a War Democrat and member of the U.S. House of Representatives, 1863-1869.

Evening
September 27, 1862

*Dearest Wife:*

I add an appendix to acknowledge the receipt of your dear letter of the 25th. It makes me very glad to read such true dear words from you. I beg of you, give me as much of your time as you can. It is a great blessing to be so near that your letters can reach me the second day after they are mailed.

Mr. Chase and his daughter Kate have insisted that I shall stay with them while I remain in Washington, and so I came here this evening with all my luggage. I have a delightful room and am much better pleased than at the Willard's. You may still direct my letters there, however, and I will get them more certainly and speedily than I should if they went to the General Post Office.

I am rejoiced that General Cox has been doing so well. It is now due to him to be made a major general, and I have been doing what I can with the heads of the Department to effect it. If they respect seniority of commission they cannot resist his claims, for his commission dates May, 1862,[20] and many who were made brigadiers since then have been promoted. I have received two letters from him. He is well, and has grown very much in the esteem of his men since the late battles.

The President's proclamation gives great satisfaction among all strong vigorous men. It can only have an adverse effect in Kentucky and Tennessee, and that, whatever it may be, is a thousand times overbalanced by the great moral force and significance which the measure will add to the war. The President's heart is right; God grant he may have the strength to stand up to his convictions and carry them out to the full.

I wrote a gossiping letter to Harry last night which I presume you will see before this reaches you. I am getting very anxious about my good Captain Swaim[21] and the rest of my staff, and particularly about my horses. They have all arrived safe in Louisville, and I hope soon to be able to order them forward here. I have met Root, a college classmate, and hear that Gilfillan,[22] another classmate, is a clerk in the Treasury Department. If so, I shall find him. I am glad you are pleased

[20] Cox was appointed a brigadier general in May, 1861. He was promoted to major general in October, 1862, but was reduced to his former rank in April, 1863, because the number of major generals authorized by law had been exceeded.

[21] David G. Swaim became an intimate friend of Garfield. A man of some financial means, Swaim loaned most of the money Garfield used to build a house in Washington after the war. In 1880 he played a major role in managing Garfield's presidential campaign. Early in 1881 President Rutherford B. Hayes, to please Garfield, appointed Swaim Judge Advocate General.

[22] James Gilfillan graduated at Williams College with Garfield and began his career in the office of the U.S. Treasurer as a clerk. He was Treasurer of the U.S., 1877-1883.

with the prospect of keeping house. Would that I could be with you to help you enjoy the reality. You had better close an arrangement with Brown soon, lest he may see that you are preparing for the work, and will keep up his price.[23]

Do write me often and long. Love again to Trot and yourself. Ever, ever your

James

Washington
October 3, 1862

*Dearest Crete:*

Your dear letter of the 29th was received yesterday. I cannot tell you how full of gratitude is my heart that your soul goes out so strongly toward me. It is so new and so delicious a joy to know that at last I have found the fountain in what I had supposed to be desert. Indeed it has sprung up joyously in the desert of my life.

But dearest, you must not be so desponding in reference to myself. I have felt, it is true, and still feel great impatience at being kept here in suspense, like Coleridge's *Ancient Mariner:*

> "Day after day, day after day
> We stuck, nor life nor motion
> As idle as a painted ship
> Upon a painted ocean."

While it annoys me very much to be kept waiting so, and particularly to keep my staff waiting so impatiently at Louisville for orders from me, I am still assured that it is meant as no lack of confidence in me, but rather the contrary, for they are endeavoring to get me an independent command. Again I have not been till very lately able to take the field. It is two weeks this morning since I arrived here and it has dragged very heavily by I assure you. But the personal discomfort of being kept here and the positive loss of reputation I shall suffer if I do not do something soon are all overborne by my painful and anxious interest in the welfare of the country. Men do not usually grieve for national calamities as for smaller specific sorrows. But when I see what is unfolding here every day of the weak timid government, on the one hand, and the deep plottings of the old Breckinridge wing

[23] In October, Garfield and his wife rented, for $100 a year, a house in Hiram owned by a Mr. Brown. During the winter they bought it. In the following summer, while Garfield was in the field, they remodeled and enlarged it. As the letters of the period show, Mrs. Garfield oversaw the work and kept her husband informed as to its progress. He in turn sent back advice, sometimes in the form of specific instructions. The Garfields owned the house until 1872, when they sold it to Hinsdale. Known now as the Garfield-Hinsdale house, the building still stands.

of the Democratic party in connection with General McClellan, when I see the criminal vacillation that has marked the course of the Government in its desire to remove him from command, and its cowardly drawing back at the very important moment when hesitation was surrender, I am filled with most anxious forebodings.

Only think of it. McClellan lay still on the field of Antietam one day and two nights and let the rebels cross the Potomac in perfect safety, when he could have destroyed them. He has been reinforced until he must now have near 140,000 men.[24] He now refuses to cross the Potomac into Virginia till the river is permanently swelled by rains so that the rebels can't get around behind him into Maryland, at which time of course the roads will be bad and the winter near. To complete the disgracefulness of this sad picture he has sent to Washington for an immense supply of intrenching tools and for all the topographical engineers that can be spared from the various departments of the Government.

You have probably seen the account of the dismissal of Major Key[25] from the army by the President. He was a brother of Key our Ohio Senator and on Halleck's staff. His crime was that on being asked why McClellan did not follow the rebels after Antietam, he answered: "It is not the plan to whip the rebels. They are to be kept from invading the North, and the two armies are to be kept in the field till both sections of the country are exhausted and the armies and the Democracy will compromise the matter." From all I can see, I am almost convinced that McClellan is not misrepresented in that statement. The President has gone out to see General McClellan and there [is] great commotion in the official circles here. No progress can be made at any other enterprise till that is settled.

Four days ago Buell was suspended from command, the papers all made out; but Crittenden and a few more half and half patriots from Kentucky protested and the Government backed down at once and restored him.[26]

[24] On September 30 McClellan reported he had 173,745 present for duty.

[25] Major John J. Key was dismissed from the service for stating that after Antietam the game was not to capture the Confederate army; rather, it was to prolong the war until both sides were exhausted. Then the country could be reunited and slavery preserved.

[26] Late in September, during Bragg's invasion of Kentucky, Stanton persuaded Lincoln to dismiss Buell and appoint Thomas commander of the Army of the Ohio. An aide was sent west with the order, but he was not to deliver it if he found Buell ready to fight or victorious in battle. Halleck meanwhile convinced Lincoln to retain Buell and wired the aide to withhold the order until further notice (September 27). The message arrived too late. Buell promptly turned his command over to Thomas, who, not wanting it, telegraphed to Halleck that Buell was ready to advance and should be retained. On September 29, Halleck, on the authority of the President, suspended the order. That morning four Kentucky politicians— Senator Garret Davis and Congressmen John T. Crittenden, Robert Mallory, and George W. Dunlap—had telegraphed to Lincoln urging him not to remove

I shall spend the day with General McDowell, who will show me the history of the Virginia campaign. I believe he has been greatly wronged. The President and Cabinet know he is a true man but dare not come out before the people and vindicate him. Do write to me. I may be here weeks, but rather than stay much longer I will take command of a brigade, regiment, or company and guard duty. I am sick and tired of such terrible weakness. I am quite well except a little diar[r]hea yesterday. I found the vial of diar[r]hea medicine in the box in my trunk. Kiss the dear little one for me. She is 27 months old today.

*Ever your own*
James

Washington
Sunday Evening
October 5, 1862

*My Dear Harry:*
At four this evening I returned from Sigel's headquarters and found yours of the 1st *inst.* awaiting at Willard's. I had all the way back been anticipating a letter from you, and its perusal gave me great pleasure. *You are very healthy;* and I begin to agree with Carlyle that to say *that* of a man is about as high an eulogy as can be pronounced upon him. You must continue to write to me often and long. Being the one that is away from home, I am in much greater need of letters than you are, and so I pray you not to forget me in my necessity. Just now, however, while being tortured by the delay and inaction which are thrust upon me unwillingly, I am, in the character of lounger and gazer enabled in part to repay you for your letters, by telling you what I see and hear. Since my last letter I have become a temporary member of Mr. Chase's family, as you probably know from my last letter to Almeda, an answer to which I await.

On Friday last Miss Kate Chase and I took their carriage and pompous liveried driver, and, allowing him to change his tall plug for a comfortable slouch, we set out for General Sigel's headquarters at Fairfax Court House. We had already telegraphed to General Schurz whose guests we were to be. Miss Chase had prepared two large baskets of provisions, partly for a present to the General and partly for our use if we should go on to the battle field.

In the beginning of our journey we had a fine opportunity to get the whole outline of Washington and its environs. The city is surrounded by a nearly complete circle of hills not unlike those at

---

Buell. It appears, however, that in making his decision Lincoln acted largely on the advice of Halleck.

Williamstown in several appearances, though much smaller and farther away from the town. In crossing over into Virginia there are three famous bridges—the Long, the Aqueduct, and the Chain Bridge —the last being furthest up stream, and around which there have been many skirmishes during the past year. The great [Chesapeake and Ohio] Canal which comes in here from the west, formerly crossed the Potomac and made its southern and eastern terminus at Alexandria. The water has been let off and it is now used as a bridge from Georgetown to Virginia. Hence its name [Aqueduct Bridge]. The heights around Washington are all crowned with formidable fortifications, mostly heavy earth works and are called Forts. We passed through Georgetown and over the Aqueduct Bridge and went via Arlington Heights, the home of Lee the rebel General in Chief.[27] He owns a large tract of land there and has a quaint old pillared residence on it with a touch of the Norman Castle style about it. He married a Custis, one of the Washington family. From there we went by Bailey's Cross-Roads to Fairfax Court House about 18 miles through a country completely devastated, it having been in turn held by both armies several times during the last eighteen months. Fairfax is an old town built mainly of stone and brick, and seems to be nearly or quite one century old.

Here we found General Schurz and his wife stopping in a fine residence with a secession family. Mrs. Schurz and their two little children have been staying there several days. She is a very fine lady and is much more accomplished than any other German woman I have seen. She has a fine form and that low musical voice which is so characteristic of the higher culture and genial good heartedness of the Germans. After a ride among the camps we accepted an invitation to take tea with General Sigel. He is a very small man, but lithe and well made.

Indeed, of the four German generals we saw there, no one of them would equal you in weight, and none but Schurz in height. Our people hardly saw a German of any talent till the revolution of 1849 threw a crowd of noble fellows upon our shores. Nearly all these have the same type of form and physique. They are of a small, well-knit frame, their heads and faces are inverted triangles of which the chin is the apex. This gives them great breadth of brain. The four I mention were Sigel, Schurz, Steinwehr, and Stahel.[28] After supper we had most splendid music from Schurz and Sigel on the piano. They are both very fine performers, among the very best I ever

[27] General Robert E. Lee, commander of the Army of Northern Virginia, was not appointed General in Chief of the Confederate armies until February 6, 1865.
[28] In the Army of Virginia, Sigel commanded the I Corps, in which Schurz and Brigadier Generals Adolph von Steinwehr and Julius Stahel commanded divisions. In September, shortly before Garfield's visit, Sigel's corps was designated the XI Corps in the Army of the Potomac.

heard. Several members of their staffs were there and sang their old Father Land songs to the music. Mrs. Schurz's fine voice added, made music rarely equalled by our best artists. Schurz told me he could form a choir from his 2,000 men, of 150 artists, men who at home even were regarded as far above ordinary musicians. It is wholly impossible for me to describe the tremendous enthusiasm of these noble fellows. Full of genius, full of the fire of their own revolution, and inspired anew by the spirit of American Liberty, and just now by the proclamation which gives Liberty a real meaning. They are really miracles of power. I am reminded of Koerner and his *Wilde Jägers* in 1813.[29] There are several young German noblemen who came over on purpose to take part in this war and are now on the staff of General Sigel or some of the four generals.

I formed the acquaintance of two brothers, the barons von Koenig[30] —one 21, the other 23. They are of an old family and their ancestral castles have been in the family over 500 years. They are the younger sons and seek glory in arms. They have been through the fights in Pope's late campaign in Virginia. The youngest, Robert, in the battle on the Shenandoah [Rappahannock] saw the 61st Ohio Infantry broken and retreating; and dashing forward [he] caught up the regimental banner and riding along the front of the line, told them to remember Ohio and their friends at home (Ohio was only a name to him), and calling upon them for three cheers for the Union, led them back again in three splendid charges, and with them pierced far into the masses of the rebels with the bayonet. Since that time, the 61st Ohio never see him without cheering him most enthusiastically. He speaks English very brokenly but he is a very finished scholar and gentleman.

The older brother is a perfect, jolly, devil-may-care sort of fellow who broke away from home when he was fourteen and became a sailor, and in a few years a lieutenant in the British navy. When in South America he took part in the late war there, was five times wounded, and on the breaking out of the rebellion, when his younger brother came over, went in with him. I should have said above that the younger brother was at Solferino and Magenta when [where] he won scars and promotion in the Austrian army. Indeed he got leave of absence from his regiment to come here and see the war. The chief reason for their going in on our side is that they hate Negro slavery.

[29] Karl Theodor Körner's poetic tribute to the wild chase and defeat of Napoleon's troops by the Lützow Free Corps in which Körner himself fought (1813). His "Battle Prayer," mentioned later by Garfield, is a short poem in which Körner glorifies God and invokes His aid in the struggle for freedom.

[30] Robert and Paul von Koenig were in the Sixty-eighth New York. Robert resigned from the service as a captain on December 24, 1862. His elder brother Paul, also a captain, served temporarily on the staff of Schurz; later he became an aide to Brigadier General William W. Averell and was killed at White Sulphur Springs, West Virginia, in August, 1863.

The elder brother, who came out with us this afternoon, had three horses shot under him at the last Battle of Bull's Run. These facts I get from General Schurz, so that I know they are correct. I give them as illustrative of the German character. Paul von Koenig, the elder, has taken quite a fancy to me and wants to be on my staff if I go to the West.

After a long evening filled with singing and playing, smoking, and wine interjected (tell Almeda that the *wine* refers principally to the Germans, except a little "domestic" Catawba, which refers to me, for both Sigel and Schurz smoked cigars in the midst of their most splendid playing) we retired; and late Sunday morning we, the gentlemen, took horses (General Schurz furnished me a fine one, and Baron Robert von Koenig loaned me his long riding boots and spurs), and Kate and Mrs. Schurz went in the carriage, and started to visit the Bull Run battle field. We reached Centerville, seven miles from Fairfax, where General Stahel is stationed with two brigades which form the advance force in Virginia, and he sent forward a squadron of cavalry to see that the country was clear and safe for us to go to the battle field.

We went on then across Bull Run to the limit of the late battle about five miles beyond Centerville, and General Schurz, who was in the engagement, gave us a fine description of the whole two days' work and the shameful and unnecessary retreat which followed. We saw hundreds of graves, or rather heaps of earth piled upon the bodies where they lay. Scores of heads, hands and feet were protruding, and so rapid had been the decomposition of 34 days that naked, eyeless skulls grinned at us as if the corpses had lifted their heads from their death beds to leer at us as we passed by. Shells and round shot lay scattered all over the field and broken muskets and dismantled gun carriages were very plenty. Hats, caps, coats, equipments, letters and all that lately belonged to life were scattered around.

I picked up a joint promissory note of $1,000, which would probably be valuable to the heirs of some poor skeleton. *"Your loving wife till death"* was the conclusion of a letter which lay near the bones of a skeleton arm which reached through the side of its grave, and had doubtless one day not long ago clasped the loving wife, but now the *"till death"* has opened for him the portal of the world where "there is neither marrying nor giving in marriage."

We followed the path where the fierce giants struggled and saw their battle tracks thick with graves. At last we stopped and took a glass of milk with the old Negro who lives on the eastern marge of the field on the bank of Bull Run (to be a sadly famous stream hereafter) and who saw both battles—of 1861 and 1862. All along the road from the Run to Centerville, and even far this side toward Fairfax, are wrecks of burned wagons and artillery carriages. Just as we were leaving the field a sunburned dragoon came up to me and reached out his hand, saying he was from Hiram and had sisters at school there this term. It was [Addison] Harrington, brother of E. N. Harrington. He belongs to the 6th Ohio Volunteer Cavalry.

When we reached Centerville I went to the camp of the regiment and found [Delos R.] Northway, now a 1st lieutenant [captain]. He spoke of cricket at Hiram and asked for Augustus! Presently [Lieutenant Elias] Shepherd of Newburgh, Captain [Norman A.] Barrett of Newton Falls, and quite a crowd of friends came around. An Irishman came pushing in and gave me his hard hand saying, "Jineral, and I've heard ye prache mony a time." Then came [Alcinas W.] Fenton—you remember him, good at cricket—from Bloomfield [Bristolville]. His fine muscles are all iron now, and his face bronze, but his heart and eyes were full of noble tenderness.

Then, Harry, I remembered the Eclectic play ground and blessed it, for you know with many of those young men it was the only, or the chief, tie that bound them to us, and now I saw in their eyes and felt in their hand-grasps that they loved me. I tell you it is a joy to fight beside such fellows, and when they told me they wished I would come and command them, I felt that we had infused some of the real Rugby spirit into our boys.

I wish you would talk to the boys there and make them feel that every noble fellow now in the field places them under new obligations to be men of muscle and nerve, clear heads and true hearts. Fenton talked with me, and I could see in his eyes the old bashfulness of the student before his teacher, the soldier before his officer, strangely mingled with the warmth of the friend with his friend, and I loved the dear fellow more than ever. He and Northway are both worthy of the good old school. Seven days before, they were in a skirmish where Orlando Ferry and the two Sager boys were taken prisoners, being surrounded by about 20 rebels. They are now in the hands of the enemy. I was very sorry to hear it, for they, especially Ferry, seemed to be much beloved by their comrades.[31] This morning I saw Jenisha[?] Ferry's husband who is a captain in that regiment.[32]

General Stahel gave us a fine lunch at his headquarters in Centerville, and then we left for Fairfax, passing through the formidable fortifactions [fortifications] which Beauregard built on the lofty ridge at Centerville, which overlooks five miles each way and is a very perfect line of defence. We saw also the thousands of log huts built and occupied by the rebels during the long "All quiet on the Potomac"

[31] On a reconnaissance from Centerville to Warrenton Junction, Virginia (September 25-28, 1862) troopers of the Sixth Ohio Cavalry Regiment encountered the enemy in force and in a sharp skirmish lost four wounded and six captured. If Ferry and "the two Sager boys" were among those taken prisoner, they were soon released. Orlando Ferry, a first lieutenant, and Jacob A. Sager, a corporal, served into 1865 Henry F. Sager, a bugler, was discharged at Washington on October 30, 1862.

[32] The only officer named Ferry on the roster of the Sixth Ohio is Orlando.

which McClellan gave them last winter. We reached Fairfax about dark and after a fine supper which we four prepared at General Schurz's headquarters, we went again and spent the evening with General Sigel, where the scenes of the previous night were repeated, only we felt more acquainted and they were more enthusiastic.

This morning the generals all turned out and took me around to visit the various regiments at Fairfax. We had a dashing gallop of five or six miles, and at noon Miss Kate and I took our leave, with many God bless ye's and *Leben sie wohl's,* and with our dashing little Koenig the elder to accompany us. (I should have told you that two days ago, he went with 12 mounted men to near Culpepper Court House, 45 miles inside the rebel lines, and took two prisoners within two miles of the village where were a thousand rebels.) We went round by Fort De Kalb, and crossing the Chain Bridge reache[d] Washington about 4 P.M.

Secretary Stanton, Colonel Hamilton of Texas,[33] and Governor Morton[34] were here this evening. The President returned from visiting McClellan last night. God grant he has come to the conclusion to remove him. Cox is to be made a major general and be sent to Western Virginia. I hear no word of my own future. I am resolved to be patient, "let come what come may."

I think we are passing through a most fearful time, and the most fearful aspect by far is the painful weakness and uncertainty of the administration. I have no words to tell you how sad my heart is over it all. With an army of the noblest men that ever took up arms, and yet nothing being done because of the jealously and selfishness of a few men. Scarcely a man that has any audacity in battle or any positive opinion about the policy of the Government has a chance to do anything.

There is that glorious Sigel stripped down to 7,000 men and placed under an inferior both in rank and ability. His men have been sent away to swell McClellan's already overgrown army, and McClellan refuses to cross the river and has sent here for entrenching tools, while Sigel could, if he had the force, strike a fatal blow upon the rebels' rear and flank. When he (Sigel) spoke to Halleck about it a few days ago he was personally insulted by him, and Halleck has also charged him with cowardice!! As well charge Marshal [Michel] Ney with cowardice.

If the Republic goes down in blood and ruin, let its obituary be written thus: "Died of West Point." Unless help comes soon, that ignominious death will stare us in the face. For myself, I say in all sincerity I have no wish to survive this republic, and if the end must

[33] Earlier in the year Andrew J. Hamilton, an avowed Unionist, fled Texas through Mexico to Washington, where, in November, 1862, he was appointed a brigadier general and Military Governor of Texas.

[34] Oliver Perry Morton, Governor of Indiana.

come I hope I may find a bed like Kearny's.[35] I am passing through a terrible ordeal of personal suffering over the whole matter. I cannot believe I shall be kept here much longer. The first day I came Stanton offered me Western Virginia, but I resolved I would not choose but let them put me where they pleased.

Oh the deep shame of Kentucky and the Army of the Ohio! The whole state, except Louisville, in rebel hands and almost the only real fighting general there righteously shot for being a brute.[36]

Stanton, Chase and Morton talk this evening like men whose hearts are sinking down in despairing shame at a condition which might be so easily remedied if only they were allowed to use bold and vigorous measures. To what a depth of disgraceful weakness are we reduced. Buell, removed one morning, for a year of unparalleled s[t]upidity and disaster, and reinstated the same evening at the request of a half dozen Kentuckians who misrepresent the army and the people of the whole West!!! If you imitate Jeremiah in his prophecies, I do in his lamentations. I visited Sigel in hope of throwing off the burden of my grief, which I believe has become quite unselfish and national. I returned with a double portion. But I still hope. Schurz says we must loose 50,000 more men and $200,000,000 more, and then we shall shake off West Point and finish the war. Must hecatombs still bleed, without avail! My heart utters Koerner's battle prayer tonight and asks God to lead us.

Should I go to Florida, I shall shall insist on your going with me. But if they will send me where there is only to be fighting, I will choose it rather though I believe the colonizing scheme to be the solution of the great problem. Harry dear, forgive me for this letter which is "drawn out to the crack of doom," and of midnight. Do write me soon. Give my tenderest love to Crete and Almeda, and think that no whit of my love for you is abated.

*Ever your brother,*
James

Washington
October 7, 1862

*My Precious Crete:*

Your dear letter of the 2nd reached me yesterday and made me very glad. Since my last letter I have had an excursion to Bull Run

[35] Major General Philip Kearny was killed while leading his troops at Chantilly on September 1, 1862.

[36] In the Galt House in Louisville, Major General William Nelson was shot to death by one of his subordinate commanders, Brigadier General Jefferson C. Davis of Indiana. The shooting followed an altercation which grew out of Nelson's recent reprimand of Davis. Governor Morton witnessed the shooting and intervened in behalf of Davis, who went unpunished and back to a command.

which I have already noticed in a long letter to Harry. You have doubtless seen that, and I will not repeat.

Yesterday I spent the early part of the day with General McDowell who is here preparing his official and private papers for the court of inquiry which he has asked from the Government. He has been in a position to know as fully and comprehensively the operations of the army in the East, and the conduct of the War Department, and the leading generals of the [Army of the] Potomac, as any man in the country; and while he has invited me to look over his papers so that an Ohio man may understand his case, and is grateful to me for doing so, I am glad of such an opportunity to learn from such a competent and reliable source the inner movements of this sadly famous series of campaigns. I have never believed the absurd stories about McDowell's being disloyal, or anything of that sort, but I was not prepared to find a man of such perfect, open, frank, manly sincerity. I believe he is the victim of jealousy, envy, and most marvellous bad luck—luck that came exceedingly near being splendid success, but failing of that turned sadly the other way. I shall have two or three more sittings with him and go over his Shenandoah campaign, which will illustrate his relations to McClellan and to the administration.

Last night General Cox and staff arrived and I was with him till a late hour. He has been made a major general and is ordered to Western Virginia; he starts today. I shall see him again after breakfast and spend all the time I can with him till he leaves. I rejoice at his good fortune, which has justly come to him after so long a time. He did finely at the battles of South Mountain and Antietam. He is looking very well indeed. I did what I could for his promotion. It is a step toward the vindication of merit vs. West Point. He is sorry to be sent away from the Grand army, but I think it will be better for him in the long run. He is so well acquainted with that country he will know how and where to strike. The Cumberland Gap boys are to be sent up the Kanawha with him. He has also got permission to take his old Kanawha division back to Western Virginia with him. I was very glad to see him. We had not me[t] for a year and a half. You must write to Mrs Cox and give her the substance of what I say. Present her my congratulations on Dolson's promotion and tell her that none of his friends are more rejoiced than I. His staff— [Gustavus M.] Bascom, [Richard B.] Treat, [Enoch P.] Fitch and [William W.] Holmes—are with him.

I do not yet hear anything in reference to myself. You can understand without my saying how keenly I feel this delay and how it makes me feel that I am not doing the service any good. But I have resolved that I will bear patiently and uncomplainingly whatever fortune awaits me. I want to correct an impression of yours—viz, that my being called here had anything whatever to do with Dr.

Robison's visit.[37] Mr. Chase says that a large command was open to me here in Virginia, but my sickness delaying me, when I came the opportunity had passed. Hence the apparent causelessness of calling me. This being so, I do not think that any but the kindest and best feelings called me here, and I will not repine at unforeseen accidents such as my sickness, though you can hardly imagine how irksome is this delay to me. At almost any other time such an opportunity to see would be welcome. But do not be sad. All will yet come out right. Thayer is still at work at his Florida plan and considers me a part of it.

With kisses and love to Trot (and I hope the little darling can understand them) and yourself, I am lovingly your own

James

I have found the diarrhea [medicine?] and also occasions to use it. I hope Dr. Briscoe will make out medicines for me soon. I have written to him. I can hardly advise you about Brown's house, but I hope you will not be obliged to pay much yourself for permanent repairs. Anything that makes the house permanently better he should pay at least a large part of. I hope you will be able to be settled soon, and pleasantly. Do write me very often. Your letters have all their new dreams and love,

James

Washington
October 8, 1862

*Dearest Crete:*

Your note of October 4th stating Mr. Brown's proposition and asking my opinion is just received. I have only time to write a word in answer, as I am about going by appointment to me[e]t Mr. Giddings[38] who is now in the city and has sent for me. Accept his proposition without hesitation. If he will let you have the house, after it is repaired according to your wishes, for $100, it will probably be as well as you can expect to do. Let it be understood in the bargain, if you can do so, that you are to have the house the next year also at the same rate, if he rents it. I think he ought to put it in a good state of repair for $100.

I have no news to write in regard to my own future. The Florida scheme is maturing but the troops are not at hand for the expedition.

[37] "I don't wish to say anything unkind," Garfield's wife had written him on September 28, "but I feel a little as though your call to Washington was but playing out one of Doc. Robison's big farces."

[38] Joshua R. Giddings, Ohio abolitionist and member of the U.S. House of Representatives, 1838-1859; Consul General to Canada, 1861 to his death in 1864.

General Halleck has got to be consulted. My heart burns with indignation when I see these beautiful autumn days pass and McClellan's army idle. In a few weeks more the rains will be upon us and the campaign will be ended. The rebels are unmolestedly moving back toward Richmond. Shame! if not treason.

Write me soon. Don't call this a letter. Love and kisses to you and Trot from your loving

James

Washington<br>October 8, 1862

*My Dear Harry:*

Your note of the 3rd *inst.* inclosing a letter from Mr. Suliot[39] was received last evening. I have just written a letter to him in answer, and here I will say that if any opening offers I hope you will give him a chance in the Eclectic. I said nothing in the letter to him which will in any way embarrass you. Indeed, I told him you were at present supplied and there was no opening.

But I have had a full examination of his credentials and a very complete history of his mental and moral character, and it was a settled purpose with me to get him into the school. I think he would be of great service. If you should go to Florida, could he not be taken in tempor[ar]ily at least?

I have nothing new since I wrote to Almeda yesterday except the accumulating evidence [that] the Army of the Potomac will do no more this season. Thayer has not yet been appointed. The only lack is a sufficient military force.

I saw *Othello* rendered very well last night by Davenport.[40] I am becoming a living monument of patient impatience, stolid unrest. I am getting a little shattered in my opinions of Sigel and Schurz.

*Ever and ever yours,*<br>James

Washington<br>October 12, 1862

*My Dearest Crete:*

Yours of the 9th came this morning. I hope you will not be sad when my letters are delayed. I have written as often as twice a week I

[39] T. E. Suliot of Mogadore, Ohio, taught at the Eclectic during the winter of 1862-1863.

[40] Boston-born Edward Loomis Davenport, internationally famous actor, was a favorite of theater audiences here and in England, where he was called the American tragedian for his performances in Shakespearean roles. Many believed his most outstanding accomplishment was his portrayal of Othello.

think, though perhaps the week of my visit to Sigel and Bull Run, I wrote but one. I assure you I am very joyful in the receipt of your letters, and I hope you will be constant in writing to me as frequently as you have. In this new life we have fallen upon, let us take large measures of hope and joy into our hearts and still cultivate that charity and patience which in the past has been our salvation. In my sad impatience and waiting here I need the presence of your love, and your letters are longed for more than they have ever been before.

I have spent my time lately in getting deeper views of men and movements, and taking observations on current events. I hope you will not be shocked at receiving such a bundle of manuscript as this letter envelope contains, but I thought you and our circle there would be glad to see some of the late movements of the army from an interior view. You will be careful that the manuscript does not get into the hands of any one who will make it public, for the interviews were private and unofficial.[41]

Your views of my friendships are just and I thank you for your consideration and kind admonition.[42] I am glad to feel that your love for me does not make you blind to my dangers nor my faults. Always tell me anything you see in me that you would have otherwise. I regret that I have become yoked to Dr. Robison, but I do not feel that I am altogether responsible for it; nor can I help Jones's saying what he pleases about Middle Creek. *He* was in the battle, and there is not an obliviousness of that fact in his own mind when he recounts and praises the work.[43]

The prospect[s] for immediate work are no better now than when I first came here; only the delay is more accumulated and hence a greater pressure is brought to bear upon the government to do something than was then. You can hardly imagine how irksome and hateful

[41] Reference is to a manuscript written by Garfield after he had had two interviews with McDowell. Because of its relevance to Garfield's service as a member of the court-martial for the trial of Fitz John Porter, the manuscript is reproduced with an introduction in Appendix A. See also Garfield's letter to his wife, October 31, 1862.

[42] The "kind admonition" had come in a letter of October 8 in which Mrs. Garfield again voiced her displeasure over the "intimacy" between Garfield and Robison. My desire, she wrote, is "that you wrap yourself in a little more *reserve* in the new circles to which you are now being introduced. Be a little more select in your choice of companions, and admit no one to *intimacy* who is not at least your equal. Now Jamie I do not think that selfish. You have done your reputation great injustice by allowing such a man as Dr. Robison to the familiarity which gives his great gross selfish nature the least reason to feel that you regarded him as an intimate friend. I do very much desire that you get no more such undesirable individuals tacked on to your skirts."

[43] In her letter of October 8 Garfield's wife had written that her cousin Mary Curtiss "says the extravagant stories that Harry Jones told concerning you and your expedition up the Big Sandy did you far more harm than good. She laughs and says tell you for her that she had not learned before what an extraordinary prodigy you were."

this delay is to me. Under almost any other circumstances, my stay here would be very pleasant. I see a large number of leading men almost every day. Last Thursday Mr. Chase had three lady relatives here from New York, and Kate being too busy, I was requested to take them out to see the sights.

We took the carriage and went across the Potomac to Arlington Heights, thence to Alexandria, thence to Fairfax Seminary, back to Alexandria, drove the carriage on board a steamer and came back to Washington by water. General Lee's house at Arlington Heights was built by George Washington Custis whose daughter Lee married. It is a quaint old building, built in the castle style, and the walls of the main hall are ornamented with the skull and antlers of stags and paintings of the chase, also several battle pictures of the Revolution. It is now the headquarters of General Heintzelman.[44] In Alexandria we saw the Marshall Home where Ellsworth was shot and visited the fort which was named after him.[45] There is an army of wounded and sick men in Washington and vicinity. Of wounded alone there are over 16,000 in the hospitals here. What a multitude of maimed old men will the next generation see! The Fairfax Seminary which was once alive with female beauty is now the center of sad scenes. There are 1,800 sick men there in the building and in the sheds around it. The graveyard in front is growing very fast. Four were buried while we were there. I would attend church today, but it is cold and snowy and I do not feel very well.

Mr. Chase is confined to the house with a sore foot (not the gout) and I have been keeping him company part of the day.

Kate is unwell and was not down to breakfast. I have not seen her today. She has promised me a card device for you. She is a woman of good sense and pretty good culture, has a good form but not a pretty face, its beauty being marred by a nose slightly inclining to pug. She has probably more social influence and makes a better impression generally than any other Cabinet lady.[46]

[44] Major General Samuel P. Heintzelman, a corps commander, was in charge of the defenses of Washington south of the Potomac. Later in the month he assumed command of all of the Capital's defenses.

[45] On May 24, 1861, Colonel Elmer E. Ellsworth, a close friend of Lincoln, tore down a Confederate flag from the roof of the Marshall House, a tavern in Alexandria, and was shot to death by the proprietor. Ellsworth's body lay in state in the White House before removal to New York for burial. Fort Ellsworth was situated a mile from Alexandria between the Little River and the Leesburg turnpikes.

[46] Garfield's remarks about Kate Chase were in response to this passage in his wife's letter of October 8: "By the way, I should enjoy very much a little *gossip*. From your letters to others I learn that you and Miss Kate are taking dinners out, visiting camps, *etc.*, and I have a good deal of woman's curiosity to hear about some of those doings; and is Miss Kate a very charming, interesting young lady? *I may be jealous if she is, since you have such a fashion of becoming enamoured with brilliant young ladies.*"

This is the transition period between the old slaveholding, aristocratic, social dynasty and the new Republican one. Indeed it is rather the absence of any, the interregnum between the one that was and the one which is to be. The old social dynasty has been one of the most powerful political elements in Washington and is the secret of a great many successes for the South. From the days of General Jackson and Mrs. Eaton it has been a great power.

If I live to enter Congress I may conclude to get a house here and bring you and Trot here with me. I am thinking the matter over. But that is too uncertain and remote to be discussed now. Meantime, I hope you will soon get into the new home and that I may some day be able to call it "ours" by helping you enjoy it.

Love to the family and love and kisses to yourself and Trot.

*Ever your* James

Washington
October 13, 1862

*My Dear Burke:*

Yours of the 7th was received night before last. I have been expecting your letter some time and am very glad to receive it. I hope we will not again allow our correspondence to drop off. . . .

The present is a period of a very peculiar character in the history of the war. It is the period of under-currents, counter-currents, and cross-currents so balanced as to cause a momentary stagnation—a sort of unstable calm. As when a huge wave breaks on the shore tossing its waifs high on the shore, and between the recoiling force and the on-rushing might of the waters behind there is a union of turmoil and stillness, so now our great armies, east and west, have been driven back upon the border, the force of the pursuing legions was stunned not shattered at Antietam, here and there generals tossed on shore with wrecked reputation, and those still in the storm struggling between death and life, wrangling fiercely to know who shall survive and who perish.

It would be a godsend to us if our father Abraham were another *"pater omnipotens* [all powerful father]" who could raise his *"placidum caput super undas* [quiet head above the waters]," drive back the ruffian winds and lead back the sun. But our President is neither Jupiter nor Neptune, though commander-in-chief of the army and navy. . . .

Another remarkable fact is that all three [Stanton, Lincoln, and Halleck] desire to get rid of McClellan and two or three times have been on the point of removing him, but have lacked the courage. Stanton would have done it, but was not allowed. The President would have done it, but feared the Border states and the army. Halleck would have done it, but claimed that the responsibility should not be placed on his shoulders. It is still being agitated, and I think is to be done soon, but I believe they are waiting for the elections to be over, lest it may strengthen the Peace Democracy, who all praise McClellan to the skies.

All my former opinions of McClellan are confirmed. His late campaign in Maryland has been most shameful. He has lain perfectly idle 27 days since the last battle with a force almost twice the number of the rebel army, and has constantly been asking for reinforcements, and at last has sent for entrenching tools and topographical engineers. Now Pennsylvania is invaded again.[47] I believe Major Key told the truth. The same weakness was manifested toward General Buell. He was removed from command one morning and in consequence of a protest from Crittenden and a few other Kentuckians was restored the same evening.

Your views are right concerning Secretary Seward.[48] He has always in the Senate made a fine oration in favor of or against any great measure and then taken his ease, enjoyed his *"otium cum dignitate* [leisure with dignity]" till the time for voting came, when he has voted right, but all the while was in good social standing with both friends and enemies. He never, like [Stephen A.] Douglas, went into a contest to contest every inch of ground against whatever odds. He was legislative rather than parliamentary or executive, and in the Cabinet he takes the same course, says his say and then lets it go. In these time[s] the Cabinet as well as the field need real muscular workers as well as thinkers.

The administration has about come to the conclusion that there is not a reliable loyal element in the South strong enough to build on again and they are now proposing to colonize the insurgent states by sending a loyal population there and making a new free system for the South. You may have notice[d] Eli Thayer's scheme for the colonization of Florida. They now propose to put me in command of the Department of Florida to help in the colonizing experiment there. If that succeeds, it is proposed to open the doors to European emigration and colonize and free the whole South. How soon we shall be ready to sail I cannot tell, but it is intended to move soon. I may be here some weeks yet.

At any rate write to me. Direct to Willard's Hotel.

Love to Mary and your folks at home.

> *Ever your friend,*
> J. A. Garfield

[47] A crack Confederate force of 1,800 cavalrymen under Major General J. E. B. Stuart rode around McClellan's army in a three-day expedition (October 10-12) through Maryland and Pennsylvania. The troopers covered over 110 miles, paroled about 280 sick or wounded Federal soldiers, captured about thirty hostages and 1,200 horses, and destroyed property estimated to be worth $250,000.

[48] William H. Seward, Secretary of State, had been Governor of New York, 1838-1842, and a U.S. Senator, 1849-1861.

Washington
October 14, 1862

*My Dearest Crete:*

I was really disappointed not to get a letter from you tonight. This is the first day for more than two weeks that I have not received a single letter from any body. Still the impatient delay continues, though there is a little streak of light on the horizon today.

Secretary Stanton gave my staff a short leave of absence and ordered them at the end of that time to report to me. I go to New York City by the morning train tomorrow with Eli Thayer. He is to hold conference with some leading men in the city in reference to the Florida [expedition] and he wants me there. The railroads in Florida are principally owned by New York men, and it is desirable to secure their cooperation and assistance in the work before us. We shall, while there, add a few pages to the manuscript now prepared and publish a pamphlet setting forth the proposed colonization scheme. Mr. Stanton approves of our going there, but says I must be back in seven days. This gives me hope that by that time he will be ready to do something. I do most earnestly hope so, for I begin to feel almost as though the uniform of a general was disgraced by being worn so long in idleness. I am seen on the street as little as possible.

If I can get the time I shall go and see Rebecca[49] and spend Sunday there. I don't know whether I can or not. I have arranged to have all letters that come here in my absence forwarded to me at the Metropolitan Hotel, New York City, which I shall make my headquarters while I am there. If you get this so as to write me by next Friday's mail, direct to New York and I shall get it before I return.

I am really lonely tonight without your letter which I expected. I should have gone this afternoon but I got the time put over till morning solely for the sake of the letters I hoped to get tonight.

Mr. Chase has been very sick for the last two days. He has been confined to his bed. I have staid with him a considerable part of the time and have been glad to feel that in some little way I was being of use.

I hope you may never feel so useless and miserable about doing nothing as I have for the last two weeks. I do but little else than write and read letters and look over the newspapers. True I am reading

[49] Rebecca Jane Selleck lived in Lewisboro, New York. Garfield had met her in Poestenkill when he was a student at Williams College. He made trips to the scenic valley town to conduct Disciple meetings, and she went there to visit Maria Learned and family, fellow Disciples and dear friends. An attractive, affectionate young lady, Rebecca fell in love with Garfield and succeeded in capturing his heart. She hoped to become his wife. Their romance not only survived his return to Hiram after his graduation at Williams College, but nearly caused him to cancel his plans to wed Lucretia Rudolph. For the latter, all this was an anguishing ordeal, and it left her with scars of distrust and doubt which remained for several years.

some poetry, but all is so foreign from the great work of the hour that it makes me sick.

With a whole heart full of love for you and Trot,

*I am your own*
James


Washington
October 14, 1862

*Dear Brother Austin:*

Yours of October 1st was received some days ago. I was very glad to hear from you and should have answered sooner but I hoped to be able to tell you that I was starting for the field and active duty. . . .

There is a very sad state of things in the Government here, especially in the War Department. There is lack of confidence in the ability of some of the leading officers and just now there is great anxiety in regard to the elections. There are so many of the Union voters of the North away in the war that it is greatly feared that the Vallandigham Democracy[50] may carry a great many districts and bring in an element of discord with [which] will strengthen rebellion and greatly weaken the power of the Union.

Today has decided the elections in three states. I hope you will tell me how the election has gone in our district. I see by the papers that Warren furnishes a congressional candidate after all. I am pleased to hear that there has been no unkind feelings engendered toward you on the part of Mr. Hutchins. I had a very pleasant visit with him here.

We have now lain still so long with our great armies that we have almost lost the great opportunities which the good weather and the good roads have afforded us. On the whole, therefore, I don't know but I am better pleased to go to Florida or some point far to the South where something can be done even in the winter season.

I go to New York tomorrow with Mr. Thayer of Massachusetts to see some leading men of the city in reference to the matter. I shall be gone about a week and then return here.

[50] Clement L. Vallandigham of Ohio, lawyer, journalist, and Democratic member of the U.S. House of Representatives, 1858-1863, opposed the Civil War and urged reunion through negotiation or mediation. This, he claimed, could be accomplished but for Lincoln's policy of prolonging the war to free the blacks and enslave the whites. Republicans generally regarded Vallandigham and his followers as traitors and used various uncomplimentary terms in referring to them, one of the mildest being the Vallandigham Democracy. In 1863, Vallandigham was arrested for treasonable utterances and banished to the Confederate states. (The order authorizing his passage through the Union line was written by Garfield.) During his exile, Vallandigham was unsuccessful as the Democratic candidate for Governor of Ohio. He returned to his state, through Canada, in 1864 and played a prominent role in the Democratic National Convention in Chicago which nominated McClellan for the presidency. Vallandigham died in 1871.

If I go to Florida I shall have command of that department and be responsible to no other commander, but make my reports to and receive my instructions from the Secretary of War. It will be much better and pleasanter for me to be independent of West Point and all its surroundings. If the colonization scheme is successful in Florida, it seems to me to offer a feasible solution for our great difficulty. The trouble is that we have at last been unwillingly forced to the conclusion that there is not a sufficiently strong loyal element in the South to build up states that will be true to the Union. Slavery has left such a blight upon them that a new and more loyal population must be sent there to possess the land and help make free institutions. As having relation to this most important and interesting question I shall be pleased to help in the experiment in Florida. I know I run the risk of making a failure, which would be very bad, but war is made up of risks and I have made up my mind to do without complaint whatever is put upon me. I know the President and his Cabinet have confidence in me and I hope I may continue to prove worthy of it.

I want you to write to me frequently. Give my love to Lottie and Minerva and all who inquire after me.

*Truly your brother,*
J. A. Garfield . . . .

Lewisboro
October 19, 1862

*My Dearest Crete:*

Your dear letter of the 12th was forwarded from Washington and re[a]ched me yesterday. I should have written you before I left the city but your letter did not come in time. I reached New York on Wednesday at midnight and last evening came here. Rebecca has been quite sick, confined to her bed and under the doctor's care. She had a very serious attack of what the doctor calls neuralgia in the chest. She is better now, is able to be around, though she has not ridden out yet. I fear the attack will leave her lungs in a bad condition. She has now as the result of it a pretty serious cough.

The place here is very pleasant looking, only [looks] more old and quaint than it did six years ago when I was here. The air is chill and cold today and the leaves are already falling. I was surprised to see how completely the autumnal tints are set on all the foliage here. I have seen hardly an indication of autumn around Washington.

In New York I heard Forrest[51] play two nights. You had told me so much about him that I was particularly anxious to hear him. I find he is regarded as by far the greatest tragedian in the country, though

[51] Edwin Forrest opened on September 15, 1862, an eight-week engagement at Niblo's Garden.

Edwin Booth[52] who is now also playing in the city has many admirers who claim for him the palms. They were both playing *Richelieu* for several nights, one at Niblo's, the other at Winter Garden. I heard Forrest first in *Virginius* and second in Spartacus, *The Gladiator*. They are both tragedies founded on Ancient Roman history and are full of classic as well as dramatic interest. I admired Forrest very much but I think his body and mind are much better adapted to the expression of strong stormy passions than of the milder and gentler ones. In Spartacus he was really sublime in some passages of his grand power. I wish you could have heard him. Our work in New York is not completed; indeed, I don't know as it will amount to anything at all. That depends chiefly upon the War Department, but I think we shall achieve something. I go back tomorrow evening and leave for Washington on Wednesday. I shall hope to find a letter from you at the Metropolitan when I get back.

I presume you have before this got my note in reference to the Brown trade. I hope you have already closed the bargain. I have had a better photographic card taken than the one I sent you, and I will send you a package of them as soon as I can get them.

I am feeling exceedingly blue over the late elections in Ohio and Indiana.[53] At that rate we shall be soon overpowered by treason at home. Do you know what my majority was? I have not seen any account of it.[54]

I hope you have received the pile of manuscript I sent you a few days ago.

Give my love and kisses to our dear little Trot, and thank her for the sweet kisses she sent me. I should be very glad, my dear Crete, to have you go with me to Florida. I should enjoy it very dearly, I assure you, and I have thought a good deal about it. I will see when I get there how the future looks and if it is at all feasible I will have you go. You know in general I am opposed to having women go into the army, but I should be very glad to have you there with me. Ever and forever your loving

James

I have had another attack of diarrhea, probably from change of diet. Rebecca sends love to you and Trot.

I will write to Joe, most cheerfully. That I may not forget it, please ask me next time you write whether I have done it.

[52] Edwin Booth opened on September 29, 1862, a seven-week engagement at the Winter Garden Theater.

[53] In both states the Democrats won control of the legislatures and sent large majorities to Congress. The terms of Governors Morton of Indiana and Tod of Ohio had not expired, but the Cincinnati *Enquirer* and other papers demanded that both resign.

[54] Garfield defeated his opponent by a two to one margin: 13,288 to 6,763.

Washington<br>
October  24,  1862

*My Dearest Crete:*

I left New York night before last, but the train missed connection at Philadelphia and I was left there till yesterday noon, and so I did not reach here till last night. I had a conference with Thayer just before leaving New York and found that the Florida plan is winning friends and supporters every day. The only thing now needed is the action of the Government, and we seem as far from that as ever. I have not learned what the War Department has been doing in my absence, but from all I can gather they have done nothing. It is exceedingly discouraging to see how weak and dilatory they are. I am growing into a feeling of personal shame at being kept here in idleness. I am really ashamed to be seen on the streets with the United States uniform on.

In New York, here, everywhere, there is a settled gloom on nearly every face; a great nation groaning in an agony of suspense and anxiety to have something done; a people that have poured out with a most lavish hand their life and treasure to save their Government, a people that have trusted their executive head with a constancy and faith, which in these degenerate days is really sublime, are now beginning to feel that their confidence has been betrayed, their treasure squandered, and the lives of their children sacrificed in unavailing slaughter. The failure at the late elections is the natural and inevitable result of the management of the war. But I will not distress you with any further views of the dark and gloomy picture of our times.

I am glad to hear that you are perfecting your arrangements for a home of our own. I only wish I were well through this war and could enjoy it with you.

I am glad to have you write me frankly and fully as you do in the last letter of the 20th now before me.[55]

I was however sorry to know that you had been sad and had passed through a struggle on account of my visit to Rebecca. I hope you will not harbor the thought that I have practised any deception toward you in my late conversation. I hope you will see me as I am conscious of being indeed a true man, and that I am true to my *whole* history. I had a very pleasant and yet sad visit with Rebecca; pleasant because I was glad to revisit the scenes of six years ago and was enabled to do

---

[55] On October 19, Garfield's wife had written that she had just passed through a great struggle. She recalled that before he had come home last summer the threads of their lives seemed almost hopelessly entangled with others. "But during your visit," she said, "we turned back together and looked through that tangled past and . . . found the links we called broken only hidden. Then from mutual explanations and confessions we found more that was unfortunate than wrong in what had once seemed *all* wrong. . . . [A new light and love blessed our marriage, but when] I read your purpose to visit Rebecca the old pain came back to my heart, and . . . I began to fear . . . [you wished only] to deceive me. . . . Most solemnly and earnestly did I pray . . . for a just and generous heart and He who hears the young ravens when they cry heard and answered my prayer."

so without having my horizon clouded, or having the thorns again pierce me; pleasant because I am more than ever assured that he that is true to his own virtue is happier and better in being so, and I can say in truth that I love you none the less for having seen Rebecca again and she is no less dear to me from the fact that the sunshine has sweetly dawned upon your life and mine; pleasant because I took pleasure in telling her that I had passed a very happy month with you and that henceforth my life with you was full of promise of sweet peace and sunlight.

It was sad in this, that I found her just arisen from a bed of pain and suffering; that I found the insidious approach of consumption; that I found her surrounded by those who do not contribute much to make her life agreeable, nor do they seem to be worthy to be companions of so noble a woman. She has been sorely disappointed in Maria's not going to visit her before her return to the West.

Eben Ayers[56] has got home from the army, sick with a fever, and worst of all has a fever sore on his knee which th[r]eatens to make him a cripple for life. Maria has been attending on him in Troy and is still there.

I received last night a letter from Dr. Briscoe, and I have this morning written him sending him $30, the amount of his bill. He will send you some medicine for me, and I will try to have some member of my staff visit you before they join me and get it and my cotton socks and whatever else you may send. Pardon this hurried scratch for I have a great deal to do today.

Kiss our darling for me. I regret that I cannot be with you on the 11th November, but I am preparing something for you which will answer nearly as well.[57]

Loving you and hoping to hear from you very often,

*I am forever your own*
James

Washington
October 26, 1862

*Dear Mother and Sister:*

It is a rainy, dreary day and I did not go to church, but am staying in my room today. . . .

[56] Ayers, whose home was in West Troy, New York, had become acquainted with Garfield during the latter's visits to Poestenkill. He was a student at the Eclectic during Garfield's principalship.

[57] Garfield's gift to his wife on their fourth wedding anniversary was a picture of himself. Mrs. Garfield liked it immensely. "The face is so grandly serene," she commented, "so unlike any picture of yourself for the last years. There is not a trace of those lines which have shown so plainly the restless chafing spirit within. In the quiet eye I see an assurance of your happiness which gives me more hope and gladness than all the assurances your *lips* could give."

I should be very glad if I could be with you again and spend my next birthday which is not far off. It really saddens me to think how the years are flying and how fast I am leaving the sweet days of boyhood. But still I believe I am about as much of a boy in my feelings as I ever was. I am still the same restless being I ever was. I am anxious to get away from here and when in the next place I suppose I shall be equally anxious to get away from there. So it goes, and always will, I presume.

I do not yet hear from Hitty, according to promise. I do wish the dear girl would write me one letter at least. I am sorry I did not have time to visit more with her when I was at home. Do tell her to write to me. I want Thomas also to write. I will always answer any letters that any of you write to me. We are only a small family of orphan children, and if we don't love each other and stand by each other, who will stand by us? We have been greatly blessing [blessed] in having such a mother and I don't know a family of nobler or better hearts than ours, the writer of this always excepted, for I don't know as I am very good. I fear not. Give my love to them all and let me hear from you again.

That picture I sent you seems to me to look gaunt and lean. They are taking a still engraving of me in New York which I will send you if it is good. Ever your own

James

I am now quite well again.

Washington
October 26, 1862

*My Dear Harry:*

It is a dreary and rainy [day] and I have been indoors all day. It is now near evening and my hand and pen cast shadows on the paper as I write. I have just closed up and laid away Coventry Patmore's second volume of *The Angel in the House.*[58] I began it three hours ago and finished just now. It is very beautiful. I can understand him when he says:

> "How light the touches are that kiss
> The music from the chords of life"

but I cannot understand this indefinable, vague sadness, partly painful, partly joyful, which falls over the spirit like a mantle that shields and yet darkens. I doubt if by the most searching analysis I could tell why I rise from the reading of that book with such sadness. It may be that the child that I still am is feeling the sense of silence and loneness,

[58] The work consisted of four volumes of poetry celebrating married love. The second volume, *The Espousals,* appeared in 1856.

the ache that comes of catching beautiful thoughts and have no one beside you to speak to; or it may be the sadness resulting from the early memories awakened by the book; or it may be that mysterious power that spirit exerts in spite of space and absence, and that my state is the result of the sadness of some distant friend. If the first supposition be correct I shall throw it off by writing to you. Hours like this make me long for a quiet life of thought and study among friends, and make me feel how poor and unsatisfying are all the places of power and dignity which men can bestow.

On my return from New York I found yours of the 17th awaiting me. You speak of having written me several times during the week before. I have had no letter except that of the 17th from you in a long time. I wrote you a long, four-sheeted letter, but have not yet received your acknowledgement of it. Your letters may have miscarried. . . .

I saw Greeley,[59] Beecher, and a number of the leading lights in New York. All grant that the prospect looks very dark, and that there is little hope while Halleck, McClellan and Buell are in command. It is becoming a settled feeling that there is some concert of purpose between the leading generals to keep the contest from being decisive. Major Key's "programme" is becoming more and more manifest every day.

Yesterday Mr. Chase had an interview with the President and Secretary of War and thinks they are now pretty fully aroused. The removal of Buell[60] evidently interfered with the programme, and I hope will pave the way to the removal of the other two.

I am thoroughly ashamed to be seen on the streets in uniform, and am seriously thinking of resigning my commission and coming out in a letter giving my reason why. Still my work is always to be assigned *very soon,* but I, like every other general of positive opinions, am kept in idleness. I shall wait a few days more. . . .

*Ever yours,*
James

Washington
October 30, 1862

*My Dear Burke:*
Yours of the 22nd came duly to hand and was read with pleasure. I had hoped by this time to be able to write you more hopefully and cheerfully than I did before, but the gloom is no less sombre and there are no more hopeful signs, unless indeed the condensing black-

[59] Horace Greeley, the outspoken and erratic editor of the New York *Tribune.*
[60] On orders of October 23, Buell was replaced by Major General William S. Rosecrans, who was appointed commander of the Department of the Cumberland.

ness indicates the bursting of a terrible storm which, though it destroy much, may clear the sky of its suffocating vapors. Of course I am glad Buell is removed, but it is locking the stable after the horse is stolen. He is superseded, not until the campaign is ended in Kentucky and the great opportunities completely lost. The Government seems to be taking a similar course with its slow generals on the Potomac. My feelings of anxiety give place to a feeling of wonder and utter amazement that any administration should permit such criminal trifling. . . .

The old time Calvinists of New England used to hold that sinners must bring themselves up to the point of willingness to be eternally damned if it were the Lord's will. Now the administration seem[s] to have gone to a much profounder depth of humility. They seem to have determined to get damned by the people, whether or no, to see if perchance it may not bring salvation. I doubt if the history of government shows anything to equal the stupidity and weakness of our war administration of 1862. Mr. Chase is the only live, strong, earnest man in the Cabinet, and he says it is a misnomer to call it a Cabinet, for there seems to be some power out of the Cabinet, and indeed out of sight which neutralizes all good efforts and makes Cabinet councils a farce. I have no hope that General McClellan will ever fight again this season unless the battle is forced upon him. I believe Major Key was dismissed from the service for telling the truth, that what he said of the military programme is McClellan's programme, and never till he is removed will anything be done here. It is now claimed that a blow will fall on him as soon as the New York elections are over, but I doubt if anything short of the overwhelming indignation of the people and Congress can do us any substantial good.

The elections in Ohio, Pennsylvania and Indiana are the natural result of the weakness of the administration. Of course the absence of voters who are in the army contributed to the result, but if we had had a vigorous campaign and a bold strong President, this disgraceful defeat could not have happened. When will our people learn that the best way to fight battles, either in politics or war, is to take bold strong ground and sometimes make the most desperate risks? Scott illustrates it in a single couplet from Roderick Dhu's and Fitzjames' fight:

> "With [Then,] foot and point and eye opposed
> In dubious strife they darkly closed."[61]

The Ohio Republican state convention affirmed nothing positive, said not a word about slavery, but went through with the platitudes of the Crittenden Compromise and put one of its resolutions in their platform. Then they nominate[d] a state ticket of conservatives as fossil as Honorable Preserved Doe. It is true they resolved in favor of prosecuting the war; but the Democrats did the same and when the

[61] Sir Walter Scott, *The Lady of the Lake* (1810) , Canto V, Stanza 14, Lines 377-378.

Democratic speaker said, "Let the inbecile abolitionists give way to the vigorous Democracy," it had some sense as well as *ad captandum* [crowd-pleasing] power. Ben[jamin] and Fernando Wood will both be in the next Congress.[62] *Par nobile fratrum* [?]. The result in New York is becoming more doubtful every day. . . .

I hope you will write me often. Give my love to Mary and Louisa, who I believe is with you.

*Ever your friend,*
J. A. Garfield

Washington
October 31, 1862

*My Very Dear Crete:*

Your precious letter of the 26th came to hand last evening and is very dear to me. It is matter of great deep rejoicing to me that you are so happy in our new-found love. Your letter expresses what I so long missed and despaired of but find at last just as it was nearly given up. Let us thank God that He has opened a way through the darkness and allowed us to walk at last in the clear calm light.

I am glad to hear that you have perfected the bargain for the house and at the very time I was reading your letter, and probably now you are in Cleveland making purchases for our home. I hope to hear soon that you are in possession. The arrangement to have Nellie with you will be very fine. But I hope you will soon find a good reliable girl so that you may be more independent. . . .

I am surprised to hear that Harvey should be taking such a strange course. It betrays a weakness and want of liberal-mindedness that I was not quite prepared to see in him. I hope the teachers will now take him at his word and let him go. He has had tantrums enough in that direction. Will they keep up the school during the coming winter?

I am glad to hear from Brother Streator[63] again. There are few men I would be so glad to meet as him. Tell me his address and I will write to him. He is one of the truest and best friends I ever had. He has a large heart and is much more of a man than he has the credit for being. If his health would sustain him, he would make a decisive mark as a preacher. I regard him as far above the average of Disciple preachers, though his manners are rather against him.

[62] Benjamin Wood of New York owned and edited the New York *Daily News* and was a Democratic member of the U.S. House of Representatives, 1861-1865, 1881-1883. His brother Fernando, also of New York, was a Democratic member of the U.S. House of Representatives, 1841-1843, 1863-1865, and 1867 to his death in 1881.

[63] Myron J. Streator was a Disciple preacher with whom Garfield conducted meetings at West Rupert, Vermont, and Poestenkill, New York, during his college days.

Thank you for the election returns. It is more than I had seen. I believe my dear friends in Hiram managed to run me behind the ticket in that place a little. I hope they enjoy the sport. I wish you would send me the *Portage Democrat* occasionally. I have not seen a copy since I left the State.

Mr. Hutchins is here and I visit him and he me quite often. He is very friendly.

I am unexpectedly placed on the court of inquiry to investigate the accusations against General McDowell. You remember that I had a long interview with McDowell and the manuscript I sent you was drawn chiefly from my recollection of his official documents. Now being place[d] on the court to try the very case it is exceedingly important that nobody shall make any use of that document I sent home, lest I be again charged with breaking the faith of a court. I had at the time not the remotest idea that I should ever have any official connection with the case. What have you done with the manuscript? What did Harry and Almeda say of it? I want it preserved, but locked out of sight for the present.[64]

Give my love to mother and father and Nell. Ask her to write to me. Please present the enclosed card to Hannah Morton[65] with my love. I wish she would write to me. She nee[d]n't wait for me to write. Let her consider this card a letter. Kiss our darling and then thank her for me that she *ain't* nobody but a sweet little somebody, and that I am ever hers and yours,

James

Washington
November 2, 1862

*My Dear Harry:*

Yours of the 30th *ult.* came last night. I am surprised to hear you say that you are not my epistolary debtor. I have received two letters from you since the 3rd of October, one bearing date October 16th and the other the one now before me. I believe you did send me some letters that had come to the Hiram office with an accompanying note about the 12th October. If you have written any more they have miscarried and I am very sorry for I am always exceedingly glad to hear from you.

I am quite unwell today and have been so since day before yesterday.

---

[64] Garfield never sat on the McDowell court of inquiry, his appointment being withdrawn when he was placed on the Porter court-martial. But, of course, he did not know this when he directed his wife to lock up the manuscript he had sent home. Obviously, he had no intention of disqualifying himself as a prejudiced party.

[65] Hannah S. Morton taught instrumental music at the Eclectic for several years.

I have been shutting myself up pretty closely to reading very heavy subjects for the last few days and have not taken exercise enough. I have taken up the subject of currency and finance and have been reading the great debates of [Daniel] Webster, [John C.] Calhoun and [Thomas Hart] Benton and comparing them with Macaulay's fifth volume.[66] At any other time than this such a pursuit would delight my soul, and even now I occasionally forget that our nation is struggling for its life and so take pleasure in these studies. I think, if we ever survive the shock of the war, the great currency question will be revived with new and interesting features resulting from our huge national debt which now amounts to seven hundred millions and will be nearly doubled before the war closes.[67]

The McDowell court has not yet assembled as two of its members, Generals Hunter and Cadwalader,[68] are on the Harpers Ferry case which is not yet finished, but will be in a day or two.

I am forced to feel that we are in the darkest place we have yet seen. Aside from our great losses and the pressure of foreign powers, the conduct of the war and its present condition have given the rebels a moral power which will be a great weight on their side. Five or six of their leading generals are almost religious enthusiasts in the cause they have espoused. General Lee, Jackson, and J. E. B. Stuart have inspired their men with a kind of Cromwell spirit which make their battallions almost invincible. All this time our own men have grown dis[couraged]. If we do not see some light break in upon us very speedily there will come an end to our hopes of restoration and union.

No government ever before went so fully on the doctrine of neglecting its friends and rewarding or propitiating its enemies as ours is doing. There is not a Republican general in the whol[e] army who has now a command of any great importance. The large majority of them have no commands at all. The defeat in our late elections is the natural result of this policy. New York is quite likely to go Butternut.[69] It is nearly certain that Ben and Fernando Wood will be elected. The rebels are delighted beyond all measure at the Democratic successes, accomplished and prospective.

The hope of having anything to do myself is becoming very faint, though I have been permitted to order my staff and horses on here. They will come in about ten days.

I am greatly surprised at the course Harvey has seen fit to take,

[66] Thomas Babington Macaulay, *The History of England*, five volumes (1849-1861).

[67] In 1862 the total gross national debt (fiscal year ending June 30) was $524,178,-000; in 1865 it was $2,677,929,000.

[68] Cadwalader served as President of the McDowell court of inquiry after completing his work on the military commission for the Harpers Ferry case.

[69] Since Confederate uniforms were commonly dyed butternut brown, Southern soldiers were nicknamed Butternuts. Butternut was also used to denote the Confederacy. Garfield used the term to refer derisively to the Democratic party, a faction of which opposed the war and sympathized with the Confederacy.

but I don't see that it need to injure the school very much.[70] I hope the trustees will be firm about it, and not allow themselves to be bullied into any concessions they don't see best to make. By getting Suliot or Mary Raff, or Burke, you will have force enough. I need not say that the success and power of the school will depend upon the harmony and hearty cooperation of yourself and Almeda, and I hope you may keep up the most perfect understanding and good feeling in every thing. I would be very glad to be back there with you, and if the door opens I will be there. I think we had better correspond with some member of the legislature in reference to a military department.

Crete wrote me that she would be glad to have you and Mrs. Martin board with her and Almeda if she could only get a good girl to work for them. Can't you find one for them?

I hope your Institute will go off handsomely. Present my kind regards to the teachers from abroad who will be there to assist you, especially Mr. Suliot. I hope you will not fail to write me often, and see that your letters do not get miscarried. Reciprocating all your love. I am as ever,

*Yours,*
James

Washington
November 7, 1862

*Dearest Crete:*

Yours of the 3rd is just received and read with the same pleasure that attends all your letters. I am glad to tell you that I am at length assigned to duty. I go with Major General Hunter to Port Royal as the second in command to operate against Charleston, and I hope to retake Fort Sumter. If I may be an assistant in that work it will compensate for all this vexatious and weary delay which has kept me in inglorious idleness so long. I beg you not to feel alarmed in consequence of Yellow Fever of which General Mitchel so sadly died, for it has never been know[n] to continue with any virulence after the frosts set in, which usually come on by the middle of November.

There will be many advantages of that climate during the winter season, and I hope to be able to give you tropical pictures which will compensate for my being so far away. I do not yet know what day I shall set sail but it will probably be in two or three, possibly tomorrow. You may write your next letter to me here as usual unless you see by the papers that I have gone. If so, send to Hilton Head, South Carolina, care Major General Hunter, until you hear from me again.

[70] Garfield learned from his wife's letter of October 28 that Harvey Everest, the Principal of the Eclectic, had resigned largely as a result of differences with Almeda Booth. Apparently he was also in disagreement with other members of the faculty and with some of the trustees.

I have drawn my pay again up to the end of October and thought it best to invest it in a safe way, as I had no time to attend to loans and security with private individuals. I will explain the enclosed bonds to you, so that in case of accident they can be made available to you. They are called registered bonds, and draw 6 per cent interest payable in Washington in gold semi-annually. The first payment of interest will be made May 1st, 1863, and then every six months thereafter. They are *registered* so that should these be lost or destroyed the money can still be paid on the register here. They can be sold, but whenever they are transferred they must be sent here and transferred to the new purchaser. I got them in five bonds of $100 each so that part could be sold, if necessary, without selling the whole. You will have them carefully preserved, and remember they are not taxable, so that when the assessor comes around they are not to be taxed. So much for the bonds.

I am glad you have got so near ready for house-keeping. I hope you are pleased with your purchases and arrangements.

I have got Lieutenant [Joseph D.] Stubbs, my old 42nd quartermaster appointed captain and quartermaster and ordered to report to me and go to Port Royal with me. I am sorry Captains Plumb and Heaton cannot go with me.

I shall write you again by tomorrow or next day. Love to Trot and all the other young ladies of my acquaintance.

*Ever and forever your* James

Washington
November 10, 1862

*Dear Harry:*

Yours of October 11th was received last night. Where it can have been wandering for the past 30 days is more than I can conceive. But I am glad to get it even after such a delay. I am today in a singularly mixed state of joy and disappointment. Disappointed at my bad fortune in not getting into the field. Day before yesterday I was ordered to go with General Hunter to Hilton Head. Eleven thousand men were ordered to go with us. I was to be second in command and have at least a division. We, General Hunter and I, held a long and most cordial interview and laid plans for making a speedy and thundery attack on Charleston and Sumter, and for 24 hours I feel [felt] more joyful then I have at any time since I left the Sandy Valley. I telegraphed for my staff to meet me in Baltimore, where we were to take the steamer tomorrow and in three days from now we should have been in the enemy's country. But yesterday a dispatch came that the Yellow Fever was raging with great malignity and that no more troops should be sent there till the black frost set it. So the order was suspended and the troops turned into another channel. General Halleck told me, however, he did not know but he should send me with General Banks. So much for bad news.

Before this reaches you, you will have read of the removal of Mc-Clellan.[71] God be praised that this act of justice to the army and the country, so long delayed, has been consummated at last. It is better to the country than a decisive victory over the enemy. Indeed, I am not sure that it is in itself a decisive victory over rebels at home. If the disastrous elections (which by the way, you prophesied in this letter of the 11th *ult.*) shall act as a spur to the President to give him some motion, I shall welcome them as messengers of mercy though they come in the guise of terrible disasters. On the whole I see a brighter prospect ahead for the country than I have at any time since I came to Washington.

There are two great expeditions maturing to clear out the Mississippi Valley, and then the grand armies of the Ohio and the Potomac will soon be at work. The day is dawning. I cannot leave the army now but as soon as I do, I shall try to do what I can for the school. I feel more and more desirous of getting with you again. Do not get me pledged in any way that I cannot perform. Keep the dear old school up in healthy and robust condition. Let me hear from you often. I am doing the most of the writing between us.

*Ever thine,*
James

Washington
November 11, 1862

*Dearest Crete:*

I take my pen on this quadrennial anniversary with mingled feelings of sadness and happiness. *Sad,* as I review the past, that it should have been so strangely, painfully, trying to us, who groped about in the darkness and grief trying to find the path of duty and peace, and being so often pierced with thorns. Sad that so much of life which can never be recalled should have been, by a kind of fatal necessity, devoted to a sadness almost bordering on despair, and that possibly those dark years may have left a residuum of bitterness which the whirling eddies of after years may stir up and mingle with the sweet waters of life.

But I am also happy in the reflection that we were both seeking the path of duty and honor and that we each bore in silence many griefs, and each drank bravely and uncomplainingly many a bitter cup. Happy that in those days we were each borne up by the trust that the other was of true noble soul, and however great the errors might be there was still integrity of heart. Happy, above all, that this patient waiting and

[71] The order relieving McClellan was dated November 5; it was delivered to him on November 7.

mutual forebearance has at last begun to bear the fruits of peace and love and that the buds of this hope give promise of a harvest of calm joyful peace as we go down the lengthening shadows of life. I have watched the new hope with great anxiety to see if it were a transient flower or a perennial growth. I have rejoiced with trembling, and I will not even yet speak with that full assurance that can lay all the future under contribution; yet as the days wear on, I rejoice more and tremble less.

I hope *strongly* and *happily* that we have passed through the valley and shadow of that death which for so long a time we "died daily." But I here pray you to be still ready to bear with me if at any future moment my heart should for a time go down again into the deeps. I do not say this because of any such experiences since I left you; I have had none. Were I with you today, I would let you see in my eyes and heart that the cloud has not returned. It would be a great joy could I go with you today and occupy our first home, and tonight kneel with you and Almeda around the new altar. I hope you have gone into the house today. I cannot tell you how I long to see our little darling Trot again. Precious little soul.

I have ordered a present sent you by express in commemoration [of] this anniversary. It is now in New York City and may not reach you for a week. I tried to have it reach you by today but could not. It will explain itself. I have directed it to be sent to Garrettsville and you may have to send for it there. It's only a little matter, but I thought you would be pleased with it. . . .

*Ever and forever your* James

Washington
November 16, 1862

*My Dear Harry:*

Your very good letter of the 10th came only to hand. It is one of the very best you ever wrote. What could be a more full and perfect substitute for being with you at the dear old seminary than to have so spirited and complete a picture of it as you gave me. You speak of the characters grouped there in such terms as make their idiosyncracies stand out in strong colors. I can see each rosy face and luscious lip, each trim ankle and nearly fitting gaiter as you describe them. I have been able to sketch some interesting objects to you since I have been here, but none I am sure which awakened so many pleasant reflections as those you have given me. In the female line I can give you but a sorry return for your radiant sketch. I have, it is true, been living at the home of the first belle of Washington, but I left there three days ago for the sake of my staff who had just arrived and I was desirous to aid them in seeing the city and learning what they could of it before we leave. Again I am anxious to preserve and deepen the affection between them and me, and I want to help them where it is in my power.     •

We have taken rooms at 119 Pennsylvania Avenue, lately occupied by General Augur.[72] There are three professors boarding here who are attached to the naval observatory in the city and are very intelligent men. But the women of the establishment! Ye Gods, what a contrast with your picture! No rosy cheeks or Lil Johnson legs here. The gynic quartette here consists of lady *Davis*, past sixty-five, and her two immaculate virgin daughters, whose years range from forty to fif[t]y, and a little wench of twelve cal[l]ed Topsy by common consent. Such a trio of toothless crones, withered ugliness, with all the outré of Washington mannerism, cannot be paralleled. They are all very deaf, so that Topsy acts as interpreter by shrieking in her shrill voice all the mild cooings of yours truly. The chief conversation of the virgins is on courtship and marriage and severe diatribes on the matrimonial tastes of men and women. I am glad to assure you that I and the two ardent young men are safe from the charms of these syrens. Our virtue is proof against their most betwitching blandishments. I think that even warmer blood than our own might be kept in the channels of continence with such surrounded [surroundings].

I have not yet any definite knowledge as to the date of our departure, but the late news from Port Royal gives promise that the fever will soon be frozen out. You say truly that I "am not destined to be the Napoleon of this war." From what has been said to me here I believe I could be made major general now if I should ask it, but I would not until I should have done something more. Do you remember that I have had no opportunity to do anything since I left the Sandy Valley? War is something like hunting. You may kill a buck the first hour, and you may hunt a week and never see a track. Indeed I am inclined to carry your remark a little further and say that nobody will be the Napoleon of this war, though it may have a Waterloo. I have been so much disgusted by the management that I could have played Cambronne's part at Waterloo so far as saying the word is concerned.[73] Indeed my prevailing malady has turned my thoughts in that direction more than has been pleasant.

I am glad to hear of your success in the Institute; it will have a good influence on the winter term and a still better one of [on] the spring term. I feel as though there were some question about the success of

[72] Major General Christopher C. Augur who, after serving on the military commission for the Harpers Ferry case, left Washington to join Banks in the Department of the Gulf.

[73] At Waterloo (June 18, 1815) General Baron von Halkett, commanding Hanoverian infantry, took as his prisoner French General Pierre Cambronne, commander of the imperial guard. It was rumored that Cambronne's defiant reply to Halkett's demand of surrender was: *"La garde meurt, et ne se rend pas."* Cambronne denied it.

Mr. Suliot as a teacher, just as there is in reference to almost all foreigners in their failure to adapt themselves to our young American habits and wants, but still I hope he may be made servic[e]able and I think he can. He is very sensitive and if he comes with you, you will of course be very tender of his feelings and make him as much at home as you can.

You had better take pains to find out what the temper of the legislature will be in regard to the military school question.

I am making a great effort to straighten myself up. I find I have fallen into a most vicious habit of stooping my shoulders and lopping around. I have put myself in back stays and am "hauling myself taut" as the sailors would say. The result is that I am just now very lame across the shoulders and breast, but I hope to become more upright by the means. Keep me reminded of it once in a while so that I may not forget it.

I see by the New York *Post* that President Hopkins has published a book on moral philosophy.[74] I have sent for it and you must. The *Post* eulogizes it in a very strong and appreciative article. I am reading Carlyle's *Friedrich der Grosse*[75] and reviewing Horace which latter has great charms for me. McClellan will soon find his level, especially if New Jersey elects him to the Senate. His playing *mum* for profound is played out.

I will try to see Hutchins, though I have no hope that it will do any good. Write me soon and often.

*Ever yours,*
James

Washington
November 16, 1862

*My Dearest Crete:*

Your good, dear anniversary letter was received last evening. Your mind, I see, took quite a similar track to that my own took over the gloomy and joyous past of our lives. I take courage and hope from your letter and am made happy by the sameness of our reflections.

Since I wrote you last I have left Mr. Chase's and [am] taking rooms and board at 119 Pennsylvania Avenue, so as to be with my staff and keep them company in the strange city till we leave. It was very pleasant, indeed, to be at Mr. Chase's, and though I had the fullest assurances that my stay was a pleasure to them, yet I could not but feel that it was staying a long time as a guest by invitation, and so I seized the arrival of my staff as an occasion to get away. I suppose it is the same kind of morbid fear that I may be in some way an intruder that

---

[74] Mark Hopkins, *Lectures on Moral Science* (1862).

[75] Thomas Carlyle, *History of Friedrich II of Prussia, Called Frederick the Great,* six volumes (1858-1865). The first three volumes appeared, 1858-1862.

made me at times quite unhappy about being there so long, but I could not help it occasion[al]ly. But I think they really regretted my coming away. Mr. Chase and I are about equal at chess and we had been averaging five or six games a day for the last two or three weeks; and when I called on him night before last he insisted on playing, though quite a large company was present, and we kept at it till eleven o'clock.

Two members of my staff, Captain Swaim, Assistant Adjutant General, and Lieutenant Lake are here; but as they could not get the horses brought with them, they left Lieutenant Farrar behind to bring them on. We expect him here by the middle of the coming week. There are as yet no indications as [to] the date of our departure for the South. The last advice from Port Royal show[s] the health of the troops improving, and lead[s] us to hope we may not be detained here long.

It was no surprise to me that you did not get into the new home by the 11th, for I know [how] many things there are to do in putting a house and its outfit in order. Then you "half expected me home." I suppose I should have gone but for my pride. I really had a struggle with it. I could not bear to be seen home again without having been in the field first. And then, I could not have had any assurance that I could have staid two days. Thank you for the election returns. I believe I have the largest majority of any one in any state, so far as I have seen. Do you remember George A. Packer of Vermont who was at the school several years ago? I met him here the other day and we knew each other. I send his picture. Harry and Almeda will remember him. He is now a lieutenant in a New York regiment.[76] I believe I told of meeting Edwin Gilbert a week or two ago. He is now lieutenant colonel.[77]

Joe writes me for my advice in reference to his trying to get a place in the regular army. What shall I tell him? Love to all. Kiss the blessed little darling for me. Ever your James.

[P.S.] Wallace [Ford] writes me about some trouble with Harry and the Institution note. What is the matter?[78] Tell me when you will need more money and how much. I am nearly laid up with my corn again. I am quite lame again today. I am wearing shoulder-braces to try to correct my very bad habit of stooping, which has been made much worse by my sickness. My shoulders are quite lame today.

I remind you that next Wednesday is my birthday. Tell Trot. Write in her book then.

[76] First Lieutenant George A. Packer of Guilford, Vermont, served in the Eighty-sixth New York. He attended the Eclectic, 1857-1858.

[77] Gilbert of the Twenty-fifth New York, had been captured at Gaines's Mill and exchanged in time to fight in the Second Battle of Bull Run. He died in February, 1863, in Rochester, New York.

[78] "The trouble between Wallace and Harry was nothing serious," Garfield's wife replied on November 24, "and is all settled now. Each wanted your Institution note, and Harry was a little displeased to give it up."

Washington
November 19, 1862

*My Dear Harry:*

Yours was received last night and read with pleasure. I have been trying all day to write, but I have not been well, a dull head ached [ache] and a kind of slow fever in the bones have kept me feeling a kind of discomfort and unrest which I am quite unable to shake off. I don't know but it results from my continued inaction. I try to neutralize that by a few games of billiards each day.

Aside from my physical discomfort and the miserable, drizzly, nasty weather which is gloomy enough to satisfy even Dickens' Dismal Jemmy (*Vide Pickwick*), I have spent a good deal of time on this 31st birthday of mine reviewing the swift years. *"Eheu! Postume! fugaces labuntur anni!"*[79]

As I look them over I am made very sad and can hardly tell why. To some men the fact that they come up from poverty and singlehandedness is a matter of pride. There is, at times, a little touch of gratification in my heart at what I have accomplished, but on the whole, reviewing it all, I lament sorely that I was born to poverty and allowed to catch up any or no chance habits of mind, body, morals and manners, and in this chaos of childhood seventeen yea[r]s passed before I caught up any inspiration which was worthy of my manhood, or which would lead me to begin to find the path of manhood and life. Precious 17 years in which a boy with a father and some wealth might have become fixed in manly ways and have attained half or all the preliminary work of books. Frederick the Great, at that age, an accomplished scholar, a colonel in the Army and a splendid tactician! Plenty of young men in this country and in all countries [were] ready for high places in active life at that period. I, an over-grown, uncombed, unwashed boy with the delicate japan of the soul tarnished past restoration, past that indeed if tarnished at all, was at that age compelled to begin the work of exhuming my manhood from the drift and rubbish which every chance had thrown upon me.

It has been a sad task, painfully toiled at, and with but poor success. Hardly a day passes in which I do not find sad traces of the 17 years' chaos; hardly a day when some fortunate young son of early opportunities does not make me feel my inferiority to him in things whereof I lament, but must always lament. Such experiences make me feel a sympathy with Spartacus.

Reduce the questions of life to fight, storm, or any main strength operations and Spartacus and I can stand up erect. *Possumus esse reges* [we can be kings], but in the thousand little great things of life, in the under-currents of the soul that should flow in the channels of virtue and high-minded royal honor, how sadly weak and inferior I feel. I can and do, by the sheer brute force of outer sense and religious obligation,

[79] See Horace, *Odes*, Book II, Line 14.

keep myself in the path of morality and public respect, but it does not come to me as an easy natural current whose fountain was opened in the far-off years of youth and whose flowery banks have become the sweet Eden of my life. I must do with a gladiator's strength what those thrice fortunate souls could do as matter of fixed habit from sweet choice.

Let no man praise me because I was poor and without a helper. It was every way bad for my life. Every way, unless perhaps it helped me as a gladiator; but like Spartacus, my soul is weary of the brutish spectacles whereat the *"mutum et turpe pecus* [the dumb and foul herd]" are so delighted. I would, God knows my heart, this hour joyfully surrender all I have attained could I have 17 years of my beginning replaced by the same number under the skillful hand of an able man, both in purse, head and heart. Let us never praise poverty, for a child at least. Better be poor in old age than at the time when money can buy culture of soul.

I cannot but be sad, though I hardly ought to communicate my gloom to any one else.

I am put on a military commission to try Fitz John Porter, Major General.[80] I think it will be rich in developments, though I hope short. Three courts are in operation—Buell's, McDowell's, and this.

I am very thankful for your good long letters. Keep writing I pray you. I suppose the term is about beginning. Poor Harvey! He inherited a jealous nature, and a hard one. My own feelings today lead me to pity him more than blame. This is the difference. His faults are not of the same kind as mine.

*Ever yours,*
James

Washington
November 21, 1862

*Dearest Crete:*
Yours of the 16th came duly to hand and made me glad. I have not been very well for the past three days though there is nothing serious the matter, unless it be the rust of idleness which is settling down upon me. It has been gloomy, dull weather. My birth-day has just passed and that is almost always a sad day to me, and on the whole I have been sadder for four days than for a long time. . . . Let me once be at the head of a colum[n] with Harry between my legs and I can bid a gay farewell to blue devils and almost all other colored friends.

I am right glad to hear that you are in our new home, and you cannot know how much I desire to be there with you. If you could see my longing, you would not doubt my deep joy at the thought of you and

[80] For comment on Garfield's role in the trial of Porter, see Appendix A.

Trot and our home. I am heartily tired of this rambling way of life I have live[d]—how long! Always I may say.

Just now I am bored by a most pungent smell of rotten potatoes which has tainted the atmosphere of my room for the past three days. It comes from a grocery store on the ground floor below us. No wonder one of [the] withered virgins of our family has the ague. I keep out of the room as much as I can. I am now writing [in] the court room, before the other members of the court, rather military commission, have arrived. General Hunter and I have been changed from the McDowell court to this because this can do its work in a shorter time than the other. I hope and believe [that] by the time this is through with its work the Fever may be fully abated and the iron-clad gun boats ready to go with us. On the whole I am better pleased to go against Charleston, especially as it is to be in winter, than to any other place in the army.

Lieutenant Farrar has not yet arrived with the horses. I hope he will do so today. Indeed I expect him.

I received another short note from Joe as he was passing through Cincinnati. He said the 42nd was on its way south. I want to write to him again but I don't know where to direct. I hope you will tell me what his address is. Don't fail.

I want you to keep a sharp eye on Mr. Brown. He will bear watching as well as any man in Hiram. I am sorry, very sorry, I could not have been there to help you. I know you have had a hard time.

Why don't Almeda write me? I haven't heard from her for near two weeks. I hope she is well. With much love, I am your

James

Washington
November 23, 1862

*Dearest Crete:*

I am sorry to tell you I am sick again, not seriously but very provokingly and disagreeably. For several days past I have felt dull heavy pains in my bones, especially my back and head, and today I have a great deal more of the same with considerable fever. They say that everybody that comes here from the North has to pass through a period of seasoning to the bilious fever, and this seems to be my ordeal. That you may not think it worse than it is, I tell you the full extent of my ailment. I am in a good deal of pain today, and my head aches so and is so dizzy that I can hardly write. But I am now taking medicine and I think [I] shall be able to throw it off in a few days. Thanks to you, that box of medicine arrived yesterday. Don't feel at all alarmed. I think I shall throw it off in a day or two. I shall let you hear often.

Your good letter came in due time. Keep writing to me. You will pardon this brief note. I am too unwell to write more now.

*Ever your*
James


Washington
November 30, 1862

*My Dearest Crete:*

Your good letter of the 24th came duly to hand with the welcome that greets all you have written since I came away. It is exceedingly pleasant for me to think of you as being the mistress of a home of our own, and from all the accounts I receive I am led to believe you are doing your part with grace and success. Almeda praises, Harry eulogizes, Burke decidedly approves, and Wallace goes into ecstacies; and were I there I should quietly and with great satisfaction enjoy it. I think our ideas of the management of a household harmonize well. I don't want a household conducted on niggardly principles, and yet we must study economy in all points. Whatever my future may be, I shall need to husband with care all the resources I may become master of. I know you are aware of this and I do not mention it because I think you have in any way neglected it. The month is now closing and I hope to draw some more pay in a day or two, when I will send you the $100 as you suggest. My expenses are very heavy here just now and I shall be obliged to use the othe[r] $200 of the past month's pay.

It has cost me about $125 to get my horses here and it is costing me full $15 per week to live. I changed my boarding place yesterday to an humbler and cheaper one. I am now at 435, 11th Street where I have a small room and my staff have two others. Brother Stubbs, the old quartermaster of the 42nd, arrived here this morning. I have had him appointed assistant quartermaster with the rank of captain to serve with me. My horses are well, although they do not look as they did when Green had the care of them. I shall miss him very much.

I expect Jim Rollins here in a few days and he will take care of them. I have purchased a sword, belt, and lash [sash?], which cost $50. I would not have gone to such expense, but my duty on the court requires it, and everything here is enormously dear.

I am now quite well again, though I only weigh 176 pounds.

We took a long fine ride on horseback this morning. I wish you could ride my horses some time. I hope you may. They really seemed to remember me.

Congress meets tomorrow and the city is alive with notables.

I think our court will really get to work in earnest in the morning, and I hope we may not make another Turchin case of it so far as time is concerned.

I intended to enclose a newspaper slip in a late letter to Almeda but forgot it. Here it is for both of you. It explains itself. I have nearly got over caring about it. You remember my habit in regard to such matters. With much love to you and Trot, I am ever your

James

Washington
December 1, 1862

*My Dear Burke:*

I was exceedingly pleased to receive such a long good letter from you, written at Hiram. The "eternal fitness of things"[81] seems to require you to be there to make everything seem right and natural. I hope the time may not be far distant when you will be there to work in the school again. Your recollections of the Thanksgiving at Hiram of two years ago awakened a long train and [of] memories in my own mind. Indeed I had almost forgotten that I had delivered the discourse you refer to, but now it comes before me in the full light of memory. I shall be anxious to hear from you of your discourse. Please send me a copy of your notes.

In regard to the point I made in my letter to Harry, I think reflection will show you, on the general ground, that culture is better than the want of it, that the early life of any man is more likely to be put to use by parents of means and culture than by those who have neither. It was for a long time with me a matter of gratification and perhaps pride that I had to do my own work alone. Indeed I have sometimes expressed my gratitude to that fortune which made me poor and forced me to make more efforts than I should have made had I been the inheritor of wealth. And I have no doubt that some natures are better developed under adversity and need obstacles and discouragements to bring out the mettle that is in them. . . .

I have been to the Capitol today and heard the President's message read by Forney.[82] I could hardly credit my ears when I listened to the whole message and heard no word or sentence that indicated that the administration intended to push the war to a triumphant conclusion. Indeed, it hardly contained a sentence which implied that we are in the midst of war at all. This omission is significant and ominous. I have no idea what will be said of the message. I only [know] of the impressions made on my own mind during the reading. The President goes into what seems to me a most weak and absurb [absurd] scheme of emancipation in the year of our Lord 1900, and goes on to say that

---

[81] See Henry Fielding, *The History of Tom Jones* (1749), Book IV, Chapter 4.
[82] John W. Forney, well-known journalist, was secretary of the U.S. Senate, 1861-1868.

this scheme will end the rebellion sooner than it can be ended by force, and much cheaper.[83]

I have lately seen some statements in the public journals which lead me to believe there is in certain [planning   ?] a scheme for affecting some sort of adjustment with the rebels. Now all I have to say is that any scheme which does not include the purpose of pulverizing the rebel armies and completely subd[u]ing them will bring upon us the most fearful future that any nation has seen. I hope with my whole heart that these fears may be groundless, but I have been made inexpressibly sad by the message and these collateral matters which its reading called to mind.

It would be a great pleasure for me to go back to the school again and I fully appreciate all you say in regard to it. If it can be brought about I shall do it. But the future from this standpoint is very uncertain.

I have been assigned to General Hunter's Department and I hope to get away as soon as this court is over.

Thank you for your suggestion about what I write to Harry. It was amazing to me that he should have read my letter in public.[84]

Give my love to Mary and your father and family.

*Ever yours,*
J. A. Garfield

Washington
December 5, 1862

*My Dear Harry:*

While there is a technical question before the court to which I need give no particular attention, I will make a few notes of persons and things for you. This court is attracting a great deal of interest and the room, during the hours of open court, is crowded with officers of rank and citizens of high standing. This interest results from the high rank and command of the accused, the accuser, the leading witnesses (to include Generals Pope and McClellan), and the number and rank of officers composing it, and more than all the gravity of the charges and the important operations which the transactions under consideration covered. The doings of this court will no doubt form an important part

---

[83] After presenting his plan for gradual, compensated emancipation by constitutional amendments, Lincoln said: "The plan would, I am confident, secure peace more speedily, and maintain it more permanently, than can be done by force alone; while all it would cost, considering amounts, and manner of payment, and times of payment, would be easier paid than will be the additional cost of the war, if we rely solely upon force. It is much—very much—that it would cost no blood at all." See Roy P. Basler, editor, *The Collected Works of Abraham Lincoln,* eight volumes (Rutgers University Press: New Brunswick, New Jersey, 1953), V, 536.

[84] Reference is to the letter of November 19, which Rhodes showed to Garfield's wife, Hinsdale, Almeda Booth, and perhaps to others. See the rebuke Garfield received from his wife, note 104, page 193.

of the future history of the war. By the custom of military courts members are seated at the table in the order of their rank. At the head of the table sits General Hunter, who by virture [virtue] of rank is President. He is a man of about sixty years of age, wears no other whiskers than a mustache which together with his somewhat thin hair is dyed black. He has keen gray eyes, a long nose, slightly aquiline, a large mouth with corners slightly depressed, and the whole shut with a sharp decisiveness. He has a habit of swaying his head from side to side when he speaks, and seems to sling his quick decisive words right and left. He is probably 5 feet 10 inches and weighs 175 pounds.

On his right sits Major General Hitchcock[85] of Bennington, Vermont, a hale looking old gentleman, a little turned of sixty, with a broad round head of the J. Q. Adams type, with a monkish baldness, having only a fringe of thin hair perfectly white on the side and back portions. He has a fine blue eye, smooth-shaven face, and probably weighs 200 pounds. He is an old army man, but I don't know what he has done in this war.

On the President's left, and opposite to General Hitchcock, sits Brigadier General King[86] of Milwaukee, Wisconsin, a man of about 40 years, rather spare built, with shaggy black hair and full whiskers of the same color, with a rugged, strongly-marked face enlightened by a steel-gray eye and surmounted by a knotty Roman nose of the Bascom sort. He has a weather-beaten, powder-blackened look which reminds us for [of] the rugged fighting he has done and the sturdy blows he has struck in the Army of the Potomac and of Virginia. Three deep, permanent, vertical wrinkles in the forehead where brow and nose join set off the expression and complete the picture of a man who has evidently got in him a large fund of hard sense and hard work.

On General Hitchcock's right sits Brigadier General Prentiss,[87] a man strongly resembling Esquire Williams, constable of Chagrin Falls, or perhaps a cross between him and the Honorable Blakessee [Blakeslee?] of the same place. His face is not sufficiently marked to lead me to take his picture *in extenso*. You rem[em]ber his Cairo-Shiloh and rebel prison experience. He is a pleasant little man, on the whole rather sensible, but will never be considered the avatar of intellect.

Opposite [Prentiss] and on the left of General King sits Brigadier General Ricketts[88] of New York, about 35 years of age, of fresh com-

[85] Ethan Allen Hitchcock, a graduate of West Point, was then the newly-appointed commissioner for exchange of prisoners of war. His *Fifty Years in Camp and Field*, published in 1909, thirty-nine years after his death, is autobiographical.

[86] Rufus King, editor and diplomat, was then nearly forty-nine years of age. King was the organizer of the famous Iron Brigade.

[87] Major General Benjamin M. Prentiss, a hero of Shiloh, where elements of his Sixth Division were surrounded and forced to surrender after a gallant stand at the Hornets Nest, went from a Confederate prison to Washington after being exchanged in October.

[88] James B. Ricketts, then in his forty-sixth year, was recovering from a wound (he was wounded six times during the war) received at Antietam, where he had led a division.

plexion, rather of the precise, clerkly sort, pointed chin, tipped with light gh [?] whiskers which mingle with a curling mustache, pale blue eyes and a smooth, fresh-looking forehead slightly marred by a scar which resembles a saber cut. He has served mainly under General McDowell and bore a brave part in the last battle of Bull Run. On the left [right] of General Prentiss sits Brigadier General Casey of New York, probably 55 years of age, badly bald, hair and whiskers white, the latter consisting only of the underchin growth. He has a florid countenance, blue eyes, a very long slender Roman nones [nose] and a very large mouth. He is a microscopic sort of man of the bookish persuasion much wedded to the school of precedents and *res judicata,* and the minutest matters of form. He is the author of three volumes on military tactics lat[e]ly published by the Government and adopted as the standard. You will rem[em]ber him as the commander of a division which suffered a defeat on the Peninsula and was blamed by General McClellan, but the blame was afterward retracted.

Opposite him, and on the right [left] of General Ricketts, is yours truly. On the right of General Casey sits General Buford[89] of Illinois (a classmate of General Polk, rebel), and on my left, General [John P.] Slough of Colorado Territory, formerly of Cincinnati and member of the Ohio House of Representatives. I am the only member of the court, besides himself, who happens to know a little item of his history. He was a little tight one day, and in debate he struck [Darius] Caldwell of Ashtabula in the face, for which he was expelled [from] the House. I of course make no reference to this, not even so much as to tell him that I beat in convention the man whom he beat with his fist.[90] Of Judge Holt,[91] General Pope, Porter, *etc.,* I will write you hereafter, if I find this is not a bore to you. It is snowing and dreary. Do write.

*Ever yours,*
J. A. Garfield

Washington
December 7, 1862

*My Dear Harry:*
Yours of November 28th, post-marked Solon, December 1st, came to hand yesterday. I had already sent an interloper written from the

[89] Brigadier General Napoleon B. Buford had distinguished himself at Belmont, Island No. 10, and Fort Pillow. He was called to Washington after suffering a sun stroke in the Corinth campaign of October, 1862.

[90] Caldwell was one of Garfield's opponents for the nomination as Republican candidate for Congress from Ohio's Nineteenth District.

[91] Joseph Holt of Kentucky, Postmaster General and Secretary of War under Buchanan, was appointed Judge Advocate General of the Army in September, 1862 and prosecuted the Government's case against Porter.

court room, which you will notice was clipped off rather abruptly by
the adjournment of the court and by the receipt of a note from Governor Chase asking me to call on him at the [Treasury] Department at
3½, or in default at his house to dinner at six. I was engaged and declined the dinner, when I received another note and went, where I had
a pleasant time with him, the Assistant Secretary of the Treasury
([George] Harrington) and Henry B. Stanton of New York. We played
five games of chess, after which I went to theatre. Mr. Chase had that
morning got the biographical sketch which you wrote of me published
in the *Chronicle* here, with some additions of his own. I did not know
how it came to get into the paper here but Chase told me he did it.

At the theatre we saw Miss Lucille Western (a new and very bright
star) in *Camille*. It is a most powerful play and was magnificently presented. If you ever come in reach of Miss Western you must not fail to
hear her. She has played here thirty-six nights without the omission of
one week-day night, and had [has] had crowded houses all the while.
I think she has more talent in some respects than any woman I have
ever seen on stage.

Today I went to Brother Campbell's on Massachusetts Avenue where
the Disciples hold their meeting. There is a small body of them here
who keep up their organization and hold social meetings and break the
loaf at private houses. I spoke a short time but was annoyed [by] their
constant reference to "their distinguished brother," *etc., etc.* On my
return from meeting I took up President Hopkins' new book on moral
philosophy, which I lately sent for to Boston (Gould and Lincoln), and
I have read the first two lectures. I want you and Almeda to read it
together. It is evidently one of the most well-weighed and elaborate
performances of the good old man's life and is full of gems. It has an
extraordinary amount of *solidarity*. Let me give you some of his clear,
compendious statements: "Whoever can answer, in all cases, these three
questions, 1st. What ought to be done? 2nd. Why ought it to be done?
3rd. How ought it to be done? has mastered the science of morals."
"Rules and laws have often been confounded, but they are essentially
different. A law is imperative; a rule is not. A law has sanctions; a rule
has not. A law tells us what to do; a rule how to do it."

This is more luminous than Blackstone himself, and if I remember
right it criticizes him. It is new to me, but very just. Here is one of his
fine touches in which he is so inimitable, "The only question is, what
is it that consciousness gives. If we say that it gives both the subject
and the object, that simple affirmation sweeps away in a moment the
whole basis of the ideal and skeptical philosophy. It becomes as the
spear of Ithuriel, and its simple touch will change what seemed whole
continents of solid speculation into mere banks of German fog." The
whole book has the genuine ring of the old President's metal, and you
must not fail to get it. It is dedicated to the graduates of the college.

He takes issue with both Jouffroy[92] and Hickok[93] on the basis of morals, but he seems to me to adopt a theory which makes the *summum bonum* consist in happiness, though that is not the final statement. Again I urge you to read the book.

Governor Dennison is here. Tomorrow evening I go with him to take dinner at Mr. [Montgomery] Blair's, the Postmaster General, and on Tuesday evening I dine at Marshal Lamon's, whose wife is a Disciple.[94]

Day before yesterday two young men came up to me and announced themselves as Bill Ogle and Chauncey Black,[95] whom we expelled from Hiram several years ago. I think it was before you were there. It was in the days of Goddard. Almeda remembers them. They laughed about their expulsion, said they deserved it, and seemed very glad to see me. Ogle is a clerk in the War Department, and Black is a lawyer. His father, late Attorney General, has lately moved to this place and fixed his residence here.

Chase's report[96] is the great state paper of the day, in some respects the greatest ever brought out in that Department. There is one matter in it about which I feel a personal gratification. We conversed a good deal on currency while I was at his house, and I read a good deal on the subject. Mr. Carey[97] of Philadelphia was sent for to be conversed with upon it. In one conversation I advanced the following about in the words in which they are written. "There are two causes, and only two which can affect a paper currency and cause it to fluctuate in value. 1st, the kind of security on which it is based, and 2nd, the amount of its circulation. To secure a uniform currency, both these conditions must be provided for by *one* power. Congress has power, by the Constitution, to coin money and regulate currency, but it has most unwisely allowed states and corporations and even individuals to make

[92] Théodore Simon Jouffroy, French philosopher and author, wrote works on metaphysics, psychology, ethics, and aesthetics.

[93] Laurens Perseus Hickok, clergyman and philosopher, was the author of several books, including *A System of Moral Science* (1853).

[94] Ward H. Lamon of Illinois, a former law partner of Lincoln, was marshal of the District of Columbia. His second wife, Sally, was the daughter of Stephen T. Logan.

[95] Ogle and Black were from Somerset County, Pennsylvania. They attended the Eclectic, 1852-1853. Among their classmates were Charles Goddard of Ashtabula County and J. T. Goddard of Macon, Georgia. Garfield later became a close friend of Black's father, Jeremiah, and was associated with him in a number of cases in law. Ogle's father, Charles, was a member of the U.S. House of Representatives, 1837-1841.

[96] In his second annual report Chase proposed an association of national banks supervised by the Federal Government and authorized to issue national bank notes based upon U.S. bonds. Chase believed his plan would create a market for U.S. bonds, establish a more uniform currency, ease the demand on legal tender notes for use as bank reserves, and thus do much to solve the nation's major financial problems. The proposal induced Congress to pass the National Banking Act early in 1863.

[97] Henry Charles Carey, economist, publisher, and author, was a leading authority on political economy.

currency. Thus we have a thousand different parties tinkering at the currency. Hence there is no uniformity in the securities on which the various currencies are based, and of course there can be no rational regulation of the amount of issue. It takes a certain amount of currency to [do] the business of the country. If the issue is less than that amount, money is at a premium, if more, at a discount. Therefore to remedy the evil Congress must assume the exclusive control of the matter and sweep away all currency but its own." It was considered a very novel proposition, but there is a good deal of it in the Secretary's Report. The court is pushing its work on, but Reverdy Johnson[98] cross examines as fierce as a tiger. I will write you more of it by and by.

No wonder you say that marginal lines are the cream of letters, when you tell me in the margin, so incidentally, that you are soon to be married; were it not nearly midnight I would undertake to write your *epithalamium*. But you know I wish you all possible joy and happiness. I shall hope to hear a full report of "your taking off."

You and Almeda are wrong in supposing that my notions about the disadvantages of early poverty are the result of my life here. The origin of that opinion is two-fold: 1st, a paragraph in one of Broderick's best speech[es] in the Senate,[99] which I read three years ago; and *second,* the experience of my life, early and late.

Do write and tell Almeda I am waiting anxiously to hear for [from?] her. With much love, I am as

*ever your brother,*
James

Why don't I hear from Charley Harmon?[100] I have written him. I wish you would find out.

I send you Secretary Chase's note as a specimen of his penmanship.

J. A. G.

If you have money to invest I think it is well to invest it in Government stocks. See a letter of mine to Crete in which I sent home $500 in U.S. bonds at six percent.

J. A. G.

[98] Johnson, one of the outstanding trial lawyers of his time, was defending Porter.

[99] David C. Broderick was a Democratic Senator from California, 1857-1859. In March, 1858, during a debate on the Lecompton Constitution, Broderick referred to his humble origins and toilsome early life as follows: "I am the son of an artisan, and have been a mechanic. . . . I am not proud of this. . . . I would that I could have enjoyed the pleasures of life in my boyhood's days; but they were denied to me. I say this with pain. I have not the admiration for the men of the class from whence I sprang that might be expected; they submit too tamely to oppression, and are too prone to neglect their rights and duties as citizens." Broderick also stated his belief that the laboring class would control "the destinies of this nation."

[100] Charles Harmon, a storekeeper and postmaster in Aurora.

Washington
December 9, 1862

*My Dearest Crete:*

Yours of the 4th was received last night. I am very glad you are pleased with the picture. It was made by Mr. Ulke,[101] my German friend here. He took a photograph, and then I gave him two sittings of half an hour each. His brush did more for the picture than the camera. When I was in New York, an engraver, J[ohn] C[hester] Buttre, wanted to make a steel engraving of me for a volume he is publishing and I sent him the picture. It was three or four weeks before he had completed the engraving. I think the engraving is very good though of course I cannot tell. I will have some copies sent you. I would not have you think I would be so foolish as to incur the expense of my face on steel, for it would have cost $80 or $100. Mr. Buttre got the engraving up on his own account. The picture I sent you was made as a present to you and cost $30. Does little Trot know it? I hope so.

I am glad that Jim is with you. He is a good boy, and will be of great service. I had sent for him to come here and go with me into the field, but I will leave it with you to determine whether he shall come or not. I have great confidence in him and I know he would serve me well, but if he is anxious to learn to read and write, and can at the same time be of service to you, I think he had better stay with you. Of course he is subjected to a peculiar peril, in case of capture, which a white man is not. I will write to him, perhaps before I close up this envelope. I want him to like me and I hope he does.

I have lately drawn my pay for the last month, and I enclose you in this letter $100, which I hope will meet the necessities of your household till I have a little more pay. I will try to get a draft. In case I do not I will enclose a $100 treasury note. I know it is not a good way to do business, but the mails are very regular and safe and there is but little risk.

I am writing in the court, which [is] now progressing finely. We have a phonographer here who takes down the testimony as fast as the witnesses can talk. General Pope and Captain DeKay[102] have been examined, and General Roberts[103] is now giving his testimony.

I this morning received a letter from Dr. Robison saying that he and his wife are now in New York and are coming here to see me before they returned home.

[101] Henry Ulke, Prussian-born artist who migrated to the U.S. in 1851, settled in Washington and painted portraits of many prominent men of his time.

[102] Captain Drake DeKay, Pope's aide-de-camp, testified on December 8 that he had delivered to Porter, on August 27, a written order from Pope which Porter was accused of disobeying without sufficient cause. DeKay's entire testimony was hostile to Porter.

[103] Brigadier General Benjamin S. Roberts served first as chief of cavalry and later as inspector general in Pope's Army of Virginia. His testimony was hostile to Porter.

I am sorry you all seem to think that my letter to Harry in regard to the advantages of wealth and opportunity in early life, and the disadvantages of being poor and having no strong and cultivated mind to direct the growth and developement of character [was unjust and gratuitous].[104] It was the farthest possible from my thoughts to find any fault with my good mother. I have no doubt, as you say, that much good has resulted to me from having been obliged to fight the battle of life alone, but it is none the less true that I lack much which I otherwise would not. The chief thought which led me into this train of reflection was in my heartlongings over our dear little Trot. I was thinking what her future womanhood would be if she had neither your counsel or mine to guide her, and were obliged to struggle along as [a] hired girl in some kitchen at one dollar a week, as compared with what it might be, aided by us and such a competency as would enable us to give her the best culture that our educational institutions can afford. Do you think I was very "wicked" in thinking that to be poor and alone in early life is not so fine a thing as poetic views of the gallant fight in life's battle would sometimes lead us to think it. I am always glad to have you speak whatever you think of all my doings and I thank you for your suggestions on that subject.

Try to tell Trot how much I love her, and how anxious I am to go home and live with her and you. Write me often *and often.*

*Ever and forever your*
James

[104] Criticism of the remarks he made in his letter of November 19 came from Rhodes, Booth, and Hinsdale. The censure from Mrs. Garfield, in a letter of December 4, reveals so vividly her common sense, spirit, faith, and wisdom—qualities which were often sources of strength and direction for Garfield—that it is quoted at length: "I felt a little sorry," she wrote, "to read such a desponding almost complaining letter as your birthday letter to Harry. It is with me a positive certainty that whatever be the circumstances *beyond our control* which surround us they are the very best. Just what we need to make us what God designed us to be, if we use them as we have the power given us to; and I believe, Jamie, if you will question yourself as to the time when you have developed most rapidly—not only *strength* but *refinement* and *purity of sentiment* and *feeling*—you will find it was not when you were *helped* in any way but when you stood all alone, and from some tendencies of your nature I do not believe you would have been as good or noble and not half as *great* had not your career been one of struggle. Jamie, how it would break your little mother's heart to read that letter and I beg of you do not indulge in any more such *wicked*—yes, I do feel they were wicked—repinings. You can be all that any man ought to be if you will continue to strengthen and cultivate the powers God has given you." To cushion the rebuke, Garfield's wife apologized for being severe and attributed his remarks to a "very morbid condition of feeling" caused by a "bilious state of health."

Washington
December 10, 1862

*My Dear Burke:*

Your note of December 4th was received day before yesterday. I had already answered your former letter which you have doubtless received ere this.

In regard to the matter discussed in the letter now before me, I will say first that I am glad you have written me in the premises and secondly, that I most fully approve of your views as therein expressed. I wrote to Hiram soon after Everest's resignation recommending the Masters to get you there as soon as spring, and yesterday I wrote again more at length. I am exceedingly anxious that you should be with the school, and I was greatly grieved that it could not have been arranged to keep you there last fall and this winter. They have got Mr. Suliot, I suppose as a temporary help for winter, and I know they all want you if the pecuniary prospects of the school will warrant it, and I think they will.

If I should not return to the school they will need you. If I should return I shall need you, for if I go back again I must have a circle of social and intellectual friends that can mutually aid each other in growth and living. I very much desire such a condition of thinks [things], and if the stormy time in which we are living will ever clear up, I may hope to reach it. But I have no good ground for hoping that I may get there next spring. I shall hope to hear from you further in regard to this matter as the negotiations progress. Of course you understand that I don't speak with any authority, for I would not in any way interfere with the teachers or trustees in any other way than that of advising, but all I can do in that way I shall do most gladly.

The court is becoming very interesting in its developement and its record cannot fail to become an important part of the future history of the war. I would write more but I must go to the court.

Love to Mary and let me hear from you again.

*Very truly yours,*
J. A. Garfield


Washington
December 14, 1862

*My Dear Harry:*

Yours of the 11th is received today. I am amazed that you think I am your epistolary debtor. You have not sent me a letter, however short, since I have been in Washington that I have not answered, and for some time I have been feeling that you were in my debt. Indeed I have suspected that the "gentle dalliance of love" had filled your heart more than the thought of writing letters to me. But I will not be jealous. Only write to me and give me credit for responding punctually. My letter to you from the court martial was an interloper and not an answer to anything I had received from you.

Today the battle is raging along the Rappahannock[105] and I hope tomorrow will reveal the features of victory and a good hope for the future.

Our Court is becoming intensely interesting in its developements and at almost any other time I should be glad of such an opportunity as this affords to become acquainted with the men and movements of the time. But I am growing more and more restless every day, and when the work of the court is done I shall make a direct issue with the War Department. They must give me something to do or they must take my commission. I will not endure it.

General McDowell was before us Friday and Saturday, and (with the exce[p]tion of about half an hour in which the grim old Dutchman, General Heintzelman, gave his testimony) he took the whole time. I admire McDowell more and more. His Saxon is a[s] clear as crystal and no amount of cross-examination can render him opaque or confused in the least degree. On the whole I have a higher opinion of McDowell's talents than of any other man's in the army, and if he is again assigned a command I would prefer to go under him rather than any other. His history will yet be vindicated.

Reverdy Johnson is the prince of lawyers in this country. He and Joe Holt form a fine group for studying char[acter?]. Johnson is more of an intellectual *bear* than any man I ever saw. He has a huge face with powerful maxillary muscles which give him a perfect mastiff look. Eyes that protrude from his head, one of them blind, a heavy, rugged nose, the longest upper lip I ever saw, face closely shaven, coarse, bristly hair, nearly white, and a heavy, surly, clangorous voice that pierces and tears at the same time. There is a direct, searching fierceness in his questions which is of itself almost enough to make a witness suspect himself to be a villain and fear that he is lying. He will make a modest, conscientious man give his testimony with so much timidity and so many modifications that the force of it is half wasted by the time it reaches the record.

Holt is genial, pleasant, wears his greatness with a dignity and grace which makes everybody love him, but is fully master of the situation and is never for a moment caught off his guard. He looks a little like Ben [jamin Franklin] Leiter, though the comparison is infinitely flattering to B. F. L.

McDowell's testimony was very direct and crushing, and whenever Johnson attempted to work a growl of discord into it, he struck a rock which flashed out fire and light upon the investigation.

[105] The Battle of Fredericksburg, fought on December 13, was a Confederate victory. On the 14th and 15th the Union army faced, but did not attack, the enemy: then it withdrew across the Rappahannock.

Dr. Robison and wife are now here and I expect to spend all my spare time for two or three days in doing the agreeable to them. The Doctor is full of beef and politics and I shall show him to some of the lions.

I have been writing an article on the currency question which I may send to the press, but anonymously if at all. Several gentlemen here have requested me to write it. I am surprised that in so short a time I should be able to get so strong a hold on the subject as to attract the attention of some men with whom I have conversed. I spent some time with Amasa Walker[106] of Boston and Judge Davies[107] of New York a few evenings ago on the subject. The former is Carey's rival and opponent in this country on the questions of social science and is Lecturer in Political Economy in Amherst College. He is now in Congress. I have promised to go to his hotel and spend an evening with him soon on these subjects. I will give you a report.

By the way, I have formed a very peculiar and interesting acquaintance with Major General Hitchcock of whom I wrote you. He is a remarkable man and has been appointed to the Volunteer army not to take a command, for he is too old, but to be an adviser of the War Department. He is full of wise saws, laws, and precedents, and, thinking this the ablest court ever assembled, he is anxious it should do a good deal in the way of making military law.

I tried myself on the old General a few days ago and I believe I have made him foolish enough to think quite highly of me. The court had got muddled up on the question of how far a witness should be allowed to give his opinion. Johnson had objected to a question which Holt had asked McDowell on the ground that his opinion was asked. I got off something like the following as an answer to Reverdy. "It is true that the opinion of a witness is inadmissible when that opinion is based on written orders or other documents in poss[es]sion of the court, or on any facts which may be fully placed before the court. In all such cases it is the business of the wit[ness] to furnish these documents and facts, and it is the duty of the court to interpret the one and draw its own conclusions, given the other. But where the opinion of the witness is a collective judgment, based on a series of complex facts and collateral circumstances which cannot in their totality be placed perfectly before the court, such opinion is not only admissible but is the court's only mode of reaching the truth. The question objected to is that General McDowell's opinion is asked—how, if General Porter had attacked the right flank of the enemy on the 29th August, as he was ordered, would it have affected the result of the battle. It is impossible for this court to know the situation of the moment as the

[106] Political economist and author; member of the U.S. House of Representatives, 1862-1863.

[107] Henry Ebenezer Davies, Judge of the New York Court of Appeals.

witness knew it. Hence it is competent for the court to propound the question." Johnson's objection was overruled and General Hitchcock asked that my exposition to [be] entered on the record as the rule of law in such cases. Since then the old man has been very deferential and old Reverdy more ursine than ever.

I find that General Hitchcock is a voluminous theological writer of the A. J. Davis[108] School. Indeed, he is quite an oracle among them. He has given me several of his works to read, which I do *"cum oculis currentibus* [with hurrying eyes]." I enclose you one of his waifs, an article on Dante which it will pay to preserve. He has written on the Rosicrucians and other wierd and occult subjects. His library is a curiosity of mysterious old books.

General Casey is quite a mathematical genius and we have been passing geometrical and al[g]ebraic problems across the table for several days while the formal [charge] was being read. Here is an equation he gave me which please show to the classes and to Almeda:

$$x - 1 = \frac{9}{\sqrt{x}} + 2$$

to find the value of x. Send me your solution.

By the way, and not to be named out of our circle, there are several leading men who are so sharp-sighted as to see very deep into political mill-stones and who say that there is a secret determination to keep me out of the field till the Ohio legislature has elected a U. S. Senator, for should I gain any considerable credit in the field it might be a disturbing element in the plans and plots relative to that event. I of course laugh at the whole thing as rash, but they are serious in the belief of it.[109] I would be exceedingly happy to be at home during the holiday and especially during your *holy-day* (may it be both holy and happy to you and to Libbie) but I have small hope of reaching it.

There are several prominent men here from the West who insist that I shall be sent to the West, and the thing is not altogether improbable. Should it be so, I might drop in for a day and night, but I dare not hope for it. For writing so long a letter I am ready to cry "peccavi" and no doubt to cry "enough."

The rebel residuum of the Democratic party will yet make us a great deal of trouble. They are getting very bold and very impudent.

Write me freely and often before you "swing out" [as] we used to say in college, and I shall be very jealous if you do not continue the same after the fatal noose has been adjusted. May your marriage prove a refutation of the old couplet,

---

[108] Andrew J. Davis, spiritualist and author, formulated the fundamental principles of modern spiritualism and gave it much of its phraseology.

[109] The term of Benjamin F. Wade was due to expire in March, 1863.

"No rogue [man] e'er felt the halter draw,
With good opinion of the law."[110]

*Ever thine,*
James

Washington
December 16, 1862

*My Dear Burke:*
Yours of the 12th came to hand last evening with a sketch of the Thanksgiving discourse enclosed, for both of which (letter and discourse) accept my thanks.

All our thoughts and feelings are just now absorbed in the blood and smoke of the Rappahannock. I hope the country is awaking to the truth of the doctrine I have tried to preach to them for the last six months—*viz.* that there is no hope of the republic unless we pulverize the great rebel armies. We may take small or large cities, girdle their country with expeditions, and blockade, but there is no end till their armies are broken. I have often thought of Coleridge's remark that "abstract definitions had done more harm to the world than famine, pestilence and war." This may be a strong statement but I think we have a most illustrious and pestilent example of the pernicious influence of a faulty illustration. It is not an "abstract definition," but it is a metaphor which were [when?] embodied in human flesh and blood ought to [be] hanged for the crime of high treason to the republic.

I mean General Scott's Anaconda,[111] which was going to make a second Laocoön of the rebellion. That brilliant but false idea has done more to shape the war policy of the rebellion than almost any other one thing I know of. We have all the time been trying to surround the rebels. We have frittered away our strength in a whole litter of small expeditions while the enemy has concentrated his forces and whipped us in detail.

We must make a center shot, hit him in the bull's eye before we can hope to see him fall. To do this, no shrewdness of maneuvering, no amount of military finesse will avail. To crush him there is a certain fearful amount of blood to be shed and we must hasten to shed it where we can make the like bloody reprisals on him. We must do

[110] From John Trumbull's "McFingal," Canto III, Line 489. On December 31, Rhodes married Elizabeth Ann Woodward, of Lordstown, who died in November, 1863, after bearing a stillborn baby.

[111] Lieutenant General Winfield Scott's Anaconda plan was to isolate the Confederacy by a tight blockade and an expedition down the Mississippi River to its mouth. Thereafter the idea was not to invade, but to hold firm. In time, Scott believed, Unionist sentiment in the South would express itself and force Confederate officials to sue for peace and reunion.

this, not by sharp practice but as you once said to me of your own literary performances, by main strength. I therefore welcome the bloody work at Fredericksburg. But I have no words to tell you the feeling of unrest and almost personal debasement and contempt for myself I feel by being compelled to stay here, digging up the records of past blunders and misdeeds on that court, while my brethren are struggling and bleeding. I would infinitely rather die on the Rappahannock in trying to do something than to be compelled much longer to stay here as I am doing.

The court, however, is developing an exceedingly rich chapter of history, which will some day be read with great interest, not unmixed with wonder and indignation. . . .

I am much pleased with your Thanksgiving discourse. The divisions and subdivisions are clear and comprehensive. You have struck "a rich lead" as the miners say, especially in your discussion of the causes of the rebellion. I thought there was a line of reflection that would have added to the interest of your second grand division—*viz.* the costly but valuable education which our people have received during the war. The epochs of growth in great ideas have been very marked during the past year. It would seem to require a more than human power to educate our people up to some of the planes they have reach[ed]. Nearly every regiment that marches up Pennsylvania Avenue, whether composed of Republicans or Democrats, go[es] singing "John Brown's body lies mouldering," *etc.* It is sung on the streets, in theaters and parlors, and is the wildest inspiration of the army. What a change since old fireworks Wise hung him.[112]

I have no other criticism to make unless I give you a hit on your chirography, the Choatean qualities of which sometimes nearly baffle my skill.

Harry is to be married New Year's Eve. I would be very glad to be there but cannot of course.

Give my love to Mary and your father's family and let me hear from you often and long.

*Ever yours,*
J. A. Garfield

Washington
December 19, 1862

*Dearest Crete:*

Yours of the 14th was received last night. Your last before this, written December 4th, was received ten days before this. Let us post up our epistola[r]y books, since you have referred to the account, and see

[112] John Brown's raid at Harpers Ferry, his capture, trial, and execution occurred during the governorship of Henry A. Wise.

how we stand. During the last twenty-nine days I have received three letters from you, bearing respectively the dates of November 20th, December 4th, and December 14th. I have never failed to answer any letter I have received from you since I came to Washington, and I think I have never delayed an answer longer than two days. Since November 20th I have written more letters to you than I have received from you.

During that period Harry has written to me nearly twice as much as any one else. I have carefully looked over my files of letters from you and there is nothing in any of them for the last month in regard to Mr. Buckingham. Either some of your letters have miscarried, or you forgot to write any Buckingham items. I have answered all the inquiries you have made so far as I now remember. I have been feeling very sad and very much alone of late, my staff having gone to Philadelphia and New York, and so few letters coming to me from home. And now if we have mutually been "hurt" a little, let's try to get well as soon as we can. I can't see how I am indebted to Mr. Buckingham. You will pay him no money without word from me. He had better address me himself if he wants any settlement with me. It will be the manlier way for him. He was none too manly in backing around as he did till I gave him $25.00 outright, by releasing that much of his lawful debt.

The events on the Rappahannock have cast a gloom over the whole country and I am not yet able to see what the effects will be. The country is so fearfully given up to partisan political strifes that I almost despair of our giving the great questions of the war any calm sensible consideration. There are scores of men who seem far more intent on crying up or down some military or political leader than in pushing the war. I am every day asking myself what this nation has done which is so much more wicked than the deeds of all others that the scourge of God should fall so heavily and not be lifted. I have never despaired, and do not now, but I feel as though there could not be many deeper deeps of humiliation than we have now reached.

Dr. Robison and wife are in the city and have been since Saturday last. The Doctor was taken quite unwell two days ago as he was about starting for home and has been compelled to stay till he gets better. I have given him ever[y] spare moment to show him around the city and to the lions here, for which class of wild beasts he has a great relish.

The court suspended its work for two days for lack of testimony, but we are now at work again. Parson Brownlow[113] is here trying to get the President to send me into East Tennessee. I have not expectation that it will be done. Give my love to mother and tell her I want her to write

[113] William G. Brownlow of Tennessee, Methodist minister and Unionist newspaper editor, became widely known as "the fighting parson." After the war he served two terms as Governor of Tennessee, 1865-1869, and was a member of the U.S. Senate, 1869-1875.

to me. I will answer Nell's letter either in this envelope or soon. Kiss our dear little one. Ever your

James

I am going to turn off my darkie this morning and try to find a better one. The rascal is not attentive. And then he has been running my horses so that the police took him up and fined him. It is hard to get a good man. Green would rave if he knew how the horses have been used by this scamp. Give my love to Jim. He must learn to write to me. Please send me an estimate of what it costs you to live per month.

Washington
December 24, 1862

*My Dear Harry:*

My dashing Harry, my philo-connubial, ante-nuptial, anti-Coelebs Harry, or fast becoming my "Old Harry"—the top o' the morning to you. Your chock-full letter written up the sides and down the middle isn't getting answered in time to give you Merry Christmas while the day is with you, but natheless it will reach you shortly after.

Since I wrote you last our Washington world has been "in a fine frenzy rolling" and the presidential eye has been rapidly "glancing from heaven to earth, from earth to h[e]aven," not to mention an occasional look (Seward) seaward. But he has at last got his cabinet-ware mended— for how long it is difficult to say, only it is well known that glue don't stand hot water very well.[114]

Burnside has come out with a letter to the General in Chief shouldering the responsibility of his late thrashing at Fredericksburg, which is rather frank and manly, but it is a kind of apology for getting whipped which might have been better omitted.

There is a very insidious and determined scheme on the part of the Democracy, especially that of New York, to make a kind of French coup d'etat in favor of McClellan. It has been brought to light here within the past two or three days that at a dinner given to McClellan

[114] As the war progressed, Secretary of State Seward became more and more the target of criticism from Chase and other radical Republicans who disliked Lincoln's policies and the extent to which Seward helped shape them. The feud reached a climax after Fredericksburg when Republican senators, after several caucuses, sent a delegation to Lincoln. The senators denounced Seward, demanded that the President reorganize his Cabinet, meet with it more often, and adhere to Republican policies only. They also implied he should make Chase the chief power in his administration. Lincoln arranged a second meeting with the delegation, which arrived to find all of the Cabinet except Seward present. In front of his colleagues Chase had to admit that on all major policies the Cabinet acted harmoniously, with the President making the decisions. Chase was embarrassed and handed in his resignation. Seward had already submitted his. Lincoln accepted neither. Seward and Chase agreed to stay on and the crisis passed.

by a member of the leading Democrats of New York City the proposition was made with closed doors to get the Army of the Potomac to declare for him or for him to assume the military dictatorship. It is now thought also that it was a member of his late staff who is responsible for the failure of getting the pontoons forward to Fredericksburg, and on that failure it is now evident that our defeat depended. The officer referred to was heard to say before the battle that he didn't "care a damn whether the pontoons got to him in time or not."[115] These things are now getting to the ears of the President and would forebode a thunder-gust if there were any lightning in him. But doubtless he will respond by an anecdote and let these rascal[s] fillip his nose or pluck his beard at pleasure.

By the way, do you know why our good friend Hall of the *Portage Democrat* has attacked Chase in such a terribly severe way? I felt exceedingly bad for Chase yesterday when he read the article. It came upon him like a bolt from the blue. Hall has been one of his firmest and truest friends for twenty years, and to come out all of a sudden and for no conceivable reason is not only a grief but a puzzle which he says he is utterly unable to understand.

It almost makes me homesick to think of you there studying French and having such a fine time of it. If I ever get the least chance in the world, I shall go on with the French. I have only begun a very little. I am reading *Frederick the Great* with a volume of plans of his battles, the text of which is in French. In connection with the English biography I am reading, I have but little trouble to make out the explanations of the plates, but it makes me feel the need of knowing that fine language—and ah! do you know you have touched me on a very tender point when you speak of our going to Europe together. I am more and more determined, if I ever get foot loose, to go and take that tour which can do so much for one's thoughts. I hope you will give your readings a current thitherward so that if the day should ever come we can be sensible about it.

Our intolerable court has finished the prosecution and the defense will begin today. We did not meet yesterday, and I took a gallop of ten miles with Kate Chase. She is a splendid rider and toward the close of our ride we came back to the city and Mr. Chase joined us. He looks finely on a horse. There was a considerable talk during the Cabinet troubles of putting him at the head of the army. . . .

[115] The arrival of the pontoons at Falmouth, on the Rappahannock opposite Fredericksburg, a week later than Burnside had expected them, prevented his Union army from bridging the river until Lee was in position to resist the crossing. Burnside promptly arrested Brigadier General Daniel P. Woodbury, commander of his engineering brigade, but released him after getting a satisfactory explanation. Some continued to believe that Woodbury was responsible and even suspected him of treachery. Halleck too was blamed. Washington buzzed with rumors. Garfield's, with its sinister implications, was probably about Woodbury, who, together with Halleck and Burnside himself, was partly though unintentionally responsible for the costly delay.

Dan Clayton—brother of the man who wrote me, *"I have been made a father by the birth of a son"* (remember this as a model of paternal literatim)—is a member of the Capitol-building police. Almeda will remember him if you don't.

I am happy to tell you that my health is now quite fine and I can say with some degree of assurance that I have bowels that can be relied on. I read *Frederick* till three o'clock this morning and got up at 6¾ feeling finely and greedy for *Frederick* and you. Having now polished you off, I turn to my other hero. I have written to Almeda in regard to Brother Munnell. I agree with your views. Write *semper, ubique* [always, everywhere].

> *Ever your*
> James

Washington
December 26, 1862

*My Dear Crete:*

Yours of the 22nd came to hand this morning as I returned from a Christmas trip across the Potomac. The Ohio people here in the city gave a Christmas dinner to the Ohio soldiers (about 800) who are located in a convalescent camp at Fort Gaines about four miles out of the city, so a large party went out to cheer the boys. There was a fine dinner given them and after it speeches made by Judge Spalding, John Sherman, Governor Chase, Mr. Hutchins, myself and others.

After the dinner was over I went to the Chain Bridge and over to the Virginia shore to visit Captain [Joseph H.] Allen of the 169th New York. He is Brother Allen of Millville, New York, whose wife visited us in Hiram in 1860. He has lately raised a company and come into the service. I was pleasantly surprised to find his wife there, and also to find some half dozen old college acquaintances. The colonel [Clarence Buell] was at Williams a few years before me. The surgeon [John Knowlson] graduated the year before me, and the major [Alonzo] (Alden) was a class-mate of Harry's. I knew several others. They had a fine Christmas supper concluding with speeches and songs. I staid over night and came into town this morning.

The court has done a good day's work and I hope we are moving with accelerated velocity toward the end of the business. I am delighted to hear all those dear little pranks and traits of our precious little Trot. I constantly feel that I am losing very much of the most interesting part of her babyhood by being away from her so much. It is very hard for me to let all that period pass without leaving my finger marks upon her childhood's history and developement, but the outlook for the future, as the war is now developing itself, is by no means flattering to my hopes of enjoying much for a long time to come.

The next sentence after this must not be mentioned. Mr. Chase told me a day or two ago that the Secretary of War said he was going to make me a Major General and give me General Wright's department with authority to go into East Tennessee and hold that count[r]y. I am now inclined to think I shall refuse the other star if it is offered. I would rather earn it in the field than to take it on trust of what I might do in the future. It may be necessary in order to settle some question of rank. But I have not much expectation that the War Department will hold one mind for a whole week. If it should, I may see the Cumberland Mountains again instead of the Palmettoes of the Carolinas. The war must be long, and the more I reflect on it the more I am doubtful about taking my seat in Congress. But we shall see when the time comes, that is if we have eyes.

### (Private and Confidential)

I have taken this new sheet to say a few words in regard to ourselves. I know you want me to be frank in everything and I want to assure and reassure you that I write what follows with the tenderest regards for our mutual happiness. In your letter which now lies before me there is the following passage: "Jamie. *I should not blame my own heart if it lost all faith in you.* I hope it may not, indeed I am not going to let it, but I shall not be forever telling you I love you *when there is evidently no more desire for it on your part than present manifestations indicate."*

I had to read that sentence over several times before I could become fully convinced that you had written the passages which I have underscored. Wa[i]ving the consideration out of which this sentence arose (my letters to you, their relative brevity and infrequency) for I have spoken of that in my last letter which you have received before this, I presume, wa[i]ving that I say, I want you to look at your words again and ask yourself whether you ought to have written them to me. A husband should not only be a faithful husband but should also be a noble, manly friend, and a wife should be a noble, womanly friend. Now Crete if a mere friend should write such a sentence to me, I should consider it an imputation upon my honor, a direct slight to my manhood which if unexplained would compel me to drop that correspondence.

I am clearly of the opinion that [it] is very wrong for you to write to me in that way, and I beg you with all the earnestness of my heart that you will not do it again. We came so much near[er] to each other and have been—oh, how much happier than before—in consequence of my late visit at home. It is a perpetual source of thanksgiving to me that we were so blessed. I am all the more rejoiced to know that that new joy was not an ephemeral existence but a fixed and permanent part of our lives henceforth, and I believe that nothing, unless it be such things as that above written, can fling me back into the old darkness and shadow of death in which my soul dwelt so long.

Understand me, I don't want you to write what you do not feel, nor indeed do I want you to conceal your real feeling from me, but it seems to me that you wrote that in a temporary feeling of dissatisfaction which was not at all an exponent of your fixed belief. If you really felt what was there suggested, I should consider it wrong for us to continue any other than a business correspondence. But I hope and most fully believe we love each other in a nobler and truer way than that. Be assured that I say all this (an hour and a half after midnight) from a heart that longs to cl[a]sp you to it and answer all your doubts by the warmth of its presence and love. Do write to me, and forgive me if I have wronged you. Ever and forever,

*Your* James

Washington
December 31, 1862

*My Very Dear Harry:*

It is January 1st, 1863, where I am, but not yet where you are. It will be in five minutes. But my heart is so much with you that I date this letter in your year instead of mine. Fourteen years ago this hour I was sitting up writing my thoughts as 1848 went out, and every New Year's Eve since I have either been writing or reading or holding low, sad, thoughtful converse with those I love.[116] I hope to keep up this custom as long as I shall live to see the face of Janus as he opens the door of the year.

The hour is always a sad one to me. It throws me back upon myself and makes me [realize] how really alone in the world every human soul is, and never before in my life did I feel how perfectly alone I am. It seems tonight so very far away to where you all are who love me and whom I love. When I think of you all, the long wintry miles rise up between us and seem very long and very dreary. I look back over the swift years and feel a shock as the realization that I am 31 years old comes down into my heart. I see so few of those [who] were my early friends. How dead and gone and scattered there [they are]! Were we all to meet today we would look upon their strange, sad, altered faces and ask their names as though we had never met.

I am made to feel more lonely by that which is your joy and indeed is mine also, but such is the strange perversity of the human heart that I cannot but feel that the event of this night has made you less mine than you were before, though I am no less yours. It is that strange, indefinable feeling that part of yourself is taken from me that will perforce make me sad. But with my whole heart I give you joy, and I

[116] The exchange of letters on or about the first of each new year was a custom which Garfield and several of his friends observed quite faithfully. He and Hinsdale continued it, almost without fail, from 1857 until Garfield's death.

ask from our Good Heavenly Father in this opening year, and this beginning of your wedded life, His blessings of love and joy upon you and your dear Libbie. I know you will kneel together and pray with a timidity and longing that you have never known before that you may live in His sight and in the sight of each other with mutual acceptance and blessing.

Don't think I would intrude a homily in the midst of your joy, but let me say one thing as the result of long observation; and some day, should I live to meet you, I want both of you to tell me whether it be not just. Do not strive to conform yourselves to each other to so great an extent as to interfere with those individual rights which every human soul possesses and which marriage by no means annuls. It is a delicate and difficult problem to lay out the exact ground and declare which is neutral, which individual, and which common; but it must be done, and I believe many noble and true natures have been dwarfed by trying to make themselves over to suit the matrimonial pattern. Don't demand of the base to sing tenor, nor the tenor base. The grandeur of harmony results from each part being true to itself and both moving in rhythmic accord.

But I weary you. Your good letter was received a few days since, but a pressure of engagements has kept me from answering hitherto. Kiss Libbie for me and let it be the Christmas[?] of love and blessing on your nuptial joy. I shall hope to hear from you both soon.

The guns are firing salvos to the New Year. May God let the light shine upon the coming twelve months and wipe out the blood stains from our dear land. Ever as ever and forever,

*Your brother,*
James

Washington
January 2, 1863

*My Dear Crete:*

Yours of December 28th, postmarked 30th, came to hand today. It is the first and only letter I have received this year. Though it is a day too late for New Year's calls, I will wish you a "Happy New Year" with the hope that its close will see a brighter prospect for our poor country.

Yesterday was a lively day here. It is a custom of many years standing, in addition to the usual New Year's calls, that all the officers of the army and navy who may happen to be in Washing[ton] at the opening of the year shall call on the President. Yesterday we met at the War Department and proceeded in a body with General Halleck at the head to call on His Excellency. There were not less than 800 officers of the army and navy there. The foreign ministers were there in the gaudy court dresses, the judges of the Supreme Court, the leading senators and representatives, and the heads of the cabinet departments were there.

I called on Judge Spalding and lady who are in the city and this evening I have been to a dinner party at Mr. Chase's, where I have had the pleasure of mul[l]ing again with Professor Monroe[117] after so long [an] absence. He is here to receive his final instructions before he starts for Rio to assume his consular duties. I greatly regret that I do not understand French. If I ever get the leisure again I want to take it up. I hope I may some day have the pleasure of having you for my teacher. I would not exchange my Latin and Greek for it, of course, but I would exchange part of my efficiency in those for a finished knowledge of French.

I am glad you are pleased with the cloaks. I did not know exactly what would suit you, and so I ran a venture. I left the selection of Trot's cloak to the merchant to whom I wrote enclosing the money.

The Buckingham matter I am glad to hear is settled, and though it is all right that you paid the $25, I can't greatly admire the whining style in which he has begged himself off from an honorable bargain in which he happened to lose, nearly as much as I. Next to my own course in the matter I admire Tilden's most.[118] Indeed, I am not sure but his is the most sensible.

I think our court will close next week, and I have now no doubt that I shall get into the field very soon after. I want to help in carrying out the Proclamation of yesterday. Strange that a second rate Illinois lawyer should be the instrument through whom one of the sublimest works of any age is accomplished.

Love to mother and Trot, and last but not least to yourself.

*Ever your*
James. . . .

Washington
January 6, 1863

*My Dearest Crete:*

Your good letter of the 2nd came to me a few minutes ago. I have just read it and will answer it at once. In regard to the letter, which [was] as painful to me to write as anything in the world could be, I will

---

[117] James Monroe of Ohio; graduated at Oberlin College in 1846 and taught there, 1849-1862, 1883-1896; member of the Ohio House of Representatives, 1856-1859, and of the Ohio Senate, 1860-1862; U.S. Consul to Rio de Janeiro, 1863-1869; member of the U.S. House of Representatives, 1871-1881.

[118] DeWitt Clinton Tilden, a native of New York who settled in Hiram and prospered as a farmer, tanner, and land speculator. With Garfield he invested and lost money in reputed oil land in Mecca, Trumbull County, Ohio.

only say I wrote it because I thought we ought to be true to each other in all the better and nobler senses of the word *"true."* And I am thankful to you with all my heart for the noble manner in which you have responded to it. Only good can come from faithful statements to each other of our convictions and mutual admonitions. I would not for a moment have it seem that I assumed to be so free from faults as to give me the right to criticise you, for I know fully and sadly how many faults I have that need to be forgiven.

In this letter you speak of a letter written to me when I was sick that I did not answer. On that, I say as I said before that I have answered every letter I have received from you, and if mine have been infrequent, yours have been equally so. But you have spoken so nobly and earnestly upon the whole matter that I hope and believe that you will not think I have meant to be in any way unkind or unjust in the premises.

I most fully believe that we can live happily and joyfully together, and never so much as now do I long to be with you and with those dear assurances of the living presence [that] make plain the obscure, render light the dark, and joyful the sad, as this poor pen is wholly unable to do. I pray you do not be sad, but hopeful about our life and love. There is more reason to be hopeful and joyful than ever before since we took up the journey of life together, and I feel sure that we cannot only "clamber up the hill of life" but "totter down the farther slope"[119] hand in hand with more light and genial warmth of heart than if we had never felt the snows about us and the cold wind blowing. And now, dearest, a truce to sadness and an all hail to happy thought of love and each other and our blessed little Trot.

The evidence is all now before the court. Tomorrow we begin to review the evidence. Saturday, the defence of the accused will be read and that day or Monday we shall give sentence and close our work. It has been a tremendous job full of difficulties, [has] require[d] a great deal of labor and patience.

I have no doubt but I shall get away into the field somewhere south or west as soon as we are through. I was told a few days ago by Mr. Chase that the Stanton plan of sending me to East Tennessee was probably vetoed by Halleck and that South Carolina stood fairest to be my destination. In regard to the Congress matter you have solved the question correctly in your remark that we "know not what a day may bring forth." I should not need to resign till late next fall, and before that time the question has a great many chances of settling itself. Of course I shall take no action without full consultation with you all and many of my leading constituents at home. Meantime let nothing be said that the thing is thought of at all. Indeed I doubt if I shall resign the seat. I shall not unless when the time comes it clearly appears as a matter of higher duty.

[119] See Robert Burns, "John Anderson, My Jo" (1789).

I hope Harry and Libbie may be happy and that all the fears we have had for Harry may be groundless. As I once said to Burke, there is a certain unknown quan[ti]ty in Harry's nature which can be represented by "XY" and whose value it is quite impossible to determine with accuracy. Whether there will ever be equations enough to enable us to eliminate and deduce the values of X and Y, I don't know. But such strange things happen in human values that we can form no judgment as to how Harry will come out at last. He and Libbie may be just fitted for each other; their mutual influence upon each other may be every way salutary. Let us hope so.

I am quite busy now with the book I am preparing for the press.[120] If I can have a week more here, I think I can have it ready. It being rather editorship than authorship, I am not yet decided whether I shall give my name to it or not. At any rate its preparation has afforded me a great deal of pleasant study.

Kiss our dear little one for me over and over again and write to me soon on the arrival of this, or it will not find me in Washington. Loving and hopeful, I am your James.

I attended the Italian opera a few evenings ago and heard the celebrated Angiolina Cordier sing. The opera was *La Traviata* which I find is the same as *Camille*. I send you copy of it.

Washington
January 6, 1863

*My Dear Burke:*

Your New Year's gift of six pages came to hand last evening. It is a great pleasure to me to receive epochal letters. They are mile stones on the dusty highway of life at which we stop for a moment and look back over the road we have travelled and again inquire of ourselves what manner of men we are becoming and what changes the swift years are making with us. The *"Eheu fugaces labuntur anni"* of Horace rise up to us with the same sad thought as they did to him, only we see more light beyond the dark river than he did. I hope you will keep up the New Year's letter to me as long as I shall live, and I here request you on such occasions so long as I shall live to write me any reflections, suggestions, conclusions or admonitions in regard to my course of life as may occur to me [you]. In answer I will do the same for you.

[120] Garfield was translating the *Secret . . . Instructions of Frederick II, for His Inspectors General.* In the preface he stated that geographic isolation, non-interventionist diplomacy, non-entanglement in foreign wars, and commercial prosperity had lulled Americans into a false sense of security and led them recklessly to neglect the art of war. He hoped his study (it was never published) would contribute to strengthening the nation's military system.

And Harry has gone too. I cannot but feel a certain sense of bereavement and loss when any dear friend is married. I know it is an unreasonable feeling and of course I do not allow it any prominent place in my thoughts, but it arises none the less. I am afraid that your apprehensions for his married life are only too true. But that "xy" in his nature may develope some unexpected functions which will pleasantly disappoint our fears.

I am sorry that the prospect does not seem promising in regard to your going back to Hiram, but I shall still hope it may be accomplished. The question you propose in reference to preaching is one on which my own mind and heart have been severely tried, and I most fully understand your feelings and sympathize with the difficulties and delicacies of the situation. Let me state my own opinions with categorical brevity:

1st.  I should be sorry to see you become a preacher as your exclusive or even chief work of life.

2nd.  I should be equally sorry to have you entirely cease speaking to the churches with which you may be in association.

3rd.  I hope to see you prove that it is the noblest type of religious character that leads it[s] possessor to choose and follow ardently his profession for life, be it law, literature or war, and at the same time be a living, acting member of religious society, speaking out the truths of philosophy, morality and religion with a freedom and freshness which as [a] regular minister he [you] would not and could not do.

This, I know, is not an easy part to act in the business of life, as the customs and habits of society now are, but I believe a large-hearted, large-minded man can be a better and truer man in that way than in any other. Such is the state of the Disciple organization and doctrine that I cannot be a preacher and that only. It is too narrow a field for the growth and developement that one feels he must have. No doubt this opinion will appear conceited and egotistical in the man who holds it, but I cannot help it and don't think you should. There are many who feel as though they could live the best and most worthy lives by devoting their whole time to the ministry. Such ought to do it and they will do great good. But each human soul must live a life of its own and be responsible to God and men for it. It may be a good thing for you to develope your views on this matter in a discourse declaring your policy and determination, which will in a measure relieve you from embarrassment. I contemplated such a work for myself but the intervention of the war postponed and possibly entirely removed the necessity of such a declaration, though should I again get back into social life I may do it yet. I shall be anxious to hear from you further on this subject and also on the question of what you propose to do with your life.

I am still in the court. I will not in this letter say anything about my disgust at being kept here so long, nor about the conduct of the war, nor about that strange phenomenon in the world's history when a second rate Illinois lawyer is the instrument to utter words which shall form an epoch memorable in all future ages (January 1st, 1863). . . .

I hope not to be here more than ten days longer, but long enough to read another of your letters before I go.

Ever your friend,

J. A. Garfield

Washington
January 9, 1863

*My Dearest Crete:*

Your good and most welcome letter of the 5th came to hand last night. I trust before this time you have got one or both of my letters which were on their way at that time and since. Do not, I pray you, take any more serious thought about that letter. It is all past now, and if you could see my heart and read what is written there of you, you would feel happy and peaceful I know. When I think of you in our quiet little home, with mother there, and surrounded by true and tried friends, dear friends of our earlier years, not those who are friendly for a consideration but for the sake of love, it makes me long with a kind of ache which I cannot describe to go away to you and enjoy it with you. I feel that what might be among the happiest and most peaceful days of our lives, while yet a part of the vivacity of boyhood and girlhood is still ours, is being irretrievably lost by me, wasted among strangers and in isolation, for in a place like this I shut up my interior nature where it must tumble into decay like a pile without inhabitant. Let us hope that this may not always be so. Should I come to Congress, I think I shall make arrangements for you and Trot to come with me. I shall certainly do so if I can.

I presume I shall be ordered to the field early next week. Indeed I have no doubt but I shall be in the field somewhere in less than two weeks. The sad loss of General Morgan[121] renders it not improbable that I may be sent to take command of his division. Indeed I wrote a letter yesterday which I have not yet sent, and am not quite sure I shall do so, asking the Secretary of War to send me to General Morgan's command. I feel sure my destination will be there or in East Tennessee or in South Carolina. Should I go West, I will if possible call at home for a few hours. If I cannot do that I will try to have

[121] The reference is undoubtedly to General George W. Morgan who was not lost in any sense of the term, as Confederates at Arkansas Post, where Morgan was leading a corps, were well aware.

you meet me at some point on the route. I shall know very soon and inform you as soon as I know.

I fear I shall not be able wholly to complete the preparation of my book before I leave, though I am giving all my spare moments to it. I feel about it just [as] I always have in reference to any of my performances; if I had begun a little sooner and could continue a little longer, I could make a better thing of it. But the study consequent upon the preparation has been exceedingly pleasant to me. I have so much needed you to help me in the French, of which I have read several hundred pages; that is, I have gone over it and have been enabled to get the general sense of the text without venturing to suppose I could give the full meaning. If I get the manuscript done, I shall try to leave it in the hands of some friend who will see to its passage through the press and get it as accurate as possible. . . .

I loaned Marenus $50 a few days ago and directed him to send the note for it to you. I have also made a deposit of $1,000 in the Treasury Department to be invested in a loan as soon as the new loans are opened, which will probably be in a few weeks. Tell me how soon you want more money, and how much.

I am greatly perplexed for want of a good servant. I have had to turn off two or three and my horses are looking badly for want of care. If I don't find any one that will do his duty, I don't know but I shall have to send for Jimmy. Give him my respects. With love to you and Trot and mother, I am as ever,

*Your own* James


Washington
January 10, 1863

*My Dear Mother:*

I was very glad to receive your good letter of January 4th. I hope you will not think I am remiss in writing to you. I wrote to you and Mary when I supposed you were with her, but I afterwards found you were with Crete. I am very glad to have you live at my home. It was one of the chief reasons for my getting a home that you might enjoy it and consider it your own home. I hope you are happy and comfortable in living there. It has for a great many years been my greatest desire to have a place and means of making your old age happy. I want you to feel that all that I have or shall ever have is yours to use and enjoy wherever and in whatever way you please. I know that whatever I may do I cannot repay you for the immeasurable blessings you conferred on me in the days of my weakness and always, since I have taken my place among men. I look forward with great pleasure and longing for the time when I may be there to enjoy that home with you and Crete and our dear little Trot. I cannot say that my expectation of ever seeing you all in peace and quiet in this life [will come true], but I know you would rather see me doing my duty in these [days] of danger and blood, even at the cost of my life than to see me leave the field and pass time in safety at home.

I am now in the court and the defence of General Porter is being read, and I think we shall close the case today. This is the 45th day since the court was called. It has been a most laborious and searching trial. Its record covers more than 900 closely written foolscap pages. The Secretary of War told me yesterday that he should send me into the field very soon. So I presume that I shall leave here in a very few days. I shall let you all know when I go and where I go. . . .

With all the love you could desire me to bear you, I am as ever,

*Your affectionate son,*
James

# PART III

*Campaigning in the Army
of the Cumberland*

Garfield's last tour of duty was in the West with the Army of the Cumberland. It began on January 25, 1863, when he reported to Major General William S. Rosecrans, his new commander.

Rosecrans was then approaching the zenith of his military career. A graduate of West Point, he had resigned his commission after teaching at the Military Academy and serving at various army posts in the East. In civilian life he engaged in engineering, architecture, coal mining and river navigation, and he was the head of an oil refining company in Cincinnati when the Civil War began. He entered the war as a colonel and was promoted shortly thereafter to brigadier general. As a result of distinguished leadership in the western theater he was advanced to major general and given command of the Army of the Cumberland. When Garfield reported for duty, Rosecrans had his headquarters at Murfreesboro, Tennessee, where he had recently defeated the Confederate army of Braxton Bragg. The Battle of Stones River was an indecisive but important victory which had made the Union commander immensely popular.

Although Rosecrans knew that Garfield had strong supporters in Washington, he decided to form his own opinion of the man before offering him a specific assignment. He made a companion of Garfield, even to sharing his quarters with him, and he engaged him in lengthy discussion of political, literary, military, and religious subjects. All the while Rosecrans studied the mind and character of his subordinate. After three full weeks of such association, he gave Garfield a choice between leading a division and serving as Chief of Staff. It was an important decision for Garfield to make, and he gave it serious thought. Then, with some misgivings about hitching his military future to Rosecrans' star, he accepted the staff position.

Rosecrans now had as his chief advisor a highly intelligent, efficient, hard-working man whose courage, initiative, and vitality contributed significantly to the command. He also had an ambitious congressman-elect with definite ideas about how the war should be fought, with

217

*powerful connections in Washington, and with every intention of participating in bold strikes against the enemy. As it was Garfield's plan to remain in uniform only until Congress convened, he looked forward to aggressive and hopefully successful military action in the months ahead.*

*Late in June, after a long delay and petulant quarreling with superiors in Washington, Rosecrans moved against Bragg's Army of Tennessee. His summer offensive began auspiciously. The Tullahoma campaign, though overshadowed by Union successes at Gettysburg and Vicksburg, was well-conceived and brilliantly executed, as was the advance across the Tennessee River. These were damaging blows to the enemy. By early September, all of Tennessee, including Chattanooga with its important rail connections with the East, West, and South, was in Union hands. The way appeared open for a strike at the very vitals of the Confederacy.*

*But after Bragg evacuated Chattanooga, Rosecrans, and Garfield too, seem to have forgotten momentarily that they had not destroyed the enemy army. During the advance south of the city, Rosecrans' left was at times fifty miles from his right. He was for several days in danger of being destroyed in detail. Fortunately for him, Bragg was slow to develop his counter-offensive. When the Confederate attack came, Rosecrans had massed his army and was ready to receive it.*

*The Battle of Chickamauga raged for two terrible days, September 19-20. Through the first day of fighting the lines changed but little; on the second, however, the Confederates broke through and routed the Union right and center.*

*Regrettably, Garfield never committed to writing a detailed account of his experiences in this battle. They were, indeed, hectic and heroic. From the opening gun until after the Confederate break-through, he worked tirelessly at the side of his commander. He was at headquarters late in the morning of the 20th when Rosecrans received an erroneous report that a gap existed between Major General Joseph Reynolds' division and the one to its immediate right, and that Reynolds needed help. The division on Reynolds' right was Brigadier General John Brannan's. Rosecrans, thinking it was Brigadier General Thomas Wood's, sent a field dispatch directing Wood to close on Reynolds and support him. To obey the order Wood withdrew his division from the line and marched it behind Brannan's division to the left. There was now a wide gap in the Union line.*

*It so happened that Garfield, who wrote most of Rosecrans' field dispatches at Chickamauga, was busy at the time and did not write the fatal one to Wood. What the order lacked was a phrase explaining its object, which was to maintain a strong, unbroken line. Had it contained such an explanation Wood probably would have realized that he was where he belonged and stayed there. Had Garfield written the order, perhaps he would have explained its purpose, but that can only be conjectured.*

*Through the gap poured the Confederates, throwing about one-third of the Union army into utter confusion. Unable to rally the panic-stricken troops, Rosecrans retreated with them to Chattanooga, sending Garfield to Major General George Thomas who was holding his ground on the left. After a perilous ride under fire, during which his horse was wounded, Garfield reached his destination about 3:45 P.M. He told Thomas what had happened and what Rosecrans was doing to prevent further enemy gains. He also informed Rosecrans of developments at the front. About dark, after one of the most valorous stands of the war, Thomas retreated to Rossville, stayed there a day, and then fell back into Chattanooga. Against the advice of Garfield and other subordinate officers, Rosecrans abandoned Lookout Mountain. The Confederates promptly occupied that vantage point and besieged the Union army in Chattanooga.*

*Although the Union defeat at Chickamauga can be explained largely in terms of bad luck, it demoralized Rosecrans enough that some of his subordinates believed him incapable of handling the crisis it had precipitated. Criticism of Rosecrans was rife. When it reached the White House, the President decided that the General had outlived his usefulness in his present position and relieved him of his command.*

*Concerning Garfield's responsibility for the dismissal of Rosecrans there is a maze of conflicting evidence. That he was critical of his superior is a certainty. As early as June he fussed to his wife about the "long delay of this army to move," but, of course, that remark never injured Rosecrans. On July 27, however, Garfield, in a letter to Secretary Chase, complained at length about the inaction of the army, saying that if it continued he would "ask to be relieved and sent . . . [elsewhere]." How much that letter turned Chase against Rosecrans can only be assumed; but the Secretary, who liked and had supported Rosecrans, did turn against him. More than that, after the Battle of Chickamauga, Chase showed Garfield's letter to Lincoln. There is also evidence that after the battle, Garfield, in interviews with a number of people, including Stanton and the President, made derogatory statements about Rosecrans' qualifications to lead an army. Such utterances could have had but one effect.*

*Still, it should be pointed out that Rosecrans would probably have been dismissed had Garfield remained silent. Rosecrans himself was partly to blame for losing his command; so was Assistant Secretary of War Charles A. Dana, whose communications to Washington after Chickamauga spoke of disaster and failing leadership. Dana, more than anyone, destroyed the administration's confidence in the Union commander. Stanton, Grant, and a few others were also partly responsible for Rosecrans' dismissal. But none of this excuses Garfield for criticizing his commanding general to a member of the President's official family.*

*To be generous, one can argue that Garfield's chief concern was the national welfare, and with that in mind he found it possible to make a distinction between Rosecrans the man, whom he liked, and Rosecrans the general, whose procrastination he abhorred. But with all due allowance for charity, is it possible to justify Garfield's disparagement of the professional reputation of the man whose chief advisor he was? In his letter to Chase he wrote that Rosecrans' almost fatal delay was losing golden opportunities to hurt, if not destroy, the enemy. If that was his considered judgment, should he not have resigned and then aired his grievances openly? If his chief concern was the national welfare, and if he believed that Rosecrans was not serving the best interests of the country, could Garfield have found a more effective way of forcing the issue?*

*The key to understanding Garfield's letter to Chase lies in its author's concern for his own reputation and the milieu in which it was written. As the end of spring approached and Rosecrans kept his army idle at Murfreesboro, Garfield became thoroughly frustrated. At length, late in June, Rosecrans opened his Tullahoma campaign. By superb maneuvering, he forced Bragg to abandon his fortified position along the Duck River and to retreat to Chattanooga. Garfield urged relentless pursuit, but Rosecrans delayed renewing his offensive for six weeks. All the while he was exchanging disputatious messages with Halleck, Stanton, and even Lincoln, who were trying desperately to get him to advance. Garfield knew that such quarreling could hurt only one man. If, as might reasonably be assumed, Rosecrans was falling from favor, Garfield had no stomach for descending with him. And yet the prospect of destroying Bragg seemed too favorable to abandon. If Garfield stayed with Rosecrans, and victory came, some of the credit and glory would go to Garfield. Garfield would see to that! If, on the other hand, Rosecrans should fail, Garfield, by criticizing him to Chase, would put himself on record as being dissatisfied with his commander's generalship. By following the course he adopted, Garfield placed himself in a position to jump in either direction.*

*It should be added that after Chickamauga, Rosecrans knew nothing of the letter to Chase, and when Garfield left for Washington, the two generals parted as friends. Years later, when Dana was part owner and editor of the New York Sun, he charged in his paper that Garfield was responsible for the dismissal of Rosecrans. Garfield denied having been untrue to his commander, but the disclosure chilled their friendship. When in the presidential campaign of 1880, in which Garfield was the Republican candidate, campaign biographers lauded his military prowess and exploits at the expense of Rosecrans, the latter spoke out angrily. The upshot was an open break, for Garfield was offended.*

*The friendship remained shattered. In 1882, a few months after Gar-* ✗
*field's death, Dana published the controversial letter to Chase.*

*Garfield's letters for this phase of his wartime career touch upon a variety of subjects. A number of them provide a revealing, inside view of the complex problems associated with commanding a Civil War army. Some deal candidly with political issues and personalities, and some are devoted entirely or in part to matters of a personal nature. Practically all of them illuminate the character of their author, whose dominant mood changed frequently and decidedly as he encountered new and different situations.*

Cincinnati
January 20, 1863

*My Dearest Crete:*

It was very hard for me to leave you and our dear home yesterday morning, far harder than any former leave-taking has ever been. The brief stay was very pleasant indeed to me and made me feel more surely than ever before that we can greatly aid each other in making a home pleasant and life happy. Doubtless in the wisdom of God it has been best for us that we should pass through the ordeal which has so thoroughly and terribly tried us, and I most firmly believe that the days of our darkness have passed away. Let us rejoice together and be glad in this new light of love and peace. . . .

I did not see anything [in Cleveland] in the way of mittens for Trot which suited me. You must tell her that Papa tried to get mittens for her.

There was no train till about seven o'clock P.M. and I reached here about 7½ this morning. The horses have not arrived and I am somewhat troubled about them. I have a letter from Ben Lake saying they had not reached Wheeling on Sunday evening. Probably the snow has delayed them. I shall go on tomorrow whether they arrive or not.

I have been nearly sick all day with my throat and have kept my room most of the time. I finally called a doctor who examined it and gave me some medicine. I feel better now.

I have just been out to hear John B. Gough on temperance.[1] I am not well enough to give you an analysis of his oratory as it appears to me. I will only say that dramatic art has done more for him than the art of speech. His words are only the accompaniment of his acting.

Brother Jones is with me. I found him here this morning waiting

[1] An inveterate drunkard at the age of twenty-five, England-born John Bartholomew Gough took a pledge in 1842. He violated it twice during the next three years, but kept it faithfully thereafter. He became famous as a temperance lecturer of remarkable oratorical ability.

for Captain [Horace H.] Willard with whom he goes down the river to join the 42nd.

I have suffered a great deal from my throat since I left you. It has nearly made me sick and I have kept my bed part of the day. I think, however, I shall be much better tomorrow. The doctor said he thought it was not Diptheria but a very severe case of inflammation.

I enclose duplicate contracts of sale of that house, already signed by me. Give one to Mr. Brown and have him sign the other for you to keep. Tell Mr. Humeston I will want the money on that note April 1st. Meantime the interest may be six per cent. Write me also in the same letter in which you speak of these things, the exact amount of the Mason Raymond note and the time when it can be paid. Harry knows about it. I want, as far as I can, to pay for the house and lot from what is due me. Certainly I do not want to draw on any stock I have invested in the Federal government. By prudence we can meet this contract [on] April 1st and not disarrange our other affairs. *si vixer* [*si vixero:* if I shall live]. Give my love to all our household and many kisses to our precious little darling. Write me to care of General Rosecrans near Murfreesboro.

*Ever and forever your* James

Murfreesboro, Tennessee
January 25, 1863

*My Dear Crete:*

I reached here at 5 o'clock this evening after a ride of seven hours in an ambulance. I had a cavalry escort of 20 men and narrowly escaped a fight with a large body of rebel cavalry which came down the Nashville pike from Franklin and destroyed a few cars and captured 25 of our men only two or three miles from us as we were on the route here.[2] But we are here safely now and will soon be in a shape to return any little affectionate compliment of that kind they may see fit to give us.

I have never seen more disagreeable weather than we have endured for the last four days. It has been one continued drizzle of dreary cold rain, soon converting the earth into the rarest mud for the last two days. Today, however, there are symptoms of returning sunshine, and it promises that for a while "the rain is over and gone."[3]

It is exceedingly strange that even the thought of camp life should bring back my old malady. For two months I have been almost perfectly well. But last night I was awakened in the small hours by a most frightful diarrhoea, which has been running riot with me all day. I presume it is the result of a sudden change of water and diet. I have

[2] A detachment of Forrest's cavalry descended on a construction train near Antioch and retired after doing about the amount of damage Garfield reported.
[3] The Song of Solomon II, 11.

one thing in my favor and that is a very slim appetite. I shall try fasting, or at least abstemiousness for a time, and hope soon to have adjusted myself to the new conditions and be all right again. Don't feel troubled about it, for I feel a great power of health in me which I think will show itself soon. I have had an interview with General Rosecrans who is now quite sick; indeed [he] has been confined to his bed for several days with an attack of lung fever. He was very friendly and received me with the familiarity and kindness of an old acquaintance. I did not introduce business but as I came out he asked me to come in again in the morning, saying he was glad to have me with him and that there were two or three divisions "fishing" for me.

I will not write more tonight but will write more in the morning when I have taken a night's rest. In these dreary days it is sweet to have a loving center to let my head wander back to, and to think of you as loving me, and to feel a warmth and glow about my heart which is full of hope and joy, and our happy home and dear little Trot! God bless you all, and may sweet dreams and loving thoughts of me visit you.

Good night, dearest. Your ownest,

James

Monday Morning
January 26, 1863

*Dearest Crete:*

I am feeling quite well this morning after a good night's rest, and though I have not yet surmounted my attack of diarrhoea, I am [feeling] better than I did yesterday.

I have met quite a large number of my old friends of this army. I have not, of course, been here long enough to form a very comprehensive judgment of the state of affairs here, nor of the prospects of our cause here. I am, however, greatly pleased with some features of General Rosecrans' character. He has that fine quality of having his mind made up on all the great questions which concern his work. In a military man this is a cardinal virtue. The whole texture of generalship is made up of theories which his mind must form of the position, force and intentions of his enemy; and he must shape his course, take his resolutions, and act upon them in accordance with his theory. Hence a man who does not think decisively and place full and implicit reliance upon his own judgments cannot act with confidence. General Rosecrans thinks rapidly and strikes forward into action with the utmost confidence in his own judgment. In this he is perfectly unlike McClellan, who rarely has a clear-cut, decisive opinion, and dare[s] not trust it when he has. The officers whom I have met since I came here seem to have the most unbounded confidence in Rosy and are enthusiastic in his praise. He is the most Spanish looking man I know of, a kind of Don Menendez face, and though he swears fiercely, yet he is a Jesuit of the highest style of Roman piety. He carries a cross attached to his watch dial, and as he drew his watch out of his side-pants pocket his rosary, a dirty looking string of friars beads, came out with it.

There is much in his appearance that is striking and singular. He remembered me very well, commenced at once to talk of my Sandy Valley campaign and our correspondence while I was there. Nearly midnight, last night, he came out after I had gone to bed; and though he was sick, he staid and talked for an hour till his darkey came and took [him] by the shoulder and led him away to bed.

I shall look for a letter from you in a short time. The mail comes here daily. Until you hear from me again, direct to care of General Rosecrans, Murfreesboro, Tennessee.

> *Ever and forever yours,*
> James

Headquarters
Department of the Cumberland
Murfreesboro, Tennessee
January 27, 1863

*My Dear Harry:*

Before this reaches you, you will have heard from me by way of my letters to Crete and Almeda, and [of] the chief incidents of my journey and arrival. I write this chiefly for the purpose of reopening our correspondence and bring[ing] epistolary returns from you, though I hope you have started a letter to me before this time.

Since my arrival here, I have done little else than keep quiet to allow my system time to overcome the attack of diarrheoa. Meantime I have been kindly and hospitably received at headquarters and have met many old companions in arms and friends whom I knew before the war broke out. For instance, this morning I met Dr. Seymour of Painesville, whom we met as a steamboat companion on our tour up the lakes. The sight of the Doctor called up our whole delightful journey and the banquet, together with Almeda's fine lines in honor of his birthday.

Bickham[4] of the Cincinnati *Commercial* is here and is preparing a volume for the press giving the history of Rosecrans' late campai[g]n, closing the battle here.

---

[4] William Denison Bickham, war correspondent for the Cincinnati *Commercial*, wrote *Rosecrans' Campaign with the Fourteenth Army Corps, or the Army of the Cumberland: A Narrative of Personal Observations with . . . Official Reports of the Battle of Stone River* (1863).

Last night I went into the General's room to see him and he insisted I should sleep in the room. We sat up till two o'clock, notwithstanding his illness and my frequent remonstrances that he should go to bed. We discussed a great range of questions of war, government and religion. I find him a man of very decided and muscular thoughts and with the rare Friedrichian quality of having his mind made up on every important question. I do not think him a great man in the sense of being [a] comprehensive and profound thinker, but for sharp, clear sense, ready, decisive judgment and bold reliant action he is certainly very admirable and hence an effective, successful general.

His religious history was particularly interesting. I cannot write it as I would be glad to tell it to you. Should I ever have the privilege of sitting down in our little circle, I know you would be interested in hearing it as he gave it to me. I can only say in brief that he came out of the Academy a shrewd, hard skeptic, believing only that there was an ego and a non-ego, that the non-ego was the affluence from some first cause, distinct from the ego, and that cause was "Jehovah, Jove or Lord," as you pleased, but yet intelligent and powerful. He next argues on the doctrine of antecedent probabilities, that God would [be] likely to communicate to man his designs and will concerning him, and that he (Rosecrans) would therefore take up the books which claimed to be revelations and read them as he would algebra. He agreed with himself, purely as an intellectual experiment, to read a chapter each day, and, as the book laid it down as a rule for reading that the man who wanted knowledge should ask of God, he would pray. He did so, not as a matter of feeling at all, or even of faith, but as an intellectual experience. He said on this point, "When I knelt down, I felt ashamed, and thought quite likely I was a damned fool, but then I remembered it was one of the conditions of the experiment and so I prayed on, though it seemed to me no more than talking to a stick or stump." He here explained that as he progressed in his experiment he found that to understand the book properly he was directed to lay aside his sins. He therefore did so, ceasing to be a blasphemer, *etc., etc.* I was curious to know what he would say about swearing, which he indulges in very freely, especially when he is roused. He said, "I do still curse and damn when I am indignant, but I never blaspheme the name of God." He made a difference between *profanity* and *blasphemy*.

He kept on reading four year[s] and more, asked baptism as a part of his experiment, decided in favor of the Bible and the Christian Religion, and then came the question of what church. I was struck at the similarity between his position and that of my friend Ulke of whom I told you. Ulke said, "I must either accept nothing on trust or everything. I must be a skeptic or a Roman Catholic. Therefore I am the first." Rosecrans came up to the same position and chose the last. He said after he had accepted the Bible he then wanted an authorized supernatural teacher, and the only three claimants for that place were the Roman Catholics, the Greek Catholics, and the Episcopalians. I cannot now give you all the details, but it was exceedingly interesting. Before retiring he took out his rosary and knelt for five or ten minutes beside his bed. It was three o'clock before our conversation closed. I don't know but he thought he could proselyte me.

I expect a command will be assigned me today or tomorrow. I have this morning received a telegram that my horses are in Louisville. It will be a week before they can arrive. I have bought Thiers' *History of the French Revolution*[5] and shall read it. . . .

It snowed last night and it is rainy now. The memory of our pleasant home and of you all is in very bright contrast with the present surroundings. . . .

> *Ever yours,*
> James

Headquarters
Department of the Cumberland
Murfreesboro, Tennessee
January 29, 1863

*My Dear Harry:*

Yours of the 21st was received a few hours after I had sent you the letter which I presume will reach you two days before this. I spent a good part of the day yesterday among the hospitals, hunting for the boys. At last I found a wounded boy of the 18th who knew the boys and learned the following: Late in the afternoon of the fight of Wednesday, Milford was wounded in the calf of the leg. It was only a flesh wound and did not at all injure the bone. He was taken to the Division hospital and one of his comrades told my informer a day or two since that Milford was nearly well and would soon go back into his regiment. I presume he is on duty by this time. His regiment is a few miles out of the place and as soon as I can I will go out and see the boys. A wound that does not disable is a feather in a soldier's cap and Milford will thus always have a personal certificate of service and bravery.

As a personal favor to me, the General has given a pass for you to come here. Don't let any one else send to me for passes to come with you, for they would hardly be granted and I would rather have you here alone with me. I can make you comfortable and I am sure we can have a pleasant time. Now you must not fail to come. By the time of your arrival I shall have my military household in order and

---

[5] Louis Adolphe Thiers, *Histoire de la Révolution Française,* ten volumes (1823-1827). By the Civil War several editions in English had appeared.

a warm corner of my blanket ready for you. You have often talked of coming to see me but have never yet done it. You must not fail this time.

The General is reorganizing the whole army and will not make an assignment to me till he gets the arrangement effected. It will be four or five days before my horses will reach here and I presume by that time I shall know what I am to do. We have a severe storm of snow and it is now very cold with snow lying cold and heavy on top of the deep coat of mud. There is nothing new to write, it being a time of prepa[ra]tion and gathering the odds and ends of the army since the fight. I will write you again by and by. Love to all.

*Ever yours,*
James

Murfreesboro, Tennessee
February 1, 1863

*My Dearest Crete:*

Your dear letter of January 26th came to hand this evening. It is the first I have received from you since I left home, but from your letter I see you have written me one before, which has either be[en] lost or miscarried. I am made very glad to hear from you and especially so to receive so good a letter. I am glad to tell you that I am now quite well again and I believe there is a good deal of potential work and endurance in me.

My horses have not yet come up, being detained by the necessity of having the gunboats to convoy the steamers up the Cumberland. Of course I can do nothing till they come.

Also there is a heavy body of troops coming on here from Kentucky[6] and I think the General is waiting for them to arrive before he assigns me to duty. He is exceedingly kind and genial. A few days ago I went and got rooms and board a few squares distant from here. Just after I got to bed and had gone asleep an orderly came in with a written order from the General, peremptorily ordering me to return and sleep in his room and board with him till I should be assigned to duty. Since then I have been staying here without any apologies.

The General is now nearly well. Yesterday I rode with him over

[6] In mid-January Rosecrans wired to Halleck that Lieutenant General James Longstreet was going to Bragg from Virginia, that enemy cavalry were constantly annoying him, and that he must have re-enforcements. Halleck immediately directed Brigadier General Horatio G. Wright, commander of the Department of the Ohio, to keep only enough troops in Kentucky to maintain order and send the rest to Rosecrans. Wright promptly complied by sending about 14,000 effectives under Major General Gordon Granger, the troops to which Garfield referred. Granger's "Army of Kentucky" became the Reserve Corps of Rosecrans' army. The report on Longstreet was incorrect. He did not join Bragg until September.

the field of battle and he pointed out to me the lines of attack and defence, showing the causes of the partial failure and the final saving of the army from defeat. If my book should ever get published I want you to notice the Battle of Prague and see how perfectly the battle here resembles it. Rosecrans was the beaten Austrians up to the point where Frederick struck the decisive blow of the battle, and then Rosecrans turned the scales in his own favor.

I have got him to send for the 2nd and 10th Ohio cavalry[7] and I hope to get Chamberlain[8] with me.

I have proposed to Rosecrans a plan by which we can rouse up more of a martial pride and a greater love of military glory. It is to have a roll of honor to which the five bravest in each company shall be chosen, and from these shall be chosen an elite corps for daring enterprises and dashing charges. Also asking Congress to strike medals of honor from captured cannon to be given to those who distinguish themselves for gallantry in action. We have been working over it and an order will be published in a few days. Our army has so little of the old Prussian and French fire, and yet I see no reason why it can't be roused.[9]

In regard to the addition to our house and the plan you sent me, I have thought a good deal. The plan I like very well, though I should want to make a few modifications. I feel very anxious to have a good and comfortable home and more commodious than it now is. But I think we had not better build till I leave the army. Should anything

[7] The Tenth went to Rosecrans, but the Second was assigned to duty in the Department of the Ohio.

[8] Hiram S. Chamberlain, a former student at the Eclectic, was a first lieutenant in the Second Ohio Cavalry.

[9] On February 14 Rosecrans issued orders prescribing the method for establishing rolls of honor for every unit in the army. In each company privates and non-commissioned officers were to elect by ballot five privates, approved by the company commander; and in each regiment the commissioned officers were to elect ten corporals and ten sergeants, approved by the regimental commander. Four lieutenants, four captains, and two field officers below the rank of colonel were to be selected from each brigade, presumably by the appropriate brigade and division commanders; and field, general, and staff officers were to be chosen from each corps, presumably by the appropriate corps commander. The commanding general was to add the names of men who performed special acts of heroism. Provision was made for the removal of selectees and vacancies that happened were to be promptly filled. Company rolls were to be added to regimental rolls, regimental to brigade, and brigade to corps, and each unit was to announce in orders its roll of honor. In addition each infantry and cavalry brigade was to organize an elite light battalion whose members were to be selected from its roll of honor, given the best available arms and equipment, excused from picket duty, and mounted as soon as possible. To the establishment of the elite battalion the Secretary of War objected, whereupon Rosecrans ordered roll of honor men to remain with their commands and authorized them to wear a red ribbon over their heart. In creating this roll of honor system for awarding distinguished and heroic service Garfield seems to have been largely responsible. It should be added that Congress had already authorized the Medal of Honor (July 12, 1862).

befal[l] that I should not return, it might be better not to build so large. To build now would require a draft on what I have invested and would cost much more than when the war is over. Prices of materials are very high, chiefly in consequence of the inflation of paper currency. Great cheapness must succeed the war. When a house is building, it is very necessary that some one interested directly and having control shall be there to see that everything is done as it should be. Let us make our calculations to build as soon as I return home, and I am sure we can make a pleasant home of it. . . .

Very sorry I could not have sent something to Trot. Give her my love and kisses. Love to mother. I believe she owes me a letter.

*Ever your own loving*
James

Murfreesboro, Tennessee
February 5, 1863

*Dearest Crete:*

Your good letter of January 22nd reached me last evening. It is one of those curious freaks of the mails that this letter which you wrote so soon after my departure should be the second to reach me. It is now eleven days since I reached here and my horses have not yet arrived. They were in Louisville on the 27th January, waiting for a boat. I have heard no word from them since. But I suppose they started down with the fleet which has been stopped near Fort Donelson to drive off a large body of cavalry which lately attempted to take that place by assault. We are rejoiced to hear that the rebels were yesterday repulsed with loss, and we hope a large part of them will be captured before they return to their main body.[10]

You have no idea of what fearfully bad weather we have here. Last night there was a furious snow storm, raging nearly all night. It ended in sleet and rain and today the roads are deep with mud, and it is a cold shivering day. I can do nothing till my staff and horses arrive, and so I try to be patient. But I have neither the opportunity to do anything very useful nor have I any opportunity to read or write except as I sit down in a public room crowded with officers and all kind[s] of people on all kinds of business. I hope soon to see my "Harry" and "Bill" and have something to do.

General Rosecrans spoke a few days ago of putting me in command of Nashville, which, though a very important command, I would not so soon have as a command in the field.

---

[10] On February 3 a Confederate cavalry battalion was repulsed at Fort Donelson with a loss of about 100 casualties. Pursuing Union cavalry, hampered by bad weather and confused by a well-informed enemy, took only twenty five or thirty prisoners.

I received a letter from Harry (of January 30th) last night in the mail with yours. I had written him two letters, neither of which he appeared to have received. I sent him a pass in the last one and I hope he will not fail to come down and see me in vacation. I have also written to Almeda but have not yet heard from her.

I wish we were in a condition to make the improvements on the house as you suggest, and I hope the time may not be far distant when we shall be able to begin. I fear I shall suffer loss to the extent of several hundred dollars through the bungling and ignorance of some of the quartermasters and commissaries with whom I have transacted public business. This makes another reason why I can't now venture to commence building.

If I knew when Harry would start I would have some messages for him.

I hope you will write me very frequently and know that I shall always be made happy by your letters. Kiss our blessed little Trot for me. Love to all the household and to you especially now and ever,

James

[Written across the face of the first page of the letter:]

I was amused at your earnest request that I should not eat oysters. You might as well caution me not to eat green peas or lettuce. I am quite safe on the bivalve question. Discussed Catholicism with the General till four o'clock this morning and then slept till ten. Has the note been signed yet? Don't think me unnecessarily careful about it.

J. A. G.

Murfreesboro, Tennessee
February 13, 1863

*Crete Dearest:*

Your two notes enclosing one a letter from Professor and the other from John Bowler. The last was one of the three letters I have received during my life that grieved and angered me at the same time. John wanted me to help him get the office of paymaster in the navy, and offered me $100 to secure it for him. He had written to me before on the same subject and I had written him a strong recommendation. The big envelope you sent contained recommendations from other parties, and he wanted me to preserve the whole to [send] to the Secretary of the Navy. I don't think that John appreciated the character of the proposal he made to me, but I wrote him a very severe reprimand and have almost come to the conclusion that if any such letter ever comes to me again I will expose the writer of it by publishing it in the newspaper. I was very sorry that John should have written me thus, but as I am going into public life I am bound to establish some rule by which I can be protected against the corrupt approaches which are so liable to [be] made to men in Congress.

I was very glad to get a letter from Old Professor. I have written to him offering him $20 per month and his board, and I hope he will come. It is so difficult to get a darkey that is at all reliable that I had almost despaired of getting any decent one.

My horses did not arrive till last night and they are in a terrible condition. I fear that Harry is badly injured by standing so long on the boat and in the cars.

Ben Lake is sick and will have to resign. I am very sorry, for I will now be obliged to take some lieutenant who is a stranger to me as a member of my military family. I think I shall be assigned a command tomorrow or next day.

But for the fact that General Rosecrans seems to want me with him all the while and occupies almost every moment of my time, I should be very uneasy at the long delay in getting to work; but I could do nothing till my horses came. I sat up with the General last night till 4 o'clock talking constantly and incessantly for hours on religion. He is the intensest religionist I ever saw. If we did not sleep till ten or twelve in the morning I should be worn out.

We are having fine sunny weather now, though there has been a great deal of rain and the roads are still bad. Reinforcements and supplies are still coming slowly up and in a few weeks or certainly as soon as the roads will allow it we shall be ready for a forward movement.

Tell Harry that the railroad is now opened so that he can come all the way from Louisville by rail. I hope he will not fail to come.

I am always glad to get your letters and want you to keep the line going as regularly as you can. I have written this with a crowd around me and the floor joggling at every word.

Love to Trot and mother and always to yourself.

*Ever yours,*
James

Murfreesboro, Tennessee
Feburary 14, 1863

*My Dear Harry:*

. . . . Since I wrote you last I have been engaged in the most fearful dissipation in regard to sleep. For ten nights I have not gone to bed once before 2½ o'clock in the morning, frequently not till four and sometimes not till [five?]. After one o'clock the General and I have given ourselves up to the discussion of religion, literature and war, but chiefly the former topic. I have never met a strong man, who [with] whose nature I have so soon become so well acquainted, with apparently such marked results of mutual confidence and respect.

My life you sometimes say has been made up of a series of accidents mostly of a favorable character. Perhaps this is true. Certain it is that I am perpetually in a series of unexpected *fixes,* not at all sure how I shall come out, nor always clear how I *ought* to come out. At the present writing I am in one that puzzles me more than almost any other of my life. Day before yesterday my horses arrived, and I was thus ready for duty. Last evening General Rosecrans spoke to me substantially as follows: "Garfield, I have now got a division ready for you, the one formerly commanded by General Van Cleve,[11] but I want to ask you what you think of staying here with me and taking the place as my Chief of Staff. I am almost alone in regard to counsel and assistance in my plans, and I want a power concentrated here that can reach out through the entire army and give it unity and strength." I evaded an answer and have taken the matter under advisement today. Considered personally, General Rosecrans could not pay me a higher compliment, nor in any way express more confidence in me.

Furthermore, if by chief of his staff he does not mean merely a chief clerk, but an adviser, a kind of alter ego, I have no doubt, while the confidence remains, I could do more service there than in any other [place] in this army. Were the staff organization here what it is in Europe that would be the most important and desirable position next to the Commanding General himself. But our staff corps is not such. Could I in this case make it so? Could I in fact do a greater service to the country in this capacity than as a general of [a] division? Would the army and the country think so? Would I be considered as having taken a step up or down? By taking that position I should make a large investment in General Rosecrans, and will it be wise to risk so much stock in that market? Quite probably I have but a limited number of months to remain in the army. To which side of this question should that fact incline me? Such are the questions both of public and personal policy which are before me and which I must decide long before this reaches you. It is a matter of great delicacy to manage. I should have added also the effect that such a course would have on the regular army officers toward the General and towards me.

Before you know what I conclude I want you and Almeda and Crete to make up your minds, and you write down for me a full sketch of the conference in which it is discussed. Do this without fail and when I see you I will tell you the reasons which decided me as well as my decision itself.

You must not fail to come to me. I think I can make you[r] stay agreeable. Bring me Carlyle's *French Revolution*[12] without fail. Give my love to your dear Libbie and to all our little circle of which she is a new and fitting ornament. With much love I am as ever yours,

James

[11] Brigadier General Horatio P. Van Cleve was wounded in the Battle of Stone River.
[12] Thomas Carlyle, *The French Revolution: A History* (1837).

Murfreesboro, Tennessee
February 15, 1863

*Honorable S. P. Chase*
*My Dear Friend:*

Your kind letter enclosing one to General Rosecrans was forwarded from Cincinnati and reached me two days ago. . . . I have been the guest of General Rosecrans since my arrival and he has shown me all the kindness and consideration I could desire. He has a division ready for me but has expressed a wish that I stay with him and serve as chief of his staff. I am considerably embarrassed by the proposition and hardly know what to say about it, but I shall consult with him more fully, and do whatever seems best for this army without regard to my personal wishes or interests. I think I have seen the interior of General Rosecrans' nature as fully as I ever did that of any man I ever knew and am glad to tell you that I believe in him, that he is sound to the bone on the great questions of the war and the way it should be conducted. I have known few men in my life whose whole being seemed so fully pervaded with the spirit of muscular religion as his. The last sentence of his admirable report of his late battle is no affectation, but an honest expression of his deepest convictions. It concludes with this fine sentence from the Catholic Church service: *"Non nobis Domine! non nobis sed nomini tuo da gloriam* [Grant glory, oh Lord, not to us, not to us, but to thy name]." If the country and the government will stand by him I feel sure that he will justify their highest expectations. I feel as though the army has the right to know one thing before it goes further in sacrifice. Will our enemies at home triumph and sell the nation or will the army be strengthened by new force and receive the support of the people? If it will not, to fight another battle, to throw away another life, is a crime.

The action of the Copperhead Democracy and the repeated rumor of the recall of McClellan, with the revival of his policy, is making this fine army fearfully anxious.

There is a matter in regard to which I greatly need your advice, and I hope you can do me the favor to give it at once. Members of Congress have written me that they think I ought to resign on the 4th of March, lest the next Congress should rule me out and increase the Democratic power over that body. I am unwilling to jeopardize our cause by any act of mine, and yet I can hardly bear the thought of leaving the army just now, when I have a better opportunity to strike at the rebellion than ever before, and of passing the months of spring and summer in safety while this army is in a death struggle. For my own part I cannot see how I can be excluded from my seat if I purge myself of ineligibility before taking the oath of office. I want to stay in the army till Congress meets, and then I would like to help fight the wild beasts in that Ephesus. Can these two things be done? If it is deemed unsafe for me to hold the commission after the 4th *prox.,* can't I send on my resignation and have the President hold it in abeyance till Congress meets and then accept it to take effect March 4th, 1863? If the pay is in the way, I don't care for that; I only want to help here till the time comes to help there. Or, if there should still be doubt, could I resign both my commission and the seat next November and let the people re-elect me? . . . I feel that I perhaps do wrong to trouble you with this matter at all, but I hope you will see how peculiarly annoying it is to me just at this time and favor me with your advice. . . .

*Very truly and sincerely yours,*
J. A. Garfield

P.S. Please direct to care of General Rosecrans. If you think I ought to act before your letter can reach me, please telegraph.

J. A. G.

Murfreesboro, Tennessee
February 18, 1863

*Dear Brother Austin:*

. . . . Since my arrival I have been the guest of General Rosecrans and I have become better acquainted with him than I ever did with any other man in the same length of time. He is one of the most devotedly religious men I ever knew, and makes all his acts in the army a matter of religion. He is a Catholic and on the morning of his great battle [Stones River] he received the holy communion from the priest before the battle began. He says he shall give me command of a division though he has invited me to stay with him as his Chief of Staff. If the government and the country will stand by him and give him the support he needs, he will give a good account of himself.

I have lately received a letter from John Hutchins telling me it is the opinion of many members of Congress that the men in the army who are elected to the new Congress ought to resign their commissions in the army by the 4th of March so that there need be no question about their right to hold their seats. I am greatly annoyed by it and have been in some doubt [as to] what I ought to do. I can hardly bear to think of leaving the army just now when I am in a position to do more service than ever before. Of course I recognize the great importance of holding up our cause in the next Congress, and my obligations to those who have elected me will not allow me to imperil their interests nor the interests of our cause in that next Congress. But I cannot believe that my serving in the army till the Congress meets and then resigning in time to be there at the opening will in any legal or equitable way invalidate my right to a seat. This was also the opinion of Secretary Chase, Benjamin Wade, and nearly all the prominent men with whom I have conversed. For me to resign now would look bad every way. I have been so long out of the field that a resignation just when I am again ready to [participate in the coming campaign] would not only be bad for the service but also for my own reputation. The very worst that could happen by my staying in the army till near the meeting of Congress would be the ordering a new election. But I do not think such a thing any way likely to be necessary.

Now I want your opinion on this, whether for the sake of having me serve the country in the field for nine months the people of the district would feel it a hardship to call another election if my seat should be considered vacant. I don't at all believe that such a necessity will arise, but if it should I ask your opinion upon it.[13]

I have written to five or six leading men in Washington on the subject and expect to hear from them soon. If I find there is really any danger I shall endeavor to forefend against it. . . .

J. A. Garfield

Murfreesboro, Tennessee<br>February 22, 1863

*My Dearest Crete:*

I have had no letters from Hiram since yours of February 7 and indeed have had almost no letters from any body for the last two weeks. Do you sometimes have come over you a feeling as if you could not write, as if the very manipulation of forming letters and words and constructing sentences were to[o] great a task to undertake? I have that experience, sometime[s] for days together when to answer even the briefest business letter seems harder than at other times to write a dozen pages. I cannot analyze the fact nor give any sensible account, but such is the fact nevertheless.

The last week has been such a time with me. I have not written a letter for the mail to anybody, and though I have done a good deal of work for the General and others here, yet I have felt it was well nigh impossible for me to write a letter. Perhaps, however, I can give one fact which helps to explain the reason of that feeling this time. The matter of my assignment still hangs fire, and I don't feel as though I could write again to anybody that I was still unemployed. If General Rosecrans cared less about me I should have been assigned to a division long ago, but he wants me with him and has telegraphed to Washington to get authority from the War Department to keep me as Chief of Staff. As soon as he hears from Stanton by mail I think a decision will be made. I don't even yet know what it will be. But aside from the irksomeness of having it supposed I am doing nothing it has been just as

---

[13] Garfield had already learned from his wife (January 2, 1863) that Austin believed Garfield should not resign his seat unless "most pressing" circumstances made it necessary.

well for me to be here. It has rained almost incessantly since my arrival and the roads are nearly impassable.

I have been taking what little spare time I have had for reading Thiers' *French Revolution* and have enjoyed it very much indeed. One cannot read it without being constantly struck with the remarkable analogy which the events of that day bear to our own rebellious times. I hope you will read it some time.

Do you hear anything yet from the book I ordered from New York for Suliot to translate? I am anxious to get it so as to finish my own little book.

There is a matter now troubling me very much which leaves [me] in quite an uncertain and uncomfortable state. I have lately received several letters from members of Congress informing me of the action taken by the House in regard to the case of Colonel Vandever[14] of Iowa, who was a member and served during the first session of the present Congress and then accepted a commission in the army. The committee appointed to report on his case reported that the acceptance of the military commission forfeited his right to the seat, and also expressed the opinion that no man could hold a commission in the army during any part of the two years for which he was elected. On this they have urged me to resign on the 4th of March, alleging their opinion that if I staid later than that date in the army I would be in danger of forefeiting my right to the seat, and it might thus cause a serious loss to our cause in the House.

For my own part I do not agree with that committee, nor do I concur in the opinion expressed by the members who wrote to me. Still, if by my act, the district should be deprived of a representative till they could re-elect, it might result in serious consequences to our cause, and the people of the district might also feel that I had not been so careful of their interests as I ought to have been. On the other hand, should I now resign just as I am in a position to do the country more service than at any time before, and lie by in ease all these coming nine months, I would be subjected to the most serious imputations. I wrote about ten days ago to Mr. Chase, to [Edward Bates] the Attorney General, to General Schenck,[15] and Messrs. Wade, Bingham[16] and Hutchins proposing the difficulties of the case and asking their full opinions in the case. I am in daily expectation of hearing from them,

[14] William Vandever, a member of the U.S. House of Representatives, 1859-1861, was re-elected in 1860 but entered the Union army on September 24, 1861, as Colonel of the Ninth Iowa. On January 20, 1863, the House finally declared his seat vacant from the date of his commission, but voted the next day to reconsider. There the matter stood at the close of the Congress, March 3, 1863.

[15] Like Garfield, Major General Robert C. Schenck was a congressman-elect. He resigned his commission in December, 1863, and took his seat in the House. For a while he and Garfield roomed together in Washington.

[16] John Armor Bingham of Ohio, member of the U.S. House of Representatives, 1855-1863, 1865-1873.

and of course till I do I don't feel very sure of anything. In that election I fear I have drawn an elephant. If it seems best to resign, I think I shall serve till Congress meets in some capacity without rank or pay so that I may do something for the country in its struggle.

I hope to hear from you often. Don't think from my disquisition on writing that I have been in any way cold. My heart is very warm and loving toward you, and it is sweet to think of you and our blessed little Trot and know that away through these stormy miles of winter you are loving me and wishing me with you. God bless you, as my heart does, and abundantly more than any human heart can. Some day I will write you about my religious reflections and invite you to a conference of some matters in that direction.

Love to mother and all. Ever your loving

James. . . .


Murfreesboro, Tennessee
February 26, 1863

*My Dearest Crete:*

Harry arrived yesterday afternoon bring[ing] your letter. It had been a long time since I had heard from you or any of the family. I am sorry that my letters have, some of them, failed to reach you. From what Harry tells me I am sure that several of my letters have been strangely delayed or entirely lost. I full[y] sympathize with all you say in regard to gloomy feelings, for though I have long made it a point to use philosophy and not give way to sad and gloomy feelings, I do so now; but the complication of questions, congressional and military, and especially my long stay here in comparative idleness and official inactivity conspire to make me dissatisfied and sad. The continual dreary rain, the broken and devastated country with its impassable roads, and the dreary batallions that go dripping and soiled to their daily monotony of mingled labor and idleness all act with depressing force on one's spirits. I am most happy to assure you that no part of my sadness is referable [to] any of the old causes of sadness which once haunted my heart. On the contrary, I turn from all this sadness here to our happy home and long with an ache and an earnestness stronger than ever to enjoy it with you and our blessed little Trot.

The question of what I shall be assigned to has not been a mere formal matter. If I was to have been put in command of a division, the decision would have been easy; but the place of Chief of Staff was one of more gravity and more important results. In the first place, General Rosecrans wanted to know me so thoroughly as to be sure that I was the man he needed. It was in the next place necessary that he should find out what the opinions and feelings of such officers as his leading corps commanders were in reference to the matter. Thus consultations have been held, and long and searching conversations between the General and myself have been held in reference to it. I have almost wholly abstained from writing to my friends till I should know what my work was to be.

I have not been unaware of the fact that I should lose credit and [that] my personal and military reputation to some extent [should be] injured by the long delay. My experience in delay, in Washington and here, has been one of the most trying of my life. It has tried my powers of endurance and my natural restlessness more than it was [they were] ever tried before. I have gone through all the cycles of restlessness and chafing impatience until I think I have learned to endure with a considerable degree of patience, if not with meekness, what is laid upon me.

Since I began to write this letter at the General's table, he has written an order and has just now shown it to me, assigning me to duty as chief of his staff. It will [be] printed tomorrow and I shall proceed to duty at once. So that the [sic] long agony is over, and true [to] the perverseness of human nature, I shall no doubt often regret that I am not in command of a division; but I shall nevertheless go to work thoroughly and vigorously to make as much out of this army as I can. I presume that the first impression of my assignment to duty will be unfavorable in the minds of my friends abroad, but I am willing to bear that from the knowledge that I am chosen here because it is regarded as a great necessity and, though I may not make as much reputation as I could in another place, yet I can exercise more influence on the army and more fully impress my views and policy on its administration.

I am very glad to see Harry. I have had a delightful visit with him, and shall hope soon to be set up in an independent mess where I can make him feel more at home. I had a telegram on the 24th from Professor saying he was on his way here. I am glad to have him come here with me.

In regard to the little addition, of which you speak, to our house, I leave it wholly with your own judgment. If you conclude to build it, try to get along with using as little of our invested money as possible. You had better have father superintend it and then settle with him, if he has the time. Will it disfigure the house any to have such an addition put on?

Tell Almeda I will answer her letter soon, probably tomorrow. One of my letters to her seems to be lost.

Give my love to all the household. Kiss little Trot and tell her it is from me. It is now 1 o'clock at night.

*Ever your own,*
James

Murfreesboro, Tennessee
February 28, 1863

*My Dear Phebe:*

Your very kind and welcome letter of the 23rd was received this morning. I was very glad to hear from you, but I am made very sad to hear that so many of our old friends and acquaintances are dying at home. Poor Cordie! My heart aches for her. No one knows better how to sympat[h]ize with her than you. It seems very strange and sad that Mary Hubbell[17] is dead. It is a most sad and painful thought to me that one has gone down to the grave with feeling in her heart that I have wronged her. God knows I never intended to do her any wrong, and cannot feel that I am guilty of any wrong in my heart towards [her]. Still I know that I was the cause of great suffering to her. She had many admirable qualities which I never ceased to admire. Nothing that she ever did or said about me destroyed my kind feelings towards her. It will be a great shock to Taylor to have lost both wife and child while away from them. This is but one of the many instances of men who, while away in the field, have lost all that they loved and that bound them to life. Should Crete and Trot die while I am in the army, I should hope never to return. This generation will not outlive the painful and [sad] memories of this terrible war.

I was very anxious to have visited your father's [home] when I was last in Ohio, but I had only time to spend a few hours at home on my way here from Washington. I need not tell you that your father's house seems to me my own home. I never expect in this life such unalloyed pleasure[s] as were mine in the days of our childhood when we were so young and so happy as children at home in Orange. It is the habit of life to look either back or forward for happiness, but never where we are, especially is it so with me while in the army. The only refuge from sadness is the constant and exciting work that crowds upon one in a great army.

General Rosecrans has appointed me chief of his staff in place of the lamented [Colonel Julius P.] Garesché who[se] head was cut off by a cannon ball at Murfreesboro. The duties of the position are very many and very great. It makes me in a great degree responsible for the policy and movement of the whole army in connection with General

[17] For several months in 1852 Garfield was, or thought he was, in love with Mary Hubbell of Warrensville, Ohio. Friends and acquaintances expected them to marry. During the winter of 1852-1853 Garfield gave much thought to his romance with Mary, decided against continuing it, and told her so in a letter. She was extremely hurt and unhappy. Garfield was severely criticized by people who thought he had toyed with Mary's affections. Although the clamor subsided in a few weeks, Garfield smarted from the criticism and never forgot the personal and neighborhood turmoil wrought by his first love affair. In 1853, after their breakup, Garfield avowed Mary he would always regard her "with warm affection," and he did. In 1858 Mary married William Taylor, who served from 1861-1868 as Colonel of the Fifth Ohio Cavalry Regiment.

Rosecrans. We are having terrible weather, with almost constant rain and nearly impassable roads. We are busy bringing up provisions, repairing roads and getting ready for a forward movement as soon as the weather becomes settled. There is fighting in a small way nearly every day, and more or less killing, wounding and capturing. There must be terrible fighting here and will [all] along our lines before the South can be subdued. But I have no doubt of the final result. It may be a year, it may be two or three, but I believe the end will be sure and triumphant.

I have no photographs with me but I will send word to Crete who I think has got some. If so, she will send one to you and one to Silas. There has been a very fine steel engraving of me taken in New York and I think some of them have been sent to Hiram by this time.

I want you to write me again, and often afterward. . . .

With much love, I am, affectionately,

*Your cousin,*
J. A. Garfield

Murfreesboro, Tennessee
March 3, 1863

*Dearest Crete:*

Your letter of February 12 came to hand today. It is very remarkable how a letter should be detained in the mail so long. But I am very glad to receive it, though it has been so long delayed.

I am exceedingly busy now, and you will pardon a brief letter this time.

Harry goes tomorrow and I am making up a package of things and letters to send by him. Among other things I send by him a series of letters from prominent men in Washington in regard to the congressional question which I desire to have preserved. I expect to make use of them in a certain contingency which may arise. I have determined to stay in the army, and when the time comes, if I can be of more service in Congress than here, I will go and make a test of my right to the seat which I think is clear.

In view of the conclusion to stay in the army and from a conversation with Harry I don't know but I was too precipitate in concluding not to build for the present. At all events, I will make some suggestions on your plan of addition, which is excellent in the main; yet there are some criticisms I will make, and ask you to send me a plan not liable to the same objections. 1st, the cellar stairs go down from the dining room which make a bad disfiguration and is not a proper room for a cellar to connect with. You might get into the cellar by a trap door from the porch or, if it be thought best to have an inside entrance, pierce the cellar wall and go down through the kitchen. 2nd, "Our room" receives light from but one point and would be too dark to be convenient. 3rd, "Mother's room" has no independent exit and makes ours a highway, whereas the latter should be retired. 4th, the closet in mother's room disfigures the double parlor and is unnecessary. A wardrobe would answer every purpose. 5th, the closet and bath rooms adjoining "our room" should change places so that there could be a window in the bath room, which is not needed in the other. I have no doubt your religious tendencies lead you to go in liberally for *closets* that have doors to shut. 6th, I don't understand your wood house. Please finish it. Does Jim need a room half the size of the kitchen? How will the landing of the hall stairs above affect the shape of the chambers? Send me a plan of the upper story and give the h[e]ight of the addition. Could father give his personal superintendence? Could lumber and materials be got soon? We want a horse barn and a lew[18] for Bill and myself when we come home.

Is Jim lazy? If he is he will have to leave. I can't have him around if he won't be diligent and helpful. If you think best read the above sentences to him.

Professor is here with me.

I wish I could send kisses to you and Trot by Harry. Loving you both with my whole heart, I am as ever your own,

James

Murfreesboro, Tennessee
March 8, 1863

*Dearest Crete:*

. . . . It brought a world of dear recollections to my heart to read your thoughts on my early home while you were on your late visit there. It makes me long with an intensity I have not felt for years to go back and visit that spot and the scenes connected with it. There is no spot where I could be more rejoiced and saddened at the same time than there. How vividly even now those places rise before me. I hope you will often visit Uncle Amos and go over the dear old ground.

That battle hymn or war anthem[19] of Theodore Tilton's is exceedingly fine. Thank you for it.

The poet Thomas Buchanan Read is here, and last evening recited several of his poems with fine effect. He recited "Drifting," which you will find, I think, in Dana's *Household Book of Poetry*.[20] Also "The Oath" and "Our Defenders," his own compositions. Gives a public reading to the army tomorrow night.

[18] A shelter, especially from the wind.

[19] "God Save the Nation, a Battle Hymn," words by Theodore Tilton, music by Henry C. Work.

[20] Charles A. Dana, editor, *The Household Book of Poetry* (1857). "Drifting," a poem of nature by Read, appears on pages 73-74 (1903 edition). The author of over ten volumes of verse, Read is best remembered for his "Sheridan's Ride."

The expeditions whose movements I sketched in a letter to Almeda a few days ago have not yet finished their work. The disaster at Thompson's Station south of Franklin is very mortifying and very severe.[21] It appears that the rebels had two Negro regiments against us in that fight.[22] Let our anti-abolition copperheads put that into their pipes and smoke it. We are not too good to be killed by Negroes but the rebels are, seems to be the Democratic doctrine. *Vibebimus* [*Videbimus:* We shall see]. Indeed, I am not sure as my Latin is correct. Tell me if it is not.

We are still having severe and heavy weather, changing from rain to snow and from snow to rain and sunshine. I long for more decisive weather. Give me a roaring New England winter when the cold is fierce enough to make a glowing grate and close[d] doors a luxury; but this southern winter, where a room is too cold if you have no fire and too warm if you have a good one, where the heavens smile with sunshine and the earth reeks with mud and there is no clear-cut enjoyment out doors nor in, is intolerable. Northern character partakes of the decisiveness of the climate and I am proud of both country and people. If I could now change my birthplace and did not leave it where it was, I would have it far up on some November hillside of Massachusetts, where the storm and the mountain oaks shook hands in joyful fierce glee.

[21] On March 4 a Union brigade commanded by Colonel John Coburn of the Thirty-third Indiana left Franklin, Tennessee, with orders to discover what was in front of Rosecrans and to bring in forage. About four miles out Confederate cavalrymen engaged the Federals briefly and slowly withdrew, lurking on Coburn's flanks until sundown. The next day, at Thompson's Station, some six miles from Franklin, the Union brigade was drawn into a trap, severely mauled, and forced to surrender. It was a complete victory for Major General Earl Van Dorn and his 6,000 cavalrymen. Union losses totaled 48 killed, 247 wounded, and over 1,150 captured. Coburn was among the prisoners. Thus the fate of the mission that was put in motion by the first operational directive written by Garfield as Chief of Staff. In his letter of March 11 to his wife, Garfield's criticism regarding scouts is significant in that it suggests grumbling about failure to deploy them. The official reports contain no such complaints. Coburn said in his own report, written after he was exchanged, that soon after daylight on March 5 he sent out patrols and scouts in all directions, and at eight o'clock, no force having been discovered, began to advance toward Thompson's Station. At no time before or during the fight did he receive reliable intelligence about the size or location of enemy troops he knew were near. Under these circumstances Coburn used poor judgment in advancing on a road flanked by hills and cedar thickets, ideal country for ambush. But others must share the blame for the disaster. Coburn's cavalry not only failed to supply much-needed intelligence, but fled from the field once the fight started. So did the artillery and a detachment of Ohio infantry sent along with the forage train. At fault too was Coburn's division commander back in Franklin, Brigadier General Charles C. Gilbert, who believed 10,000 enemy cavalrymen to be on his front, had well-prepared defenses to fall back on at Franklin, knew Coburn was engaged on the 4th and heard his guns on the 5th, but sent not a single soldier to help.

[22] There were no Negro troops in the engagement. Not until March, 1865, did the Confederate government pass legislation authorizing the use of Negroes as soldiers, and the war ended before any entered combat in the Confederate army.

In regard to mother's money, I hardly know what to do with it; but I will keep it if she desires it. Should there be any slip about Mason and Humeston's payment so that the purchase money of the house is not at hand April 1st, you can use it to make the amount up. There must be no slip about the exact time and other terms of [the contract]. I was not able to draw any pay from the Pay Department when Harry was here or I would have sent some by him. I hope to do so before the end of the month. If not perhaps Harry and Almeda will help me meet the contract. I hope soon to hear from the letter I wrote to you by the hand of Harry. . . .

Love to Trot, mother and all. I am ever and forever your loving and own,

James

Murfreesboro, Tennessee
March 9, 1863

*My Dear Harry:*

Like one who has lighted a slow match to fire a magazine and is waiting for the explosion, so am I waiting the results of last night's work. Take Almeda's letter, in which I sketched the outline of our plan of movements upon the enemy, and I will add a chapter showing how this game of chess has become complicated since that letter was written. The enemy, after repulsing Gilbert's [force?] at Spring Hill,[23] appeared in force in front of Franklin and menaced that place. A brigade was ordered up from Nashville to Franklin, and Sheridan's division,[24] which was at Triune, was moved to a point half way between the last named places. [Brigadier General James B.] Steedman, who had advanced from Nolensville to Triune, was ordered to fortify his position and two regiments were sent to him from La Vergne so that he had six good regiments of infantry, one of cavalry, and a battery.

Such was the situation when late last evening a deserter came in giving us the information that three rebel brigades had crossed the Duck River at Shelbyville and were last night encamped eight miles out on the Unionville and Triune pike. An hour after this news, came a telegram from General Granger at Franklin saying that he had reliable information that a large part of the rebel force in his front had moved back via Raleigh Hill and were hurrying toward Triune. This made it clear that two rebel columns were converging upon Steedman, each larger than his own, and both these columns were at

[23] Gilbert commanded the division to which Coburn's brigade belonged and selected that unit for the assignment that ended in disaster at Thompson's Station, near Spring Hill.

[24] Major General Philip H. Sheridan commanded the Third Division, XX Corps.

that time probably much nearer Triune than either Granger or we were. We immediately telegraphed to Granger to send out to Sheridan —whom we had left, as stated above, half way between Franklin and Triune—[orders to go] to the relief of Steedman. We were greatly alarmed and indignant to find that Granger had ordered Sheridan to report to him and that he was at that moment entering Franklin without our order or knowledge, and that the road he had passed over was left almost impassable.

Thus Steedman was in imminent danger and how to extricate or relieve him was the question. To reinforce him before the enemy could attack him was impossible, or in the language of chess he was en prise and there was no piece which we could interpose. We must either withdraw him or attack a more valuable piece of the ad[ver]sary. General Rosecrans was at first strongly in favor of ordering Steedman to retreat. I opposed this, arguing that he could only withdraw in one of three directions—viz. Nolensville, Stewartsboro, or Murfreesboro. If he should take either of the former two routes, the rebels could follow him with cavalry and destroy him much more easily than they could in his fortifications at Triune. If he took the latter route, they could strike across to Lizzard and capture him and escape.

I earnestly urged to have him stand and fight in his intrenchments; meanwhile we should push a heavy force from Franklin to Raleigh Hill, and another from here via Versailles to Eagleville, and either attack the rebels in the rear while they were fighting Steedman or catch them on their return if they had captured him, should they go back toward Shelbyville; and if they attempt to fall back via Chapel Hill or Raleigh Hill, Granger's Franklin force could catch them. This view was finally adopted and I have just finished instructions to all the forces to be sent out. During the night I wrote more than 25 pages of dispatches and letters of instruction, and now at a quarter before six in the morning I am scratching this word to you and shall soon lie down to get a little sleep.

Of course, I am exceedingly anxious to know the developements but I believe when the rebels come to know our movements they will back out. I ordered artillery to move down from La Vergne to reinforce Steedman and exhorted him to hold out till noon and we will attack the rear of his adversary. I feel that this plan which is my own, will do me personally great harm or a considerable good. General Granger's unwarranted removal of Sheridan from the place where we posted him has brought Steedman into peril, and if he suffers it is by Granger's fault. I am not sleepy at all but I must close and rest a little.

I hope to hear from you soon and I do implore you and Almeda and Crete to write to me very often. You can't know how much I want to know all you think and feel.

*Ever and forever yours,*
James

Murfreesboro, Tennessee
March 11, 1863

*Dearest Crete:*

In a few moments' lull of business I have scratched off for you a little plot of the late disaster at Thompson's Station south of Franklin, where the rebels drew our military fools into a regular cul-de-sac and then closed up on them and captured them. I also enclose you a private letter I received this morning from Colonel Opdycke[25] giving his views of the affair. The rebs on the hill and behind the stone fence and cedar thicket kept concealed until our fool[s] got into the bag, going up to charge the batteries on the height above the church. You can see how perfectly they might have avoided the whole disgrace by keeping out scouts a mile on each side and a mile ahead, as they ought to have done. [See Garfield's map on following page.]

I haven't the time to tell you of the problem we were solving when I last wrote to Harry, only to say that the enemy's advance attacked Steedman, but fearing our rear movements, only waited long enough to get their noses bloody and then ran off. Granger is still out after them south of Franklin.

I have been interrupted six times since I began this half sheet and now four telegraphic dispatches have come and I must close. I hope to hear from you often. Don't call this a letter, only a budget of stuff.

Love to Trot and all.

*Ever and forever yours,*
James

Murfreesboro, Tennessee
March 14, 1863

*My Dearest Crete:*

Your good letter of March 8th came to hand yesterday. Before this Harry has reached home and you know more about me and my doings than I can write. I am very hard at work and can get but very little time for writing. At the next to the last word of the preceding sentence I was interrupted, and stopped to read and answer three dispatches, which will illustrate the quiet I get in my correspondence. Mrs Rosecrans[26] and one of her little girls arrived last night to visit the General who expressed the wish that you were here too. You may know that I very cordially seconded the wish. If we were to be here any considerable time I should ask you to come. Some time in the summer, if I am alive, I hope you can come and see me a good deal further south than we now are.

[25] Colonel Emerson Opdycke of the 125th Ohio was not in the engagement at Thompson's Station, but he knew the area well and had undoubtedly heard eye-witness accounts of the fight.

[26] Rosecrans' wife was the former Anna Elizabeth Hegeman.

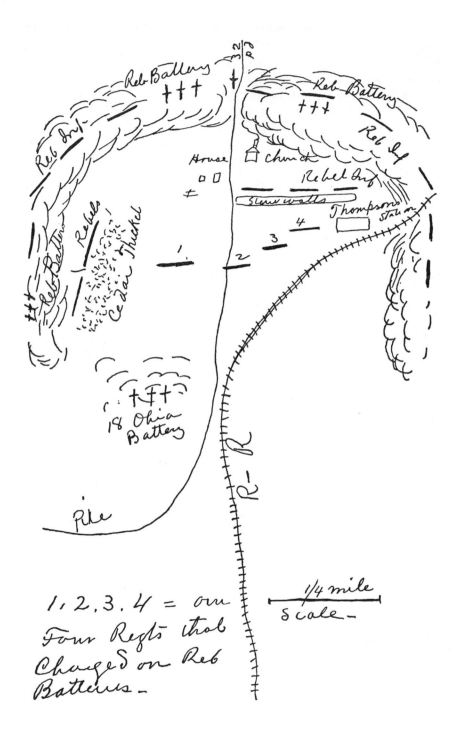

Reb Battery

†††

Reb Inf

Rebels

Cedar Thicket

Reb Battery

††

18 Ohio
Battery

Pike

Reb Battery

†††

House

☐☐

†

Reb Battery

†††

church

Rebel Inf

Stone walls

Thompsons Station

4

3

2

1

R-R

R-R

1, 2, 3, 4 = our
Four Regts that
Charged on Reb
Batteries —

1/4 mile
scale —

After a fearful series of rains which have kept the rivers and streams in a fearful state of flood we are now having a few days of fine weather, though the signs of the sky are treacherous, and cannot yet expect settled weather for some time.

The indications seem to show that Vicksburg will be abandoned by the rebels before very long and that a large part of their army will be sent here. I feel sure we shall see the great struggle of the war on this part of the line.

I am grieved and astonished at what you write in regards to the 42nd. Indeed, I cannot believe that the regiment has come to hold such absurd and wicked notions. To doubt the justice of our cause as compared with the infernal wickedness of the rebel cause is not only treason but the supremest nonsense and folly. If the dear old regiment has come to that I hope it will be publicly and perpetually disgraced before the army and the country, and the man or men who have instilled such venomous poison into it is worthy of ignominious death. I beg you write to Joe, and have all our friends in Hiram who write to the boys, not to listen to such talk nor harbor such thoughts in their hearts. Nations less powerful and far less wealthy than we have waged fierce wars for 30 years continuously and still not gone to ruin. If this war lasts seven years yet I do not, cannot, would not if I could, doubt in the final success of God's immutable justice and the terrible and complete overthrow of the rebellion. I will write to the regiment as soon as I can get time.

We have withdrawn our forces from the pursuit of Van Dorn after chasing him across the Duck River and are getting ready to open another course of operations.

I shall hope soon to hear from you how the money matters come on. We must make that horse trade sure.

I have now a mess of my own and am getting along very well, only I am greatly in need of butter that is not rancid. Should anyone be coming down here please send a firkin of fresh yellow W[estern] R[eserve] Butter. Potatoes are $5.00 per bushel as purchased from sutlers.

Professor is in his glory and doing finely. . . .

Kisses innumerable to our little blessed Trot and all love to yourself. Love to mother and the whole household.

*Ever and always your*
James

Headquarters
Department of the Cumberland
Murfreesboro, Tennessee
March 22, 1863

*My Dear Mother:*

Your letter accompanying Crete's was received in due time. I am always glad to hear from you. And would write to you oftener, but I write so often to Crete that you always hear from me. I have very seldom in my life had so much to do as now. I do not get to bed on an average before two o'clock, but on the other hand I don't get up till between seven and eight. I am in most excellent health and am growing fat and strong. I don't know how much I weigh but I think it is not much short of 200 pounds.

We are having little fights with the rebels almost every day. This town was a great nest of them and I am getting up an arrangement to send them out.

The principal church in this place is owned by the Disciples. It is a very large, fine building, and there was before the war a flourishing congregation; but the minister was a rebel and is now a chaplain in the rebel army and the church is scattered. The building is now used for a hospital. There were a great many Disciples in this country but you would hardly know that there was any such thing as religion on Sunday. We know no difference in our work from one day to another. General Rosecrans, however, has Catholic service in his room or mine every few days. I sometimes attend and as I can understand the Latin service it is not altogether unmeaning to me. I hope you are not alarmed about my becoming a Catholic. You ought to be glad that I take time to think and talk about religion at all. I have no doubt the Catholics have been greatly slandered. I am very sorry to hear of the sickness and deaths among our friends. Poor Cordelia, she has a great load of sorrow to carry with her.

Crete tells me you have place[d] some money in her hands. I send you a note for it. It is hard to dispose of it and any time you get a good chance to loan it you can have it. . . .

I hope you are enjoying yourself at my home. . . .

*Your affectionate son,*
James


Murfreesboro, Tennessee
March 25, 1863

*Dear Brother Austin:*

. . . In regard to the appointment of Major Wood, I would like to consult you. For that position it needs a man of the energetic working stamp, one who is full of enterprise and will have the nerve to do his duty thoroughly and faithfully. I don't know much about Major Wood, but from what I saw of him at Howland, I did not get the impression that he would ever set the Mahoning River on fire, though perhaps he may. There have been several applications to me for the position, among others one from Asper of Warren. I couldn't recommend Asper unless a very large number of good men should tell me that I was mistaken in supposing him to be an ass. I think much better of Wood than of Asper. Still, as I do not desire to act in any of these appointments on my own private judgment alone, I will delay till I can hear from you again. I want you to tell me how the people of the district would be likely to choose as between Asper and Wood, or whether there are other prominent candidates who would be more acceptable.[27]

I send you a pamphlet on the war, which, if you have not seen, I hope you will read carefully. It gives us a good basis of hope and confidence in the final outcome of the war. I trust our people will not give themselves up to despondency. I have never for a moment doubted the final result, provided always that our people at home shall stand by the government and the army. The rebels have brought about all the force in the field they can, and now if our government puts the conscription law into vigorous operation we shall soon see the power of the rebellion broken.

This is a splendid army, not so much in numbers as in its character. Nearly every man is a veteran and has been tested in battle. It is in a fine state of health and discipline, and it will make a terrible fight when it next meets the enemy. I feel full confidence that our Heavenly Father has a better future in store for us than to allow this great country to be overthrown.

Give my love to Minerva and Lottie. I hope to hear from you all. With kindest regards, I am

*Very truly yours,*
J. A. Garfield

[27] George L. Wood, a lawyer from Trumbull County, entered the war as a first lieutenant in the Seventh Ohio. He was severely wounded and discharged late in 1862. He died soon after the war. Joel F. Asper was a lawyer and journalist who entered the war as a captain in the Seventh Ohio. He was discharged in 1863 as a lieutenant colonel and in the following year he served one hundred days as Colonel of the 171st Ohio. After the war he moved to Missouri, practiced law, founded a newspaper, and served in the U.S. House of Representatives, 1869-1871. He died in 1872. What position these men were being considered for in 1863 I cannot say; but in view of Garfield's reservations about Wood, and his disdain for Asper, it is pertinent to note that in 1861 both men had supported Tyler, not Garfield, for the colonelcy of the Seventh.

Murfreesboro, Tennessee
March 26, 1863

*Dearest Crete:*

Your two letters of the        and        were duly received two days
ago; but I am literally covered up with work so that I have barely
found time to answer a few business letters only, for the past four
days. I would be very glad had I the time to tell you some of the new
problems we have got up in our movements of this army and I hope

March 28

You may think it strange when I tell you I have not been able for the
last two days to finish even this little sheet, but such is the fact. We
had reviews both yesterday and the day before which consumed five
hours each and I have had my hands overflowingly full of work on my
return. Night before last I got to bed at half past one and last night
at 2 o'clock. I take this morning while the General is at his breakfast
to write a few words with a pile of telegrams beside me to be answered.
I have been laying out two plans which I very much desire that you
and our little circle shall know, and yet I dare not write it to you,
except in cipher. I enclose a cipher which I will use when I describe
it and which you can use when you write to me anything that, being
cap[tured], might do harm to our cause. The great struggle is coming on
slowly but surely and I want you all to know how it progresses. The
troubles in Kentucky[28] make it necessary to use great caution in what
goes from here to you by mail. If Burnside has been reinforced as reported it will settle the Kentucky question and greatly aid us.

I have hardly a moment to think of anything but this struggle.
It will well be worth ten thousand lives if we can break the power
of the rebellion this season. I don't think the conflict will be tried here
for some weeks yet, but it must come. These two armies can no more
live in this present situation long than wild tigers and lions can
dwell in the same lair.

Captains Swaim and Farrar are in the scout department and dwell
under my charge. It opens gulfs of intrigue and treachery on the part
of the rebels. We must oppose cunning to cunning. It is a singularly
curious and interesting department.

I have drawn pay for one month and send you $183.29 draft on
New York. If you do not need to use it turn it in on Harry's note and
have it endorsed. I cannot now talk of the house as I would like. You
have greatly improved the plan, and I will try to get time to think

[28] On March 22 Brigadier General John Pegram led a brigade on a horse-raiding
expedition into Central Kentucky. He was defeated by a Union force near Somerset
a week later and retired across the Cumberland River. Although Confederate operations behind Union lines induced Garfield to try writing in cipher, he gave it up
after garbling a coded letter that went to Hiram. All letters in this volume were
written in the clear.

of it more as soon as I can. I wrote to mother not long ago. I will write to Almeda soon and use the cipher in a part of that letter.

Preserve the key to the cipher and in your next letter to me write a few lines in cipher to let me see if you fully understand it. Kiss our blessed little Trot a hundred times for me. Darling little love, how I want to see her. With love to mother and all,

*I am ever and forever your own,*
James

| 1 | 15 | 28 | 39 | 48 | 55 | 60 | 63 |
|---|---|---|---|---|---|---|---|
| 16 | 2 | 14 | 27 | 38 | 47 | 54 | 59 |
| 29 | 17 | 3 | 13 | 26 | 37 | 46 | 53 |
| 40 | 30 | 18 | 4 | 12 | 25 | 36 | 45 |
| 49 | 41 | 31 | 19 | 5 | 11 | 24 | 35 |
| 56 | 50 | 42 | 32 | 20 | 6 | 10 | 23 |
| 61 | 57 | 51 | 43 | 33 | 21 | 7 | 9 |
| 64 | 62 | 58 | 52 | 44 | 34 | 22 | 8 |

In deciphering what I may write to you, make a square like this and write my words down in order from left to right, commencing at 1 and going to 63, then from 16 to 59, and so on. You will read them following the numerals. Of course you will then have to use a new square, or the same one over again, for every 64 words. In order to aid you in dividing the squares, I will write the word "Kensington," "Toodles," or "Bluff" to mark the blocks of 64 words. The word used of these three is not to be counted.

Murfreesboro, Tennessee
April 1, 1863

*My Precious Little Crete:*
Yours of the 26th March came to hand yesterday, but the letter of the 22nd did not reach me till today. From the office marks on it, it appears to have had a trip to Cairo and left that place on the 26th of March. I am glad always to receive a letter from you, but this last that should have been first of the two is most welcome. From my heart, dearest, I thank [you] for writing it and the beautiful and tender way in which you wrote is only surpassed in my regard by the message itself. I thank you for the fact even more than for the record. You know how I have felt on that subject for a long time. The heading to this letter was written late last night and just as I was ready to

commence the first line, a pile of dispatches was brought in which occupied me till past one o'clock. I then went to my cot and for nearly an hour my thoughts of you and your letter were very sweet, solemn, and joyful.

There is such a mystery about life in any form that the contemplation of it always fills me with awe. But of incipient life, of life that is to be,[29] with all the grand and fearful possibilities which may attend it, I have no words to tell you what my thoughts were. And then the thought that it is my life, a life which I may never see, that there may be a period of oblivion between the sunset of my own and the morning of that new life. Should this be true that little life will be so strange and singular a one in its history. It is impossible for me to tell you how overwhelming and deep an interest I feel in the future of that precious hope. I beg you to be happy and cheerful during all the awfully mysterious days through which you will live till the consummation. It is a matter of great regret to me that I cannot be with you and share with you the hopes and thoughts that shall be yours during those sacred days, but you must write to me frequently and fully.

I agree to your last views in regard to the house. Can't you make the library and parlor a little longer by reducing the width of the hall or by letting the hall run out a few feet into mother's room? Do so if you can. I fully agree with father's views, that the house can never be made to suit us by additions. It is like the prayer that old Brother John Smith of Kentucky was asked to finish. He declined, saying he had rather make a new one than to try to patch up that one. Get some thorough man to build it and bind him to finish the work by a given time and not far distant. A horsebarn must be built under the same contract, as it will cost less. Also a *lew.* Toodles should furnish the plan for the latter and send me a drawing. I want the *horse barn* large enough so that a carriage may stand in between the stalls and the opposite side and still have full room to lead horses out and in. I want some good plan made out and sent to me. If I had time I would get one up but it is not possible for me to do it. I want the barn finished with upright boarding, battened over and painted some light color, say slate trimmed with white. Economy is the word in all this work.

I sent you a draft on New York of $183+ in my last. I forgot to enclose the stanza. I send it now together with a song which General McCook sings. His wife copied it for me. The General (McCook) sings it finely. It is very beautiful. Kisses and love to Trot, and always to you.

*Ever and forever yours,*
James

[29] At this point in the letter an asterisk appears, and at the bottom of the page opposite another asterisk these words are written: "This alludes to Harry A. Garfield. Note, June 30, 1872, J.A.G." Harry was born on October 11, 1863.

Murfreesboro, Tennessee
April 10, 1863

*My Dearest Crete:*

Yours of the 6th is this moment read. I am greatly distressed that my letters should not reach you. I have received all those you refer to and have answered each of them very soon after they came. In one I sent you the diagram by which you might decipher anything I might write which it would not be prudent to send in the usual manner. If that letter is lost you can decipher Almeda's letter by making a diagram of eight squares each way and writing down the words of my letter from left to right, one word in each square. Then read diagonally commencing with the lefthand upper corner and return by the next parallel row of squares above, then descend below. The word "Toodles" marks the divisions of 64 words. In another I sent you a draft of $183+ which I hope is not lost. I shall constantly write to you even if my letters do not reach you for I think they cannot all be lost. Besides the letters I have sent several papers with documents sometimes with a few lines in them and sometimes not. I have also sent a large topographical map of this country to Almeda so that you may all trace our movements.

I received your letter of the 22nd March was [which] was so deeply interesting to me and answered it within an hour of its reception. I very much hope that answer will reach you. The letter, however, was much delayed, having been sent by way of Cairo, and did not reach me till after your next of the 26th came to hand.

I have had the entire burden of getting up and fitting out the expedition of Colonel Streight.[30] It has embarked at Nashville this morning. I will as soon as it is safe send you my letter of instructions to him. You can hardly imagine how deep is my interest in the result. Our forces are now in a very interesting position. We have gained some brilliant little successes lately but shall very soon test the strength of the mass of the rebel army. The General has now gone out of the fortification and told me to lay a plan for the capture of Van Dorn and present it to him when he came in. I shall go at it as soon as I close

[30] On April 7 Colonel Abel D. Streight of the Fifty-first Indiana led a small brigade of infantry and cavalry out of Murfreesboro on an expedition whose purpose was to cut the railroad from Atlanta to Chattanooga, one of Bragg's supply lines. Streight marched to Nashville, went down the Cumberland by boat to Clarksville, disembarked and marched to Fort Henry, and thence by boat up the Tennessee River to Eastport, Mississippi. From there he struck across Northern Alabama, with a force under Brigadier General Grenville M. Dodge acting as a decoy. Unable to elude Forrest, who was not long fooled by Dodge, Streight was constantly annoyed by enemy cavalry after reaching the vicinity of Blountsville, about fifty miles southeast of Decatur. Continuing eastward to Gadsden, he headed for Rome, Georgia, but on May 3, at Cedar Bluff, Alabama, on the Coosa River near the state line, he was attacked by Forrest and forced to surrender his exhausted and poorly equipped command. This was deeply distressing to Garfield, who had labored hard and hopefully on the expedition.

this letter which must be soon. Tell me how you get on in paying for the house. I must close. I sent mother a copy of an intercepted letter a few days ago. Lest that may have been lost I send you the original together with another captured at the same time. Do write to me very often. Love and kisses to Trot and all.

*Ever your own,*
James

As Chief of Staff, Headquarters
Department of the Cumberland
Murfreesboro, Tennessee
April 12, 1863

*My Dear Secretary:*

Yours of 6th has just come to hand. I should have written you long ago, but the great amount of work we have had on hand for the last three weeks has left the General and myself but little respite or rest day or night. You have probably seen from the papers that General Rosecrans has chosen me as his chief of staff. I have now been serving in that capacity for nearly two months. During that time we have been steadily at work to prepare this army for its great work, and I am glad to tell that it is now nearly *ready* to work.

One thing was settled soon after my arrival, and that was that it is useless to advance into the rebel territory unless we are prepared to hold the ground we win in battle. This cannot be done until we make our supplies secure. We have therefore established a triangle of posts with Nashville as its northern apex and Franklin and Murfreesboro its base, facing south. These points we have strengthened by erecting by far the best fortification built during this war. At the same time we have used every available pound of transportation power to bring up supplies and store them in their several places, so that we now have rations to last till September and forage till July.

We have communicated with General Burnside, who responds generously to all our requests and has promised to move forward and hold the lines of the Cumberland, thus securing our rear. At the same time he will push a column into East Tennessee, and put his New England troops abreast of us in line of battle. His forces are now in motion to take the place assigned them. That done, it relieves four of our brigades, now doing garrison and railroad duty in the rear. The army will then be foot loose and will move. As we climb we can pull the ladder up behind us without danger. The enemy may then cut off our railroad if he can, and we will not be compelled to turn back.

This army is in most excellent condition. The froth has run off and the weak elements are worked out. There is scarcely a regiment that has not been in more than one hard-fought battle. The men are reduced to solid muscle and brawn and they have that *esprit de corps* which I have never yet known in any other army. The country has a right to expect great things from this army and I do not believe it will be disappointed.

I hope the government is fully awake to the probable movements of the enemy in this direction. The impression is very general, both among the rebels and ourselves, that the grand expedition is a failure, and there is every reason to believe that the rebels contemplate an early removal of a large part of their Vicksburg army to this front. They have already sent a large force to Tuscumbia and Florence and are rapidly building boats and bridges to pave the way for the transfer when the time is ripe. When the movement begins, if not sooner, Grant's main force should be sent here or up the Tennessee with all dispatch.

I should be glad to tell you, once the mails [are] entirely safe, of a plan of mine which is now being put into execution to disturb the equanimity of the rebels in a very unexpected place. I hope you will hear from it in the course of a fortnight.

The Negro question is becoming one of very great practical difficulty. We cannot easily dispose of all the able-bodied male Negroes here, for we take all we can find for teamsters and for workmen on our fortifications. I am urging, and I believe with success, that when the works are finished these Negroes shall be drilled and organized for their defense. But the trouble arises with the swarms of Negro women and children that flock to our lines for protection and support. This country is fearfully devastated and destitute, and I am totally unable to see how its people and especially its Negroes will escape actual starvation. Thousands have been abandoned by their masters, who have lost all hope of gain by keeping them and now cruelly turn them out to perish or to become a burden which this army cannot safely assume. We should be obliged to duplicate our issue of rations in less than two months if we took them up to feed and protect. It is one of the saddest pictures I ever witnessed to see these only innocent people in the South should *per necessitatem* be the greatest sufferers. The General and I have spent many earnest hours in studying the question, but we fail to solve it in any way hopeful for them. I wish the Government would try some plan of alleviation.

Lest you may not have a good map of the country in which we are operating, or trying to, I send you one which has been gotten up by our topographical department and which will aid you in understanding any fixes we may get into.

I congratulate you on the brilliant and solid success of your financial measures; there could hardly be built a broader and firmer basis for the country's prosperity and your own future. The American people owe you a debt of gratitude.

We shall be glad to receive any suggestions. I hope you will write when you can.

*Very truly your friend,*
J. A. Garfield

Honorable S. P. Chase, Secretary of Treasury.

Murfreesboro, Tennessee
April 21, 1863

*Dearest Crete:*

Yours of the 13th came only to hand. I have but a moment that I can spare today. I wrote Almeda a long letter a day or two since, but the expedition I spoke of in that letter has drawn heavily on all my hours since. I did not get to bed till 4 o'clock this morning and I am not very *pert* (purt) as the Southerns say. Everything seems thus far to be working well and I hope good results from the expedition. You will probably see in the papers before this reaches you that General Dodge's force from Corinth has fought the rebels near Tuscumbia and driven them. This is all right and just in the line of our wishes. Colonel Streight will make himself heard from in the course of a week or two from now I think. I drew two months' pay a day or two ago, and I send you a draft on New York for $500 which I have made payable to your order. I want you to take up all the interest bearing notes against me that you can. I don't quite know the state of your finances and I wish you would make a report in the next. How has the house trade come out? Of course you will keep what you need for present expenses, and to carry on the necessary present work of building; but you had better use all you can to pay our debts for in a few weeks I can send you more and keep you supplied as you may need it. How is Jim doing? I am not well please[d] with his lack of manliness in not coming with me, though I have a good horse man now and of course Professor is all right.

I send you a poem said to be by [Edgar Allan] Poe which I found in a Louisville paper yesterday. Do you get time to read all budgets I send to you?

I thank you for your good and frequent letters. Don't let them become more infrequent nor shorter. Kisses and love to Trot and mother.

*Ever yours,*
James

Murfreesboro, Tennessee
April 25, 1863

*Dearest Crete:*

Yours of *April 19th* came to hand yesterday. Indeed, I did remember your birthday. There was heavy cannonading heard by nearly everybody in camp and the troops were ordered under arms, but strange to say we could not learn of any firing at any of our outposts. I told General Rosecrans that it must be a salute to the first battle of the revolution, or to the slaughter of Massachusetts men in Baltimore, 1861, or to your birthday. He adopted the latter suggestion.

The occurrence was exceedingly strange. The General and I went out and listened and could hear rapid and heavy firing as of a whole battery in close engagement. It continued for nearly half an hour and yet we are now sure there was no firing in any of our camps nor outposts. I am half inclined to be superstitious about it. Do you remember the appearance of armies and battles in the clouds during the siege of Jerusalem (*vide* Josephus).[31]

In my last I forgot to speak of the city lot in Chicago. I don't know anything about its value. Indeed no one can tell where this war will leave us financially, or how much any kind of property will be worth. If you will find out how much Mattie holds it at, I will tell you more about it in my next. I presume I can take it off her hands, on that debt, if she desires it. It will be a long time before such property has any fixed value and I presume she had better dispose of it. Please tell me where and how it is located.

I sent you $500 in my last and suggested how it should be applied. Your report of family finances is satisfactory. Remember when you settle with Brown not to pay him any interest after the time you were ready to pay the principal. I don't care about the amount, but I won't be *hornswoggled* by him.

In your arrangement of the house, put transoms over the doors between rooms whenever you can. Tell Trot I want her to "top the doors off" since she is in the "topping off" business. How is the school getting along? Love to all.

*Ever your*
James

Murfreesboro
May 1, 1863

*My Dear Harry:*

Yours came to hand day before yesterday. I am very glad to hear that you are convalescent after so long a sickness. I am myself just getting up from a sharp attack of fever which kept me in bed three days. It was probably the result of continued loss of sleep and nervous prostration consequent upon it. I am much better but am still feeling quite unwell. I am surprised that you upbraid me with not having written you. I supposed you had been very sick and not able to read letters and so I

---

[31] Flavius Josephus, *History of the Jewish War*, Book VI, Chapter V. Josephus wrote that while Jerusalem was besieged by Titus, many reported seeing chariots and troops of soldiers in their armor running among the clouds. Soon after the appearance of this and other signs, the city fell.

would wait till you were in better condition. I think on the whole however that I was wrong and would not like to have been treated so myself. It was my thought at the time that you would not be well enough to enjoy a letter. Please grant me *novas tabulas* [new accounts, i.e., a clean slate] and we will start anew.

Our mails have lately been interrupted so much that I will not say much in this letter in regard to our operations present and prospective. Suffice it to say we as an army are in a state of indefinite expectation of active work. The rebs have been reinforced from Mobile and their main force has been readvanced to the line of Duck River and strong outposts several miles this side. I hope they will attack us but I have no good ground to believe they will.

I wish I could see you and tell you how much disgust I feel over the whining of that fool Treat[32] of whom you speak in your letter. It is 18 months since I have thought of him, and might never again but for the reminder. This, however, brings him to mind and I will give you the story as an instance of total depravity. When I was in Camp Chase, Treat came to me and wanted me to recommend him for some military office. Not being acquainted with him I of course refused, but as he was from my county I told him if he would bring me recommendations from E[zra] B. Taylor and such men as I knew I would then recommend him. He hung around Columbus a week or two waiting for his papers to come, and when they did come to my address he was gone. Notwithstanding this I sent them in to their destination with as good a recommendation of my own as the case would warrant. Now it appears [that] by his own neglect they were lost, and he pitches into me. There are plenty of people, and he seems to be one of them, who think a public man was born for the single purpose to honey fugle around after office for others. I don't want the personal or political friendship of any such ass and I don't care whether he ever learns that I forwarded his papers or not. There are a good many of my keepers, particularly in Trumbull County, who think I am a piece of glass ware bound to be smashed up whether or no. If I leave the army, "I am ruined." If I don't go to Congress when the time comes "it will kill me with the people of the 19th District," and such other pleasant and beautiful suggestions. On the whole I begin to be disgusted with these Trumbull sages. "Sufficient unto the day is the evil thereof."[33] When the time comes I will counsel with you all, if I am in a co[u]nselling condition.

Then you are to have a house are you? That is a good thing. Get

---

[32] Lieutenant Samuel W. Treat was in Battery G, First Ohio Light Artillery Regiment, Army of the Cumberland. Later, on May 14, Treat offended Garfield in a letter which was answered on the same day. Garfield's reply closed with this rebuke: "I did what I could to assist you and your note shows how my efforts were appreciated."

[33] Matthew VI, 34.

a house and have a good horse barn built. I want you to send me a plan for one. Now write me right soon and I will write you promptly. Love to Libbie and remember me as

*Ever yours,*
James A. G.

Murfreesboro, Tennessee
May 2, 1863

*My Dear Crete:*

The last two pages of yours of the 27th *ult.* were received yesterday and read with great pleasure. I have been pretty sick since my last to you but I am now nearly recovered. The doctor said it was an attack of bilious remittent fever, probably occasioned by malaria and loss of sleep. I never suffered more continuous painful unrest for the same length of time in my life. There was no position in which I did not toss and turn in discomfort and pain. I am trying to mend my ways by going to bed earlier than before. This sickness is only an episode I am sure for my general health has never been better than since I commenced duty here.

We had news last night from Colonel Streight which was very satisfactory. The force from Corinth in conjunction with Streight and Ellet's Marine Brigade[34] drove the rebs after a sharp battle and took possession of Tuscumbia, the enemy retreating towards Decatur. On Sunday night (26th) Streight started for the mountains. General Dodge moved towards Decatur and attacked the rebs in Town Creek and repulsed them. Just then a heavy detachment from Van Dorn reached Florence from the neighborhood of Columbia and Dodge retreated to Tuscumbia, the enemy whom he had fought at Town Creek following. He continued to retreat, they following as far as Bear Creek, at which place they were when the messenger left for Corinth to send us the news. If you will look at the map you will see that the rebels' movement shows that they did not on the 28th know of Streight's whereabouts, so that he had two full days' start. Dodge just shoved back the folding doors of the enemy and Streight slipped through. They have closed behind him and we shall not hear a word more till we hear it through rebel sources. The plan has thus far worked admirably. I could not wish it changed in any particular, only I wish I were at the head of it. I offered to go and General Rosecrans could not spare me. It is nearly time for him to strike the road. By our calculations before, he would probably reach it today. I shall watch the rebel papers and movements with the greatest anxiety to see the developements.

[34] Brigadier General Alfred W. Ellet, commander of the Mississippi Marine Brigade, accompanied Streight's force from Nashville to Eastport. After completing his part of the mission, Ellet returned to Fort Henry. Garfield erred in reporting Ellet with Streight at Tuscumbia.

I can't imagine why you feel bad about my using the frank. That is what the law was made for and if I am entitled to the seat in Congress I am also entitled to the frank. Every member-elect is entitled to it after the 4th of March, and use[s] it. Letters come to me *free* and when I send a large package I frank it, all my official correspondence here being at the expense of the Government. I prefer to use the Government stamps though I might just as well use the frank.

Captain Plumb owes me $200 on an old Sandy Valley account which he writes to know where he shall pay. I have told him to send it to you which he will probably do soon. Make the same disposition of it as I suggested for the $500 lately sent. Sell my gun. It cost $17. It ought to bring $15. Don't sell it for less than $10. Do as you think best in regard to the piano. It ought not to be sold for less than $160. How do you come on with your building? Glad the deed is made. Love to Trot and all.

*Ever your*
James

Murfreesboro, Tennessee
May 4, 1863

*My Dear Crete:*

I have received my pay for April and enclose in this a draft for $300, payable to your order. As soon as it is received and you get the data, I want you to give me a full statement of the several amounts received from me lately and the dispositions made of them. . . . This draft is on Louisville and you will probably have to pay from ½ to one percent to get it cashed. . . .

The rebels have been reinforced from Mobile and they have advanced their lines from Tullahoma to this side of Duck River. A council of war was held last evening and though I cannot here speak of the result I will say that from all the facts in regard to the relative situation I do not think two weeks can pass without a collision. Hooker seems to be in motion now. Banks has been and is doing gloriously. There seems at last to be hope in the Vicksburg expedition and when we meet the enemy the fire will flash all along the line.[35] This will be a *Battle Summer*. The collision of arms will be more terrible here than at any other point for there are two veteran armies nearly equal in strength and discipline to contend with each other. Some day I hope to tell you

[35] Although Garfield did not know it, Hooker, now commanding the Army of the Potomac, was being defeated at Chancellorsville. But Banks was making good progress (in four days he would capture Alexandria, Louisiana) in his Port Hudson campaign; and Grant, now across the Mississippi River below Vicksburg, had taken Port Gibson and Grand Gulf and was advancing toward Jackson. On May 9 Rosecrans received from Washington a reminder that "The rebels will never be conquered by sitting in their front."

of the council of last night. It is one think [thing] to express an opinion at home. It is quite another to express one and stake your life on it a few hours afterward. It tries the stuff that men are made of.

John McGowan and Ebbie Ayres are here. I send you a letter from Corydon, also a photograph is enclosed which General Rosecrans sends to you.

Love to our little precious and to all.

> *Ever and forever your own loving*
> James

> Department of the Cumberland
> Headquarters
> Murfreesboro, Tennessee
> May 4, 1863

*My Dear Corydon:*

. . . . I have now fully recovered my health and for the last three months have been very hardy and robust. My duties are very full of work here, and I have never been more pressingly crowded with labor than now. I have not retired on an average before 2 o'clock for the last two months and a half. General Rosecrans shares all his counsels with me and places a large share of the responsibility of the management of this wing upon me — even more than I sometimes wish he did.

This army is now in admirable condition. The poor and weak material has been worked out, and what we now have is hard brawn and solid muscle. It is in an admirable state of discipline and when its engineries are fully set in motion it will make itself felt. From all the present indications it cannot be long before we meet the rebel army now in our front and try its strength again. When that day arrives, it bids fair to be the bloodiest fighting of the war.

One thing is settled in my mind. Direct blows at the rebel army, bloody fighting is all that can end the rebellion. . . . Hence our real objective point is not any place or district but the rebel army wherever we find it. We must crush and pulverize them and then all places and territories fall into our hands as a consequence. These views lead me to a hope and belief that before many days we shall join in a death-grapple with Bragg and [Joseph E.] Johnston. God grant that we may be successful. The armies are nearly equal in number, and both are filled with veteran soldiers, well drilled and disciplined.

The little circumstance you related to me of the soldier in the Fifty-first Indiana touches my heart.[36] I wish you would write a letter for me to Joseph Lay, the young man's father, and express my sympathy with

---

[36] Private Thomas O. Lay who died on October 7, 1862, in Nashville, Tennessee, after campaigning in Garfield's Twentieth Brigade. While in the field Lay became the father of a son and named him after Garfield.

him for the loss of his brave son who was many times with me under the fire of the enemy. I want to know of the health of his family and especially of that little one to whom the affection of the father gave my name.

With the love of other days, I am, as ever, your brother,

James

Murfreesboro, Tennessee
May 4, 1863

*Dear Brother Austin:*

Yours of the 13th April was duly received. I see from that that one of your letters to me must have been lost in the mail. I am sorry, but a good many of my letters have gone into rebel hands also. The[y] have several times attacked our trains and got possession of our mails. My friends must not charge me with neglect if the[y] sometimes do not hear from me, for I cannot tell what letters get lost and what do not.

I am glad Major Wood has withdrawn his application, though I do not yet know whom the district wants. Perhaps the man is already appointed.

In regard to the congressional question, I hardly feel as though it is necessary to agitate it yet. There are so many chances hanging over the coming months that many troublesome questions may find a settlement of their own by the time action is necessary. Certain it is that I shall remain in the army as long as I can before I decide the matter for myself. When the time is ripe and we have all the light which the summer can give to the question, I then want a full examination of the matter.

I fully agree with Brother Wallace in regard to the necessity of having a principal for the school at Hiram. I am compelled to the conclusion that it is not best for the trustees to expect any help from me. The future is too uncertain to base any action on it. If I am ever able to assist the school I shall gladly do it. The trouble with my mind is about the person to be chosen. I do not know who he is. There may be plenty [of qualified people available] but knowing the teachers now there, if it is proposed to get some one from outside, I don't know of one I would be willing to have them work under. I wish the customs of the world would allow you to appoint Miss Booth. I know of no one more competent to manage a school. She has never been half appreciated by the mass of our patrons and brethren.

In regard to the non-confirmation [of] General Cox as major general, I did not know the case in full till a few days since when I had a letter from him giving the case in full. He says the President did not send his name in to the Senate because there was so great a pressure in favor [of] generals of the Regular army. There was an attempt made to injure

Cox by some parties in Gallipolis by trying to fix the charge of corruption on his quartermaster and then make it appear that he was implicated in it. Stories were circulated that his property in Warren was in a more flourishing condition than his salary would warrant. But all these wanton and wicked lies failed of any other effect than perhaps to delay his confirmation. I hope he will yet be better appreciated by the country than he has been. It is really too bad to keep him shut up as he has been, where he could do but little.

Give my love to Lottie and Mrs. Austin. Lottie owes me a letter. When will she pay it? Let me hear from you again.

With much love, I am,

*As ever yours,*
J. A. Garfield

P.S. I send a photograph of General Rosecrans to Lottie.

J.A.G.


Department of the Cumberland
Headquarters
Murfreesboro, Tennessee
May 5, 1863

*Honorable S. P. Chase*
*My Dear Friend:*

Yours from New York of April 25th came duly to hand and yesterday your package of letters to the Union League was received. I am exceedingly gratified with your letter. It is an opportune moment to advance those views. The time is ripe in the army, and there will be heard only a feeble voice of dissent. We are gradually getting educated up to the point of willingness to use the means which God has placed in our hands for ending the war. General Rosecrans read the letter and was greatly pleased with it. He sends his best regards and tells me to say that he fully concurs in the views expressed in your letter.

The situation here is now very interesting. The rebels have been reinforced from Mobile and have advanced their lines to this side of Duck River. The two armies now confronting each other here will, I think, have a collision soon. General Hartsuff[37] was sent here by General Burnside, and night before last a council was held to determine upon a plan of operation by which General Burnside's force, a part of it at least, should move in conjunction with ours.

[37] Major General George L. Hartsuff, who had been Rosecrans' Chief of Staff in 1861, was commander of the XXIII Corps, Department of the Ohio. The conference mentioned by Garfield ended with a decision to have Burnside's IX Corps relieve Rosecrans' force at Carthage, but the plan was changed when Burnside was called upon to aid Grant at Vicksburg.

I am [have] been anxious to impress upon the General [Rosecrans] the truth that our true objective point of operations is the rebel army and not any particular position or territory. In Europe, if an army becomes master of London, Paris, Vienna or Berlin, it has conquered England, France, Austria or Prussia. Not so with the Confederacy. We may take Richmond, but they can put their government with all its archives on wheels and trundle it away into the interior in 48 hours. Nothing but hard blows that will break their armies and pulverize them can destroy the Confederacy. I am, therefore, for striking, striking, and striking again till we do break them.

The two armies here are in fine condition. Indeed, they are veteran armies and there will be a fearfully bloody struggle when they grapple again; and I think the day of conflict is now very near.

The movement at which I hinted in my last is now so far in progress that I may speak of it safely. We have sent a force of near 2,000 men that went down the Cumberland, up the Tennessee, and on the 26th of April under cover of a force from Corinth, which we had engaged to act in concert with our own, it left Tuscumbia, Alabama for the mountains, and I hope and believe that it has by this time reached the Georgia railroad system and broken it between Rome and Atlanta. I have set my heart on this expedition more than on any one thing since I have been here. In order to secure it, after I had fully canvassed the ground, I offered to lead it myself. General Rosecrans could not spare me, but we chose one of my old officers that served with me last year, Colonel Streight of Indiana, who will make thorough work and if at last surrounded he will sell his command as dearly as possible. When the blow has fully fallen upon the rebels, I think we can successfully meet them in front. Should this rear movement be successful its results can hardly be estimated. The loss of the whole force would be trifling in comparison with the advantages to us.

I hardly know what I ought to do in reference to the congressional question. But there are so many contingencies hanging on the events of this "Battle Summer" that the question may have adjusted itself long before the time for decision arrives. When the time comes I shall be glad to hear from you. Of course I shall stay in the army for the present.

Remember me kindly to Miss Kate. . . .

With kindest regards, I am,

*Very truly your friend,*
J. A. Garfield

Murfreesboro, Tennessee
May 6, 1863

*Dearest Crete:*

Yours of May 1st is just received. I am now quite recovered and hard at work again and in good condition. You can hardly imagine how great consequences hang on the military operations of the next few weeks here, on the Potomac, and at Vicksburg. I have hardly a thought for anything but these events and hence you will excuse me for only a hurried note this time. I have sent you $300 in a letter since I sent the $500 which I hope will reach you safely. It was my pay and a little more for April. I indicated in that letter the disposition I desired made of it. I am sorry you have trouble in your work of building. Who have you got to do the work? Please tell me your arrangements about the whole matter.

I am disgusted with Jim. I don't want anything to do with that stubborn kind of laziness and wrong-headedness which he has manifested. As soon as you can get along without him, send him off. I would keep him and help him as long as he seemed willing to help himself, but no longer. You may read this to him. If there is anyone who will give him work, he had better go and hire out. The Beechers will do well by him, I have no doubt. Whatever of demoralization there is in them is not of a kind to influence Jim unfavorably. After all, it is the curse of bondage that is more responsible than he is.

I feel very keenly for poor Mary Curtiss and would be glad to assist her but I know of no way in my power to do it. If Lester is in the state of mind indicated in her letter, I fear he would be made worse rather than better by being in the army in the midst of such excitements as are now before us. It is a very sad case.

The letter of old Professor Reinman[38] is as odd as ever. He seems now to have changed his former name and gone down from a professor to a private in "bed 46 ward 48 of the Chestnut Street Hospital." I am a little puzzled to know what application he makes in his own case to his passage from Ovid: *"Major sum quam cuiquam [sic] Fortuna nocere possit* [I am too great for Fortune to harm]"—for Dame Fortune seems to have been inclined to *"nocere"* and knock him around very vigorously for the last ten years. Did you translate his letter to me? It is rich and odd as possible.

Love and kisses to Trot and yourself.

*Ever and always your own,*
James

Department of the Cumberland
Headquarters
Murfreesboro, Tennessee
May 9, 1863

*Honorable S. P. Chase*
*Dear Sir:*

In my last I gave you a brief outline of a movement we were making to cut the rebel railroad system in Alabama and Georgia. I enclose you

[38] An eccentric German who frequently wrote to Garfield asking for money.

copies of two dispatches we received yesterday from General Hurlbut,[39] giving an account of his progress up to last intelligence from him. I hope, and believe, he has by this time cut the road between Rome and Atlanta. If he has reached the latter place he has done them irreparable mischief. From the dispatches it appears that the rebels had taken the wrong scent, and in preparing to meet him at Chattanooga they would fail to ward off his blow further south. We are exceedingly anxious to know the exact truth in regard to the situation on the Rappahannock. The relation of that situation to our own here is too important to render it admissible that anything in reference to Hooker should be covered up from us. I hope you will feel at liberty to tell me so much of the situation there as will give us an assurance that the rebel force in our front is or is not likely to be reinforced from Richmond or Charleston.

We are holding everything in suspense here till we have solid ground to go on. Hoping to hear from you soon, I am,

*Very truly yours,*
J. A. Garfield
*Brigadier General, Volunteers*


Murfreesboro, Tennessee
May 12, 1863

*Dearest Crete:*

Yours of May 5th came to hand yesterday. I am always made glad by your letters and this good cheerful letter did me good and made me glad. I am quite well now and hard at work. Our news from the Rappahannock last night was more cheering than any we have had for a week and I hope there will yet come good results out of their operations. If General Dix can get up on the south side of James River and threaten Richmond, Lee's army must fall back.[40] The rebels are steadily creeping up on us here. Breckinridge's advance is now only seven or eight miles from our outposts at Readyville and Cripple Creek east of here.[41]

Did Almeda receive a large map I sent her? If so, you can see these

[39] The information in Major General Stephen A. Hurlbut's dispatches to Rosecrans had come from Dodge and was, of course, about Streight.

[40] Major General John A. Dix, commander of the Department of Virginia with headquarters at Fortress Monroe, did not cross to the southern side of the James River; but on May 11 he did begin advancing up the Peninsula. His purpose was to threaten Richmond, destroy railroad track and bridges, and keep a large enemy force occupied. Dix's operation was interrupted by orders to help Major General George Meade in the Gettysburg campaign.

[41] Major General John C. Breckinridge commanded a division on the Confederate right near Wartrace. Later in the month he and his command were sent to help General Joseph E. Johnston in Mississippi.

points on the Woodbury pike east of us. Hazen holds Readyville with his brigade. It appears that the rebels intend some kind of a flank movement. Our movements are greatly delayed by the slow motions of Burnside, who ought by this time to have reached Carthage or James-town. It is very trying to the patience to stand here like a wrestler tripping and making feints at his adversary and watching his move-ments, keeping the muscles strained all the while, yet never grappling and making decisive end to the delay and struggle. Still, if our people are to succeed at Richmond we had far better wait here till that work has its full effect on the rebellion. There is a report in the rebel papers that gives us some ground to hope that Streight's force was not all cap-tured. Still we have no very solid ground to stand on. Colonel Grierson's raid in Mississippi was an associate part of the plan and that has been a brilliant success. I hope you have traced his movements from near Corinth to Baton Rouge.[42] . . .

Everything in Grant's department augurs success just now. His late movement on Grand Gulf and his advance up Black River must result in the evacuation of Vicksburg if he has force and subsistence sufficient. Banks's operations have also been very successful and exceedingly im-portant. If you will trace on the map his track from Baton Rouge by way of Grand Lake, St. Martinsville, Opelousas and Washington to Alexandria and his junction there with Farragut's fleet in the Red River, you will see that he has conquered nearly all the alluvial lands of Louisiana and got the sugar region in his possession. . . .

I am sorry to hear that you get along so poorly with your building. Don't start unless you can get a good man. I don't want this work botched. . . .

Tell Trot I always send love and kisses to her. Bless her little soul.

> *Ever and always your*
> James

Murfreesboro, Tennessee
May 23, 1863

*Dearest Crete:*

I am sorry to tell you that I have been sick again, very much as I was a few weeks ago. I have kept [to] the bed four days and this morning for the first time have got up and put on my clothes. This time, how-

[42] On April 17 Colonel Benjamin H. Grierson left LaGrange, Tennessee, with 1,700 cavalrymen and a six-gun battery and swept southward the length of Mississippi destroying railroad track and bridges, trains, telegraph lines, mills and factories, ammunition and supplies, and capturing and paroling hundreds of officers and men. On May 2 Grierson's tired but triumphant troopers rode into Union-held Baton Rouge, Louisiana, bringing to an end an immensely destructive raid which not only terrified a vast section of the deep South, but helped Grant in his Vicksburg campaign by keeping troops and supplies away from the enemy on his front.

ever, I was very sick at the stomach and vomitted nearly half a day till I was very weak. Dr. [Glover] Perin, the Medical Director of the Department, came and gave me his personal attention and has treated me most kindly and skillfully. He brough[t] me some hair mattrasses and sheets and pillow, mosquito bars, and made me as comfortable as nausea would let me be. I am better this morning but the Doctor forbids me to go over to the offices or do any work for a day or two yet. I do think this time I will be a little more careful of my health, but I have but little confidence in a sick man's resolutions. You remember the old stanza:

> "The Devil got sick
> The Devil a monk would be
> The Devil got well
> The Devil a monk was he."[43]

Hence I will not speak of reform with much confidence.

Yours of the 15th came to hand day before yesterday and it lay in bed with me five hours before I could read it I was so sick and dizzy. I was very glad indeed to have it come to me when I was in pain; next to a visit from yourself it was the pleasantest thing you could have done for me.

I am hardly well enough to give the new house the attention I desire to but I will say a few things in answer to your letter. I think you will find it better and cheaper to buy not only your door, windows and shutters in Cleveland, but also your siding and flooring already dressed at the planing mills. If the whole house does not need repainting, the addition better be white. If, however, it does and it can be changed from its present color I would prefer a slate or some color different from white. Don't have the doors grained by any means. Let the doors outside and in, and all the inside work be painted with white zinc paint. I can't tell you what I would like in regard to wall paper. If you leave the house white on the outside, it may be best to have the outside doors some other color than white.

I send you Mr. Gilmore's[44] new book which I have read with pleasure. I have much to say to you about him when I see you.

Give my love and kisses to Trot and mother. Excuse this badly written letter for I don't feel very steady in the hand.

*Ever your*
James

---

[43] See *The Works of Rabelais*, Book IV, Chapter 24.

[44] James Roberts Gilmore (pseudonym, Edmund Kirke) *My Southern Friends* (1863). Gilmore was with Rosecrans' army in 1863 and worked on a peace movement in which Rosecrans was involved. It collapsed with the unsuccessful Gilmore-Jaquess mission to Richmond in 1864. In 1880 Gilmore wrote a campaign biography of Garfield.

Headquarters, Department of the Cumberland
Murfreesboro, Tennessee
May 26, 1863

*My Dear Burke:*

Your two favors of the 11th and the 20th are before me. I have been sick for nearly a week and have written but few letters during that time.

In regard to the subject matter of your last letter, I had written quite fully to Harry several days before the receipt of yours. Tell all those Copperhead students for me that were I there in charge of the school I would not only dishonorably dismiss them from the school, but if they remained in the placed [place] and persisted in their cowardly treason, I would apply to General Burnside to enforce General Order No. 38[45] in their cases. They entirely mistake and misapprehend the character of the times if they suppose that the same license can now be used as in the days of peace. It is a grievous and shameful wrong to the memory of all our brave boys who are dying in front of Vicksburg and suffering everywhere, for the country to have these misguided ones at home permitted to spume out their silly treason at Hiram and in the country around them. They ask that if they are not permitted to speak, neither should Union boys speak their views!! Fools. There is a place for all such. This is a time when men who take sides on the great questions at issue do so in a brave way and go to their party, North or South. If these young traitors are in earnest they should go to the Southern Confederacy where they can give and receive full sympathy. Tell them all that I will furnish them passes through our lines, where they can join Vallandigham and their other friends till such time as they can destroy us and come back home as conquerors of their own people, or can learn wisdom and obedience. I know this apparently [is] a small matter, but it is only *apparently* small. We do not know what the developements of a month may bring forth, and if such things be permitted at Hiram they may be anywhere. The rebels catch up all such facts and sweet morsels of comfort, and every such influence lengthens the war and adds to the bloo[d]shed. Let me hear what disposition is made of them. You may [make] whatever use of this letter you choose.

The news from Vicksburg is very encouraging, and indeed I have many new reasons for believing that the catastrophe of the rebellion is not far off. Still it cannot be reached except through much blood. There is economy even in the shedding of blood, and the faster it flows now the sooner our national wounds can be staunc[h]ed and our health restored. God grant that the hour may come soon.

[45] Issued on April 13, 1863, by Burnside, who commanded the Department of the Ohio, March-December, 1863. The order threatened persons "declaring sympathies for the enemy" with arrest and trial by military procedure as spies and traitors. Those convicted were to be executed or sent to the enemy. For violating this order Vallandigham was sentenced to imprisonment for the duration of the war, but Lincoln commuted his sentence and banished him to the Confederacy.

I hope this army will move in a day or two.

I am made sad and anxious by what you write me in regard to the school, and what is the worst feature, I do not see the remedy.

What news do you hear from the 42nd boys? They have been through the fire. They are noble men. Poor Olds, he was one of the best of men.

Let me hear from you often.

Are we to be afflicted with Tod again for another biennium?

Love to Mary.

*Ever yours,*
J. A. Garfield

Headquarters
Department of the Cumberland
Murfreesboro, Tennessee
May 30, 1863

*My Dear Smith:*

I have just seen in the Cleveland *Herald* of May 23rd an editorial notice of yourself which pleases me very much and which I enclose to you. It has been a long time since I have heard from you. I sent you a letter several months ago but never received an answer. I am very glad to see that the people are looking toward you in connection with the government of Ohio.

I desire to hear from you on this subject and also to communicate my views of the matter from this standpoint. From what I can learn there seems to be a general tendency in Ohio to renominate Tod. I do not know what your own views or feelings may be in reference to him; but I will say what I thoroughly know, that the Ohio soldiers are greatly opposed to him. He has wronged nearly every Ohio regiment in this department by the unjust way in which he has made appointments in total disregard of the wishes of both officers and men. He has repeatedly foisted in upon regiments his particular friends, or their sons, nephews or cousins who were strangers to the regiments and who had no claim either by fitness or past services. I feel sure that if he should be nominated the majority of the soldiers would vote for any War Democrat that the opposition would nominate.

I earnestly hope our friends at home will not force such an alternative upon the army.

So much for the feeling among the soldiers. For myself I was opposed to taking up Tod from the start. I believed him then and believe him now an ass—a man destitute of those high qualities of manhood and moral excellence which he should possess who is entrusted with so important duties as belong to that station in time of war. To repeat the folly of two years ago will be more than double folly now. My attention has been more particularly called to this matter from the fact that a deputation of officers came to me a few days ago and said the Ohio soldiers wanted to nominate me. I of course told them I deemed it impracticable and had no desire for the position if it were practicable. A good many papers in northwestern Ohio have proposed General Steedman's name. I write thus fully and frankly for you are one of my best friends and I want you to tell me what you think the people are going to do. I assure you that I do not desire my name used in that connection, unless there is what I do not [at] all believe there is—a general wish in that direction. I dislike to have anything said to lead the people to believe I am aspiring in that direction.

Vallandigham assured us that he believe[d] he should be nominated by acclamation.

I hope you will soon hear that this army is in motion. It is in admirable condition and ought to give a good account of itself. I am extremely busy and have not time to write you on the great matters of the war, only to say my faith is stronger than ever in the final overthrow of the rebellion. Hoping some time to grasp your hand in peace, I am,

As ever your friend,

J. A. Garfield

Murfreesboro, Tennessee
June 2, 1863

*My Dearest Crete:*

After an unusually long silence yours of the 28th has come to hand. I am very glad to hear from you for I had begun to fear you were unwell. There seems to have been some break in the transmission of my letters, and perhaps of your own. I am very greatly obliged to Uncle Thomas for his kindness to you. He can aid you more than anyone I know of. His acquaintance in Cleveland and his experience in business are very extensive. Thank him for me.

Your financial report is all satisfactory except that it is not good policy to loan money at the same rate we are paying to another. It doubles the risk you know and leaves the debt unpaid. As soon as practicable I hope you will get it liquidated. It costs me about $30 per month to live here. I will save all I can and I know you will be as economical as possible.

A *transom* is a sash with two or three panes of glass in it over a door. It answers the double purpose of window and ventillator, as the sash should be arranged to open on a pivot or on hinges. It is a good way to give light to a room where windows are scarce. I don't know as your arrangement of rooms will require them, but in your former plan there was some trouble in getting sufficient light into one of the rooms, I remember.

After our long delays we have at last reached the verge of a movement. Indeed the movement has begun and I confidently expect to be in the saddle by Saturday. Bragg's army has been reduced by two divisions of infantry and two brigades of cavalry which have gone to reinforce Johnston at Vicksburg.[46] It is our purpose to go out and offer battle and if he declines it we shall drive him away from the line of Duck River as far towards Tullahoma as we can. I expect it will be a fearful struggle and a severe campaign. By the aid of the map which I sent to Almeda you can trace our operations pretty accurately. Study particularly the country on the Manchester pike in the direction of Beech Grove, Wartrace, and Manchester. I would be glad to tell you of our plan but I dare not entrust it to the mail. I know your heart will follow me and the army. I ask you to pray for me and still more for the success of this army. I am very anxious about Vicksburg and painfully anxious to hear from the 42nd. I see by the papers that several of my acquaintances are killed and wounded.

I want you to tell me particularly and fully about your health and the health *filii nostri* [of our child]. I have thought and felt more than I can tell you on this subject, but have not felt as though I could write my thoughts on paper. Tell me your own thoughts, feelings, and experiences, your hopes and fears and joys and all that relates to this and to yourself. You cannot understand what my thoughts are at this distance and under all the peculiar circumstances which surround me. I would not if I could have you know all the thoughts that throng around my heart just now on the eve of the great movement.

Be hopeful for me and do not allow yourself to be in any way depressed. Make yourself feel that our good Heavenly Father has our future with all its results in His hand and whatever be, betetides [betides] it will be well. Give my love to our precious little Trot and cover her lips and cheeks with kisses for me. . . .

*With all my heart I am your*
James


Murfreesboro, Tennessee
June 6, 1863

*My Dearest:*

Your dear letter of the 1st came to hand yesterday with one from mother enclosed. I was very glad to have you write me in such sweetly tender way. Do not be so anxious for my health. I think I shall stand the season very much better than I did last year. I am much stronger than I was one year ago this time and I think when we are fully in the saddle it will be better for us all in the way of health. It is this long

[46] On May 26 Bragg reported that he had ordered two divisions of infantry and one of cavalry to re-enforce Johnston, the commander of Confederate troops in Mississippi, who was in Jackson, not Vicksburg.

confinement and late hours that are wearing on me. The change will be effectual. We have had a series of brisk skirmishes during the past three days and should have gone out with the whole army but for some delay occasioned by Burnside's change of plan in sending an army corps away to Grant.[47]

Since writing the above some scamp came in and tore off the other part of this sheet and I have not time to rewrite it. So you will excuse this torn paper.

The movement of which I told you in my last began four days ago by withdrawing the mass of our force from Franklin and bringing up several detachments from posts in the rear. On the 4th the rebel cavalry attacked Franklin thinking they would be able to take the small garrison lef[t] there, but they failed after a desperate attempt. We do not want to begin a general movement on Sunday and so I think we shall have no more fighting before Monday next. It is quite impossible to tell in so large an army as this precisely when any general movement will be made, but nothing peculiar preventing I think the army will move at that time. I had a photograph of my horse, Harry, which I will send you as soon as it is finished. He is a glorious old fellow and I wish you knew him as I do. . . .

With much love I am as ever,

*Your* James. . . .

Murfreesboro, Tennessee
June 11, 1863

*My Dear Harry:*

A sense of disappointment and mortification almost akin to shame has kept me from answering any letters for some time. I have delayed answering yours in hopes of having something decisive to say. I have written a number of letters within the last fortnight in which I have said, "Before this reaches you I hope you will hear that the army has moved upon the enemy." I have made my personal preparation, said my good-byes to absent friends by letter, commended the cause and myself to God, and nerved myself up for the shock, intending to send a few words of parting to you all after my horses were saddled and the great columns were in motion. Now I write to tell you that I have given up all hopes of either dying or fighting at present. I had drafted a plan of campaign, drawn the first rough draft of the order for movement, fixed the times of departure, arrival and attack, entered minutely into all the details, and submitted the document to General Rosecrans who had approved it, and all things seemed ready. But there have been most strange and unexpected interferences. The chess board is now indeed muddled and no man sees through it. Just on the eve of our move

[47] In compliance with Halleck's order of June 3 to send 8,000 men to Grant at Vicksburg, Burnside sent two divisions of his IX Corps.

ment there seemed to fall down upon the leading officers of this army as suddenly as a bolt from the blue a most determined and decided opinion that there ought to be no immediate or early advance. Officers who to my certain knowledge were restless and impatient for a forward movement became suddenly conservative and cautious, and think masterly inactivity the chiefest of virtues. The reasons given are legion and among them all there are some that have weight, such as that Hooker is placed *hors du combat* for the present and nothing offensive is to be expected from him. Grant is involved (?) in a terrible struggle and the Army of the Cumberland is the only one that can elect to give, accept or refuse battle as it chooses, and in case of a reverse at Vicksburg it would be every way desirable to have one great army free and intact. Again should we advance, say some, the enemy in our front would rapidly fall back behind the Tennessee River and there, seated in the fastness of the Cumberland Mountains, could hold us at bay with so small a force as to be able to send heavy reinforcements to Johnston. An advance would lengthen our line of communication and shorten the enemy's, and leave us in a relative position of disadvantage. I will not repeat the many reasons assigned why and how not to do it. The most weight I give to all this is the conclusion that it may be best to wait a short time to see what are the developements at Vicksburg. When they are learned, or if it should appear that the fate of the Mississippi will hang in suspense for a considerable time yet, all these reasons will be to my mind totally insufficient to balance the reasons why we should strike. So be at rest about this army and your friend for the present, and be content to hear that we are picking up a ragged rebel now and then, or hanging spies à la the late Franklin tragedy.[48]

I have become acquainted with Mr. Swinton,[49] political and military editor of the New York *Times* who has lately come here. He is a very able writer. He lately wrote an article for the *Times* which the President ordered should not be published on pain of sending the writer into Fort Lafayette. It was in type at the time when the casemates yawned. He struck off a slip and gave it to me. I enclose it. It is contraband and you must not let it get to the public. Read it to Almeda, Crete and Burke, and give me the comments of the circle. I am glad you have struck the Copperhead students from the rolls. Love to Libbie and all.

*Ever yours,*
J. A. G.

[48] On June 8 two Confederate officers, dressed as Union officers, entered Union lines at Franklin to get information about Rosecrans' army. They were captured, tried by a military commission, and hanged for spying.

[49] William Swinton, journalist, educator, and author, was a war correspondent for the New York *Times*. A severe critic of leading generals, Swinton often exceeded the bounds of propriety in his quest for news. In 1864 the War Department stripped him of his privileges as a war correspondent and forbade him to remain in the battle zone.

Murfreesboro, Tennessee
June 12, 1863

*Dear Mother:*

Your letter was received the same time that Crete's last came. I was glad to hear from you and know that you were well and that you had had a pleasant visit to Solon and Orange; but I am glad that you felt on returning that you had come back [home]. When you are with any of your children you are at home; but I want you to feel that your permanent home is with me, or rather with Crete and Trot, for if my future life is as broken up as my past, I see but little chance of my ever enjoying my home and family only for a few days at a time. I have been married four years and five months and have been away from home more than two years and a half of that time and even while I lived at home I was away a great deal. If there were not such great matters at stake I should feel as though I would leave public life and live at home. If anything should happen to me that I should not return *Trot* would hardly remember me. She certainly would not long. But we must all be cheerful and hopeful. When the war is over we will hope to meet again.

Kiss the dear little creature for me and tell her papa loves her more than she knows of. Write to me. With much love, I am your son,

James

Headquarters
Department of the Cumberland
Murfreesboro, Tennessee
June 12, 1863

*General:*

In your confidential letter of the 8th *instant* to the corps and division commanders and generals of cavalry of this army, there were substantially five questions propounded for their consideration and answer, *viz.*:

1. Has the enemy in our front been materially weakened by detachments to Johnston or elsewhere?
2. Can this army advance on him at this time with strong, reasonable chances of fighting a great and successful battle?
3. Do you think an advance of our army at present likely to prevent additional reinforcements being sent against General Grant by the enemy in our front?
4. Do you think an *immediate* advance of this army advisable?
5. Do you think an early advance advisable?

Many of the answers to these questions are not categorical, and cannot be clearly set down either as affirmative or negative. Especially in answer to the first question there is much indefiniteness resulting from the difference of judgment as to how great a detachment could be considered a "material reduction of Bragg's strength." For example, one officer thinks it has been reduced 10,000 but "not materially weakened."

The answers to the second question are modified in some instances by the opinion that the rebels will fall back behind the Tennessee River and thus no battle can be fought, either successful or unsuccessful.

So far as these opinions can be stated in tabular form, they will stand thus:

| Answer to 1st question | 6 yes, | 11 no. |
|---|---|---|
| " " 2nd " | 2 yes, | 11 no. |
| " " 3rd " | 4 yes, | 10 no. |
| " " 4th " | 0 yes, | 15 no. |
| " " 5th " | 0 yes, | 2 no. |

On the fifth question, three gave it as their opinion that this army ought to advance as soon as Vicksburg falls, should that event happen. The following is a summary of the reasons assigned why we should not at this time advance upon the enemy:

1. With Hooker's army defeated, and Grant's bending all its energies in a yet undecided struggle, it is bad policy to risk our only reserve army to the chances of a general engagement. A failure here would have most disastrous effects on our lines of communication and on politics in the loyal states.

2. We should be compelled to fight the enemy on his own ground or follow him in a fruitless, stern chase, or if we attempted to outflank him and turn his position we should expose our line of communication and run the risk of being pushed back into a rough country well known to the enemy and little known to ourselves.

3. In case the enemy should fall back without accepting battle he could make our advance very slow, and, with a comparatively small force posted in the gaps of the mountains, could hold us back while he crossed the Tennessee River, where he would be measurably secure and free to send reinforcements to Johnston. His forces in East Tennessee could seriously harrass our left flank and constantly disturb our communications.

4. The withdrawal of Burnside's 9th army corps deprives us of an important reserve and flank protection, thus increasing the difficulty of an advance.

5. General Hurlbut has sent the most of his forces away to General Grant, thus leaving West Tennessee uncovered and laying our right flank and rear open to raids of the enemy.

The following opinions are expressed incidentally, *viz.*:

1. One officer thinks it probable that the enemy has been strengthened rather than weakened, and that *he* (the enemy) would have a reasonable prospect of victory in a general battle.

2. One officer believes that the result of a general battle would be doubtful, a victory barren, and a defeat most disastrous.

3. Three officers believe that an advance would bring on a general engagement. Three others believe it would not.

4. Two officers express their opinion that the chances of success in a general battle are nearly equal.

5. One officer expresses the belief that our army has reached its maximum strength and efficiency, and that inactivity will seriously impair its effectiveness.

6. Two officers say that an increase of our cavalry by about 6,000 men would materially change the aspect of our affairs and give us a decided advantage.

In addition of the above summary, I have the honor to submit an estimate of the strength of Bragg's army gathered from all the data I have been able to obtain, including the estimate of the General commanding in his official report of the Battle of Stone River, and facts gathered from prisoners, deserters, scouts and refugees, and from rebel newspapers.

After the battle Bragg consolidated many of his decimated regiments and irregular organizations, and, at the time of his sending reinforcements to Johnston, his army had reached its greatest effective strength. It consisted of five divisions of infantry, composed of 94 regiments and two independent battallions of sharpshooters, say 95 regiments. By a law of the Confederate Congress, regiments are consolidated when their effective strength falls below 250 men.[50] Even the regiments formed by such consolidation (which may reasonably be regarded as the fullest) must fall below 500. I am satisfied that 400 is a large estimate of the average strength. The force would then be:

| | |
|---|---:|
| Infantry, 95 Regiments, 400 each | 38,000 |
| Cavalry, 35 Regiments, say 500 each | 17,500 |
| Artillery, 26 Batteries, say 100 each | 2,600 |
| Total | 58,100 |

This force has been reduced by detachments to Johnston. It is as well known as we can ever expect to ascertain such facts, that three brigades have gone from [Major-General John P.] McCown's division and two or three from Breckinridge's—say two. It is clear that there are now but four infantry divisions in Bragg's army, the fourth being composed of fragments of McCown's and Breckinridge's divisions and must be much smaller than the average. Deducting the five brig-

[50] Not until 1865 did the Confederate government pass legislation providing for consolidation of skeleton regiments.

ades, and supposing them composed of only four regiments each, which is below the general average, it gives an infantry reduction of 20 regiments (400 each, 8,000) leaving a remainder of 30,000 [50,000].

It is clearly ascertained that at least two brigades of cavalry have been sent from Van Dorn's command to Mississippi and it is asserted in the Chattanooga *Rebel* of June 11th that General Morgan's command has been permanently detached and sent to Eastern Kentucky.[51] It is not certainly known how large his division is, but it is known to contain at least two brigades. Taking this minimum as the fact, and we have a cavalry reduction of four brigades. Taking the lowest estimate, four regiments to the brigade, and we have a reduction by detachments, of 16 regiments, 500 each, leaving his present effective cavalry force 9,500.

With the 9 brigades of the two arms, thus detached, it will be safe to say there have gone six batteries, 80 men each—480, leaving him 20 batteries—2,120, making a total reduction of 16,480 and leaving of the three arms 41,680.[52] In this estimate of Bragg's present strength I have placed all doubts in his favor, and I have no doubt [that] my estimate is considerably beyond the truth. General Sheridan, who has taken great pains to collect evidence on this point, places it considerably below these figures.

But assuming these to be correct, and granting what is still more improbable, that Bragg would abandon all his rear posts and entirely neglect his communications and would bring his last man into battle, I next ask what have we with which to oppose him?

The last official report of effective strength now on file in the office of the Assistant Adjutant General is dated June 11th and shows that we have in this department, omitting all officers and enlisted men attached to department corps, division and brigade headquarters:

1st. Infantry, 173 regiments
       "       10 battalions, sharpshooters
       "       4    "   , pioneers
       "       1 regiment, engineers and mechanics
with a total effective strength of 70,918

[51] The *Rebel* was most unreliable for such information. Knowing the enemy read the paper, Confederate commanders sometimes attempted to confuse him by directing the editor to publish misleading intelligence. With respect to Brigadier General John H. Morgan, only a part of his division, a force of about 2,500 men, was detached for duty in Kentucky; and, what is more, he was apparently ordered only to raid Louisville, destroy the Louisville & Nashville Railroad, and return before Rosecrans learned he was away. Morgan seems to have undertaken his spectacular but inconsequential raid through Indiana and Ohio on his own volition.

[52] Considering the intelligence available to him, perhaps Garfield did as well as could be expected in attempting to determine Bragg's strength. It is not at all surprising that he misjudged enemy numbers by about 5,000; but in view of the tendency in the Civil War to overestimate enemy strength, it is interesting to note that Garfield erred in the other direction. On June 10 Bragg reported that he had 46,260 effectives.

2nd. Cavalry, 27 regiments
    and one unattached company 11,813
3rd. Artillery, 47½ batteries field artillery, consisting of 292 guns and
    5,069 men, making a grand total of 87,800 men.
Leaving out all commissioned officers, this army represents 82,767
    bayonets and sabers.

This report does not include the 5th Iowa Cavalry, 600 strong, lately
arrived, nor the 1st Wisconsin Cavalry, nor Coburn's brigade of
infantry now arriving,[53] nor the 2,394 convalescents now on light duty
in "Fortress Rosecrans."
There are detached from this force as follows:

| | | |
|---|---:|---:|
| At Gallatin | | 969 |
| Carthage | | 1,149 |
| Fort Donelson | | 1,485 |
| Clarksville | | 1,138 |
| Nashville | | 7,292 |
| La Vergne | | 2,117 |
| Franklin | | 900 |
| | Total | 15,130 [15,050] |

With these posts as they are, and leaving 2,500 efficient men in addition to the 2,394 convalescents to hold the works at this place, there
will be left 65,137 bayonets and sabers to throw against Bragg's 41,680.
I beg leave also to submit the following considerations:

1st.  Bragg's army is now weaker than it has been since the Battle of
    Stone River or is likely to be again for the present; while our
    army has reached its maximum strength, and we have no right
    to expect reinforcements for several months, if at all.

2nd.  Whatever be the result at Vicksburg, the determination of its
    fate will give large reinforcements to Bragg. If Grant is successful
    his army will require many weeks to recover from the shock and
    strain of his late campaign, while Johnston will send back to
    Bragg a force sufficient to insure the safety of Tennessee. If Grant
    fails, the same result will inevitably follow so far as Bragg's army
    is concerned.

3rd.  No man can predict with certainty the result of any battle how-
    ever great the disparity in numbers. Such results are in the hand
    of God. But viewing the question in the light of human calcula-
    tion, I refuse to entertain a doubt that this army which in
    January last defeated Bragg's superior numbers, cannot over-
    whelm his present greatly inferior forces.

[53] Soon after his capture at Thompson's Station, Coburn was exchanged. He returned to the Army of the Cumberland in May and two months later assumed
command of a brigade in the Reserve Corps.

4th. The most unfavorable course for us that Bragg could take would be to face back without giving us battle; but this would be very disastrous to him. Besides the loss of material of war and the abandonment of the rich and abundant harvest now nearly ripe in Central Tennessee, he would lose heavily by desertion. It is well known that a widespread dissatisfaction exists among his Kentucky and Tennessee troops. They are already deserting in large numbers. A retreat would greatly increase both the desire and the opportunity for desertion and would very materially reduce his physical and moral strength.

While it would lengthen our communications it would give us the possession of McMinnville and enable us to threaten Chattanooga and East Tennessee, and it would not be unreasonable to expect an early occupation of the former place.

5th. But the chances are more than even that a sudden and rapid movement would compel a general engagement, and the defeat of Bragg would be in the highest degree disastrous to the rebellion.

6th. The turbulent aspects of politics in the loyal states renders a decisive blow against the enemy, at this time, of the highest importance to the success of the Government at the polls and in the enforcement of the Conscription Act.

7th. The Government and the War Department believe that this army ought to move upon the enemy. The army desires it and the country is anxiously hoping for it.

8th. Our true objective point is the rebel army whose last reserves are substantially in the field, and an effective blow will crush the shell and soon be followed by the collapse of the rebel Government.

9th. You have, in my judgment, wisely delayed a general movement hitherto till your army could be massed and your cavalry could be mounted. Your mobile force can now be concentrated in twenty-four hours and your cavalry, not equal in numerical strength to that of the enemy, is greatly superior in efficiency and morale.

For these reasons, I believe an immediate advance of all our available forces is advisable, and under the providence of God will be successful.

*Very respectfully, your obedient servant*
J. A. Garfield
*Brigadier General, Chief of Staff*

Major General W. S. Rosecrans
Commanding, Department of the Cumberland

Murfreesboro, Tennessee
June 14, 1863

*Dearest Crete:*

Your good letter of June 8th came duly to hand. I am sorry to hear that my letters do not reach you regularly. I write punctually on receipt of yours. Please don't entertain a thought that I am neglecting your kindnesses to me. I think of you lovingly and in the happiest way.

Besides being intensely busy I will say, as I told Harry in my last to him, that I have been so distressed at the long delay of this army to move and the unreasonable way in which some treat the whole manner, that I could hardly write to anyone more than to utter my disgust. I have for several days past been diligently at work collecting all the facts I could of the strength of the rebel army in our front and comparing it with our own. I have just completed a carefully written paper which I shall present this evening to the General. I argue the state of the case and urge an immediate movement upon Bragg. I don't know what the result will be. I know the General desires to move but it is hard to go with so many unwilling men in high places.

I have had a long good letter from Joe which rejoiced me very much, and yet you cannot know how sad I was at the havoc that battle has made in the ranks of the dear old 42nd. How many times I have wished myself with them to share their sufferings and dangers.

What is Will Clapp at home for? I had a letter from him some weeks ago. He was then in Missouri.

I hardly know what to say in regard to your plan of building. I would rather leave the whole matter to your own judgement. I will only say here that I do not think it wise to make a very great outlay on our house in Hiram. I fear that the future of the school does not promise very highly for corner lots.

Almeda tells me that the Trustees were to discuss the question of shutting it up for a time. Of course I can't have a very intelligent opinion at this distance but I shall be very sorry if it is done.[54] I suppose commencement is over. Tell me all about it. When it occurred last year I was in Alabama. How long the war has lasted, and the future——

Kiss our dear little Trot for me over and over again. . . .

I am as ever and always yours and hers,

James

Murfreesboro, Tennessee
June 21, 1863

*Dearest Crete:*

"The sweet church bells are pealing out a chorus will [wild?] and free" and should I close my eyes and listen I should seem again to be

[54] The Eclectic remained open throughout the war.

in some quiet little village where the people were gathering for the worship of God. It is a dear delusion to fancy that all is peace and the holy time is to be marred by no sound of war, but I have only to look out of my window [in] or[der] to dispel it. The tramp of the sentinel, the long line of courier horses, the passers-by, all tell me we are in the midst of volcanic elements ready to break forth in fury and wrath. How I wish I could be with you and Trot this quiet Lord's day in Hiram. It would fill a great void in the hot, duty-path of this wild life of mine. Your very dear letter of the 15th came to hand day before yesterday. I was glad to know you were cheerful and happy in the prospects of the dear new life. Cherish it my dear one, that it may be cheerful, happy, and noble. How long will it be before its advent upon the earth?

Why didn't you tell me something about commencement? Neither you nor Almeda sent me a programme, nor tell me a word about the exercises. Harry has not written to me for a long time. I don't know what is the reason. What is he doing now?

What are the Trustees going to do with the school this fall?

I had hoped Captain Plumb would have paid you the $200 by this time, or I would have drawn my pay for last month. There is no paymaster here now, and I don't know as I can get any more before the last of the month. Captain Plumb is still sick and I cannot expect him to pay it till he is able to return to Cincinnati and draw his pay. It will come all safely as soon as he can get it. I hope the delay in sending it will not interrupt your work of building. Tell me how you are getting along with it.

My health is pretty good now, though I think I am constantly inclined to torpidity of liver. I want to tell you some things about our affairs here, but don't regard it as prudent now. I am having a great deal of anxiety about our affairs, but hope we shall see our way through before long. George Garfield goes home today. I hope you will see him before he returns. I send you a photograph of my friend General Stanley our chief of cavalry. He is an able and gallant officer. We are delighted with the nomination of Brough,[55] and the defeat of Tod.

Kisses to Trot and with much love to you and mother,

*I am ever your*
James

[55] John Brough of Marietta, journalist, lawyer, and railroad president, ran as the candidate of the Union party and defeated Clement L. Vallandigham in Ohio's gubernatorial campaign of 1863. The campaign attracted nation-wide attention. Brough served from January 11, 1864 to his death on August 29, 1865.

Murfreesboro, Tennessee
June 24, 1863

*Dearest Crete:*

The whole army is in motion. Headquarters moves at 1 P.M. I have only time to tell you this for we are very busy. I have just issued an order interdicting all telegraphic dispatches to the press until further orders. You may not hear from us for several days. We shall test the strength of Bragg's Army before this reaches you. I send you love and a thousand kisses to Trot. Love to mother. I shall send you a line when I can.

*Ever your own,*
James

Beech Grove, Tennessee
June 27, 1863
8:15 A.M.

*My Dear Crete:*

We have driven the enemy back upon Fairfield and our advance is now close upon Manchester. We have lost about 300 men thus far.

The rebs are not disposed to give us a general battle this side [of] Duck River. We shall push for Tullahoma and try to get in their rear. If we succeed we shall then test the metal of both armies. We have 100 prisoners.

I am well, though I get but little sleep. It has rained fearfully and almost constantly since we started.

Love to Trot and mother [and] all our folks. Write me often. Letters will come without any place named on envelope.

*Ever and always yours,*
James

Manchester, Tennessee
June 29, 1863

*Dearest Crete:*

Yours of the 21st reached me yesterday morning. It was a pleasure that you cannot realize to have a letter full of love and tenderness follow me on such a march as this and find its way to me with all its blessing.

We reached this place Saturday evening, captured a small force of rebels that were here, and found the mass of their army was in full retreat toward Tullahoma. Yesterday we threw forward our extreme right and seized Shelbyville, taking 400 to 500 prisoners and a battery. Yesterday we brought up our trains and we are now preparing for an immediate advance on Tullahoma. If the rebels stand we shall give them the biggest fight we are able. We somewhat expect they will retreat beyond the Tennessee River, but hope not. If they stand, I think we shall be able to damage them materially. Our operations thus far have been successful beyond the expectations of every one outside headquarters. I have studied all these movements carefully beforehead, and I am delighted to see how fully my judgment has been vindicated. I have enjoyed excellent health since we started though I have been drenched in rain nearly every day. I felt a little unwell last night and my head aches this morning, but when Harry is under me again I think I shall be all right. You will forgive these hasty letters for I have only time to tell me [you] where we are and how.

Kisses innumerable to Trot. Love to mother and write me often, remembering that I am always your own,

James

Tullahoma, Tennessee
July 8, 1863

*Dearest Crete:*

Your two good letters of June 28th and 30th came duly to hand. It gave me peculiar pleasure to know in the midst of our hurried marches and fights of the last ten days that you were well and happy. I am glad to tell you that I am well and safely through the campaign, which is ended. The rebels are now wholly driven from Middle Tennessee. The[y] crossed the Tennessee River at Bridgeport yesterday, and burned the long bridge behind them.

I will give you a brief outline of our operations. Look on Almeda's map and you will understand my statements. The rebel outposts extended from Spring Hill south of Franklin across by way of Rover to McMinnville, their pickets reaching within five miles of Murfreesboro. There is a ragged ridge of hills extended across from Fosterville to Beech Grove with only three gaps—Guy's, Liberty and Hoover's—through which an army can pass. This was their first line of defence and they held the gaps in strong force. The position is exceedingly strong. Their second line was a strongly built chain of fortifications from Fairfield in a semicircle to Duck River northwest of Shelbyville. Their third line was Duck River itself, a stream difficult to cross and of course all the bridges were in their possession. The fourth was the ridge between the Duck and Elk crowned by this place [Tullahoma] which the[y] had surrounded with five miles of fortifications with a strong fort mounting 12 siege guns in the center. The fifth is Elk River, the sixth, the jagged spurs of the Cumberland Mountains, and the last is the Tennessee River. On the 23rd [of June] we threw forward a strong force to attack Rover and Middleton and attract the enemy's attention from our real purpose. On the 24th another strong force seized Liberty Gap after a severe fight. The same day another force seized Hoover's Gap after a very severe fight. Meantime a heavy column was marching around by way of Readyville and old Fort Nash upon Manchester. The troops on our right were suddenly drawn over to Hoover's Gap, a part sent down to attack Fairfield, while the main body was thrus[t] forward to Manchester. The rebels were completely out-generalled, for while we were far on the way to Manchester they were defending Fairfield and the gaps. They retreated in confusion across the Duck River and gave up their first two lines. Tullahoma had then only a small garrison and we could have got in ahead of Bragg as our plan was, but for the extraordinary rains which rendered the roads almost impassable. I have never seen so much rain fall in the same length of time. It began the morning we started and it has rained every day since. If we had reached Tullahoma before Bragg, we should have destroyed his army. As it was by the aid of the railroad he got into this place before us, strengthened his works, and prepared for figh[t]. In the meantime we sent a cavalry force to his rear and broke up the railroad and threw our columns in motion to attack him, when he made a hasty retreat. We pursued to Cowan and University and he has got across the Tennessee at last with a shattered and greatly de-moralized army. It may be said of him and [as] Cicero said of Catiline: "*Abiit, excessit, evasit, erupit* [He has gone out, he has departed, he has escaped, he has rushed away]."

We have not lost over 1,000 killed and wounded, and have killed and wounded over 1,500 rebels and have over 1,000 prisoners.[56] His Tennessee troops have deserted in great numbers and it will be difficult for him to repair his losses of war material. Again the rich harvest of Middle Tennessee were [was] ready to be gathered and he has lost that. The news of the fall of Vicksburg and our successes in the East are most cheering and lead me to hope we may soon see signs of light and hope for our poor country. No man will hail the return of peace more joyfully than I. Still there is much hard fighting to be done yet.

We are restoring burned bridges and bring[ing] up supplies prepara-tory to pushing forward upon a new campaign. Our hands and heads are very full of work.

Please read this to our friends as I may not have time to write it again.

I am really not able to say much about your plan of horse barn. I

[56] Rosecrans reported 84 killed, 473 wounded, and 13 missing; Bragg did not report his losses, but they exceeded those of the Union and included over 1,600 prisoners.

To the success of the Tullahoma campaign Garfield made an enormous con-tribution, for which his grateful commander paid him a handsome tribute. In his official report Rosecrans said: "All my staff merited my warm approbation . . . , but I will state that I will not consider it invidious if I especially mention Brigadier-General Garfield, ever active, prudent and sagacious. I feel much indebted to him for both counsel and assistance in the administration of this army. He possesses the instinct and energy of a great commander."

like it so far as I can see. I think you should have two or three small bins rather than one large one so that we may have corn and meal as well as oats. I am expecting a paymaster here in a few days, and I will be able to send you some money. In the mean time you must make arrangements not to let the work [of] building stop. Is Almeda with you? Tell Harry I have written him twice without response. Give my love to mother and Trot and for yourself. You are always thought of as you would wish to be.

*Ever your*
James

Nashville, Tennessee
July 17, 1863

*My Dearest:*

Your last of July 6th reached me just before I left Tullahoma to come to this place. The General and I are on a tour of inspection preparatory to an advance upon Chattanooga which will be made as soon as our railroad is repaired and supplies can be sent forward. We have been to Manchester and McMinnville and since our arrival here have visited Franklin and the fortifications at that place. We have a great work on hands to visit all the hospitals, forts, troops, and quarter-master and commissary departments in this place. We shall also make out the official report of our late campaign before we leave this place w[h]ich will be probably three days hence.

I have only time to write you a word and enclose $500 on New York. I have sent it in two drafts hoping you will be able to get along by using one and I think it will be best for you to deposit the other ($300 or $200) as you find necessary in the Bank of Commerce at Cleveland where it will draw interest. I will write you soon.

*With much love, I am as ever your*
James

Nashville, Tennessee
July 23, 1863

[Telegram to]
*Mrs. J. A. Garfield*
*Hiram, Portage County*
*via Cleveland*

If you can come do so at once. There will be time for you to arrive before we leave here. Mrs. Rosecrans is here. Answer when you will leave Cleveland. This dispatch will be a pass.

J. A. Garfield
*Brigadier General*
*Chief of Staff*[57]

---

[57] On the same day Rosecrans also wired: "Come without delay bringing daughter to Nashville on a jaunt. We want to see you."

Headquarters
Department of the Cumberland
Nashville
July 27, 1863

*My Dear Governor:*[58]

I have for a long time wanted to write to you, not only to acknowledge your last kind letter, but also to say some things confidentially on the movements in this department; but I have refrained hitherto, lest I do injustice to a good man and say to you things which were better left unsaid. We have now, however, reached a point upon which I feel it proper and also due to that kind opinion which I believe you have had of me, to acquaint you with the condition of affairs here. I cannot conceal from you the fact that I have been greatly tried and dissatisfied with the slow progress that we have made in this department since the Battle of Stone River.

I will say in the outset that it would be in the highest degree unjust to say that the 162 days which elapsed between the Battle of Stone River and the next advance of this army were spent in idleness or trifling. During that period was performed the enormous and highly important labor which made the Army of the Cumberland what it is—in many respects by far the best the country has ever known. But for many weeks prior to our late movement I could not but feel that there was not that live and earnest determination to fling the great weight of this army into the scale and make its power felt in crushing the shell of the rebellion. I have no words to tell you with how restive and unsatisfied a spirit I waited and pleaded for striking a sturdy blow. I could not justly say we were in any proper condition to advance till the early days of May. At that time the strings began to draw sharply upon the rebels, both on the Mississippi and in the East. They began to fear for the safety of Vicksburg and before the middle of May they began quietly to draw away forces to aid Pemberton. I plead[ed] for an advance, but not till June began did General Rosecrans begin seriously to meditate an immediate movement. The army had grown anxious with the exception of its leading generals, who seemed blind to the advantages of the hour. In the first week of the month a council of war was called, and out of eighteen generals whose opinion was asked seventeen were opposed to an advance. I was the only one who urged upon the General the imperative necessity of striking a blow at once, while Bragg was weaker and we stronger than ever before. I wrote a careful review of the opinions of the generals, and exhibited the facts, gathered from ample data, that we could throw 65,000 bayonets and sabers against Bragg's 41,000, allowing the most liberal estimates of his force. This paper was drawn up on the 8th of June. After its presentation and a full canvassing of the situation an advance was agreed upon; but it was delayed through days which

[58] For a discussion of this letter and its significance, see the introductory remarks on pages 219-221.

seemed months to me till the 24th, when it was begun, and ended with what results you know. The wisdom of the movement was not only vindicated, but the seventeen dissenting generals were compelled to confess that if the movement had been made ten days earlier, while the weather was propitious, the army of Bragg would in all human probability no longer exist.

I shall never cease to regret the sad delay which lost us so great an opportunity to inflict a mortal blow upon the center of the rebellion. The work of expelling Bragg from Middle Tennessee occupied nine days and ended July 3, leaving his troops in a most disheartened and demoralized condition, while our army, with a loss of less than 1,000 men was in a few days fuller of potential fight than ever before. On the 18th *inst.* the bridges were rebuilt and the cars were in full communication from the Cumberland to the Tennessee. I have since then urged with all the earnestness I possess a rapid advance while Bragg's army was shattered and under cover, and before Johnston and he could effect a junction.

Thus far the General has been singularly disinclined to grasp the situation with a strong hand and make the advantage his own. I write this with more sorrow than I can tell you, for I love every bone in his body, and next to my desire to see the rebellion blasted is my anxiety to see him blessed. But even the breadth of my love is not sufficient to cover this almost fatal delay.

My personal relations with General Rosecrans are all that I could desire. Officially I share his counsels and responsibilities even more than I desire, but I beg you to know that this delay is against my judgment and my every wish. Pleasant as are my relations here, I would rather command a battalion that would follow and follow, and strike and strike, than to hang back while such golden moments are passing. But the General and myself believe that I can do more service in my present place than in command of a division, though I am aware that it is a position that promises better in the way of promotion or popular credit. But if this inaction continues long I shall ask to be relieved and sent somewhere where I can be part of a working army. But I do hope that you will soon hear that this splendid army is at least trying to do its part in the great work. If the War Department has not always been just, it has certainly been very indulgent to this army, but I feel that the time has now come when it should allow no plea to keep this army back from the most vigorous activity. I do hope that no hopes of peace or submissive terms on the part of the rebels will lead the government to delay the draft and the vigorous prosecution of the war. "*Timeo Danaos et dona ferentes* [I fear the Greeks, especially when bearing gifts]." Let the nation now display the majesty of its power and the work will be speedily ended.

I hope you will pardon this lengthy letter, but I wanted you to know how the case stands, and I was unwilling to have you think me satisfied with the delays here. With kindest regard, I am as ever, your friend,

J. A. Garfield

Honorable S. P. Chase

Winchester, Tennessee
August 1, 1863

*Dearest Crete:*

Yours of June 27th came to hand last evening. I had been waiting anxiously to hear from you not knowing whether to look to the mail, the telegraph, or the cars for the first intelligence. I knew it would be a question of some doubt in your own mind what you ought to do and I did not feel sure myself, but yet I hoped it might be consistent for you to come and visit me. While thus waiting I did not write and in addition to this reason I was so overcrowded with business that I did not write to anybody. I have never passed so long a time before for years without writing a letter, but from the date of my last letter to you (in which I enclosed $500) I have not written a private letter till today. We staid in Nashville much longer than we at first intended to. We did not come back here till the 29th July. In addition to my work I had a very severe return of the piles which made me a great deal of trouble all the time I was there and I have not yet entirely recovered. I hope, however, the worst is over.

We are busy again preparing for another advance and I earnestly hope it will be begun soon. I don't feel at all satisfied with the slow progress we are making and I expect to hear complaints and just ones, soon. There are the strongest possible reasons for using every moment now before the rebels can recover from their late disasters.

I have been paid for the month of July and I enclose you a government check for $200. I hope you are using the funds as economically as is consistent with our wants and decent appearance. I don't say this to intimate that I have any doubts on the question but only to show my anxiety on that point. I am running myself rather shabby in the way of clothing, thinking to keep but a small amount of military clothing on hand this fall in case I should quit the service, but I presume I shall be compelled to get one more suit at any rate. I am living as frugally as I consistently can. I hope the aspect of the war may be such that I can go to Congress this fall, but I will defer a decision for the present.

Tell mother I will write her in answer to her letter soon. Dear little Trot, how much I long to see the little cog[g]er! Kiss her for me and tell her the "webbles haven't hurt papa yet."

*Ever your own,*
James . . . .

Winchester, Tennessee
August 5, 1863

*Joseph Lay, Esq.*
*Akron, Indiana*

Your letter of July 2nd, 1863, reached me while the Army of the Cumberland was taking up its new positions, consequent upon the expulsion of the rebels from Middle Tennessee, and in the hurry of business I have been unable to answer it hitherto. I thank you with all my heart for the letter which assures me I was loved by your noble son. I cannot remember your son by name but I know almost every face in that gallant 51st Indiana regiment, which was so brave and true to the country and to me in every place of duty and danger. Accept for yourself and the bereaved widow of your dear son my deepest sympathies; and if the little boy who bears my name shall ever be in want of any favor I can bestow, tell him to come to me.

I hope some day to see him in the happiness of that peace which his father fought and died for.

*Very truly your friend,*
J. A. Garfield
*Brigadier General, Volunteers*

Winchester, Tennessee
August 14, 1863

*Dearest Crete:*

I have not set up an hour for the last seven days, but I have put on my clothes this morning and am sitting at my desk for a few minutes. The fever is broken up, and I think the diarrhea is somewhat checked. The diarrhea appears to be the resulting reaction from my severe attack of costiveness and piles at Nashville. I don't believe the fountains of my great deep are being again broken up as they were last season. For a long time I have had no appetite and feared another attack of the jaundice but I think that danger is now nearly past. I am trying to starve the diarrhea out by reducing myself to the minimum amount of eating. I am very weak but I am now, I hope, over the worst. I think I will be in the saddle soon.

I hope to hear from you often and know how you get along.

Build an ice house or make arrangements for keeping a good store of it in the cellar. I think it will be best to build a separate house for it.

I must go back to bed. I am urging a movement, and think I will be ready to accompany it. Love to mother and Trot.

*Ever your own,*
James

Stevenson, Alabama
August 23, 1863

*My Dearest Crete:*

By having my cot taken into the car I came through from Winchester to this place on the 18th *inst.* without injury. Captain Swaim found a quiet room for me apart from the camp, and I have bound myself down ever since by the most rigid rules of the doctor and have been gaining slowly and steadily. I now sit up two or three hours at a time and take a turn or two in the yard morning and evening. I am now wholly free from disease but oh how puny I have become in so short a time. For once in my life I am being very careful. You came [near] having me at home in the midst of your house-building troubles, and nothing but my will and the great work before this army, in which the General says he don't know how to spare me, kept you and the *little cog[g]er* from seeing me. We are now on the bank of the Tennessee with the army. I hope to see and help direct the crossing from my ambulance, if not from Harry's back, before this week is past. There is so much of myself in the plan of this campaign that I must help realize my ideas. It looks now as though we should have a bloody crossing but we may not. It is the greatest undertaking of the kind during this war. The river is from 500 to 900 yards wide and pretty deep, averaging ten feet. I appreciate what you say in regard to my work in this army and I thank you for the kind and loving words you wrote. I believe my army life has been as free from self-seeking and pride as any part of my whole life. I am doing a work here for which I shall never get a tithe of the credit that others will. Let it pass. I am glad to help save the republic.

I hope you are progressing well with your house. Give me a drawing of it in pen from the southwest front.

Then Trot dislike[s] to be called a *little cog[g]er* does she? Then I shall call her a little *quid.* How will she like that? Wouldn't she like to have me write her a letter? I think [I] shall do so before long. . . .

Love to Trot and Almeda and all, and write soon. Forgive my sick silence.

*Ever your own,*
James

Stevenson, Alabama
September 1, 1863

*Dearest Crete:*

Yours of August 24th came duly to hand. I am grateful for your tender solicited [solicitude] for me and I would dearly love to go home and spend the remaining weeks between now and the time of my departure for Washington (in case I go) with you. Especially do I want to be with you in your approaching trial. But I know you will appreciate the situation of affairs here when I tell you that all the fruits of the past operations of this army since I opened its first gun and won its first victory at Middle Creek and [are] now about to be crowned or lost in a great and trying campaign beyond the mountains on the soil of Georgia. It is not vanity for me to say that no man in this army can fill my place during this movement. It would take him several months to learn the character and condition of affairs as I know them and to hold that influence with the commanding General that I do. For these reasons I believe I can more ably serve the country during this campaign than ever before in my life and anything short of breaking down my constitution and destroying my efficiency altogether I feel like doing to help carry out our plans. I am glad to tell you that I am much better and have now been on duty for nearly a week, and though I have lost much flesh and strength, I am regaining it slowly and hope, though not with full assurance, to be able to get through the season without another breakdown.

This is a very peculiar climate. In the daytime it is fiercely hot but at night so cold that we build fires in front of our tents and put on thick overcoats. Day before yesterday the thermometer ranged through 41 degrees between noon and midnight. Our second bridge across the Tennessee will be finished today and I hope we shall not long delay on this shore. A good part of our army is already across but [there was] a rumor last night that Bragg was crossing the river above Chattanooga and attempting to come in on our rear and cut our railroad. We must delay our movement till we can ascertain the truth of this rumor. If it be true we will turn back and fight him on this side. If not we will try to find him beyond the mountains.

How do you get on with your horse barn and ice house? I am very anxious to see your buildings. Harry complimented you on your business ability. How many horses shall I bring home? I have four. Are they bringing good prices now at home? What? Give my love to little Trot the Cog[g]er and let me hear from you soon.

Ever your own,<br>James

Cave Spring, Alabama<br>September 6, 1863

*Dearest Crete:*

We are all across the river and are closing in on the rebel army at Chattanooga. They must fight us or run before many days. The situation is one of intense interest and great results may hang upon the issue. The rebels are making some demonstrations in the direction I spoke of in my last letter to some of you. Yesterday they built a pontoon bridge at Chattanooga and are threatening to cross. Our forces are shelling them and trying to destroy their bridge before they swing it across. I am glad to tell you that I am better as I always am on campaigns, though not as robust as I could wish. Your letter of the 30th came yesterday. You will probably hear of us through the papers before you do from me. Harry is saddled and we leave for Trenton, Georgia in a few minutes.

Love to dear little Trot and all our folks. Excuse this short pencilled note. I can do no better this morning.

*I am as always, your own* James

Chattanooga, Tennessee
September 13, 1863

*Dear Harry:*

I am just leaving for the center of the army 30 miles from here in Georgia. A battle is imminent. I believe the enemy now intends to fight us. He has a large force and the advantage in position. Unless we can outmaneuver him we shall be in a perilous situation. But we will try. Our strategic suc[c]ess has been most brilliant thus far. I am hard at work but am not well yet. For my special delectation I have a terrific boil on my hand. *Felix Eques* [Fortunate Knight]!

Do write to me. Love to Crete and Almeda.

In haste,

*Ever yours,*
J. A. Garfield

Crawfish Spring, Georgia
13 miles from La Fayette
September 16, 1863

*Dearest Crete:*

I received yours of September 4th just before I left Chattanooga. Since then we have been 30 miles along the crest of Lookout Mountain, and concentrated the three colum[n]s of the army so as to be able to use its power on one point either for offense or defense as may be necessary. That done, we have moved eastward and northward and ordered our tents and wagons forward to join us. Six miles and the slender range of Pigeon Mountain now separates us from the rebel army. Whether they will fight us or will run again is not yet certain but they have been reinforced heavily from the Mississippi army and perhaps some from Virginia,[59] and are better able to fight us now with

[59] At Chickamauga Bragg was re-enforced by Longstreet's corps from Virginia, a corps from Eastern Tennessee, and two divisions from Mississippi.

some chance of success than they have been before for a long time. We are expecting Burnside to close down on us in a few days and then I think we shall give the rebs a chance to try the chances of battle again. I think you can find our position on the map I sent to Almeda. La Fayette is the center of the rebel position with the circumference resting along the crest of Pigeon Mountain. Our army has the line of West Chickamauga Creek to the northwest of La Fayette; half of our line [stands] with its back against Lookout Mountain. The situation is one of great interest and great results are depending on the outcome of the contest or retreat which must occur soon.

My health is improving as we advance. I have ridden on a very bad boil till I have broken and finally nearly overcome it. I think I shall get through the campaign without a broken constitution, though I think the war will have shortened my life a few years if not more than a few. Just at this point of my writing, a telegram has been received from Washington confirming the rumors we have already had the [that] Longstreet has reinforced Bragg with three divisions from Lee's army, and that Sherman and Hurlbut have been ordered to the Tennessee River.[60] This being so the day of the struggle will probably be deferred but it will be great when it comes. Thank God that the forces concentrating on both sides are being concentrated for a final struggle. It will, I believe, be the finishing great blow.

With love to Trot and tenderest love to you and keenest solicitude and anxiety for your next six weeks. I am, as ever, your own

James

Chattanooga, Tennessee
September 23, 1863

*Dearest Crete:*

I know you will pardon me for not writing sooner, and even now I have only time to write a few words. I would not now, had I time, recount the events of Saturday, Sunday, and Monday. The recollection of them fills me with pride and grief commingled. We are now in the peninsula which this place fills, and the masses of the rebel army are closed in around us. There is no doubt that they have double or triple our numbers.[61] Burnside will not reach us for six days. We must there-

---

[60] At Chickamauga the Union army received no re-enforcements, not even from Burnside, who defied repeated orders from Washington and refused to join Rosecrans. Burnside's performance throughout the campaign is a sorry chapter in the nation's military history.

[61] Throughout the Chickamauga campaign Bragg sent out scouts, spies, and "deserters" with rumors about the size, location, equipment, and morale of his army. They helped convince Rosecrans and his lieutenants that the Confederates outnumbered them two or three to one. At Chickamauga Rosecrans' army of 58,000 was smaller than Bragg's by about 8,000. Since each lost about 16,000 in the battle, Bragg had about 50,000 men confronting 42,000 Federals at Chattanooga.

fore save ourselves if saved at all. I expect the battle will be renewed this morning and with fury. If calamity befal[l]s us you may be sure we shall sell ourselves as dearly as possible. It is now the early morning and all is still. I would not, if I could, tell you all that is in my heart. I will only say that a picture of unutterable dearness is in my soul as I think of you and Trot and our dear circle of precious ones at Hiram. Give this word to them for me. Yours of the 14th came to me yesterday and made me glad. Keep up a brave cheerful heart. The country will triumph if we do not. Kiss little Trot for me a hundred times. Write to me frequently as usual. What ever betide, I hope you will never have cause to blush on my account. Love to mother when she returns to you. I hope she is well.

*Ever your own,*
James

Chattanooga, Tennessee
September 25, 1863

*Dearest Crete:*

I have been so perfectly overwhelmed with work and weariness for the last three days that I have not been able to write to you or any of our friends at home, and I will only now write to assure you that you need have no apprehension for the safety of the army. I will not attempt now, perhaps not till I see you, to give you a history of the battle which was much the fiercest we have had in the West, perhaps any where during the war.[62] I will only say it was won and then abandoned, giving the enemy an opportunity to follow and injure us, but he was too much crippled to do so till we had strengthened ourselves in this place and were able to repulse all his attempts. The campaign is successful and Chattanooga will be held; thus the great end of our movement has been accomplished, even if the battle be considered lost.[63] I am very much worn down with fatigue and diarrhea. I kept up finely till the trouble was over, and now [that] the reaction has come on it will take me some days to gather up again.

I hope I shall be able to spend some weeks with you before Congress convenes. Let me hear from you soon. Tell Mary that Marenus' brother is probably taken prisoner. He may have been killed or wounded but I hope not. Love to all our friends, and kisses to dear little Trot.

*Ever your own,*
James

[62] Chickamauga was the greatest battle of the West and, with the exception of Gettysburg, the greatest of the war to that time.

[63] Halleck's orders to Rosecrans were to drive Bragg out of Tennessee. In this Rosecrans succeeded, and the importance of his capture of Chattanooga cannot be denied. But he had another and more important objective, as Garfield well knew. That was to destroy the enemy army. This "great end" was unfinished business.

Chattanooga, Tennessee
October 13, 1863

*Dearest Mother:*

Your good letter of the 2nd *inst.* came to hand last night. I was very glad to hear from you and to know that you are well. Our railroad has been cut by the rebel cavalry and no mails have reached us for a week till last night. It is now restored, and I hope we shall be able to keep open communications hereafter. You can have no idea of the amount of work I have had to do for the last two months. You must not feel that I have ever forgotten you. That would be impossible. I knew you had heard from me often through Crete, though I have written very few letters to her or any body else during the late movements.

I am glad to tell you that I am well, and I have great reason to thank our Heavenly Father for his mercy to me in saving my life where so many fell. I had very little expectation of passing through unharmed and how I escaped death I do not know. I do not know the name of the orderly who fell by my side. My horse *Billy* was not killed. He was slightly wounded but he is now well again, and I love him all the more for being hit. Frank Larabee was taken prisoner; whether he was wounded or not I don't know. Our whole loss was about 16,000, of whom nearly 12,000 were killed and wounded. The rest were taken prisoners. We took over 2,000 rebels prisoners, and I think we killed and wounded 15,000 of them. General Rosecrans is going to send me to Washington on business for this army in a few days and I shall go back home from there, and I hope I shall be able to get there early in November so as to spend as much time at home as I can. I cannot now tell what time I shall get home but hope it will not be far from the first of November.

I wrote to Thomas several weeks ago but have not heard from him. I send you a general order by which I am relieved from duty as Chief of Staff[64] and am now preparing our reports of the battle to take to Washington.

Give my love to all our folks. Kiss little Trot for me a dozen times. I am very anxious to see the little rascal.

*Always your affectionate son,*
James

[64] In the orders, dated October 10, Rosecrans lauded Garfield: "His high intelligence, spotless integrity, business capacity and thorough acquaintance with the wants of the army, will render his services, if possible, more valuable to the country in Congress, than with us. Reluctantly yielding to this consideration the General Commanding relieves him from duty as Chief of Staff. In doing so he returns his thanks to Gen. Garfield for the invaluable assistance he has rendered him by wise councils and assiduous labors, as well as for his gallantry, good judgement and efficiency at the Battle of Chickamauga."

Washington, D.C.
October 30, 1863

*Dearest Crete:*

I arrived here day before yesterday morning and had hardly got my blue overcoat off before Secretary Chase sent a demand that I should go with him to Baltimore to an emancipation meeting. I did so and found from 15,000 to 20,000 people assembled on Monument Square, and the speakers, many of them life-long slaveholders, made the square bold issue for immediate and unconditional abolition in Maryland. I was never more delighted and astonished, and when I spoke to them the same words I would address to our people on the Reserve and heard their long applause, I felt as if the political millennium had dawned. The people of Baltimore insist that I shall go and help them through their campaign, which closes on the 4th *proximo* and the Secretary of War gave them permission to have me go. I was very reluctant to make speeches, but I unfortunately made the impression upon the people there that I had some fervor on the stump, and I go this noon to spend a few days on the eastern shore of the Bay. I shall try to hurry up my business so as not to delay my return home any longer than is absolutely necessary.

I need not tell you that I am exceedingly anxious to spend as much time with you and our precious little ones as possible. I hope you are being careful and will soon be quite well again. I am very proud of you for your brave and successful management of exterior and interior affairs during the past season. Do write me; direct to Willard's. Give my love to Trot and Chickamauga and all the smaller members of the family such as mother, Miss Booth, Mollie and Bell and remember me as ever.

*Your own,*
James

**P.S.** What do you want me to get in the family line while here and in New York?                                                J. A. G.

Hiram
December 1, 1863

*Dear Brother Austin:*

We have been watching for 12 hours to see our darling die. She is still alive but cannot last till noon. You and yours know how our hearts are breaking.

We thank you for your loving, tender words of sympathy. I will write you again when the light of our home goes out.

*Ever yours,*
J. A. Garfield

Hiram
December 1, 1863

*Dear Brother Austin:*

Our darling Trot died at 7 o'clock this evening. We bury her day after tomorrow morning at 10½ o'clock.

I have sent a letter accompanying this to Brother Lanphere asking him to conduct the service, which will be at the house only.

If it be possible, we shall be glad to see you and Minerva and Lottie with us.

Only such as you can know how desolate our hearts are tonight. Will you write me?

*Ever your brother,*
J. A. Garfield

Washington, D.C.
December 6, 1863

*My Darling Crete:*

I arrived here at six o'clock last evening having been detained at Harrisburg six hours by our train failing to connect with the one for Baltimore. Mrs. Parmlee and her friend did not get the morning train at Bedford but came on in the afternoon and overtook me at Harrisburg next morning. I cannot tell you what a lonely dreary ride it was to me. On reaching Pittsburg, I fell in company with Captain [Alex] Pearce of Cincinnati whom I knew in the days of my senatorship. He was accompanied by his wife and her sister and all were accompanying the remains of a third lovely sister of 19 to their former home in Washington. I joined the party and seemed far more at home with stricken mourners than with any others. I told them the story of our precious little Trot and they told me of their grief. The way seemed very long and very dark.

I reached here just in time to attend the caucus at 7 in the evening where we selected Mr. Colfax of Indiana as our candidate for Speaker.[65]

Today I have resigned my commission in the army and am now for the first time since August 12th, 1861, a citizen [civilian].[66]

I have come away this evening to my rooms at the corner of New York Avenue and 13th Street and am now here alone. The rooms are very large and I more alone than ever before in my life. It does seem to me that I cannot stay here alone this whole winter and spring and Heaven knows how much of the summer besides.

[65] Schuyler Colfax, an Indiana Republican, was Speaker of the House, 1863-1869, and Vice President of the U.S., 1869-1873.

[66] Garfield resigned as a major general. His commission for that rank was dated September 19, 1863, and was conferred in recognition of "gallant and meritorious services" in the Battle of Chickamauga.

How constantly the image of our precious lost one leaps into my memory and heart! I took dinner with Secretary Stanton today and his little ones were there to haunt me with contrasts between them and Trot. Her brightness so far outshines theirs that I almost wondered anyone could love them and not worship her. I find myself sitting alone, calling her by her pet names, and asking her if she loves me, and almost hoping to hear an answer. Precious little darling, I wonder if she can know how her papa loves her and longs for her! I find here awaiting me your letter of November 6th in which you tell me of her crying that I came away without kissing her. On my leaving for Washington this last time, I could say that the little darling had left without kissing me. I grieve more than she did.

I find a ponderous pile of letters awaiting me and I sit down drearily to the task of answering.

Secretary Stanton assures me that he will hold my place in the army open for me at any time I choose to return, and if this terrible weary work and desolateness of heart continues it seems as though I must go back into the wild life of the army. . . .

*I am as ever your own,*
James

# Appendix A

## Notes of an Interview with Major-General McDowell at Washington, October 6th and 10th, 1862

Major General Fitz John Porter, a corps commander in the Army of the Potomac, was accused of disobeying orders during the Second Battle of Bull Run. Since some of the charges against him implied cowardice and treason, a verdict of guilty could have meant a death penalty. Porter's trial was originally entrusted to a military commission to which Garfield was appointed, but on November 25, 1862, the commission was dissolved and a court-martial ordered. Garfield was again detailed for duty. After a trial that dragged on through December and into the middle of January, 1863, Porter was found guilty of most of the charges, cashiered from the service, and forever disqualified from holding any office of trust or profit under the Federal government.[1]

The Porter case produced highly partisan debate among contemporaries and is the subject of a considerable body of literature by twentieth century authors whose works have kept the controversy alive and spirited. One writer devoted an entire volume to denouncing the trial and verdict as a travesty of justice from start to finish. Included in his list of injustices against Porter is the charge that Secretary of War Stanton packed the court with anti-Porter men.[2] This is denied by Stanton's most recent biographers who point out that no evidence has been uncovered to support the charge and claim that Stanton "awaited the court's decision . . . with considerable uneasiness and suspense."[3]

At any rate, by its rulings on important points during the trial, to say nothing of its verdict, the court left ample ground for accusations of gross unfairness. The purpose here, however, is neither to condemn the court nor to explore the question of its fitness to sit in judgment of Porter. It is intended only to determine whether Garfield was a prejudiced judge and, if so, the nature of his bias and why it existed. This requires consideration of certain of his friends, notably Salmon P. Chase and Major General Irvin McDowell, his opinion of McClellan, and his own stake in the court's findings.

Not directly involved in the case but watching its every development with keen interest was Garfield's good friend Secretary of Treasury

*Chase. There may be no truth to the story, reported to Porter, that Chase told Garfield, "Great things are expected from you on the court."⁴ But there can be no doubt as to Chase's feelings. Well before the trial he had lost all confidence in McClellan and his friends and was openly critical of the General, one of whose favorites was Porter. On the other hand, Chase was extremely fond of McDowell, a key witness against Porter. The Secretary of Treasury enjoyed entertaining Mc-Dowell as an overnight guest in his spacious Washington home and was advising him on matters of great importance to his career, including that of requesting a court of inquiry which was to have a significant relationship to the Porter court-martial. Suffice it to say that on fundamental points at issue in both tribunals it was impossible to be for McDowell without being against Porter. Chase was for McDowell and Garfield knew it.⁵*

*McDowell's testimony against Porter must be assessed in the light of his own precarious position. It is a fact that his own military reputation and career were then, like Porter's, in jeopardy. To be sure, no formal charges were drawn up against McDowell, but after Second Bull Run a torrent of harsh criticism, some of it from congressmen, was aimed his way. McDowell, spurred on by advice from Chase, decided to ask for a court of inquiry to investigate any or all aspects of his Civil War military career. His request was granted. Thus at the very time of the Porter trial his own conduct at Second Bull Run was under investigation. As could be expected, McDowell's testimony in the Porter case was of crucial importance on several key points on which the court could find for Porter only at McDowell's expense. Thus, in order to save himself, McDowell found it necessary to malign Porter.*

*In addition to all this there was bad feeling between McDowell on the one hand, and McClellan and Porter on the other. It originated some six months earlier, during the Peninsula campaign, when Mc-Dowell moved into the Shenandoah Valley instead of joining McClellan for the pending attack on Richmond. Although McDowell had acted on orders from Lincoln, McClellan and Porter blamed him and attributed their failure on the Peninsula to his failure to cooperate. The extent to which all this soured McDowell can be gleaned from the document which appears below. No wonder McDowell's testimony was immensely damaging to Porter!*

*It remains to consider Garfield himself and his fitness to serve on the Porter court. Of his scorn for McClellan and his supporters there can be no question. He was, and had been for weeks before the trial, severely critical of the General. That Chase whetted his antipathy is more than likely. But Garfield knew that other leaders in the administration, including Stanton, disliked, and even questioned the loyalty of, McClellan, who, by the time of the trial, had been relieved of his command. Considering these circumstances, and that it was quite contrary to Garfield's nature to buck what appeared to be the wishes of those in power, to frustrate the men who were at that very moment trying to find him a suitable military assignment, it is difficult to believe that Garfield could have ignored existing pressures and judged Porter objectively.*

*But there is more convincing evidence with which to demonstrate Garfield's anti-Porter bias. In Washington he met Irvin McDowell, a man who was to become such a dear friend that Garfield named a son after him. From the moment of their meeting Garfield liked McDowell and, in October, about six weeks before the Porter trial, held with him two interviews out of which came the document reproduced below. The prejudice disclosed by that document is clear and decided, and because of it Garfield's proper course was to ask to be disqualified from serving on the court. This he did not do; yet, even in 1879, when a court-martial reversed the decision, Garfield insisted, as always, that Porter had been fairly tried and judged in 1862-63.*

*The record shows that Porter, when asked if he objected to any member of the court, replied in the negative.[6] Had he known of the existence and contents of Garfield's lengthy statement on the McDowell interviews, he doubtless would have challenged its author as a prejudiced party, unfit to serve on the court.*

*The text of the statement is presented without explanatory notes for the reason that its numerous inaccuracies would have required extensive documentation, for which there is no place here. Moreover, considering the use made of the document in this work, the omission of explanatory notes in no way detracts from its value.*

At this time Major General Irvin McDowell is under a cloud before the American people, being accused of treason, inefficiency, and indeed almost everything that can throw an officer's name into infamy and contempt. He is from Ohio, and is an intimate friend of Governor Dennison's family and I have been anxious to know the facts in relation to his case. For some reason he seemed to have a desire to show me the record of his military operations, and I accepted his invitation to look over his official records and hear from him the history of his part in the war. This I did at two sittings of nearly four hours each. In these interviews he gave me the free reading of all his dispatches, received and sent, his general orders, letters of instruction, and even his private journal containing notes of some most important interviews with the President and Cabinet. The important though unfortunate part that he has played in the war makes the history of his doings almost the whole history of the Army of the Potomac. I have therefore concluded to note down in brief the substance of the conversation and readings from official records during our interviews as throwing light upon many important transactions and going far to give correct views of the leading men who have borne a part in these stirring events.

General McDowell was a major in the Regular army when the war began and was one of the chief officers who organized our three-months levies that came to Washington and put the Capital in a state of defence.

When Ohio was permitted to have a major general for her three-months men, Governor Dennison proposed to appoint Major Mc-Dowell, but when Cincinnati was threatened a pressure was brought to bear from that city to have George B. McClellan appointed, and McDowell wrote to Governor Dennison telling him to appoint McClellan, saying that McClellan was a more thoroughly educated soldier than he. Governor Dennison appointed McClellan and showed him McDowell's letter, which led McClellan to have a deep sense of gratitude for the manliness and generosity displayed in it.

McDowell was made brigadier general in the Regular army and commanded at Bull Run, though the battle was planned by General [Winfield] Scott. McDowell performed his part with success. The failure of [Major General Robert] Patterson lost us the day.

McClellan assumed command at Washington and McDowell was his second in command and, at first, shared his councils and confidence. The fall of 1861 passed away and part of the winter. The rebel army lay between Manassas and Centerville and were strongly fortified at the latter place. The patience of the people became at length exhausted by the delay of our army and Congress was becoming fearfully clamorous for action. In the month of December General McClellan was taken sick. The gloom grew deeper. Finally on the 10th of January 1862, the President sent for Generals McDowell and [William B.] Franklin and with several members of the Cabinet a conference was held. The President said the bottom of the Government seemed about ready to drop out; he reviewed our relations with foreign governments, the state of the treasury, the feeling of the people and the Congress, the sickness of General McClellan, and in conclusion said: "If General McClellan don't want to use the army, I want to borrow it and get someone to use it for me, and I have sent for you generals to ask what plans you have to propose." They appointed a meeting for the next day and General McDowell proposed to move the army on Richmond via Manassas and the [Orange & Alexandria] Railroad, holding it to be quite easy to dislodge the rebels at Centerville. General Franklin, who was in McClellan's confidence, opposed this plan and proposed to take the army via Annapolis down the Chesapeake Bay and up the York River to West Point and thence along the [Richmond & York River] Railroad to Richmond. Several of these meetings were held and the two plans discussed, when finally, about the 15th of January, McClellan was able to meet with the President and these generals. He listened to their opinions and when all was said he very curtly remarked to McDowell: "You can have whatever opinion you please." He refused to divulge his own plans unless he was ordered to do so. When he declared that he had a plan and a time set for its execution, the President said he would now put the whole matter in General McClellan's hands and dismissed the conference.

But January and February passed with no movement whatever. Congress took the matter in hand and several prominent generals were brought before the Committee on the Conduct of the War. McDowell was among those called and he told them of the two plans. They favored his. Finally the pressure became so great the President was obliged to take the chief command of the army from McClellan and put him at the head of the Army of the Potomac only. The President also ordered him to hold a council of his chief officers and vote on the plan of the campaign. The council was held and the vote stood 8 for McClellan's plan to 4 for McDowell's.

Meantime the rebels, who had staid at Centerville as long as they could, left their Quaker guns and retired to Richmond, at the same time raising the blockade of the Potomac. With a sullen kind of desperation, McClellan marched his vast army out to Fairfax, more to stop the popular clamor than for anything else. The Potomac being now open he so far modified his plan as to bring his fleet of transports around from Annapolis to Alexandria and began to send his army, one division at a time, down to Yorktown.

McDowell, having failed to get his own plan adopted, now went heartily to work to help make the chosen one succeed, though his own was preferred both by Congress and the administration. This difference of opinion in regard to the plan and the fact that McDowell had been consulted so freely by the President, seemed to have soured the mind and awakened the jealousy of McClellan toward him, and from that time forward the advocates of McClellan became the critics or defamers of McDowell.

The different corps d'armee moved down the river successively and to conceal their real design made a diversion on Norfolk. McDowell expected and desired to go to the Peninsula, but when all the other corps had been sent the President became alarmed at having no army left between Washington and Richmond, and said in his quaint style that "McClellan might take Richmond, but the rebels might at the same time come and take Washington, and he was not willing to swap capitals." He therefore ordered McDowell to remain with his corps between Washington and Richmond. McClellan and his friends blamed McDowell for this and represented him as wanting to get a separate command at the expense of McClellan's success. But the President informed McClellan that it was wholly his (the President's) own work. McDowell was thus left in command of a separate army corps of 40,000 men and this leads us to

### McDowell's Rappahannock Campaign

Being kept back from the Peninsula expedition for the protection of the Capital, he determined to accomplish this purpose and aid McClellan against Richmond at the same time. He therefomed [therefore] moved from his camp at Fairfax and proceeded to the Rappahannock near Fredericksburg, at the same time sending supplies and a naval force down the Potomac to Aquia Creek and to Belle Plain a little below, from which point supplies could reach his army by waggoning them eight miles. He immediately went to work to rebuild the [Richmond, Fredericksburg & Potomac] Railroad from Aquia Creek to Fredericksburg and to rebuild the bridges across the rivers and creeks and open the road on toward Richmond, at the same [time] thoroughly organizing his army and bringing up his supplies and putting everything in order to move toward the rebel Capital. The President, seeing this and being timid lest the Capital might be still in danger, sent a positive and peremptory order that McDowell should only hold Fredericksburg for defensive purposes and that he should not go south of the Rappahannock until further orders. By this positive order he was for weeks kept in camp while the people were cursing him for his idleness. Meantime he was preparing his pontoon trans[portation], putting himself in order to move when he should get the President's permission.

By looking at the map it will be seen that General Banks's Department of the Shenandoah and Frémont's Mountain [Department] were important auxiliaries in this work of defending the Capital, and hence their troops occupied Franklin and Harrisonburg and part of Banks's command actually joined McDowell at Fredericksburg. Finally, the President, [and] Secretaries Stanton and Chase on the 22nd [23rd] of May visited McDowell at that place, saw his fine large army and gave him permission to move upon Richmond. The time was then fully ripe. McClellan had crossed from West Point, passed along the Pamunkey, and his right flank rested at Hanover Court House. This left the way open for McDowell to go down upon Richmond from the north while McClellan should attack it from the east (I should have remarked that Franklin's division of McDowell's corps had already, at General McClellan's request, been sent [a]round from Aquia Creek to West Point). The President allowed McDowell to go, but placed one restriction upon his movements. He must always keep his army in a body between the enemy and Washington. In every other respect it should be under [the] command of McClellan. On Saturday [Friday] night, May 23rd, McDowell announced himself ready to move but the President deemed it best not to begin the expedition on Sunday, and so the hour of moving was set for early Monday morning, the 25th [26th].

The President and suite returned to Washington Saturday evening. On Sunday news reached Washington that Banks was attacked and a strong rebel force under Jackson had gone from Richmond via Gordonsville and were sweeping up the Shenandoah. This event marks the end of the Rappahannock campaign and the complete frustration of McDowell's designs on Richmond, and also inaugurates a new chapter, *viz.*:

### PRESIDENT LINCOLN'S VIRGINIA CAMPAIGN

for you must know that he took the command and managed one expedition himself. (He had a little while before been to Fortress Monroe and returned nearly determined to remove McClellan when he found on his return that Owen Lovejoy had passed through Congress a resolution of thanks to McClellan for his glorious victory at Williamsburg, and the tide of popular approval, that moment setting toward McClellan, the President had not the nerve to do it. It is a remarkable fact that the Battle of Williamsburg was fought without his orders and against his will, and he sent on a request to the President to suspend from command the general who fought it. But when he found it applauded by the people, he took it under his wing and reported it as his work.)

Jackson went plunging up through the Virginia Valley driving Banks before him, beating him badly at Winchester and driving him to Harpers Ferry; and also he went through the Blue Ridge [Mountains] and made a bold demonstration toward Washington with about 20,000 men in his whole column. The President and Government were thoroughly alarmed for the safety of the Capital and before night of Sunday [Saturday] the 24th McDowell was ordered to leave Fredericksburg with nearly his whole force and hurry with all possible speed to Front Royal and cut off the rebel retreat. Frémont was ordered to cross over into the Shenandoah Valley to cooperate in the movement. McDowell immediately obeyed but telegraphed the President that the expedition must of necessity be a failure; that Jackson could pass Front Royal in retreat before he (McDowell) could possibly reach it; that it was changing a certainty at Richmond for an uncertainty in the Shenandoah; that there were men enough around Washington to protect that city and that Frémont and Banks could harrass the rebels on their retreat. He said in his telegram: "I am obeying your order with all possible speed, though it is a terrible blow to us." He made a very rapid march through Warrenton and the Manassas Gap Railroad to Front Royal, but not until the mass of the rebel army had passed that point on its way up the Shenandoah. However a part of McDowell's force united with Frémont's and some of Banks's and pursued the enemy, fighting the battles of Harrisonburg and Port Republic, in which we lost more than we gained and Jackson carried the laurels back with him and joined Lee in time to take part in the Battle of the Seven Pines. It was then a question whether McDowell should continue the chase up the Shenandoah or return to Fredericksburg to pursue his original plan of aiding against Richmond (that question was the subject of the President's visit to General Scott).

The President's campaign had been a complete failure and by this time McClellan was so beaten that he was on the point of capitulation at one time. The cry was raised by the press that the Shenandoah campaign failed in consequence of the unwillingness of the three department commanders—McDowell, Banks and Frémont—to cooperate with each other, and the President, true to his timid policy, not daring to take the responsibility and say which one of the three should command, dodged the difficulty by making a new Department of Virginia and calling [John] Pope to the command of it. The great problem now was how to rescue McClellan from his position of danger and inutility on the James River. It was therefore determined that Pope's whole army should hold the attention of the rebels while McClellan should use his legs and get home. This brings us to

## POPE'S VIRGINIA CAMPAIGN

It must be understood that Pope was not to make offensive war, only so fas [far] as was necessary to keep the enemy away from Washington and from McClellan, until a junction could be formed between the two armies. His orders were to *"fight and fall back,"* retreating as slowly as was consistent with safety. Accordingly, while McClellan was secretly making his preparations to leave the James River, Pope massed his army east of the Blue Ridge and threw it across the *Rappahannock* and *Rapidan,* and started as if to attack Richmond. Of course his force was much smaller than Lee's. As soon as McClellan embarked Lee moved his whole force against Pope with the design of crushing him up and taking Washington before McClellan should reach it. With the map before you, you will see that the axis of Pope's operation was the Orange and Alexandria Railroad. After a series of skirmishes, in which the enemy's advance was delayed by disputing his passage of the Rapidan, the battle of the campaign was fought by Banks at Culpepper. Then Pope's army fell back and disputed the passage of the Rappahannock. McDowell was specially charged with this work, and made Warrenton the center of his defense and the Rappahannock his circumference. The rebels attempted to cross at five different points, but were foiled till they got so near the source of the river that they could ford it. A strong rebel column was at the same time moving down the valley of the Shenandoah, part passing the Blue Ridge through Manassas Gap and part through Ashby's Gap, the former part pushing on toward Alexandria and the latter making its way toward Leesburg. That point gained, there would have been three rebel columns bearing down on Washington, one from Leesburg, one from Manassas Gap, and the other from the headwaters of the Rappahannock near Warrenton.

In the movements to resist their approach, McDowell was in immediate command of both Banks's and Sigel's (late Frémont's) corps, and had his headquarters at Warrenton. Pope, their common superior, had his headquarters at Manassas Junction. To protect the Potomac, and also Pope's left flank, Fitz John Porter's division had been sent from McClellan's army. While on its passage up the Potomac and turning off at Aquia Creek, [it] went up the Rappahannock by boats to Catlett's Station where the Orange and Alexandria Railroad crosses that river, and joined Pope. While that part of the rebel force in front of McDowell were [was] engaging all his attention, another column passed through the Thoroughfare Gap of the range of hills running parallel to the Blue Ridge and known as the Bull Run Mountains, and were [was] bearing down upon Centerville to form a junction with the column from Leesburg. Pope, discovering this movement, immediately set about the attempt to catch them. They had gained his rear. On Monday [Tuesday] the 26th [of] July [August] the head of McClellan's army reached Alexandria, and though Pope was partially surrounded by the rebel army, he had no doubt of McClellan's hearty cooperation, or rather the country had no such doubt, though Pope predicted that Mc-Clellan would not help him. Pope's army was set in motion for Centerville. McClellan was asked for troops to move up from Alexandria, only 20 miles distant, and on Thursday and Friday, July 29th and 30th [Friday and Saturday, August 29th and 30th] was fought the

### SECOND BATTLE OF BULL RUN

The whole of McClellan's army lay at Alexandria, and most of it had lain there since the previous Sunday. One division (Franklin's) was sent part way, halted a day, then sent forward again and reached Centerville the morning after the battle. McClellan and his army heard enemy cannon that was [were] fired at Bull Run.

It would be too tedious, and without proper drawings not sufficiently clear, to write here a detailed history of that battle. Suffice it to say that after two days [of] terrible fighting (in which there is the best evidence that McDowell did his duty bravely, and, from his knowledge of the topography of the country, was of invaluable service to Pope) we were badly beaten, driven back to Centerville, and thence to Fairfax, where a sharp battle was fought and the rebels routed and driven back; it was here that General Kearny, one of our bravest and most valuable generals, was killed.

The people, disgusted at Pope's failure, and some of his corps commanders, particularly Sigel, finding much fault with his management, his prestige was lost and he was sent away to fight the Indians. Every prominent general in Pope's army either had his reputation ruined or badly damaged in that campaign except Banks.

Pope preferred charges against Fitz John Porter and Franklin and deeply blamed McClellan. In his dispatches previous to the battle at Bull Run, he says, "Sigel must be crazy," and the leading officers with Pope agree in the opinion that Sigel is a humbug. The storm that had long been gathering over McDowell's head burst when he was a second time beaten at Bull Run. The letter of the dying Colonel Morehead, charging him with treason, was the match that ignited the magazine of popular veng[e]ance. McClellan was to be removed at once and the only question was how should it be done, suddenly or gently. The President, true again to his timid policy concluded to do it by a weak indirection. McClellan was made commandant of the defences of Washington, a mere post commander of less active consequence than a commander of division in the field. The Army of the Potomac was to be put in the command of Burnside or Hooker. It was drawing toward the close of August. September was to inaugurate the new order of things, when the rebel [army] made its movement upon Maryland.

Again all was agitation and alarm at the Capital. Halleck, Stanton and the President bent before the storm and it was concluded to let McClellan try his hand again. Then followed the Maryland campaign with its bloody and indecisive [fighting] (for the generalship of which see George Wilkes) and the month's idleness that has succeeded, and now tonight (October 11th) the rebels hold Chambersburg, Pennsylvania.

## REMARKS

I. *General McDowell:*

(a) In the preceding history it will be seen that in no case has General McDowell been permitted to operate on his own plan. 1st, He opposed the Peninsula expedition and filed written objections against it which events have proved to be correct and his plan has at last been adopted as the only possible one. But he was overruled and worked on McClellan's plan. 2nd, His plan of moving on Richmond from Fredericksburg to aid McClellan was delayed for near two months by express order of the President, and he was cursed by the country for being so long idle on the Rappahannock. 3rd, When at last he was about to put his plan into execution, he was peremptorily ordered by the President to go away into the Shenandoah campaign, in which he had no faith and his dispatches to the President giving the reasons why it would fail proved true in almost every particular. 4th, In his campaign under Pope he was helping carry out the plan of one general to enable another to back out of a bad predicament.

(b) He has fallen into odium. 1st, By the attacks of McClellan and his friends who, after McDowell was called into consultation by the President and by Congress and had dissented from McClellan's plan, seemed jealous of his power and omitted no opportunity to disparage him. This they did by saying he did not want to help McClellan on the Peninsula, and so got himself appointed commander of a separate army. 2nd, The people blamed him for lying so long on the Rappahannock and letting Jackson get up behind him and in general for being unlucky. 3rd, Sigel disliked him because he was made subordinate to him, McDowell, at Warrenton, but this was Pope's order. Sigel's Dutchmen attributed their Bull Run defeat to McDowell. 4th, He treated army correspondents rather cavalierly and thus brought them down upon [him]. 5, He is a strict disciplinarian and would not let his men pillage and hence was charged with being tender of the rebels and finally of being a traitor. Of there being any open quarrel between him and Sigel—shooting, stabbing, etc.—of his being drunk, and a score of such rumors, there is not the least foundation in the world.

(c) *My Opinion* General McDowell is a man of far more than ordinary ability and culture. He is frank, open, manly, severe and sincere. He is truly patriotic, but is not a politician. He does not deem it a discredit to be a *mere soldier*. His military education has led him to obey, without question, his military superiors and to make no explanation of his orders or movements to those under him. He says he is a living illustration of the truth that no man's reputation is safe who *merely* goes forward and does his whole duty. I add to this statement the reflection that his military education has brought him to feel a kind of lofty contempt for the press and politics, and civil life generally, which has kept him stiff and reticent where he ought to have spoken. If he had asserted himself more, it would have been better for him and for the country. Whether he has the dash and audacity to make a good general I do not know. That he is a true brave man I have no doubt. *I like General Irvin McDowell.*

II. *Major General Pope*:

(a) He was wronged by the President in being placed in the most trying position of any officer since the war began. 1st, He was placed over at least three officers who outranked him and felt injured by it. One (Frémont) resigned in consequence and there was much ill feeling in the army. 2nd, He was ordered to move at once a great distance in a country with which he was totally unacquainted and whose topography was very complex and difficult to be learned. 3rd, He was ordered to one of the most difficult, dangerous, and inglorious enterprises known in war, a retreat from what he must make the enemy and hence the country believe was a determined attack.

(b) He was deeply wronged, one might almost say shamefully and treacherously betrayed by General McClellan, who could easily have turned the tide at Bull Run by sending promptly forward to Pope's assistance a part of that great army which he had saved.

(c) Pope was successful in the purpose for which he went out, but his general orders were full of claptrap and braggadocio and his return seemed to be much more of a failure than he was.

(d) *My Opinion*: Pope has been greatly wronged, is a man of some considerably [considerable] ability and vigor, but given to fanfaronade and on the whole I don't admire him very much.

III. *Major General McClellan:*

(a) His loyalty has not been above suspicion. 1st, It is well known that he was a member of the Quitman scheme for separating New England from the Union and acquiring Cuba and Central America. 2nd, The rebel press openly assert that early in the rebellion he held correspondence with them and they regarded him as ready to accept a command there. 3rd, Major General Hunter has an adopted daughter who is a wife of the rebel General Stuart and is now in Georgia. She got a letter through to General Hunter a few days ago complaining of her loss in being shut off from her Union friends, and in this letter she says she has seen the evidences that General McClellan made overtures to Davis for a command before he was appointed to a position in the

Union army. General Hunter told me this last night (It is now October 12th).

(b) He has seriously thought of assuming the military dictatorship of the Government, nor is such a purpose yet wholly dismissed from his mind. He is a very weak man, distrusts his own judgment, is easily led and flattered by others. Probably his worst advisor is Judge Key, my old brother senator, who is a most artful, cunning and dangerous man. He covers up his real designs under patriotic platitudes. He said to General Cox, lately, substantially as follows: "I have greatly changed in my opinions since you and I were in the Ohio Senate. Then I was in favor [of] conservative and conciliatory measures. But now the events of the war have really destroyed our simple form of civil government. The President has suspended the chief civil processes and ours is no longer a government of law but of force. The army is the embodiment of that force and is in fact the government, though the civil forms are still retained by the administration. The emancipation is of course not a matter of law but of force, and hence I approve it." The drift of all this is that whenever it may seem best to McClellan he may throw off the pretence of civil forms and become the ruler in form as well as fact. Such sin is whispered into his ear with honied words of flattery and they have made him very vain and egotistic.

(c) I consider him one of the weakest and most timid generals that ever led an army. This opinion is held by General Hooker and nearly every prominent one of his field marshals.

(d) He is constantly scheming in politics, and I think the Government would at once remove him but for the fear that it would strengthen the Democratic party too much in the coming election, especially in New York. Unless some new complication arises, I think he will be removed as soon as the New York election is over.

(e) I have no hope for the success of our arms in the East till McClellan is removed entirely from active command. The loss of the last 27 days since the Battle of Antietam has addead [added] at least six months to the war.

IV. *Major General Franz Sigel:*

I am more perplexed to reach a satisfactory judgment concerning General Sigel than any other man I know. I halt between two veins— one leading me to earnest admiration of high qualities, the other to a sad contempt of his charlatanry and unfounded pretensions. On the whole I suspend judgment in regard to him, though I think he has been overestimated and I shall not be greatly surprised, though much grieved, to find that his fame will grow less hereafter.

V. *General Reflections and Conclusions*

The coming men of the eastern army are Hooker, Burnside, Banks and Heintzelman. We have the material for splendid field marshals, and Napoleon's staff of marshals could be twice duplicated from our army if only we had the Napoleon to develope them.

It is doubtful whether McDowell can ever be in favor again so as to have a high place. Indeed if the Government gives him such a court of inquiry as he asks and lets its proceedings be published, the President and the Cabinet will be far more damaged by it than General McDowell. I therefore doubt if it will ever see the light.

I have taken these notes wholly from memory, but with the exception of here and there a name or date, I am very sure they are in the main correct. In going over the documents, which were nearly all official and incontrovertible, we (General McDowell and I) must have read more than 200 manuscript pages. The current of this sketch may be tinged with McDowell's own views and feelings, but I have tried to make allowances for that, but I must say he did not impress me as at all biased by prejudices or hate. My sketches of men were not drawn from that interview alone, but from my impression from all sources.

NOTE:

I would like to have you and Harry and Almeda and such others as you may deem prudent read this, with the map of Virginia before you. But it must not get into any hands that will make it public. I desire to have it preserved carefully, not for any merit in its preparation, but for the important facts it contains.

Washington, D.C., October 12, 1862

## NOTES

1. For the record of the Porter court-martial see *War of the Rebellion: A Compilation of the Official Records of the Union and Confederate Armies,* 130 volumes (Washington, 1880-1901), series I, volume XII, part II, 505-536 and supplement.

2. Otto Eisenschiml, *The Celebrated Case of Fitz John Porter* (Indianapolis, 1950), 72-81.

3. Benjamin P. Thomas and Harold M. Hyman, *Stanton: The Life and Times of Lincoln's Secretary of War* (New York, 1962), 260.

4. Quotation is from Eisenschiml, *The Celebrated Case,* 80.

5. For Chase's feelings toward McDowell, McClellan, Porter, John Pope, and other principals in the trial, see David Donald, editor, *Inside Lincoln's Cabinet: The Civil War Diaries of Salmon P. Chase* (New York, 1954) and Donnal V. Smith, *Chase and Civil War Politics* (Columbus, 1931).

6. *Official Records,* series I, volume XII, part II, supplement, 824.

# Appendix B

*Acknowledgments*

Financial assistance from the Penrose Fund of the American Philosophical Society and from the All-University Research Fund of Michigan State University defrayed most of the expenditures required for travel, research assistance, and materials in preparing this volume. For this support I wish to express my sincere gratitude.

I also wish to thank members of the staffs of the following institutions for factual information and assistance in locating source and reference materials: the Rutherford B. Hayes Memorial Library, Fremont, Ohio; the Cleveland Public Library, and the Western Reserve Historical Society, Cleveland, Ohio; the Hiram College Library, Hiram, Ohio; the James A. Garfield Museum in Mentor, Ohio; the Ohio Historical Society in Columbus; the Bethany College Library, Bethany, West Virginia; the Williams College Library, Williamstown, Massachusetts; the Disciples of Christ Historical Society, Nashville, Tennessee; the New York State Library in Albany; the St. Louis Public Library, St. Louis, Missouri; the Alabama Department of Archives and History in Montgomery; the Department of Lincolniana, Lincoln Memorial University, Harrogate, Tennessee; the Michigan State Library; the Michigan State University Library; and the Manuscript Division of the Library of Congress.

I am indebted to a number of persons who contributed in various ways to this study. The late Abram Garfield of Bratenahl, Cleveland, a son of President Garfield, made available scores of manuscripts, including almost all of the letters in this volume. He also loaned me books and gave me access to the library of the Garfield Museum in Mentor. His son, Edward Garfield, also of Bratenahl, more than once went out of his way to assist me in getting books, manuscripts, and newspapers. Professor Harry J. Brown, a colleague with whom I am preparing a multi-volume edition of Garfield's diary, helped enormously by making available the fruits of his extensive study. Professors Arthur Adams, Alan Schaffer, and Harold Fields, all colleagues, read and criticized parts of the work and made suggestions which improved it. Professor William Seaman translated most of the Latin. Mr. John T. Houdek of Western Michigan University, who is preparing a doctoral dissertation on a phase of Garfield's congressional career, was also very helpful. Mrs. Margaret Leech Pulitzer, among whose distinguished accomplishments is an immense knowledge of Garfield, permitted me to see many of her notes and made numerous insightful observations about his personality and private life. Mr. Charles Henry of Geauga Lake, Ohio, allowed me to see letters his grandfather had received from Garfield. Mrs. Edward C. Betts of Washington, D.C., Mr. Maclin Frierson of Athens, Alabama, Mrs. R. H. Collacott of Cleveland, and Mrs. James C. Cooper, librarian of the Garfield Museum, supplied information for several annotations. Caroline Gasaway Weng and Linda Graham assisted in the research, and Russell Buhite, Calvin Enders, and my daughter, Sandi, helped proofread the manuscript. To all of these people, and especially to my wife, Florence G. Williams, whose patience, encouragement, and suggestions contributed immeasurably to this work, I am deeply grateful.

East Lansing                                                    F.D.W.
February, 1964

# Index